Russian and East European Studies

Charles Jelavich,
TSARIST RUSSIA AND BALKAN NATIONALISM:
Russian Influence in the Internal Affairs
of Bulgaria and Serbia, 1879–1886

Nicholas V. Riasanovsky,
NICHOLAS I AND OFFICIAL NATIONALITY
IN RUSSIA, 1825–1855

Charles and Barbara Jelavich, eds.,
THE EDUCATION OF A RUSSIAN STATESMAN:
The Memoirs of Nicholas Karlovich Giers

Simon Karlinsky,
MARINA CVETAEVA:
Her Life and Art

Richard A. Pierce,
RUSSIAN CENTRAL ASIA, 1867–1917:
A Study in Colonial Rule

Jerzy F. Karcz, ed.,
SOVIET AND EAST EUROPEAN AGRICULTURE

THE LIFE AND WORKS OF EVGENIJ ZAMJATIN

N. È. Radlov. A portrait of Evgenij Zamjatin, c. 1928

THE LIFE AND WORKS OF EVGENIJ ZAMJATIN

Alex M. Shane

UNIVERSITY OF CALIFORNIA PRESS
Berkeley and Los Angeles — 1968

University of California Press
Berkeley and Los Angeles, California

Cambridge University Press
London, England

L.C. 68–19643
Printed in the United States of America

To Milla

Preface

I wish to express my gratitude to the many persons who helped me in the course of my work on Zamjatin. I am most deeply indebted to Professor Gleb Struve for the direction of my doctoral dissertation (University of California at Berkeley, 1965), from which this work is adapted, and for his continued advice during the writing of this book. I am grateful also for the suggestions and encouragement of two other members of my dissertation committee, Professors Oleg Maslenikov and C. Bickford O'Brien, and for the comments of Professor Nicholas Riasanovsky on the biographical chapters.

To the late Mme Ludmilla N. Zamiatine and Professor Philip E. Mosely I am indebted for permission to use the Zamjatin materials at the Archive of Russian and East European History and Culture at Columbia University. I am very grateful for the help extended by archive curator Lev F. Magerovsky, and I am forever in debt to Professor Herman Ermolaev of Princeton University for performing the invaluable and herculean task of cataloging the Zamjatin materials and preparing them for microfilming.

I owe special thanks to the many librarians who made possible the acquisition of materials for this study — in particular, the staffs of the Hoover Institution at Stanford University, the inter-library loan departments of the University of California at Berkeley and Davis, and the Slavonic section of the Helsinki University Library. I am also grateful to the University of California Humanities Institute for the grant which enabled me to complete this study, and to the American Council of Learned Societies for a grant-in-aid which enabled me to use the Helsinki University Library. I also thank Professor Marc Slonim, Joan London, and the late Charles Malamuth for sharing their memories of Zamjatin with me. And I wish to express my unlimited gratitude to my wife Milla for her suggestions, encouragement, and patience, as well as for endless typing and proofreading. Finally, I should like to acknowledge my debt to Mrs. Judith Kartman of the editorial staff of the University of California Press for her numerous helpful suggestions in editing the final version of this book.

The transliteration generally accepted by Slavic scholars has been used throughout this work. For the uninitiated, it may be helpful to note that *j* is pronounced as *y* in *boy* or *you*, *x* as a guttural *h*, *c* as *ts* in *boots*, *č* as *ch* in *cheer*, *š* as *sh* in *shop*, *šč* as *shch* in *fresh cheese*, and *y* as *i* in *bit*. Old orthography has been transliterated as new. Dates prior to February 1, 1918, have been given in Old Style (add thirteen days for twentieth-century dates, twelve for nineteenth, in order to convert to the Gregorian calendar used in the West).

A.M.S.

Introduction

More than thirty years have passed since the Russian writer Evgenij Zamjatin died in self-imposed exile in Paris. To call him a "White émigré," as several scholarly Soviet publications have recently done, however, would be not only inappropriate, but highly misleading. The basic facts of Zamjatin's biography differ greatly from those of most White émigré writers, artists, and scholars who emigrated from Russia during the civil war and the early twenties to settle in such European capitals as Berlin, Prague, Paris, Belgrade, and Riga. There, they created an active émigré press in their Russian cultural communities, through which they loudly voiced their irrevocable hostility to the Bolshevik Revolution and the Soviet regime. Although highly critical of many aspects of the Soviet regime, Zamjatin did welcome the Bolshevik Revolution, and he remained in the Soviet Union until November 1931, when he went abroad with the consent of Stalin himself. During his fourteen years (1917 to 1931) in Soviet Russia, he was extremely active in Petersburg/Leningrad literary life as a writer, lecturer, editor, and playwright. More than two dozen monographs bearing his name were published in Soviet Russia. Despite being close friends with such émigrés as the writer Aleksej Remizov, literary critic Marc Slonim, and artists Jurij Annenkov and Boris Grigor'ev, Zamjatin did not frequent Russian émigré circles when he was abroad, nor did he contribute to émigré periodicals. In June 1934, although he had been absent from the Soviet Union for almost three years, he was nevertheless elected to the newly created Writers' Union, as some of his Soviet friends were still expecting his return. He apparently retained his Soviet passport to the day of his death, March 10, 1937. Although he was an émigré, Zamjatin clearly was not a White émigré writer in the usual sense of the term.

On the other hand, Zamjatin cannot be labeled a Soviet Russian writer without some qualification. He *was* a Soviet Russian writer in that he lived, wrote, and published his works in the Soviet Union; that is one reason why most histories of Soviet literature which have been written by Western critics include a section — frequently an entire chapter — on Zamjatin. From the Soviet critic's point of view, however, Zamjatin was in no way a Soviet Russian writer, for, as Professor L. I. Timofeev has stated in his extensive introduction to the three-volume Soviet Academy of Sciences *History of Soviet Russian Literature*, "the concept Soviet writer was by no means a geographical concept; it was from the very beginning a political concept, and herein lay its strength, value, and honor." [1] With the end of the civil war, the introduction of the New Economic Policy (1921 to 1928), and the resumption of extensive publication in the early twenties, Communist critics branded Zamjatin an anti-Soviet, bourgeois writer who championed bourgeois individualism, apoliticalism, and hostility to the October Revolution. In 1929 he came under especially severe criticism in connection with the purge and reorganization of the All-Russian Union of Writers (Vserossijskij sojuz pisatelej, VSP), and, since his departure in November 1931, none of his works have been published in the Soviet Union. His name all but disappeared from print in the Soviet Union during the thirties, reappearing briefly in 1946 in Andrej Ždanov's attack on Anna Axmatova and Mixail Zoščenko as one of the sources of Zoščenko's apoliticalism and lack of ideology. It was only in the late fifties that he at last received mention, albeit cursory and negative, in standard scholarly histories of Soviet Russian literature; there, several of his works were cited as examples of bourgeois works directed against young Soviet literature and "Soviet reality." No attempt at literary analysis was made, and there was no description of his literary activity or his influence on young writers. In this respect the recently published *History of the Russian Soviet Novel* marks a step forward, for it speaks of Zamjatin, with Andrej Belyj and Aleksej Remizov, as one of the "decadent" writers who "exerted a definite influence on young writers." It mentions that in the years immediately after the October Revolution their works "seemed to be almost masterpieces," although subsequently Zamjatin was criticized as a proponent of "linguistic naturalism" and "formalistic refinement." [2] Since 1934 only two of Zamjatin's works have elicited more than a sentence or two of negative commentary: "Uezdnoe," which, in an interesting, seven-page analysis by Sergej Kastorskij, was viewed as a continuation of the Gor'kian antiphilistine tradition, and the anti-utopian novel *My*, which was considered by Mixail Kuznecov to be symptomatic of bankrupt modernism and was rather unimaginatively labeled a "straightforward, maliciously lucid, rationalistic piece of propaganda." [3] O. N. Mixajlov's well balanced article in the recently published *Concise Literary Encyclopedia*, which gives a fairly accurate sketch of Zamjatin's literary production, represents the current Soviet view of Zamjatin: his post-Revolutionary output is "permeated with hostility to the Revolution and a deep pessimism," while *My* is branded a "malicious pamphlet on the Soviet government." [4]

Fundamentally different approaches to literature by Soviet and Western literary scholars have resulted in extremely divergent — indeed irreconcilable — assessments of Zamjatin's role in Russian literature. For the Soviet critic today, Zamjatin remains a bourgeois, anti-Soviet writer of no consequence, an inner-émigré who left the Soviet Union rather belatedly. For the Western critic, Zamjatin is a talented writer of considerable originality, who influenced some of Soviet Russia's most promising young writers and wrote a remarkably prophetic anti-utopian novel. Wherein lies the truth?

At issue is Zamjatin's anti-utopian novel *My*. From the Soviet point of view, the novel not only lacks the proper ideology, but actually propounds an ideology hostile to that of the Communist party. Therefore, it was unacceptable to the Soviet government in the early twenties and remains so today. Consequently, the inclusion of this work in the category of Soviet literature by Western scholars has been consistently viewed as anti-Soviet propaganda in the hands of "reactionary imperialist groups."[5] Furthermore, Soviet scholars completely reject the anti-utopian novel as a legitimate genre because it attempts "to destroy faith in the coming happiness of man" and because it is "permeated with an incurable historical pessimism, a zoological hatred for the people and for democracy."[6] Accordingly, none of the classic twentieth-century anti-utopias — Zamjatin's *My*, Aldous Huxley's *Brave New World*, or George Orwell's *1984* — have been published in the Soviet Union, although the titles are familiar, and they are the objects of negative pronouncements. In the West *My*, aptly described by George Woodcock as the "first of the significant contemporary anti-utopian novels,"[7] has become a classic in this genre. In view of the growing number of translations, it may justifiably be considered Zamjatin's lasting contribution to world literature. The appearance of half-a-dozen new translations of *My*, as well as a spate of articles (both scholarly and popular) on Zamjatin during the past decade, reflect a growing interest in the West toward this original writer. Regrettably, however, most of the articles have dealt exclusively with *My*, ignoring the rest of Zamjatin's creative output, which by and large has remained unknown to the general reader. Fortunately for the English reader, Random House has recently published *The Dragon*,[8] a good collection of Zamjatin's stories translated by Mirra Ginsburg, and the University of Chicago Press plans to release a collection of his essays soon.[9] Although *My* probably will remain Zamjatin's sole contribution to world literature, it is his other works that have played an important role in the development of Russian literature and, through their technical excellence, have exerted considerable influence on the younger writers in the early twenties. The negative evaluation of Zamjatin's "linguistic naturalism" and "formalistic refinement" expresses Soviet critics' avowed opposition to stylistic and structural experimentation. This, coupled with Zamjatin's ideological unacceptability, means that no scholarly studies of his life and works will be made by Soviet critics until there is a radical change in their basic conception of literature and its role in society.[10] The task of evaluating Zamjatin's literary heritage till then is left to Western scholars. To date, only one monograph, D. J. Richards' *Zamyatin: A Soviet Heretic* (London: Bowes and Bowes, 1962), has appeared, but, since it was published in the popular series "Studies in Modern European Literature and Thought," the work lacks both the extensive bibliography and the critical apparatus that could facilitate further research.

In this book, which consists of three major parts, I have attempted to lay a foundation for the further investigation of Zamjatin's work and his role in Russian literature. In the first, Zamjatin's life and literary activities are described in detail, and an attempt is made to trace the evolution of some of the ideas expressed in his critical essays. The second part consists of a critical analysis of all of his known published prose fiction, organized according to chronological, thematic, structural, and stylistic considerations. The third part, the bibliography, is of particular importance to further study, because no extensive bibliography on Zamjatin has been published previously. It should be noted that, although the Zamjatin materials in the Archive of Russian and East European History and Culture at Columbia University have been used extensively in this study, archives in the Soviet Union, which undoubtedly contain much unknown and interesting information, have not been consulted. It is hoped that, on the basis of the material presented here with an aim of objectivity and thoroughness, the reader will evaluate for himself Zamjatin's importance in Russian and — depending on his definition — Soviet Russian literature.

Contents

PART I

The Biography of a Heretic

And the world lives only through its heretics, through those who reject the seemingly unshakable and faultless today. Only the heretics discover new horizons in science, in art, in social life; only the heretics, rejecting today in the name of tomorrow, are the eternal ferment of life and ensure life's unending movement forward.

Zamjatin, *Robert Majer*

CHAPTER ONE

Early Years, 1884-1917

If I mean anything in Russian literature, I owe it all to the Petersburg Secret Police.

Zamjatin, *Autobiography*

On the steep west bank of the River Don, some two hundred miles south of Moscow, lay the sleepy nineteenth-century town of Lebedjan'. Across the Don to the east and to the south stretched broad, flat plains which were frequently cut by deep ravines. Here began the rich, black soil characteristic of southern Russia and the Ukraine, and here was the center of old provincial Russia — the Russia of Tambov, Tula, Orel, and Voronež — unhurried and untouched by the changing times. Foreigners had not penetrated this virgin corner. Almost the entire population of Lebedjan' County, which was famous for its craftsmen, consisted of native-born Russians. Even the names of the major rivers — Don, Voronež, Krasivaja Meča — and their numerous but insignificant tributaries — Glinka, Rakitnaja, Skvirnja, Semenek, Skromna, Gaek, Ust'e — reflected the Russian character of the area.

Founded late in the sixteenth century, Lebedjan' had grown by the 1880's into a town of 700 buildings and 6,500 persons. It had become notorious for its swindlers, gypsies, horsefairs, and robust Russian language and had been immortalized in Ivan Turgenev's story "Lebedjan'." Although the town was the commercial center and county seat, its dusty streets were overgrown with wild mallow and were used as much by pigs and chickens as by people. The educational needs of the populace were served by four schools — a county school, a Progymnasium, and two church schools — one for men and one for women.

Evgenij Ivanovič Zamjatin was born in Lebedjan' on January 20, 1884. Very little is known of his family. His father, Ivan Dmitrievič, taught at the local Progymnasium. His mother, Marija Aleksandrovna, was a competent musician under whose piano young Evgenij spent many childhood hours. Other members of the household included a grandmother and Evgenij's sister. Apparently the only other relative was a maternal aunt who lived in Voronež and whom Evgenij had once seen bathing naked in the river. Rather massive (polar bears wallowing in a pool were later to remind him of her), she inspired both curiosity and trepidation in her young nephew. The bathing incident gave early meaning to the boy's concept of woman, and some incidents later depicted in his stories about the provinces seem to recall this aunt.

Equally little is known about Zamjatin's childhood, and biographers must rely solely on what he himself chose to reveal in three brief autobiographies, all written and published in the 1920's.* Some of the incidents that he described are of purely biographical interest and are not revealing of the future author and his work: for example, his childhood impressions of melting snow, a near-fatal illness during his second year, a cholera epidemic with his awareness of death, his first walk to the Progymnasium in long trousers and tunic, and so forth. More interesting are those incidents and details that underline themes later predominant in Zamjatin's life and works: solitude, books, analytic scepticism, a perverse stubbornness, revolution, and things provincial.

A sense of loneliness was characteristic of Zamjatin's entire life. One of his few recorded impressions of early childhood describes being separated from his parents in a large holiday crowd at a Zadonsk monastery: "The service ended, people shoved, I — a fragment — am carried out with the crowd, now

* Quotations from Zamjatin's three autobiographies are identified in the text as A.I (written in 1922), A.II (1924), and A.III (1929). Page citations refer to the place of first publication. For more information, see [177], [178], and [179]. (Bracketed numbers refer to entries in the bibliography.)

I am alone in the crowd: father and mother are gone and they will never return, I am alone forever. I sit on some sort of grave; the sun is shining, I cry bitterly. For a whole hour I lived alone in this world." (A. III, 8.)

Zamjatin himself stated that as a child he had been without companions and that later, during his school years, he also had experienced much loneliness. His awareness of being alone undoubtedly contributed much to formulating the outward restraint and reserve typical of his mature years, a reserve well illustrated by the opening lines of his first autobiography: "So you still insist on having my autobiography, but you will have to limit yourself only to an outside inspection and perhaps a glimpse into half-dark windows. I seldom ask anybody to enter, and you will see little from the outside" (A. I). It is also significant that in Zamjatin's earliest published stories, "Odin" ("Alone") and "Devuška" ("The Girl"), loneliness is a dominant theme.

It is natural for a lonely child to turn to books for companionship, and Zamjatin was no exception. Books took on human characteristics and replaced the childhood friends he never had. Years later, long after he had achieved literary fame, books still retained their human qualities for him and even replaced the children he also never had. Zamjatin himself made the comparison: "When my children go out in the street poorly dressed — I am sorry for them; when boys throw rocks at them from around corners — I am hurt; when a doctor approaches them with forceps or a knife — I would rather have him operate on me. My children are my books; I have no others." [1]

Zamjatin learned to read at the age of four. His father subscribed to *Syn otečestva* (*Son of the Fatherland*), a Petersburg political, literary, and scientific newspaper whose inexpensive edition was very popular in the provinces during the late 1880's and 1890's. Zamjatin would wait in a high state of excitement till dinnertime in order to unfold the newspaper and ceremoniously spell out the title.

In 1892, at the age of eight, he entered the Progymnasium and began in earnest the reading of Russian classics. Among his favorite authors were Fedor Dostoevskij, Ivan Turgenev, Nikolaj Gogol', and — considerably later — Anatole France. In his writings Gogol' seemed to be a friend, while Dostoevskij and Turgenev seemed older and more frightening. Works like "Netočka Nezvanova" and "Pervaja ljubov'" ("First Love") sent shivers down the young boy's spine and did much to develop his already active imagination and sensitivity.

From 1896 Zamjatin attended the gymnasium at Voronež, a city of 60,000 persons located ninety-five miles south of Lebedjan'. Voronež, the birthplace of the poets Aleksej Kol'cov and Ivan Nikitin, was situated on a high, steep bank overlooking the Voronež River and at that time was considered one of Russia's most beautiful provincial towns. Evidently, the beauty of the town was lost on young Zamjatin, who recalled only the dull, gray years of school life, whose monotony was broken at infrequent intervals by a wonderful red flag which signaled that the temperature had dropped to five degrees below zero, Fahrenheit, and that classes were canceled. As a student Zamjatin excelled in Russian composition. Upon graduation in 1902, he was awarded a gold medal, which he pawned for twenty-five rubles promptly on arriving in Petersburg. Indifferent to tokens of honor, he rarely sought after public success.

The first indications of the future heretic became manifest during Zamjatin's gymnasium years. At the age of twelve a healthy skepticism was fostered in him by an older student's fist. Zamjatin's description of the incident includes a clever play on the word *fonar'*, which denotes a lantern, but which colloquially can mean a "shiner" or black-eye: "At the age of twelve — Diogenes' lantern of skepticism. The lantern was lit by a brawny second grader and — blue, purple, red — it burned under my left eye for two whole weeks. I prayed for a miracle — for the lantern to go out. The miracle did not happen. I began to think" (A. III, 9–10).

During his years in Voronež, Zamjatin sought to analyze and test himself in various ways. This self-experimentation became, along with Russian composition, his major special interest; but, unlike his composition, his testing was carried out in strict secrecy. Once, bitten by a rabid dog, Zamjatin decided to await the first symptoms of madness. His feelings and sensations were duly recorded in a diary, the first and the last he ever kept. Two weeks later, when no signs of illness had appeared, he told school authorities of being bitten and was immediately rushed to Moscow for immunization.

In addition to skepticism and analysis, a rather perverse stubbornness emerged in his teens which even motivated his career choice. Zamjatin's description of this provides an insight into the motivation of his actions thereafter: "In the gymnasium I would get *A* plus for composition and was not always on good terms with mathematics. Perhaps because of that (out of sheer stubbornness) I chose the most mathematical of all careers — the Department of Naval Architecture at the Petersburg Polytechnic Institute" (A. I).

Zamjatin displayed a similar obstinacy during the 1920's. Remaining true to his own views on man, literature, and the writer's role in society, he courageously persisted in expressing them, despite continued harassment by Communist critics which culminated in public defamation.

Zamjatin's decision to become a writer also can be attributed in part to the same stubborn perversity. On the day of his graduation the vice-principal had admonished him against becoming a writer and sharing the fate of Pavel E. Ščegolev (1877–1931), a native of Voronež who had been arrested and exiled in 1899 for participating in the revolutionary movement, but who later was to become a well-known historian, literary scholar, and editor of the journal *Byloe* (*The Past*):

> I remember: the last day, the vice-principal's office (according to the gymnasium system of rank — "the old nag"). His glasses up on his forehead, he hitches up his trousers (his trousers were always slipping down), and hands me some sort of a brochure. I read the author's inscription: "To my *alma mater*, of which I can remember nothing but the worst. P. E. Ščegolev." And the vice-principal, admonishingly, speaking through his nose, rounding his *o*'s: "Good? He also graduated with a medal, but look what he writes! And he was put in jail. Take my advice: don't write, don't take that road." The admonishment did not help. (A. III, 11.)

History repeated itself: Zamjatin did become a writer and was twice imprisoned. The vice-principal's admonishment turned out to be an accurate prophecy.

The first eighteen years of Zamjatin's life, spent in provincial Russia, did not pass without leaving their mark on him and his works. Raised in a family of at least moderate education, Zamjatin hardly felt himself to be a part of provincial life. In his autobiographies the reader senses a distinction between life inside Zamjatin's home and the provincial life outside: "My mother used to play Chopin at the piano. Two paces from Chopin was the provincial: geraniums in the windows, and in the middle of the street — a little pig fastened to a stake and hens flapping their wings in the dust" (A. I).

From the general tone of his autobiographies it is apparent that Zamjatin did not look back on his childhood in the provinces with affection. To the contrary, he viewed provincial life as he did in the gymnasium: gray, boring, set to a single pattern. Nonetheless, Zamjatin's childhood did provide ample material for his early stories. He rarely modeled his characters on real people, but when he did, the literary character would be so much altered that only Zamjatin would know whose shadow it was. The one exception to this was the unforgettable Čebotarixa of "Uezdnoe" ("The Provinces"), who was patterned after an aunt of the writer Mixail Prišvin: "I had seen this aunt of Prišvin's many times in my childhood; she became firmly imbedded in me and — perhaps in order to rid myself of her — I had to tear her free and put her in a story. I didn't know her life, all her actions are imagined, but she really did own a leather factory and her external description in 'Uezdnoe' is true to life." [2]

It is highly doubtful that works such as "Uezdnoe," "Na kuličkax" ("Out in the Sticks"), and "Alatyr'" could have been successfully created without the experience and insight acquired during Zamjatin's early years. Only after Zamjatin's departure from the provinces did his rebellion against the boredom of provincial life find expression in the revolutionary movement.

Upon enrolling at the Petersburg Polytechnic Institute in the autumn of 1902, Zamjatin was immediately caught up in the ferment of Petersburg life, a striking contrast to the torpor of the provinces. In retrospect, this era with its demonstrations on the Nevskij Prospect, galloping cossacks, and huge meetings at the university and various institutes seemed to him a whirlwind. During the winters he attended lectures at the institute, but in the summers he worked at shipyards and factories along the Kama River and in such cities as Nižnij Novgorod, Odessa, and Sevastopol'.

The summer of 1905 was especially memorable because Zamjatin's assignment included a trip to the Near East, with stopovers at Istanbul, Izmir, Salonika, Beirut, Jaffa, Port Said, and Alexandria, and a glimpse of Mt. Athos. The high point was a week's stay with an Arab family in Jerusalem, which he described as "extraordinary, distinct from everything, astonishing" (A. III, 12). The journey must have been rich in experience for Zamjatin, but, surprisingly, it found no direct reflection in his later literary work.

Zamjatin's winter activities were not confined to his technical studies, and the rebellious energy which had been pent up at last found direction in the revolutionary movement of the early 1900's. His decision to join the Bolshevik party was motivated more by his rebellious spirit and craving for excitement than by concrete political considerations. As he himself wrote in the 1920's: "To be a Bolshevik in those years meant following the path of greatest resistance, so I was a Bolshevik then" (A. III, 12).

In 1903 he first saw a public demonstration. Soon after, he became involved in subversive activities, and at one time he had an illegal printing press in his room. The year 1905 was eventful for Zamjatin, as well as for Russia; he returned from his Near Eastern trip in time to witness the June general strike in Odessa and the "Potemkin" mutiny, an experience which eight years later was to serve as the basis for an impressionistic sketch, "Tri dnja" ("Three Days"). Upon returning to Petersburg, he continued his revolutionary activities throughout the turbulent autumn of 1905, with its strikes, mass meetings, and the famous October Manifesto.

In December the Petersburg police dissolved the soviet of workers' deputies, arrested the leaders, and began ferreting out revolutionary groups throughout the city. A surprise raid on the revolutionary headquarters of the Vyborg District caught thirty persons, including Zamjatin, bent over battle plans and a cache of arms. The culprits were arrested, searched, beaten, and imprisoned. Zamjatin spent several months in solitary confinement at Špalernaja Prison, where he studied shorthand and English, was in love, and wrote verse (which he termed an inevitable consequence of confinement). A source of some anxiety during the months of isolation were recurrent nightmares about a bag of pyroxylin that had been left on a windowsill in his quarters and a stack of leaflets hidden under his bed. Zamjatin had no way of knowing that his friends had received the hastily scrawled note which he had thrown from a prison window and that they had cleared his room of the compromising materials prior to the police search.

Released in the spring of 1906, Zamjatin was exiled to Lebedjan'. He was unable to bear the provincial quiet for long and during the summer returned illegally to Petersburg. By July he had made his way to Helsinki, where he rented a room on the cliffs of Erdholmsgatan, overlooking the Gulf of Finland. It was a time of unrest and expectation. The workers' demands for a more representative reorganization of the Finnish parliament, which had been triggered by the Russian October Manifesto, were on the verge of at least partial fulfillment. From his window in the summer twilight Zamjatin could make out the faces of the people who gathered on the granite banks at midnight meetings. On Sundays the workers' Red Guard, organized during the general strike the previous November and grown much larger under the able leadership of the famous Captain Kok, would parade gaily through the streets of Helsinki with unfurled banners on their way to practice maneuvers and exercises in Tele Park. Rumors of disquiet in the Sveaborg Fortress were rampant. Two days after the Duma was dissolved in Petersburg on July 9, a public meeting was held by the Bolsheviks in Helsinki's Kaisaniemi Park. The main speakers were Mixajličenko, a member of the Duma, and Leonid Andreev, who was well known as a decadent writer, but who now was to speak out as an antimonarchist revolutionary. Tickets sold quickly, as the entire Russian colony rushed to see Andreev in his new role. Assigned to look after the guest of honor, Zamjatin had ample opportunity to converse with Andreev; and sixteen years later, in a collection dedicated to Andreev, Zamjatin described the vibrant atmosphere in Helsinki and narrated an amusing anecdote about Andreev, who had playfully given a young admirer his governess's wet umbrella as a souvenir.[3] A week later, Zamjatin witnessed the outbreak of the Sveaborg Revolt, but before the fortress had been subdued he was on his way back to Petersburg in a disguise complete with pince-nez.

That summer marked the apogee of Zamjatin's romantic attachment to the Bolshevik cause. For him the Revolution was not yet a legal wife, jealously guarding her legal monopoly on love, but was rather a young, fiery-eyed mistress whom he loved very much. Perhaps this erotic comparison (Zamjatin's own) was prompted by his love for a girl with whom he shared his evenings on the quay in Helsinki and whose identity remains as much a mystery as do most of his personal relationships.

In Petersburg, Zamjatin resumed his studies at the Polytechnic Institute, was elected to the student parliament (which he served once as chairman) and was active in party propaganda and electioneering. He was soon discovered by the police and called in to the district office. Shown an official document about the exiling of "a university student Evgenij Ivanovič Zamjatin," he was able to declare honestly that he had never attended the university and that obviously there was some mistake in the document. He then moved to another district. A year and a half later, the police called him in again, but the mistake was still unrectified. It took five years for the officials to correct the error, so not until 1911 was Zamjatin exiled again from Petersburg. By then, he had finished his studies at the institute, was a practicing naval engineer, and had written a few short stories.

> Russians are justly accused of easy morals," "I, for example, am a bigamist, and what is even worse — I am not ashamed to declare it openly. As justification I can say only this: I am neither the first nor the only one, for in the history of Russian literature there have already been such cases. In his letters Anton Čexov has confessed that he also had two wives: a lawful wife — medicine — and a mistress — literature. My two wives are shipbuilding and literature.[4]

The duality of Zamjatin's interest was already manifest by the spring of 1908, when he concurrently worked on his degree project (the blueprints of a turreted warship) and his first short story "Odin."[5] That summer the story was submitted to the pedagogical and popular scientific monthly *Obrazovanie* (*Education*), where it appeared in the November issue. Although inspired by his prison experiences of two years earlier, "Odin" was more the product of romantic imagination than of fact and clearly showed that Zamjatin had much to learn before attaining recognition as a master stylist. "Odin" was not only unusually prolix for Zamjatin, but also bore the unmistakable imprint of Leonid Andreev at his worst, especially in its abstract, seemingly symbolic beginning, as well as in a final tasteless paragraph describing a suicide's crushed and oozing skull. Perhaps these were the features, however, that prompted the literary editor of *Obrazovanie*, the very popular sensationalistic novelist Mixail Arcybašev, to publish the young author's work. The mature Zamjatin twenty years later ruefully admitted that "when I now meet with people who have read this story, I feel just as embarrassed as when I see an aunt of mine whose dress I publicly wet at the age of two" (A. III, 15). Harsh but equitable, Zamjatin's judgment explains why "Odin" has not been republished in any of the numerous Zamjatin collections.

Zamjatin's graduation from the Polytechnic Institute and withdrawal from the Bolshevik party marked the end of him as a student revolutionary.[6] He chose shipbuilding as his lawful wife and, upon graduating, was retained by the institute's Department of Naval Architecture. He became a lecturer there in 1911. The intervening three years were spent in the construction of ships, the consideration of problems relevant to naval architecture, and the publication of highly technical articles in such journals as *Teploxod* (*The Ship*), *Russkoe sudoxodstvo* (*Russian Navigation*), and *Izvestija Politexničeskogo instituta* (*Proceedings of the Polytechnic Institute*).

His work entailed much travel throughout European Russia, from the far north (Murmansk and Arxangel'sk) to the distant south (the Crimea, the Caucasus, Astraxan'); and he traversed the full length of the Volga River, as well as the Kama and Donec regions. In March 1916, he was commissioned to supervise the construction of Russian icebreakers in England. Prior to World War I Russia had possessed only two icebreakers, the "Ermak" and the "Car' Mixail Fedorovič." During the war ten additional icebreakers, all bearing the traces of Zamjatin's work,[7] were built in Armstrong, Whitworth's shipyard at Newcastle upon Tyne. The "Aleksandr Nevskij" (later renamed the

"Lenin"), whose supremacy among icebreakers was challenged only by the famous rescue ship "Krasin," was Zamjatin's special project from conception to completion. Not only were the original drafts drawn up by him, but all subsequent blueprints were subject to his examination and bore the signature, "Chief surveyor of Russian Icebreakers' Building, E. Zamiatin." After a year and a half in England, Zamjatin, not without considerable danger, returned to Russia a month before the Bolshevik Revolution.

Despite his many creditable achievements as a naval engineer, Zamjatin did not remain faithful to his "lawful wife" and devoted much time to his mistress, literature. Although he claimed not to have published any of the stories written between 1908 and 1911 except for "Odin," at least one other, "Devuška," is known to have appeared in print. More concise, better structured, and less sensational than "Odin," "Devuška" represented an important step in Zamjatin's literary evolution. The two stories, as well as Zamjatin's reluctance to publish other early efforts, indicate the experimental nature of his earliest stories and suggest that he sought to develop a definite literary style. He was aware of the shortcomings in his early stories and later wrote that "in each I felt something that was 'not quite it' " (A. III, 16). "It" finally came late in 1911 when he began work on his first tale, "Uezdnoe."

It should be mentioned that the Russian term *povest'* (here rendered as "tale") refers to a fictional narrative of intermediate length and frequently has been translated into English by the somewhat nebulous terms "long short story," "short novel," or the pejorative "novelette." The distinction between *povest'* and *rasskaz* (translated here as "short story" or "story") is both valid and useful in an analysis of Zamjatin's fiction.

Oddly enough, it was the Petersburg police in 1911 who had provided Zamjatin with the opportunity to devote himself to literature. After five years, the error in the document concerning Zamjatin's exile had been rectified, and in 1911 he had been deported again from Petersburg. Seriously ill, he first settled at a summer home in Sestroreck, but, with winter impending, soon moved to Laxta, a small village six miles west of Petersburg on the Gulf of Finland. There he wrote "Uezdnoe." Completed during the summer of 1912 and published in the May, 1913, issue of *Zavety* (*Behests*), "Uezdnoe" was widely reviewed and acclaimed. Extensive excerpts were reprinted that autumn in *Bjulleteni literatury i žizni* (*Bulletins on Literature and Life*), a publication similar in character to the *Reader's Digest*.

In most sources the date of first publication is erroneously cited as 1911, an error that stemmed from Zamjatin's second autobiography where he stated, "I began to write in earnest in 1911 ("Uezdnoe" in *Zavety*)." This statement should have been interpreted as, "In 1911 I began writing 'Uezdnoe,' which was first published in *Zavety*." Since *Zavety*, a literary and political journal with a strong Socialist-Revolutionary inclination, commenced publication in April, 1912, "Uezdnoe" could not have appeared there in 1911!

With the publication of "Uezdnoe" began Zamjatin's lasting friendship with Aleksej Remizov, Prišvin, Ivanov-Razumnik (the pen name of Razumnik Vasil'evič Ivanov), and others of the *Zavety* group. In 1913, due to the tercentenary of the Romanov dynasty, Zamjatin was granted permission to live in Petersburg again, but his return to the city was short-lived. Because of ill health, he traveled south and spent the winter of 1913–1914 in Nikolaev, a large military and commercial port on the Black Sea at the mouth of the Bug River. Zamjatin continued to play the role of bigamist with great success: in Nikolaev he "constructed several steam shovels, several stories, and the tale 'Na kuličkax'" (A. III, 16), a satire on army garrison life. The March, 1914, issue of *Zavety* (No. 3) featuring "Na kuličkax," was quickly confiscated by the censor, who found that, "according to Zamjatin the conduct of Russian officers is utterly disgraceful and reveals them to be crude, torpified people devoid of human qualities and lacking consciousness of one's own dignity—which, undoubtably, is most insulting to military honor." [8] The censor also contended that Zamjatin's description of the intimate details of marital life and his use of "pornographic expressions" were offensive to a sense of decency. On April 22 the Petersburg District Court upheld the censor's decision to deny the distribution of *Zavety*, No. 3, until Zamjatin's story had been expunged. A second edition, numbered 3*a* and without "Na kuličkax," was issued and circulated thereafter.[9] Due to the circumstances "Na kuličkax" reached but few readers, and no extensive reviews or criticisms of it appeared in print until the publication of three editions of the tale in 1923.

Zamjatin's literary output in the four years immediately preceding his departure for England was considerable. During that period he wrote and published three of his five tales: "Uezdnoe," "Na kuličkax," and "Alatyr'"; seven short stories: "Aprel'" ("April"), "Neputevyj" ("The Ne'er-do-well"), "Črevo" ("The Womb"), "Staršina" ("The Elder"), "Krjaži" ("The Diehards"), "Pis'menno" ("In Writing"), and "Afrika" ("Africa"); the sketch "Tri dnja"; and at least four of his twenty fables.[10] In October 1915 (notwithstanding the 1916 date on the title page) "Uezdnoe" was published as a separate book, and in February 1916, it appeared as title piece in a collection of Zamjatin's stories. The collection was favorably reviewed by most of the leading "thick" monthly journals, as well as by many newspapers. Zamjatin was, according to general consensus, a very talented, original, and interesting young author who displayed an extraordinary verbal mastery, although several critics did express serious misgivings about his excessive use of dialect and hyperbole. Representative of contemporary critical opinion was the statement of the popular and influential critic Julij Ajxenval'd, who claimed that with this book Zamjatin "undoubtedly enters our imaginative literature as a master with very distinctive characteristics and with a lively and brilliant talent,"[11] an appraisal which is still valid for the literary historian today.

CHAPTER TWO

Man of Letters, 1917-1929

There is no target at which he, the Scythian, would fear to draw his bow.

Ivanov-Razumnik, *Skify* I

From the Revolution to the mid-twenties Zamjatin occupied a prominent position in Russian literature. Even the Communist critics, while continually hounding Zamjatin for "anti-Revolutionary" ideology, freely admitted his artistic mastery and his influence on the younger generation of writers. His numerous interesting articles, written in a sparkling prose style that rivaled that of his fiction, revealed him to be an astute critic and an incurable heretic imbued with a passionate love for man and literature. Acquainted with the foremost literary figures of Petrograd, he played a leading role in professional writers' organizations and taught creative writing in several literary studios. He also served on the editorial boards of several publishing houses and did editorial work on numerous publications, including three magazines. Because of his heretical views and his stubborn refusal to follow the dictates of the Soviet regime, Zamjatin's name has all but disappeared from Soviet histories of Russian literature, and the Soviet reader has been denied knowledge of his significant role in the early, formative years of Soviet literature. In view of this, it is all the more important that an objective and detailed account of Zamjatin's activities and ideas be presented here.

Upon returning from England to Petrograd in September

1917, Zamjatin devoted all his energies to writing and to the literary life of the nation's capital.* Through the renewal of his acquaintance with Ivanov-Razumnik, a leader of the prewar *Zavety* group, Zamjatin met the Scythians, a loosely organized circle of philosophers and writers that published two miscellanies under that same title (*Skify*). Ivanov-Razumnik was the chief theoretician of the Scythians, and both miscellanies carried his programmatic articles. *Skify* I was published in the summer of 1917, prior to Zamjatin's return; *Skify* II appeared early in 1918 and included Zamjatin's fourth tale "Ostrovitjane" ("The Islanders"), which had been written in England and which was praised by several critics as the best work in the two miscellanies.[1]

Several aspects of Zamjatin's world view — his romantic conception of the Revolution, his idea of an infinite series of revolutions, his intellectual heresy, and his violent opposition to philistinism — were akin to views prevalent among the Scythians. However, his agreement with them was not total. Evgenij Lundberg, a minor writer and critic who in the early twenties organized the Scythian Publishing House in Berlin, described some lively Scythian evenings in January, 1918, in the Carskoe Selo home of Ivanov-Razumnik, where Zamjatin opposed certain views expressed by the host and A. Terek (pseudonym of Ol'ga Forš):

> Calmly, having assimilated something from "the islanders," E. I. Zamjatin speaks of England.
>
> Ivanov-Razumnik tells about Kerenskij's deviations, about nuclei, about the death of the Carskoe Selo priest, about the non-battle nature of civilian battle paintings.
>
> E. I. Zamjatin is in opposition. Ivanov-Razumnik expounds permanent revolutionism, the eternal oscillation of the crests and troughs of the populist wave. Terek measures the present epoch with a multitude of her gods — morality, faith in good taste, anthroposophy, etc. . . . and cannot reconcile them in any way.[2]

* Apparently Zamjatin also resumed lecturing at the Polytechnic Institute, which he did until his emigration from the Soviet Union in 1931 [434], 160, but it seems doubtful that an engineer of his caliber and experience would have "taught only English" and not technical subjects as has been stated in Mme L. N. Zamiatine's letter of December 9, 1962, to me.

His opposition was also reflected in Zamjatin's 1918 article "Skify li?" ("Scythians?"), published under the pseudonym of Mix. Platonov.[3] A sharp polemic on aspects of Ivanov-Razumnik's Scythianism, the article proved to be of paramount importance, for it represented Zamjatin's first published expression of philosophic conceptions which were not only the basis for future essays, but which also altered the very nature of his prose fiction.

The essence of the spiritual revolutionary was captured by Zamjatin's description of the Scythian: "Over the green steppe speeds alone a wild horseman with streaming hair — the Scythian. Where is he speeding? Nowhere. Why? For no reason. He speeds simply because he is a Scythian, because he has become one with his steed, because he is a centaur, and because freedom, solitariness, his steed, the wide steppe are most dear to him."[4] The galloping Scythian symbolized freedom, unending movement, and solitariness — freedom to reject the present in the name of the distant future, unending movement as a guarantee of man's progress in the face of universal philistinism, and solitariness because the spiritual revolutionary and heretic was always an isolated figure who stood apart from the masses. In the last point, Zamjatin took sharp exception to Blok's poem "Skify," which spoke of "hordes, and hordes, and hordes" of Scythians.

Ivanov-Razumnik's assertion that the spiritual revolutionary "works for the near or distant future" was the point of departure for Zamjatin's polemic. Unequivocally rejecting the middle-of-the-road conjunction "or," Zamjatin argued that the true Scythian works

> *only* for the distant future, and never for the near future, and never for the present. Therefore he has only one path — Golgotha, and there is no other; therefore he has only one conceivable victory — to be crucified, and there is no other.
>
> Christ on Golgotha, between two robbers, bleeding drop by drop, is the victor, because He is crucified, defeated in fact. But Christ, when in fact the victor, becomes the Grand Inquisitor. And worse: Christ, the victor in fact, is the potbellied priest in a purple robe with a silk lining, giving benedictions with the right hand and collecting gifts with the left. The Beautiful Woman in legal marriage is simply Mrs. so-and-so, with curlpapers at night and

> a migraine in the morning. And a down-to-earth Marx is simply a Krylenko.*
>
> Such is the irony and such is the wisdom of fate. Wisdom, because this ironical law guarantees unending movement forward. The realization, the bringing to earth, the victory in fact of an idea immediately philistinizes it.[5]

The true Scythian, for Zamjatin, invariably devotes his life to revolution, to an endless seeking that promises no attainment. Should a Scythian achieve his idea, then the idea becomes philistinized, and for him to retain the idea proves that he is not a true Scythian.

Remaining a true Scythian, Zamjatin rebuked Ivanov-Razumnik and the Scythians for extolling the Bolshevik Revolution which, by accepting the official title of "The Victorious October Revolution," had flouted the need for unending movement and had succumbed to philistinism, whose surest symptom was the hatred of freedom. Four years later the same thought underlay his fond recollections of the year 1906: "The Revolution was not yet a lawful wife who jealously guarded her legal monopoly on love. The Revolution was a young, fiery-eyed mistress, and I was in love with the Revolution."[6] This does not imply that Zamjatin decried the October Revolution as did the émigré writers, for he welcomed sincerely both the February and October revolutions and very much regretted his absence from Russia during the former: "I am very sorry that I did not see the February Revolution and know only October. . . . It is as if I had never been in love and then awoke one morning to find I had been married for some ten years" (A. I).

The heretic Zamjatin's objections to the Bolshevik dictatorship and to the dogmatic glorification and canonization of October did not represent a disillusionment with the Revolution; they were rather the logical consequence of his conception of heresy and his belief in never-ending revolution. For him the October Revolution always remained a positive, elemental force that did not need the protective armor of dogma and deification, as was

* Ensign N. N. Krylenko, who was arrested in early August 1917 for circulating Maximalist propaganda among the Russian troops, was appointed Commander in Chief of the Soviet Army by Lenin in November 1917, a position which he held until March 1918.

also evident in his 1923 defense of the Serapion Brothers, a group of young writers who were attacked by Marxist critics for the lack of Communist ideology in their works: "There are no writers now in Russia who are hostile to the Revolution — they have been invented in order to alleviate boredom. This was prompted by the fact that [the Serapion Brothers] do not consider the Revolution to be a consumptive maiden, who must be protected from the slightest draft." [7]

Although Zamjatin's basic attitude toward the October Revolution had been determined by philosophical rather than political conceptions, political commentary on subsequent events did enter into his minor writing during the turbulent year after the Revolution. Despite his polemic at Ivanov-Razumnik, his political views probably were close to those of Socialist Revolutionaries of the Left. Highly critical of some post-October Bolshevik policies, Zamjatin attacked them in a series of political fables in *Delo naroda* (*The People's Concern*), a left-wing Socialist Revolutionary newspaper whose moving spirit was Viktor Černov and which at one time carried a literary page edited by Ivanov-Razumnik.

In the fables Zamjatin ridiculed the proclamation of ineffectual decrees, the irresponsible destruction of cultural monuments, and the results of a socialist equality carried to absurdity. A strange little fellow named Fita, who came into being under a pile of reports in the basement of the police department and was adopted by the district police inspector Ul'jan Petrovič, figured in four of the fables. The stepfather's name, Fita's general appearance (honorable, bald, with a small protruding belly) and his innate ability to produce a prodigious number of reports and orders (chancery ink flowed from his lips) left no doubt as to his true identity — the Bolshevik leader Lenin (pseudonym of V. I. Ul'janov). Zamjatin also published several fables and critical articles in *Novaja žizn'* (*New Life*), a Social Democrat newspaper financially supported and edited by Maksim Gor'kij. In the article "Elizaveta anglijskaja" ("Elizabeth of England"), Zamjatin deplored the mass terror propagated by the Bolsheviks, comparing their role to that of Queen Elizabeth in the execution of Mary Stuart. In the later article "O belom ugle" ("Concerning White Coal"), he criticized the grandiose

Bolshevik schemes for electrification and proposed instead a very inexpensive and practical solution that could be effected immediately. Within a year after the October Revolution, however, all dissenting publications had been closed down, and Zamjatin ceased writing political articles and fables.

The arrest of Ivanov-Razumnik on February 13, 1919, by the secret police (known then as the Cheka) led to the arrest of many acquaintances. On the following day they were shepherded to Cheka headquarters at No. 2 Goroxovaja Street and were questioned about a supposed Left Socialist Revolutionary conspiracy. All were detained for many hours, except Zamjatin, who managed to free himself within two hours. Ivanov-Razumnik's written version of Zamjatin's account deserves to be cited in full, for it graphically illustrates Zamjatin's nimble thinking, daring, and great sense of humor:

> Having roared with laughter at the accusation leveled at him, he described in detail our acquaintance and relations, and also filled out the inevitable questionnaire, where in answer to the question "Have you ever belonged to any political party?" he answered briefly: "I did." After this the following dialogue took place between him and the interrogator:
>
> "To which party did you belong?" asked the interrogator, anticipating the possibility of a political accusation.
>
> "To the Bolshevik party!"
>
> During his student years E. I. Zamjatin had indeed been a member of the Party, but became a violent opponent of it during the years of Revolution. The interrogator was completely nonplused.
>
> "What! To the Bolshevik party?"
>
> "Yes."
>
> "And are you now a member?"
>
> "No."
>
> "When and why did you leave the Party?"
>
> "A long time ago, for ideological reasons."
>
> "And now, when the Party has triumphed, aren't you sorry you left?"
>
> "I'm not sorry."
>
> "Please explain. I don't understand."
>
> "But it is quite easy to understand. Are you a Communist?"
>
> "I am."
>
> "A Marxist?"
>
> "Yes."
>
> "Then you are a bad Communist and a bad Marxist. If you were a real Marxist, you would know that the petit bourgeois layer

> of Bolshevism's fellow travelers has a tendency to self-dissolution, and that only the workers are invariably the class base of Communism. And since I belong to the class of petit bourgeois intelligentsia, I can't understand why you are surprised."
>
> This ironic argumentation so affected the interrogator, that he immediately signed the order for his release, and Zamjatin was the first among those arrested to walk out of jail.[8]

After this episode Zamjatin was not bothered again by the Cheka until his arrest in 1922. His breach with the Bolsheviks, unlike those of Gor'kij and Aleksej Tolstoj, was never repaired. As a Scythian he objected to the canonization of Bolshevik Communism as the sole truth, and as a humanist he deplored the terror and repression that were rampant during the civil war of 1918–1921. He astutely discerned Communism to be a religion and, as such, subject to a tripartite development common to all religions — through the prophetic, the apostolic, and the ecclesiastical periods:

> The *prophetic stage*, of course, contained most of the peaks, the grandeur, and the romanticism. The Christians in the catacombs. In the *apostolic stage* they preach openly, but they still struggle ideologically, they have not conquered. And, finally, in the *ecclesiastical stage*, they have conquered on the *earthly* plane. And as all conquerors, the Christians begin forcible salvation: by force, by sword, by fire, by prisons. Christ becomes the Grand Inquisitor.[9]

As an avowed romantic, Zamjatin was interested only in the prophetic stage of any cause he championed. His ardor would cool at the apostolic stage, and the attainment of the ecclesiastical stage, with its concomitant philistinism, would turn him against the very cause he had supported. To the question, "which stage of religious development is Communism undergoing at the present," Zamjatin gave no answer, but it seems clear that he greatly feared a transition to the third and final stage. The subsequent history of the Soviet Union has borne out his fears.

Two of Zamjatin's basic theses — unending movement forward and the rejection of the present in the name of the distant future — were fundamental to his view of the Hegelian dialectic as the true representation of man's historical progress. Considering yesterday, today, and tomorrow to be immutably hostile to each other, Zamjatin saw them as the three members of Hegel's dialectical formula — thesis, antithesis, and synthesis:

> Today is doomed to die, because yesterday has died and because tomorrow shall be born. Such is the cruel and wise law. Cruel, because it dooms to eternal dissatisfaction those who today already see the distant heights of tomorrow; wise, because only eternal dissatisfaction is the guarantee of unending movement forward, of unending creativity. He who has found his ideal today, has already been turned into a pillar of salt as was Lot's wife, has already grown into the earth and moves no further. The world lives only by heretics: Christ the heretic, Copernicus the heretic, Tolstoj the heretic. Our creed is heresy: tomorrow is infallibly heresy for the today which has been turned into a pillar of salt, for the yesterday which has crumbled into dust. Today negates yesterday, but tomorrow is the negation of negation: always the same dialectical path, which carries the world into infinity along a grandiose parabola. Thesis yesterday, antithesis today, and synthesis tomorrow.[10]

This conception of the dialectical process, which represents a grafting of Hegel onto the eternally dissatisfied Scythian, underlay all of Zamjatin's future thinking. It ultimately was to lead to the extreme contention that "fortunately, all truths are false: the essence of the dialectical process is that today's truths become errors tomorrow; there is no final number."[11] He maintained that this sole truth existed only for the strong, not for the weak who needed the "crutches of certainty" and lacked the strength to include themselves in the dialectical process.

The key figure of the Hegelian dialectical spiral is the heretic who rejects the accepted canons, be they social, political, scientific, religious, or artistic, and looks ahead to the future. Without him, progress would be impossible. Zamjatin chose the role of heretic and in the ensuing years wrote several critical and philosophical articles in which he boldly developed his ideas. As Soviet Communism moved into the ecclesiastical stage, the heretic became more and more isolated, but not before he had played a very important role in Russian literary life of the first post-Revolutionary decade.

The pressures created by Russia's prolonged participation in World War I led to an economic breakdown, and the vicious civil war that followed the Bolshevik coup intensified existing shortages and resulted in extensive destruction of factories and estates. The subsequent three winters were a time of widespread famine, extreme cold, and unrelieved privation. That literature continued in any form during those terrible years is remarkable. The grim years of War Communism have been dubbed the Café Period in Russian literature, because verse, which is not dependent upon the printed word, could be transmitted to eager audiences at all hours in all places. The prose writer, however, fared considerably worse than the verse writer, for by the middle of 1918 the non-Bolshevik press had been silenced and all the traditional "thick" journals had ceased publication. Prose fiction ranked very low on the priority list for that very scarce commodity, paper; and most of what little was available passed into the hands of proletarian cultural organizations whose zealous but inexperienced authors produced prodigious quantities of naïve tedium. For most writers, artists, and musicians the need to survive supplanted the need to create. And their survival depended in part upon receiving regular rations from the government in return for serving in one of several benevolent organizations aimed at saving Russian intellectuals from starvation:

> For three years we were locked up together in a steel shell, and cramped in darkness we hurtled into the unknown with a whine. In these seconds-years before death, we had to do something, to accommodate and live in the hurtling shell. Humorous projects in the shell: "World Literature," "The Union of Practitioners of Imaginative Literature," "The Writers' Union," the Theater . . . And all of the surviving writers jostled one another in these cramped quarters — side by side were Gor'kij and Merežkovskij, Blok and Kuprin, Mujžel' and Gumilev, Čukovskij and Volynskij.[12]

The history of Zamjatin's publications and of his organizational activity accurately reflects the general situation during the civil war, but it is surprising that the years 1917–1920 marked Zamjatin's most intense and productive period of literary creativity.

When Zamjatin returned from England, he brought with him two completed works: a short story, "Pravda istinnaja" ("The Real Truth"), and the tale "Ostrovitjane." Cast in the form of a servant girl's letter which reveals her longing for the country despite her eulogy to town life, "Pravda istinnaja" thematically and stylistically is most closely related to Zamjatin's pre-Revolutionary works. On the other hand, "Ostrovitjane," with its stylistic innovations and new handling of the old themes of love, revolution, and philistinism, inaugurated a new phase in Zamjatin's literary evolution.

During the "gay, frightful winter of 1917–1918, when everything broke loose and flowed somewhere into obscurity" (A. III, 17), Zamjatin remained in Petrograd and continued writing. His most Čexovian story, "Zemlemer" ("The Surveyor"), was written late in 1917,[13] as was "O svjatom grexe Zenicydevy" ("About the Sacred Sin of the Precious Virgin"), the first of several irreverent stories in which sexual themes were treated in the ecclesiastical style of saints' lives. Written the following year, "Znamenie" ("The Sign") also touched on a sexual theme, but lacked the ecclesiastical style. "Lovec čelovekov" ("The Fisher of Men"), which originally had been conceived as the denouement to "Ostrovitjane" and then discarded, became an excellent story in its own right and continued the innovations of the mother tale.* In addition to the political fables and articles that appeared in Gor'kij's *Novaja žizn'* and Černov's *Delo naroda*, Zamjatin contributed several short fictional pieces, such as the allegory "Glaza" ("The Eyes") and the descriptive sketch "Drakon" ("The Dragon"), both of which reflected his keen concern for the preservation of human values at a time when conditions tended to destroy them.† The same theme underlay "Spodručnica grešnyx" ("The Protectress of Sinners"), the first in a series of satirical stories playing on incongruities of old

* Zamjatin expounded on this at length in his contribution to the collection *Kak my pišem* [156], 29–47, even appending his original outline and a variant ending for "Ostrovitjane." This material, when compared with the two works in their final forms, gives an excellent insight into his creative process. Unfortunately, the four-page appendix (pp. 44–47), as well as some extremely interesting comments on consonant and vowel instrumentation (pp. 38–39), were deleted in "Zakulisy," the widely read version reprinted in *Lica* [38], 259–274.

† Since the holdings of *Novaja žizn'* and *Delo naroda* in such Western libraries as the Hoover Institution in Stanford, Calif., and the Helsinki University Library are incomplete, other stories, fables, or articles by Zamjatin may have been published during this period (September 1917 to July 1918).

habits in post-Revolutionary Russia. He also penned four finely wrought vignettes which appeared together as *Vereški* (*Fragments*) in an attractive eight-page booklet graced with N. Ljubavina's illustrations; characterized by remarkable brevity (none exceeded eighty words), each vignette implicitly conveyed an idea through a combination of realistic and impressionistic description of concrete detail. That summer Zamjatin also contributed two chapters from an unfinished tale "Kolumb" ("Columbus") to a short popular miscellany edited by Gor'kij and Vl. Rozanov.

Since the impending winter of 1918–1919 promised the Petrograd intellectuals no relief from the shortage of food, fuel, and employment, many traveled to the country in search of provisions during the late summer months. Zamjatin returned to his home town of Lebedjan', where he completed his fifth and final tale, "Sever" ("The North"). On September 8 he delivered a lecture entitled "Sovremennaja russkaja literatura" ("Contemporary Russian Literature") at the recently established People's University of Lebedjan' (Lebedjan'skij narodnyj universitet).[14] In this lecture, which may be his most significant work of criticism, Zamjatin defined the essence of what he termed the Neorealistic movement in Russian literature. Applying the Hegelian dialectic to literary development, he effectively demonstrated that the Neorealism of the decade after 1910 could be considered a synthesis of nineteenth-century Realism (thesis) and early twentieth-century Symbolism (antithesis).

It is quite probable that Zamjatin had returned to Petrograd by December 1 in time to witness the opening of the House of Writers (Dom literatorov) on Bassejnaja Street. In any case, by January 1919 he was again immersed in the literary life of the capital. His activities at first centered around two organizations, both literary in character: the Union of Practitioners of Imaginative Literature (Sojuz dejatelej xudožestvennoj literatury, abbreviated SDXL) and the publishing house World Literature (Vsemirnaja literatura); but within two years his activity spread to include several others. Zamjatin's participation in these organizations strengthened his friendship with Gor'kij, whom he had first met in the autumn of 1917. This explains why the image of Gor'kij in Zamjatin's memory was invariably connected with post-Revolutionary Russia. During the years of War Communism (1918–1921) Gor'kij became an unofficial minister of culture and sought to alleviate the terrible privations of Russian intellectuals by the creation of numerous institutions and establishments that provided employment and housing for them. He was the chairman of virtually all such undertakings, and Zamjatin, who was elected to the boards of directors of three or four, met with Gor'kij frequently throughout this period. It is known that Gor'kij praised Zamjatin's mind and talent and that he considered him to be a connoisseur of the Russian language. But by the mid-twenties Gor'kij's opinion had apparently changed, for he was highly critical of one of Zamjatin's stories and especially of his novel *My*.* Nonetheless, in 1931 Gor'kij gave Stalin Zamjatin's frank letter protesting his intolerable position, and it was through Gor'kij's influence that Zamjatin was able to obtain a visa to go abroad.[15]

The SDXL was organized by the symbolist poet Fedor Sologub and his wife Anastasija Čebotarevskaja in March 1918, in an effort to provide material aid to Petrograd writers. Membership numbered forty at the first general meeting on May 20. Evidently, Zamjatin was a charter member, because two weeks earlier, on May 7, he had been one of eleven writers participating in an afternoon SDXL public reading at the Academy of Arts (Akademija xudožestv).[16] Offices and a meeting hall, as well as a dormitory and dining hall, were set up later in what had been the mansion of M. A. Ginzburg, which the government as-

* In his recollections, "Gor'kij sredi nas" [569], Fedin mentioned that Gor'kij "praises Evgenij Zamjatin's talent and his intellect," and Gor'kij himself called Zamjatin a "fine connoisseur of the Russian language" in his essay "Gor'kij o molodyx," [582], 19. Yet the following year in commenting on Zamjatin's "Rasskaz o samom glavnom" in a letter to the émigré poet V. F. Xodasevič, Gor'kij wrote: "I am in complete agreement with your evaluation of Zamjatin. Having read his story, I made a mental note: 'a surplus of intellect hinders Zamjatin in making a proper assessment of the extent of his own talent. Zamjatin's intellect is not bright and deceives him. His thoughts are blind.' " *Novyj žurnal*, No. 31 (1952), 194. Five years later in a letter to I. A. Gruzdev, Gor'kij again criticized Zamjatin's excessive intelligence: "And Zamjatin is too intelligent for an artist and should not allow his reason to direct his talent to satire. *My* is hopelessly bad, a completely sterile thing. Its anger is cold and dry; it is the anger of an old maid." *Sobranie sočinenij*, XXX (Moskva, 1955), 126.

signed to the SDXL on July 4. Because the governing body of the SDXL was inactive, a new council, headed by Viktor Mujžel', was elected on October 30. Appointed director of World Literature in September 1918, Gor'kij conceived of the SDXL as a parallel publisher that would print Russian literary works, ranging from the late eighteenth century to the present.

On January 13, 1919, a nine-man editorial board was elected by the SDXL with Gor'kij as chairman and Zamjatin as a member, and ambitious plans for various publications were drafted. Two series of works by contemporary authors were projected and approved; each series consisted of ten titles by ten different writers, and 50 per cent advances were actually disbursed to authors represented in the first series, which included Zamjatin's "Uezdnoe."

Plans for the publication of a journal titled *Literaturnyj sovremennik* (*The Literary Contemporary*) were worked out in great detail. Gor'kij was designated chief editor, with Zamjatin and Čukovskij as co-editors, but the actual duties of editing were assigned to Zamjatin. Conceived as a bimonthly, *Literaturnyj sovremennik*, like all other projected publications of the SDXL, failed to appear, even though manuscripts were solicited, selected, and edited. In Zamjatin's account of SDXL's magazine project, the title was cited as *Zavtra* (*Tomorrow*), and he was entrusted with the task of writing a literary manifesto.[17] Zamjatin's account made no mention of *Literaturnyj sovremennik*, just as P. Širmakov's account of SDXL activities made no mention of *Zavtra*; thus, it is not clear whether there were two different magazines or one under two names. In any case, Zamjatin did write a short programmatic article ("Zavtra") which was published that same year; and, interestingly enough, he helped edit a miscellany under the title *Zavtra* four years later for the Berlin publisher Petropolis.

The SDXL editorial board also projected a series of literary almanacs. At the third meeting of the editorial board on March 5, 1919, the contents of the first almanac were determined, and Zamjatin's most recent tale "Sever" was included. Although none of the publication plans were realized, some forty manuscripts (excluding books) were read and edited by Gor'kij, Kuprin, Gumilev, Šiškov, Zamjatin, Mujžel', and Čukovskij for the SDXL publications.* In addition to its ambitious publication projects, SDXL organized a series of literary evenings. Altogether, six such evenings were held in March and April of 1919, and Gor'kij and Zamjatin were among those who participated in the first, which took place on March 24 at the Grotesk Theater. On April 25 at a joint meeting with the SDXL council the entire editorial board gave notice of its resignation from the SDXL. Although the reason has not been revealed, the exodus may have been due to protests by SDXL founder Sologub against government interference. The SDXL nominally continued its existence until August, but actually ceased functioning in May.

World Literature, the second organization to which Zamjatin devoted much time during the first half of 1919 (as well as in later years), had been conceived by four men — Gor'kij, Aleksandr Tixonov (who wrote under the pseudonyms of A. and N. Serebrov), Zinovij Gržebin, and Ivan Ladyžnikov. It had come into being on September 4, 1918, when an agreement with the People's Commissariat of Education (known as Narkompros) was signed.[18] Aimed at making world literary classics readily available to the Russian people, World Literature was to have been the most extensive translation enterprise in Europe, thereby demonstrating and propagandizing the international scope and cultural benefits of the proletarian revolution.

Specifically, it was the task of World Literature to select, translate, and publish non-Russian literary works of the nineteenth and late eighteenth centuries, but later the program was expanded to include works of earlier periods and of the twentieth century as well. Each volume was to be annotated, illustrated, and supplied with an introductory essay. Gor'kij, as head of the publishing house, was granted complete autonomy and administrative control in carrying out the project. An editorial board of eleven experts, consisting of Professors Fedor Batjuškov and Fedor Braun, Blok, Čukovskij, Gor'kij, Gumilev, Andrej Levinson, Grigorij Lozinskij, A. Tixonov, A. Volynskij

* Kuprin is said to have edited Zamjatin's "Žizn' nesmertel'naja" ("Life Immortal"), but the work was probably written by Remizov and not Zamjatin, as claimed by Širmakov, [694], 471.

(pseudonym of Akim Flekser), and Zamjatin, drafted a detailed program and selected the authors and works to be translated. Two hundred translators were employed, and an additional one hundred and fifty writers and scholars were engaged to write introductions and edit the texts.

The original program included only the literatures of Western Europe and the Americas, but early in 1919 a section devoted to literatures of the East was created. On April 29, only four days after the editorial board of the SDXL had resigned, Narkompros allowed World Literature to take over the documents, manuscripts, and funds of the "liquidated" editorial board and establish its own section on twentieth-century Russian literature. SDXL's first series was adopted with a few changes (Zamjatin was still included), and soon most of the SDXL second series evidently was approved, bringing the number of books planned for the Russian section to twenty.[19] Thus, the work of the SDXL editorial board was not wasted, but merely was placed under the jurisdiction of a different organization, made up of essentially the same people.

Although five hundred printer's sheets (the equivalent of twenty-five good-sized volumes) had been dispatched to the typesetter, and manuscripts ready in the editorial office amounted to another three thousand printer's sheets, World Literature was able to publish only two books during the first nine months of its existence (September, 1918 to June, 1919).* The meagerness of its output was due solely to the lack of paper, which was impossible to obtain despite Gor'kij's desperate pleas to various agencies and even to Lenin, himself. During the next twelve months some paper was obtained, and fifty-two titles were published by July 1920. The paper shortage continued to limit the number of publications drastically, and although five hundred printer's sheets had been published by February 1921, the backlog of manuscripts had risen to eight thousand printer's

* [647], 85–86. Twenty-five good-sized volumes is only a rough estimate. World Literature published books of two sizes: basic editions of 20 printer's sheets (16 pp.) each and people's editions of 4 printer's sheets. In practice, the basic editions numbered about three hundred pages, and the people's editions, about one hundred; but the size limitations were not rigorously followed.

sheets. Thus, the publishing house was functioning at only 6 per cent of its capacity.

Zamjatin's role in the activities and projects of World Literature was threefold. First, he served on the eleven-man editorial planning board. Second, he personally edited and wrote introductions for many volumes. Among the first fifty-four publications were three volumes by H. G. Wells and three by Jack London, all edited by Zamjatin.[20] In the following four years Zamjatin edited two more volumes by Wells, two volumes by Bernard Shaw, another volume of London's stories, a collection of Romain Rolland's plays, a collection of O. Henry's stories, and the magazine *Sovremennyj zapad* (*The Contemporary West*, 1922–1924). Zamjatin's third and perhaps most important contribution was the many hours he spent in World Literature's studio for translators. Established in February 1919, the studio was conceived as a practical workshop for literary analysis and the composition of prose and verse translations. At first, regular seminars were conducted by Gumilev, Levinson, Mixail Lozinskij, and Valerian Čudovskij; and Zamjatin and Čukovskij delivered lectures on various subjects.[21] The results were so gratifying that by June it was decided to enlarge the scope of the studio and to grant admission to anyone interested in the study of literature and composition. Apparently the studio was still active four years later, during the spring of 1923. Although Zamjatin was engaged in editorial work for World Literature as late as 1924, it is not known how long he continued teaching at the studio.

As new organizations continued to spring up and develop, Zamjatin became more and more involved in an organizational web, which, although it enabled writers to live, nevertheless often diverted their energy and talents to activities that hindered free creative expression. In an outspoken criticism of "nimble" authors who changed their attitude to suit the prevailing political breeze, Zamjatin cleverly illustrated the problem of subsistence for the "non-nimble" writers, who remained silent during the civil war years:

> The writer who cannot become nimble must go to work with a briefcase if he wants to stay alive. In our day Gogol' would run with a briefcase to the theatrical department; Turgenev would un-

doubtedly be translating Balzac and Flaubert for World Literature; Gercen would be lecturing at the Baltic Fleet; and Čexov would be working in the Commissariat of Public Health. In other words, in order to live — to live as a student lived on forty rubles five years ago — Gogol' would have to write four *Revizors* [*Inspector Generals*] a month, Turgenev — three *Otcy i deti* [*Fathers and Sons*] every two months, and Čexov — a hundred stories a month. This may seem an absurd jest, but unfortunately the figures are true and not a jest.[22]

Late in May 1919, at a meeting of the Major Art Council of the Department of Theaters and Spectacles in Petrograd (Bol'šoj xudožestvennyj sovet Otdela teatrov i zrelišč v Petrograde), Gor'kij presented his idea for the creation of a cycle of plays that would depict the history of the world. The unifying theme was to be man's intellectual development: the rise of superstition and religious cults on the one hand, and the development of scientific thought on the other. In Gor'kij's own words: "It is necessary to guide two-legged mammals through all earthshaking events which are accessible to their senses and to show what forced them to create a world of benevolent and evil deities around and above themselves. Along with this should be developed the process of systematic observation — the work of the practical mind, which in due time becomes scientific." [23]

Gor'kij envisioned the myth of Prometheus as the beginning of this vast history to be followed by dramas on such subjects as the Idylls of Theocritus, the life of Christ, the sermons of Buddha, the Nicene and other church councils, Byzantium, Saint John Chrysostom, and various barbaric tribes. A committee consisting of Blok, Gor'kij, Gumilev, Tixonov, and Zamjatin, to be known as the Section of Historical Pageants (Sekcija istoričeskix kartin), was established, and its members proceeded to work out a detailed program for the cycle. Topics were assigned, and several plays were written — among them, Blok's *Ramzes* and Zamjatin's *Ogni svjatogo Dominika* (*The Fires of St. Dominic*). The section was promised its own theater, but when that failed to materialize the plays were first assigned to the People's House (Narodnyj dom) and then passed on to Vasileostrovskij Theater. Rather than having their plays performed in theaters of such poor quality, the section chose to veto production. The section was disbanded in 1921.[24]

Zamjatin's participation in the section marked the beginning of an active involvement in drama. His first play, *Ogni svjatogo Dominika*, written for the section, was completed by the spring of 1920.[25] Although set in sixteenth-century Spain during the Inquisition, the play was contemporary in thought, for it centered on Zamjatin's favorite themes of heresy, humanism, and the fallibility of all monolithic "truths." During the following summer, he collaborated with Blok in translating and staging *King Lear* at the Bolšoj Dramatic Theater.[26] Zamjatin's interest in the theater proved to be a lasting one — for once, his organizational activity led him to creative experimentation in a new genre.

The House of Arts (Dom iskusstv), with the aid and blessing of the Narkompros, was established in the autumn of 1919 to unite the writers and artists of Petrograd and to use their talents in cultural and educational projects. At the same time, provision of work and lodgings would enable them to devote themselves to their chosen professions. The initiative again belonged to Gor'kij, who, naturally enough, emerged as the head of the new establishment. The governing council of the House of Arts at first consisted of two sections, of writers and of artists. A third section, of composers, was added in February 1920. Zamjatin, a member of the original council, was reelected when the council was reorganized in March 1921, and again in December 1921,[27] which attests his popularity and competence in literary affairs.

Mondays at the House of Arts were devoted to literary evenings and lectures open to the public, while Friday evenings were for more intimate gatherings restricted to members and their friends. The House of Arts was officially opened December 19, 1919,[28] and on the following Friday Zamjatin read his story "Lovec čelovekov." The first Monday evening was devoted to the memory of Leonid Andreev (who had died on September 12), and Zamjatin was among those who read their recollections. Throughout the next two years Zamjatin was a frequent contributor to the literary evenings and lectures. On October 7, 1920, at an evening devoted to the magazine *Dom iskusstv* (of which Zamjatin was an editor), he read his new story "Detskaja" ("The Nursery"). Later that month at an evening dedicated to the second issue of *Zapiski mečtatelej* (*Dreamers' Notes*), Zamjatin read his most recent story, "Mamaj," and also his "Tulumbas; poslanie smirennogo Zamutija, episkopa obez'janskogo" ("Tulumbas; the Epistle of Humble Zamutij, Bishop of the Apes"), a clever satire on conditions in Russia, cast in the form of a sermon. During the first half of 1921 Zamjatin, in connection with his work for World Literature, contributed two lectures on the novels of H. G. Wells; and at the first of two evenings devoted to imaginative prose he read his tale "Sever" and the story "Peščera" ("The Cave"), which depicted the personal tragedy of two people during a cold Petersburg winter.

Another organization which helped revive cultural activity in Petrograd was the House of Writers (Dom literatorov). Organized in the autumn of 1918 chiefly to relieve the material hardship of writers' lives, it opened on December 1, 1918, and soon became the gathering place of the older intelligentsia. In January 1919, the House of Writers began publishing *Vestnik literatury*, which was the major magazine devoted solely to literature that managed to appear with some semblance of regularity throughout the terrible years of War Communism.[29] The House of Writers continued to function as a gathering place and refuge (it had a dining room and warm reading rooms) for its members throughout 1919. On January 22, 1920, it launched an ambitious cultural program of two hundred and seven evening gatherings in one year. Included in the program were thirty lectures on literature and twelve "live almanacs," where contemporary authors read their works. This intensive program was continued for the next two years. In 1921 the House of Writers began issuing *Letopis' Doma literatorov* (*The Annals of the House of Writers*). Three issues (unnumbered) appeared in the *Vestnik literatury*, but beginning on November 1, 1921, the annals were published separately as a bimonthly scholarly journal of literature, criticism, and bibliography.[30] Both the *Vestnik literatury* and the *Letopis' Doma literatorov* ceased publication early in 1922. Another magazine, *Literaturnye zapiski* (*Literary Notes*), replaced the former and first appeared in May, but it also ceased publication after only three issues.

Evidently, Zamjatin was as active a member of the House of Writers as he was of the Petrograd House of Arts. He contributed several articles to its various publications. One of the live almanacs for 1920 was dedicated to him,[31] and he was a major speaker at an evening dedicated to the memory of Blok.[32] When the House of Writers announced a literary contest in September 1920, Zamjatin was appointed one of eight judges, and it was he who delivered a sparkling analysis of the fourteen winning stories at an open meeting of the judges the following June.[33] On December 27, 1921, he was elected to the nineteen-member committee that governed the house and its activities.[34]

In view of Zamjatin's numerous literary and editorial activities, it is not surprising that he was active in the formation of the Petrograd section of the All-Russian Union of Writers (Vserossijskij sojuz pisatelej, abbreviated VSP), which was organized in the spring of 1920. The VSP was the leading writers' organization throughout the twenties. The constituent meeting took place July 4, but the members vigorously protested the proposed bylaws, which had been set up by the already established Moscow section. Among other things, the Petrograd writers refused to be subordinated to the Moscow section and demanded that the criteria of admission be considerably widened. Zamjatin was one of nine members elected to a three-month provisional directorate, empowered to carry out the changes requested by the assembly; and he was among those retained on the directorate when (with some changes in size and membership) it acquired permanent status in October.[35] With time, the need for an independent professional publication of literary criticism became acute, and the Petrograd VSP (with the agreement of the Moscow section) decided to launch a biweekly paper, *Literaturnaja gazeta* (*The Literary Gazette*). Elected as editors were Čukovskij, A. Tixonov, Volynskij, and Zamjatin. The publication of a newspaper was denied by the appropriate government agencies, but they did grant the VSP permission to publish a bimonthly magazine. The first issue, which included Zamjatin's essay "Pora" ("It's Time"), was sent to the typesetter, but "due to circumstances beyond the editors' control" it failed to appear.* In December 1921, at the yearly general meeting of the VSP, Zamjatin presented a detailed report about the ill-fated publication;[36] unfortunately, that report has never been published, although it may still be in the Soviet archives. At the same December meeting, Zamjatin was elected to the board for another year. Although no other information is available concerning Zamjatin's activity on the VSP board, he must have continued to play a leading role until he resigned in September 1929. In an article dated July 1, 1926, militant Communist critic Georgij Gorbačev complained that "the Union of Writers in Leningrad did not elect leftist fellow travelers time to its board at the present, but chose Zamjatin, the publisher of the *Russkij sovremennik* Tixonov, [and] Šiškov. . . ."[37] In 1927, when the Leningrad section of the Federation of Soviet Writers' Organizations (Federacija ob"edinenij sovetskix pisatelej, abbreviated FOSP) was being organized, Zamjatin was one of four VSP members elected to its governing Soviet.[38] Then, or perhaps somewhat later, he also served as chairman of the Leningrad VSP.[39] The reluctance of Leningrad's VSP to censure him when he was denounced in 1929, as well as the heated debates which took place at that time, testify to Zamjatin's popularity and the support which he enjoyed among Leningrad writers throughout the 1920's.

The importance of Zamjatin's role as editor and administrator during the early years of the Soviet regime cannot be denied. Of greater and more lasting importance were his own creative work and his influence on young writers. His work with beginning writers started in 1919 at the literary studio of World Literature, which has been described already. Among his pupils were three gifted young prose writers—Lev Lunc, Nikolaj Nikitin, and Mixail Zoščenko.[40] In December 1919, when the literary studio of the House of Arts opened, its teachers included most of the World Literature staff. At the new studio Zamjatin conducted a class in creative writing entitled "The Techniques of Imagina-

* Anon., "Sojuz pisatelej," *Dom iskusstv*, No. 2 (1921), 122. Xodasevič [727] mentioned his own lead article and a revolutionary story by Zamjatin as the reason for the closing of the paper. Two sample copies, which had been run off before the type was spilled from the galleys by Cheka officers, may be extant today in the archives of the Pushkin House or of the House of Writers.

tive Prose."[41] Of the numerous students in that course, some, like Lunc, Nikitin, and Zoščenko, were continuing their studies with him; others, like Veniamin Kaverin (pseudonym of V. Zil'ber), were just beginning.[42] In February 1921, a group of young authors, including several of Zamjatin's pupils, formed a literary circle called the Serapion Brothers. Zamjatin frequently visited their meetings, where he often spoke to them of plot, rhythm, and instrumentation. Evidently, his efforts were not wasted. In a House of Writers short story contest which attracted one hundred and two entries, five of the top six places went to students of Zamjatin or members of the Serapion Brothers.[43] In addition to his work at the two studios, during the winter of 1920–1921 Zamjatin lectured on modern Russian literature at the Gercen Pedagogical Institute (Pedagogičeskij institut imeni Gercena).

Despite his extensive organizational, editorial, and pedagogical activities, the four years from mid-1917 to mid-1921 marked Zamjatin's most intense and productive period of literary creativity. During that time he wrote a novel, a play, two tales, fifteen stories, fourteen fables, four vignettes, and a dozen articles. The year 1920 had been the zenith of Zamjatin's imaginative fiction, for, in addition to the anti-utopian novel *My* (*We*), he had produced "Detskaja," "Mamaj," "Tulumbas," "Pirog" ("The Pie"),[44] and "O tom, kak iscelen byl inok Erazm" ("How the Monk Erazmus Was Cured"), which was the best example of Zamjatin's unusual satiric combination of sexual and religious themes in a pseudo-ecclesiastical form and style. The adverse effect of his numerous activities upon his creative writing was manifest earlier, if at all, during 1919, when Zamjatin apparently failed to produce even one work of prose fiction. However, it is quite possible that he had already begun marshaling ideas and drafting plans for *My*. The thought of writing a fantastic novel had occurred to him as early as the winter of 1917–1918, but the conception he had then described to Gor'kij bore no resemblance to the finished product.[45] The necessary stimulus for *My* undoubtedly came from Zamjatin's editorial work in 1919 on translations of H. G. Wells's sociofantastic novels and perhaps from acquaintance with some works by Anatole France as well. Apparently *My* was written in 1920, but Zamjatin spent considerable time polishing and revising it the following year.* Although its publication was announced late in 1921 and throughout the next two years, the novel has yet to be published in the Soviet Union. Translated into at least ten foreign languages, *My* remains Zamjatin's major literary work, his lasting contribution to world literature.

The marked decrease in the quantity of Zamjatin's new prose fiction after 1921 was obscured because much of what he wrote from 1918 to 1920 was first published in book form under his name in 1922 and 1923.[46] This has led literary historians to attribute the bulk of his literary production incorrectly to the twenties. During the period 1921–1927, the time of the New Economic Policy (NEP), his output of imaginative prose dwindled to seven short stories, an average of only one a year. In the fall of 1922, Zamjatin was asked to review a collection of Boris Kustodiev's watercolors entitled "Russkie tipy" ("Russian Types"); instead he was inspired to write the story "Rus'" ("Old Russia"), which was published the following year in a slender

* The date of writing the novel is subject to question. In A. II [178], 43, Zamjatin wrote that "*My* was written in 1921–1922; the novel has been translated into English in New York," but in his letter to the editors of *Literaturnaja gazeta* on September 24, 1929 [188], he stated, "the novel *My* was written in 1920. In 1921 the manuscript was sent . . . to the Gržebin Publishing House in Berlin." There is good evidence that the novel had not been completed before 1921. Three contradictory announcements in the "Sud'ba i rabota russkix pisatelej, učenyx i žurnalistov za 1918–1921 g." section of *Russkaja kniga* stated that "a large fantastic novel has been completed" (Apr. 1921); Zamjatin "is working on a long novel" (June 1921); and that he "has written the novel *My*, which depicts a Communist society 800 years from now" (Sept. 1921). From this, one may postulate that in the spring of 1921 the novel was near completion and was at last finished by that September. Other evidence supports this assumption. In his memoirs of Zamjatin [300], 62, Ju. Annenkov stated that during the summer of 1921 "Zamjatin 'cleaned up,' as he used to say, his novel *My*," which implies that Zamjatin had already written the novel but was in his customary process of rewriting and polishing. The publication of *My* in No. 5 of *Zapiski mečtatelej* was announced in "Xronika; v Petrograde," *Pečat' i revoljucija*, No. 3 (Nov.–Dec. 1921), 301, and elsewhere often throughout 1922. Gregory Zilboorg was already translating *My* into English in 1922: "Evgenij Zamjatin's novel *My* will appear in English translation in New York prior to its publication in Russian; the translator M. [sic] Zil'burg is also busy with an English translation of some of Blok's works." Anon. "Literaturnaja xronika," *Literaturnaja mysl'*, No. 1 (Petrograd, 1922), 251. When taken together, these announcements indicate that Zamjatin completed *My* during the second half of 1921.

volume together with Kustodiev's drawings. Stylistically a refinement of the *skaz* manner of Zamjatin's early tales, "Rus'" stood apart from them in its positive treatment of the love theme and its eulogistic tone in describing a world that was no more. The same mood prevailed in "Kuny" ("Midsummer Games"), which was written at about the same time and in which the love theme was expressed in midsummer day folk customs of northern Russia. Zamjatin's major work of this period, the long story "Rasskaz o samom glavnom" ("A Story About the Most Important Thing"), was written in 1923 and represented his sole attempt to use the method of broken narrative conducted simultaneously on several parallel planes. That story was followed by "O čude, proisšedšem v Pepel'nuju Sredu" ("The Miracle That Happened on Ash Wednesday"), a naughty anecdote about a gullible homosexual canon who gave birth to a son.[47] Several years later Zamjatin used the same comic situation of a pregnant monk when he parodied the history of his own play *Bloxa* (*The Flea*) from the moment of its conception to its closing night at the Leningrad Bol'šoj Dramatic Theater. The parody "Žitie Bloxi . . ." was written for a special evening of parody held at the House of Arts early in December 1926 by the Physio-Geocentric Association (Fizio-geocentričeskaja associacija, abbreviated FIGA, a pun) and its publication three years later included Kustodiev's humorous illustrations. Earlier in 1926 he had written the stories "Iks" ("*X*") and "Slovo predostavljaetsja tovarišču Čuryginu" ("Comrade Čurygin Has the Floor"), affectionate satires on the superficial adaptations of some people to the new Soviet environment.

Zamjatin's rather meager production of imaginative prose during the NEP can be attributed to several factors. First, with maturity Zamjatin became more and more exacting and sought to achieve the utmost in stylistic precision. He himself was among the first to admit this early in 1922: "Now I write little — evidently because I am becoming more and more demanding of myself," (A. I). Second, having essentially perfected the literary technique of what he considered to be neorealism in such works as "Detskaja," "Peščera," and *My*, Zamjatin, true to his belief in unending revolution and avowed heresy, wanted to continue blazing new trails in literature. "Rasskaz o samon glavnom" represented such an attempt, but evidently it was not the answer.

A third inhibiting factor was the atmosphere of constant criticism from Communist and proletarian critics, increasing difficulty in finding publishers, and surveillance by the government. From the very beginning Zamjatin was branded a bourgeois writer and inner émigré who was antagonistic to the Revolution and the Soviet regime. In the fall of 1922 he was arrested by the Soviet government, along with one hundred and sixty other intellectuals whose activities were considered to be oppositionist and undesirable.[48] Most were given Soviet passports and sent permanently abroad, but Zamjatin, unfortunately, was reprieved through the intervention of his friends. He had been overjoyed at the idea of being sent abroad and was extremely disappointed when he learned that his friends had "helped" him. Immediately afterwards Zamjatin requested permission to be deported, but was categorically refused.[49] Examination of a bibliography of Zamjatin's works will reveal that they were published exclusively in miscellanies and such short-lived, politically "right-wing" journals as Isaj Ležnev's *Rossija* (*Russia*) and Zamjatin's own *Russkij sovremennik* (*The Russian Contemporary*), but never in such leading Soviet "thick" journals as *Krasnaja nov'* (*Red Virgin Soil*), *Oktjabr'* (*October*), and *Zvezda* (*Star*). It is also highly significant that the leading critical and bibliographical journal of the twenties, the Communist *Pečat' i revolucija* (*Press and Revolution*), conspicuously ignored Zamjatin and failed to review any of his more than twenty-five books in the period 1922–1930. The publication of *My* has never been permitted in the Soviet Union. And apparently Zamjatin's foreign correspondence was subject to censorship.[50]

A fourth factor limiting Zamjatin's literary production was his ever-expanding editorial work and his continued activity in literary organizations and studios. Although the latter have been discussed, it should be added that when the Petrograd Institute of the Living Word (Institut živogo slova) was reorganized and expanded in 1923, Zamjatin was one of the instructors actively employed there.[51] When the Z. I. Gržebin Publishing House was established in Stockholm in the spring of 1919 as an independent and privately owned foreign extension of World Literature, Gržebin drew heavily on the staff and manuscripts of the parent publishing house.[52] Invited to collaborate in the section on Russian literature, Zamjatin edited and wrote an introduction for a three-volume collection of Čexov's works. He also wrote a brief but very interesting biography of the nineteenth-century German physicist Julius Robert von Mayer (1814–1878) and was rumored to have done a biography of Thomas Edison.[53] Zamjatin also served as editor for the Alkonost Publishing House, founded by S. M. Aljanskij in 1918, and contributed to Alkonost's periodical *Zapiski mečtatelej* (*Dreamers' Notes*), published from 1919 to 1922 and edited by Andrej Belyj (pseudonym of Boris Bugaev).[54] His excellent study on the novels of H. G. Wells was published by Epoch (Èpoxa), a Petrograd publishing house founded in 1921 in which Zamjatin and Čukovskij were co-editors.[55] Soon after, collaborating with Mixail Kuzmin and M. Lozinskij, he edited the miscellany *Zavtra* for Petropolis; and from 1924 to 1926 he prepared a twelve-volume edition of H. G. Wells' collected works for the Thought (Mysl') Publishing House.[56] In 1924, with A. Tixonov, Abram Èfros, and Čukovskij, he edited *Russkij sovremennik*, the best privately owned journal in the Soviet Union. Gor'kij, who was living abroad and boycotting all Soviet publications at that time because the Soviet government would not allow the distribution of his Berlin journal *Beseda* (*Discourses*) within the Soviet Union, agreed to contribute to *Russkij sovremennik* and was listed as one of its editors. The address of the editorial offices was the same as Zamjatin's,[57] which would indicate that the bulk of editorial duties had fallen on him. The journal ceased publication after four issues, due to financial difficulties, and desperate efforts the following year failed to resurrect it. When one considers that Zamjatin also had been actively engaged in editing the magazines *Dom iskusstv* (1921) and *Sovremennyj zapad* (1922–1924), then it becomes obvious that his editorial work must have become a major occupation during the early years of the NEP.

Zamjatin's preoccupation with such nonfiction genres as biography, essay, criticism, and book reviewing during the early twenties also helps account for the corresponding decline in the amount of his prose fiction. It is true that many of his essays stemmed from his editorial activities and were simply introductions to articles or collections by such writers as Jack London, H. G. Wells, O. Henry, Čexov, Georges Duhamel, and Bernard Shaw, while others were inspired either by death (Andreev, Blok, Anatole France, Kustodiev) or by anniversary celebrations (Čexov, Sologub) and ranged from purely personal recollections to critical commentary. In addition to a handful of book reviews, Zamjatin did write two extremely perceptive and interesting critical articles on the new literature that had begun to appear in 1922 and 1923, "Novaja russkaja proza" ("New Russian Prose") and "O segodnjašnem i o sovremennom" ("On the Topical and on the Modern"). But of greatest interest were his three programmatic essays "Ja bojus'" ("I Am Afraid"), "O sintetizme" ("On Synthesis"), and "O literature, revoljucii, èntropii i o pročem" ("On Literature, Revolution, Entropy, and Other Things"), in which he further developed the philosophic ideas expressed previously in "Skify li?" and "Zavtra."

The sixth and probably decisive factor was Zamjatin's growing interest in drama and the theater after 1924. That spring Aleksej Dikij, director of the Second Moscow Art Theater (MXAT 2-j), visited Leningrad on tour with his troupe and asked Zamjatin to write a stage adaptation of Nikolaj Leskov's popular story "Levša" ("Lefty").[58] Zamjatin's adaptation, *Bloxa* (*The Flea*), was written that summer and was first performed by MXAT 2-j on February 11, 1925. The play, acknowledged as one of Dikij's most significant productions, was "astonishing in the audacity of staging, richness of fantasy, emotion, and love for the Russian craftsman Levša and for the Russian land."[59] During the summer of 1924 Zamjatin also wrote an adaptation of "Ostrovitjane" which he called *Obščestvo početnyx zvonarej* (*The Society of Honorable Bellringers*). The play was approved for performance by the local repertory committee on September 29, 1924, but was first performed a year later, on November 21, 1925, by the Mixailovskij Theater in Leningrad.[60] The second play, however, was well known in literary circles long before then; a week before the premiere of *Bloxa* Zamjatin had given a public reading of *Obščestvo početnyx zvonarej* at the Moscow House of Scholars (Dom učenyx).[61] With the staging of *Bloxa* and the rehearsals of *Obščestvo početnyx zvonarej* in progress, the autumn and winter of 1924–1925 were indeed busy for Zamjatin. He wrote in March 1925: "The theater interests me very much, but takes much time. The theaters and magazine *Russkij sovremnnik* have eaten up five months of my time; with the exception of two or three essays I have written nothing during this time." [62]

In the same letter Zamjatin announced that he had given up writing prose to take up a much more prosaic profession — that of playwright. In the fall of 1924 he had begun work on a long tale dealing with the struggle between dying Rome and the barbaric hordes of the East, but by March of 1925 he was already considering the possibility of turning the same material into a play.[63] Zamjatin continued working on this theme simultaneously in the two genres. By 1927 the play *Attila*, a tragedy in verse, had been completed, and the tale had begun to assume the proportions of a novel, although it was still very much in the drafting stage.[64] The actual conception of the basic theme undoubtedly goes back to May 1919 when Gor'kij, in presenting his idea for a cycle of historical plays, suggested the topic, "The Huns — Attila's reception of the Roman envoys." [65] Thus it can be said that Zamjatin's participation in the Section of Historical Pageants inspired his first two original plays, *Ogni svjatogo Dominika* and *Attila*.

By 1927 the theater had begun to attract many young writers, and Zamjatin devoted more and more time to it. His two-scene adaptation of "Peščera" was accepted by the Vaxtangov Studio of MXAT after the first reading. Furthermore, at the request of Vsevolod Mejerhol'd, Zamjatin made a stage adaptation of Mixail Saltykov-Ščedrin's novel *Istorija goroda Glupova* (*The History of Sillytown*).[66] The following year in collaboration with Dmitrij Šostakovič he wrote the first act libretto of *Nos* (*The Nose*), an opera which was included in the repertory of the Malyj Academic Opera Theater.[67] It is probable that his interest in writing plays was to some degree stimulated by the promise of lucrative royalties at a time when few of his works were being published. In his own words, "The successful playwright, who gets his 5 or 6 per cent of the box office receipts, is the only legitimate bourgeois in Russia today; and nobody interferes with his wealth." [68] Zamjatin's skill in handling dialogue, his tendency to show (*pokazyvanie*) rather than to narrate (*rasskazyvanie*), and his predilection for dynamic plots with a prominent love interest in his prose works made the transition to writing plays both natural and easy. The very same features did much to assure his success as a scenarist in the rapidly expanding motion picture industry. He first tried his hand at that "in self-defense" in 1927, but then unfortunately he devoted most of the last five years of his life to it:

> It happened like this. There is a story of mine called "Northern Love" ["Sever"], a bit Knut Hamsun-ish, full of Laplanders and reindeer. Ivanovsky, who afterwards did *Decembrists*, produced it. He shot most of the scenes at Alexandrovsk, on the Murman Coast, and there is some glorious Arctic scenery in the film. It was a great success in the heydey of the silent film. When I say that I had to act in self-defense, it was simply because they gave my story to one of their sworn-in scenario hacks; so I had to take it away from him.[69]

The filming of *Severnaja ljubov'* (*Northern Love*), which was closely followed by Soviet theater magazines, was filled with incident. On the Murman Coast the troupe found an unnamed waterfall which they promptly christened "Northern Love." Later during the shooting of a bear hunt in Moscow's Sokol'niki Park, the bear, frightened by a random shot, attacked the actors, severely mauled his trainer, and had to be caught by a detachment of police.[70] This incident was caricatured by A. Radakov in a cartoon showing several policemen at the precinct station holding a shackled bear who is testifying, "Comrade chairman, if you read that scenario, you'd start attacking people, too!"[71] Evidently Zamjatin was in full agreement with the bear; in disgust at Sovkino's script changes, Zamjatin requested that his name be withdrawn from the film. The premiere took place on February 24, 1928, and Zamjatin's name appeared both on the film and in newspaper advertisements.[72] He immediately published a letter protesting that "a trite, middle-class happy ending had been added, a series of cuts which weakened the moments of highest tension had been made, stylistically inappropriate titles had been added," and rejecting any responsibility for the artistic "merits" of the film.[73]

Zamjatin's second attempt at scenario writing, an adaptation of "Peščera," proved to be even more abortive: "I started writing the scenario; but when I saw what they were doing with it I gave it up. My story was the tragedy about two ordinary human beings; they turned it into a propaganda film about the 'rotting ex-upper classes'—though Ermler, I admit, is a pretty able producer." [74] The scenario was eventually done by Leonidov, although Zamjatin was credited with the original story, and the film *Dom v sugrobax* (*The House in the Snowdrifts*) was released on March 23, 1928.[75]

After this brief excursion in the world of cinema, Zamjatin returned to prose. During the following two years he continued work on his novel about Attila and also wrote three stories—a brief anecdote entitled "Desjatiminutnaja drama" ("A Ten-Minute Drama"), and two excellent long stories, "Ela" ("The Yawl") and "Navodnenie" ("The Flood"). These stories, which marked the beginning of a new period in Zamjatin's prose, were characterized by greater simplicity, less elaborate imagery, and a noticeable affinity to contemporary European models. Unfortunately Zamjatin's new direction was cut short by a vicious campaign to destroy his position of influence among fellow travelers.

Zamjatin's provocative articles of the early twenties are the key to understanding the significance of the campaign directed against him by Communist critics. At stake were not merely a few political fables and an unpublished satire on collectivism; the real issue was the definition of the writer's role in a socialist society. Since Zamjatin's views were incompatible with those of his critics, he eventually had to be silenced and discredited. But before the fascinating mechanics of the campaign are unfolded, the ingredients and developments in Zamjatin's philosophy should be examined.

The basic elements of Zamjatin's world view, as expressed in his earliest essays "Skify li?" and "Zavtra," had included acceptance of the Hegelian dialectic, a denunciation of absolutism and the topical with a corresponding assertion of relativism and revolution, and the glorification of heresy as the sole means of human progress. These ideas found concrete expression in his exciting biography of the founding father of modern thermodynamic theory, Julius Robert von Mayer, whom Zamjatin depicted as a heretic and prophet, a scientific romantic whose heresy had exploded the stagnant inertia of scientific dogma. The opening three pages of the biography, published in 1922, are the best articulation of Zamjatin's conception of human progress and the heretic's role in society:

> Between the old and the new, between tomorrow and today, there exists an eternal struggle. This struggle exists in all walks of human life — including science, and science too has its own tomorrow and today. Today consists of everything that has already been mastered, determined, generally recognized, and is considered to be incontestable and infallible. And this belief in their own infallibility sometimes makes the representatives of "today's" science a conservative element, retarding the never-ending movement of science forward. . . . Even now, when science has adopted the correct view that everything which seems infallible is infallible only relatively, is infallible only today — even now traces of former reverence before dogma occasionally crop up. So recently, in our time, the miraculous properties of radium were discovered, which upset the seemingly most infallible scientific laws — and in our time more than one orthodox scientist skeptically mocked the heretics who had encroached upon these still recently sacred foundations. And the world lives only through its heretics, through those who reject the seemingly unshakeable and infallible today. Only the heretics discover new horizons in science, in art, in social life; only the heretics, rejecting today in the name of tomorrow, are the eternal ferment of life and ensure life's unending movement forward.[76]

As he traced the evolution of Mayer's thought from his first primitive formulation of the law of the conservation of energy to his teachings on entropy, Zamjatin's interests and excitement grew. Undoubtedly he was struck by the analogy between Mayer's thermodynamic concept of entropy and his own idea of human society, as reflected in such recent works as "Ostrovitjane" and "Sever." Mayer defined entropy as the "tendency of the universe's energy toward rest — toward death," as the gradual dissipation of energy (in the form of heat) from concentrations capable of work in hot bodies toward a passive energy equilibrium among warm bodies incapable of work.[77] For Zamjatin, entropy represented the universal tendency toward philistinism, toward spiritual death, while solar energy (Mayer's energy source corresponded to Zamjatin's symbolism) stimulated the ardent passion, spiritual or corporeal, which disrupted the tendency toward a lukewarm philistine equilibrium. Zamjatin considered Mayer's conception of entropy to be one of "the greatest *philosophic* deductions of all contemporary teaching on energy," [78] and immediately used it in his novel *My*, where the heroine I-330 says "there are two powers in the world—entropy and energy. One leads to blissful rest, to a happy equilibrium; the other—to the destruction of equilibrium, to a tormentingly endless movement." [79]

Although Zamjatin had originally drawn the analogy between his own views of human society and Mayer's thermodynamic theories in 1920, he did not elaborate on the energy-entropy relationship until October 1923, when the summation of all his basic philosophical thinking was cast in the form of the brilliant essay "O literature, revoljucii, èntropii i o pročem." [80] The stimulus for this final crystallization probably was an unusual essay on solar energy by the British physicist and physiologist Frank C. Eve.[81] Examining life and its origins in terms of energy, Eve concluded that the tendency of energy to flow to a lower potential, which admittedly was the motive force in the physical universe, was also the basic motive power of life itself. In so doing, Eve was essentially removing the barriers between organic and inorganic chemistry. Entranced by the scientific extension of physical (thermodynamic) concepts to biology (life itself), Zamjatin went a step further and extended the concepts of energy and entropy to the social sciences and philosophy. Conversely, he extended socio-philosophic concepts, such as revolution, to the physical and biological sciences.

> Revolution is everywhere, in everything; it is infinite, there is no final revolution, no final number. The social revolution is only one of innumerable numbers; the law of revolution is not social, but immeasurably greater—a cosmic, universal law—like the law of the conservation of energy, of the dissipation of energy (entropy). Someday the exact formula for the law of revolution will be established. And in this formula nations, classes, stars, and books will be numerical quantities.[82]

Revolutions were vast, flaming bursts of energy ignited by heretics, and, having disrupted existing dogmas, each revolution was followed by gradual evolution (entropy), which consisted in the loss of ardor and the growth of new dogma:

> When the flaming, boiling sphere (in science, religion, social life, art) cools, the fiery magma becomes covered with dogma — a hard, ossified, immovable crust. Dogmatization in science, religion, social life, in the arts, is the entropy of thought. That which has become dogma no longer burns, it only warms; it is warm, it is cool. Instead of the Sermon on the Mount under a blazing sun, above uplifted arms and groans, a drowsy prayer in a splendid abbey; instead of Galileo's tragic "But nonetheless it revolves," calm calculations in the warm office of an observatory. On the Galileos epigones slowly, polyp-like, as corals, build their own edifice: this is the path of evolution, until a new heresy explodes the crust of dogma and all the most solid stone structures that have been raised on it.[83]

The slow building process of evolution is, Zamjatin admitted, beneficial and useful to man today, but tomorrow, he said, it will lead to the entropy of human thought, "Someone today must already see and heretically speak of tomorrow," and that is why "heretics are the sole (bitter) medicine against the entropy of human thought." [84] Since heretics are pernicious to slow, beneficial evolution, they are quite properly persecuted and destroyed. The crucifixion of heretics ensures the intellectual health of humanity by stimulating thought, but the victory of heresy results in gradual ideological entropy that can be stopped only by a new heresy. A true heretic, like a true Scythian, can never be victorious; victory is defeat, because victory is inevitably followed by dogma and philistinism. The essence of Zamjatin's doctrine, although cast in a new scientific form, had remained unchanged.

Although Zamjatin maintained that the entropy of human thought was an ever-present tendency among the masses, his outlook was essentially optimistic, for he believed that the universal law of infinite revolution would prevent man from reaching a state of complete entropy. Late in 1921 he wrote: "Fortunately, this idyll [the cessation of all polemic] will never come to pass. Because as long as human thought lives, there will never be ideological entropy and there will be revolution, storms, rebellions, explosions, whirlwinds, no matter how much others may desire constant zephyrs." [85] For Zamjatin, who viewed the world in terms of Platonic becoming rather than being, the process was of much greater importance than the final results, and his ultimate hope was the guarantee of unending movement forward, not the attainment of some preconceived goal or utopia. This was clear in his answer to Fedin's review of "Ja bojus'":

> "It is better to be silent now, if there is no music," says Blok. And this is true. But children should not be allowed to play with Brownings and with quotations: Fedin does not understand that these words of Blok are deadly for him. Yes, the essence of the matter is precisely that now "*there is no music*," that "the great music of the future," of which Blok spoke, is absent: the future has become the present; it has taken on flesh, earth, and steel, grown heavy, become topical, and because of this it no longer has music, there is no pathos of a utopia of dreams, and a new utopia, tomorrow's and the day after's, must be created for man. . . . That which *everyone* knows and accepts as something true is a sure sign that it is something false.[86]

This was a reaffirmation and restatement of the ideas symbolized by the galloping Scythians: a never-ending denial of the present in the name of the future, so that goals would remain ideal and not be philistinized in their realization. As this concept was typical of most Romanticist thinking, B. G. Guerney's comparison of Zamjatin to Lermontov's lonely white sail was quite appropriate.[87]

Zamjatin's conception of man might best be characterized as a mixture of uncompromising individualism and idealistic humanism. Uncompromising individualism underlay the galloping Scythian, the stubborn heretic, and Zamjatin's criticism of the Bolshevik Revolution: "Yesterday there was a tsar and there were slaves; today there is no tsar, but the slaves remain; tomorrow there will only be tsars. We march in the name of tomorrow's free man — the tsar. We have experienced an epoch of the oppression of the masses; we are experiencing an epoch of the oppression of the individual in the name of the masses; tomorrow shall bring the liberation of the individual in the name of man."[88]

Most of Zamjatin's essays were dedicated to the liberation of the individual from the ever-present threat of philistine conformity. In "Skify li?" he cautioned against the philistinization of ideals; in "Ja bojus'" he warned against the growth of a catholicity spawned by nimble authors who slavishly followed changing political winds; in "Raj" ("Paradise") he ridiculed the "majestic, monumental, all encompassing unanimity" of the proletarian poets which produced gray, monophonic banality. In "O literature, revoljucii, èntropii i o pročem" he hailed seditious literature as the only means of combating ideological entropy. Again, in "O segodnjašnem i o sovremennom" he criticized the nimble writer who wrote with fearful glances over his shoulder, and he ended with a passionate warning against the growth of the philistine who, sprouting from all crevices like a weed, was stifling mankind; and in "Belaja ljubov'" he again warned of the return of the cowardly, limited, stupid, self-assured, and all-knowing philistine, who, after apparently having been burned to the ground by the Revolution, was again creeping out from under warm ashes like some form of mold.

Zamjatin's frequent and repeated attacks against philistinism and fawning servility expressed the central idea of the Scythians — the struggle for the spiritual liberation of mankind, waged against universal philistinism and the spirit of minimalism.[89] This idea was not peculiar to the Scythians, but had for many years concerned a large portion of the Russian intelligentsia and was reflected in the works of such disparate writers as the nineteenth-century revolutionary exile Gercen and the twentieth-century symbolist Merežkovskij. If, for example, the latter were divested of his Christian mysticism, the similarity between his impending boor and the universal philistine of the Scythians would be striking.

Zamjatin's faith in the ability of the self-determining man to strive for self-protection, and his belief in an all-encompassing brotherly love, were the basic elements of his idealistic humanism. His criticism of the Revolution was directed not only at the oppression of the individual, but at the release of degrading, destructive animal passions: "Man is dying. The proud *homo erectus* is getting down on all fours, is growing fangs and fur, the beast is conquering in man."[90] Zamjatin's solution to such growing primitivism was to recognize that all men were brothers, and he envisioned the future in the classless society as a "time of a tremendous intensification of man's loftiest emotions, a time of love."[91] Although his belief in the positive power of a universal brotherly love was a recurrent theme in his essays, his conception of this love was not consistently drawn, and it sometimes took on a decidedly nationalistic coloring: "Ivanov-Razumnik is blind to the basic, best, and greatest quality in the Russian soul: Russian nobleness, Russian gentleness, the love of every last man and every last blade of grass. And it is precisely this best quality of the Russian soul that is the basis of the invincible Russian yearning for peace on all earth. The love for the sickle and the hatred for the sword is truly Russian, of the people."[92]

Six years later, in the essay "Belaja ljubov'," Zamjatin concluded that Sologub's intense "hating love" of his most beloved literary creations stemmed from a boundless love of man, which Zamjatin again proclaimed to be a basic trait of the Russian soul:

> But beneath the austere, sustained European dress, Sologub preserved an impetuous Russian soul. The love which demands all or nothing, that absurd, incurable, beautiful disease, is not only Sologub's, Don Quixote's, or Blok's disease (Blok actually died of it), but it is our Russian disease — *morbus rossica*. The flower of our intelligentsia suffers from this disease and, fortunately, always will. Fortunately, because a country in which there are no more irreconcilable, eternally dissatisfied, ever-restless romantics and in which there remain only the healthy, only the Čičikovs and Sancho Panzas, sooner or later is doomed to snore beneath the quilt of philistinism. Perhaps this Russian disease could be born only in the huge expanse of the Russian steppes, where recently, as it were, galloped the Scythian that knew no settledness.[93]

The love described in the two passages quoted above differed in some respects: one was a gentle love that yearned for universal peace and was rooted in the Russian people; the other was an all-devouring love, a disease that was consuming the Russian intelligentsia. The important thing, however, was that both types were rooted ultimately in a boundless love for man, and both were qualities peculiar to the impetuous Russian soul, which Zamjatin contrasted to the mechanical and spiritually bankrupt soul of the European. Yet Zamjatin greatly admired European refinement and the European's verbal whip of irony, sarcasm, and satire, which he considered to be the most effective means of ensuring human progress, of raising *homo erectus* up from all fours and freeing him of his unquestioning servility. The contrast of the European and Russian cultures was evident in Zamjatin's comparison of Anatole France and Lev Tolstoj, which reflected the two basic but divergent modes of dealing with life — the ironic, with unbounded relativism and skepticism, and the tragic, with unbounded love and hate.[94] Perhaps through his own life and work he had sought to create a synthesis of the two.

Zamjatin's conception of the writer and the social function of literature was derived from his general view of mankind. By his definition the writer inevitably was a romanticist,* and real literature could be created only by "madmen, hermits, heretics, dreamers, rebels, and skeptics, not by reliable executive functionaries,"[95] for genuine literature, like any other genuine discipline (whether scientific or humanistic), was a rejection of existing canons and dogma. Zamjatin was never an advocate of "art for art's sake." For him the writer had a definite social role — that of a prophet. The writer-prophet was a man of the distant future, and his task was to struggle in the name of the future. His fate was a Faust's eternal dissatisfaction with the present and the attainable. The comparison to Faust was not accidental, for Zamjatin's essentially romanticist philosophy stemmed in part from Goethe and the nineteenth-century representatives of romanticism, as is evidenced by his definition of literature, written in answer to Fedin's assertion that the concept of real literature is relative and changes with each period or generation:

> No, real literature says "no" to that to which everyone says "yea." Real literature is a carrot hung in front of a mule's snout, a carrot which he cannot reach and which continually forces the stubborn mule to go forward. For mules are stubborn, their essence is an inertia toward rest, a desire to rest on laurels, to set themselves a daily, attainable task. Real literature must speak of tomorrow's unattainable tasks in the realm of the beauty of form, in the realm of the beauty of life, in the social realm. And if the mule today devoured the carrot of paradise, of earthly paradise, then it is my

* In an unpublished lecture, Zamjatin had defined romanticism as "*Two psychological moments*: (1) negation with regard to today and (2) aspiration to unending movement forward. These two moments comprise that attitude to the world which is called *romanticism. Any true*, living artist is inevitably a *romanticist*." "Xudožnik i obščestvennost'," *ZA* 4:177.

> task to find and fasten to his shafts a new carrot, tomorrow's. Paradise for me is not at all a utopia; it shall be, it is almost here today, but that is precisely why it already does not exist for me. I want to think, speak, and write about that which will be *tomorrow*, after this paradise, because in this corporeal, physical, Euclidean paradise with its excellent electrification, canalization, and assonantization, man will not stop: a real man is always Faust, and real literature is without doubt Mephistopheles. And Mephistopheles is the world's greatest skeptic and at the same time the greatest romanticist and idealist. With all of his devilish poisons — pathos, sarcasm, irony, gentleness — he destroys any attainment, any today, not at all because he is amused by the fireworks of destruction, but because he secretly believes in man's power to attain godly perfection.[96]

In denying the present, real literature looked to the future, to the ultimate aims of mankind, to a classless society without government, in which freedom was supreme.[97] Zamjatin's primary goal was the guarantee of man's spiritual freedom, the freedom of human thought. He opposed any attempts by critics to standardize art or to impose a "social order" on writers[98] and fervently believed in the free, anarchic competition of ideas.[99] Zamjatin demanded that literature above all be truthful, that it comprehend the current epoch, depicting repulsive features along with the fine and creating a truthful transcription of it for posterity.[100] This did not mean that literature should simply mirror life, for Zamjatin believed, on the contrary, that literature should organize life, that it should infect and excite the reader by means of pathos and irony (the cathode and anode of literature), and that it should speak of the great goals of humanity.[101] With respect to infecting the reader, Zamjatin came rather close to Tolstoj, who believed that the one indubitable sign distinguishing real art from its counterfeit was its infectiousness.

As a writer and avowed heretic, Zamjatin was not concerned with creating a well developed and consistent philosophic system. Most of his essays represented a fascinating patchwork of a few basic conceptions artistically stated and restated in varying contexts and reducible to one basic, paradoxical premise: that the sole, unchanging truth consists in the recognition of the fallibility of all truths, that through the dialectical process today's truths become tomorrow's errors. From this stemmed Zamjatin's stubborn refusal to accept the finality of any dogma, his rejection of all authority other than himself, and his dedicated struggle in the name of man against any form of philistinism. The incompatibility of such principles with those of any totalitarian society was obvious, and with the Soviet consolidation of power and the emergence of a monolithic Communist party, Zamjatin's presence became intolerable. The alternatives were clear — enforced silence, or a public recantation of errors, as was to become so fashionable in the early thirties.

CHAPTER THREE

Denunciation and Defamation, 1929-1931

Service to the ruling class based on the fact that the service is profitable should by no means arouse mooncalfish raptures in the revolutionary; the revolutionary should be sickened by such "service," which soon turns into fawning. Only the typical products of a transitional epoch like Gorbačev or Lelevič (perhaps others, like Averbax, are not far from them), who completely lack a sense of smell, can rejoice in this.

Zamjatin, *Lica*

The New Economic Policy, with its accompanying relaxation of controls in all branches of national life, was recognized from its beginning in 1921 as a temporary tactical retreat. With the death of Lenin in 1924, factional differences among the Communist leaders came to the surface, and the ensuing power struggle resulted in Stalin's victory, the termination of the NEP, and a retightening of controls in all areas. Since Marxism demands that the writer be responsible to society for his actions and that his works be imbued with the proper ideology, writers like Zamjatin who championed maximum individualism, who had been tolerated during the NEP, now had to be either converted or divested of power and eliminated. An examination of the sustained hostility of Communist critics toward Zamjatin will not only delineate Zamjatin's role in Russian literature in the twenties, but will also give an account of the attempt to impose political and ideological conformity on an intellectually responsible and creative community of writers.

Negative Soviet criticism of Zamjatin dates from the first few years of the NEP, when most of his works were being published and widely circulated. Marxist critics branded Zamjatin as a bourgeois writer who had rejected the October Revolution, although many of them admitted both his excellence as a literary master and his influence on noted young writers like those of the Serapion Brothers group.

In 1922 Nikolaj Aseev, a disciple of the futurist poet Majakovskij and a bitter enemy of the "bourgeois" NEP, deplored the lack of an integrated ideological world view in contemporary literature and spoke of Zamjatin's works as a thing of the past, as "dad's old frock coats and cutaways, carefully stored in the closet." [1] At about the same time the prolific Soviet novelist Il'ja Èrenburg, who was then living abroad, stated that "a deep organic estrangement from the upheaval . . . in the real world hindered the great master Zamjatin in becoming the architect of the new prose." [2]

Zamjatin's estrangement from the present became an often repeated condemnation among Communist critics. It was the keynote of an article later that year by Aleksandr Voronskij—the first extensive Soviet criticism devoted exclusively to Zamjatin and his works.[3] Voronskij, the editor of *Krasnaja nov'* and one of the most broad-minded Marxist critics, regretfully asserted that Zamjatin "had approached the October Revolution obliquely, coldly, and with hostility: the Revolution was alien to him not in its details, even though of essential importance, but in its essence." [4] While criticizing Zamjatin's world view, Voronskij retained a high degree of objectivity in praising his verbal mastery, epic *skaz* style, and irony, even going so far as to state that *My*, from the artistic point of view, was excellent. Unlike Aseev and Èrenburg, Voronskij did not pass by or even minimize Zamjatin's influence on contemporary literature; on the contrary, he ended his eighteen-page analysis by stressing its importance: "Our article would be incomplete if Zamjatin's influence, his specific gravity in contemporary imaginative life, were not noted. Undoubtedly he is important. It is enough to say that Zamjatin to a large degree determined the character and direction of the Serapion Brothers' circle." [5]

A similar opinion was expressed by Valerian Pravduxin, an eclectic critic, contributor, and one-time editor of the magazine *Sibirskie ogni* (*Siberian Lights*) and the husband of the novelist Lidija Sejfullina. Pravduxin's generalizations and statements about Zamjatin were never supported by literary analysis and rarely exceeded a page or two in length. In his earliest articles on contemporary literature he described Zamjatin as a writer embittered by the Revolution and on the verge of joining the ranks of grumbling philistines, but saved for the moment by his immense talent.[6] He admitted Zamjatin's influence on the younger generation of writers, but described him as an evil master who had tempted more than one of them.[7] In later articles Pravduxin labeled Zamjatin a "haughty Salieri"* who envied the progress of young literature that had passed him by and sought to poison it with his ill-intentioned sarcasm.[8] In view of these pronouncements, it is somewhat incongruous that Pravduxin named Zamjatin and Gor'kij as the "two most powerful artists in Soviet Russian literature,"[9] and, along with Andrej Belyj, as the three masters of Soviet literature, each with pupils of his own.[10]

Since Zamjatin's talent and literary mastery were taken for granted by most Marxist critics, it is not surprising that all but one of the few who approached his works from a literary point of view passed highly favorable judgments. Late in 1922 the literary scholar and folklorist I. N. Rozanov placed Zamjatin first among young writers who had gained recognition prior to the Revolution, describing him as "an experienced master, who had pupils and followers."[11] In 1923 Jak. Braun, who was active in Petrograd literary circles, wrote the second extensive criticism of Zamjatin's literary production. Braun, unlike Voronskij, mentioned Zamjatin's "reactionary" ideology only briefly and devoted most of his attention to a formal and thematic literary analysis. His evaluation of Zamjatin's formal achievements was high:

> Of course, Zamjatin's work on the form — refined, engineered — of the plot and characterizations, the condensed (under the pressure of 100 atmospheres) expression of images, the rough economy of the word (which brings to mind only Gustave Flaubert), a European erudition set in an artistic mold — all this will become a rich treasure in Russian, perhaps, world literature. Zamjatin is the most polished, the clearest (despite his much beloved, deliberate, slyly ironic device of leaving things unsaid) Russian artist. . . .[12]

* The reference is to Aleksandr Puškin's "little tragedy" *Mozart i Salieri*, in which the competent but ungifted Salieri poisons Mozart, the genius whom he envies with all his soul.

Equally high—and unusual among Marxist critics—was Braun's enthusiastic appraisal of Zamjatin's philosophical vision in the novel *My*, a philosophy which he correctly traced back to Dostoevskij's Grand Inquisitor and Underground Man. To this day Braun's article remains the most fruitful general survey of Zamjatin's works to have appeared in the Soviet Union. Some years later the well known formalist critic Viktor Šklovskij wrote a very thorough article on Zamjatin's use of images, but it dealt only with the imagery in "Ostrovitjane" and "Lovec čelovekov." [13] Although Šklovskij fully appreciated the mastery with which Zamjatin created and developed his images, he nonetheless considered this technique to be limited and ended his article with a brief mention of *My* as an unsuccessful work and a proof that Zamjatin's methods had exhausted their potential. The article contained nothing new; several years earlier Šklovskij had succinctly stated the same thesis (that Zamjatin's stories were merely highly developed images and comparisons which in technique were similar to Belyj) and also admitted that he had never cared much for Zamjatin's works.[14]

The appreciative articles of Braun and Šklovskij (which both had very limited circulation) were the exception in Soviet criticism, although one should also mention Jurij Tynjanov's interesting article on contemporary literature in which he gave a positive evaluation of Zamjatin's novel *My*, pointing out that the fantastic was a logical development of Zamjatin's stylistic devices.[15] Voronskij's more ideological article, which was much more typical of the prevailing view and which was twice reprinted in the twenties, represented the moderate range of Marxist judgments. At the extreme end of the spectrum stood critics like Semen Rodov and Petr Kogan, the latter being a most utilitarian Marxist critic who voiced his utter contempt for all problems of form. In reviewing the literary output of 1922, a year which he believed to be a turning point in Russian literature, Kogan criticized Zamjatin for viewing the Revolution "through the eyes of a malevolent intellectual whose finer feelings had been insulted." [16] In an article attacking all writers who were antagonistic to the Soviet regime, Rodov, a leading spokesman of the newly formed October group (Oktjabr'), branded Zamjatin as an anti-Soviet writer who could not be considered a part of the world of Soviet literature.[17]

The view of Rodov and other radical Communist critics prevailed. In 1924 half a dozen short, damaging criticisms of Zamjatin's attitude toward the Revolution (including Lev Trockij's label of "inside-émigré") were published together in the form of a unanimous negative appraisal.[18] In that same year the *Russkij sovremennik*, the journal to which Zamjatin gave much time, energy, and several contributions, first appeared and was promptly branded by the journal *Oktjabr'* as "an attempt to organize the *right wing* of literature ranging from inside-émigrés to fellow travelers who were most alienated by the Revolution." [19] In the following year, in one of the earliest histories of Soviet literature, Georgij Gorbačev, an Onguardist (militant Communist) critic, devoted less than a page to Zamjatin and denounced his post-Revolutionary works for "ridiculing and humiliating the people of October" and for "lamenting over poor Russian intellectuals who had perished under the conditions of collapse and War Communism." [20] Zamjatin's formal and stylistic influences on young prose writers were duly but briefly noted.

The original position of the Onguardists with respect to the fellow travelers was to declare open and irreconcilable hostility. Their belligerence was very slightly modified by the admission that the fellow travelers were not a homogeneous group and that it would be possible to work with a few of them. In essence, this position was affirmed by the resolution of the First All-Union Conference of Proletarian Writers in January 1925. The resolution maintained that some fellow travelers — by far the minority — served the revolutionary cause and should be used under the guidance of proletarian leadership. The majority, which slandered the Revolution, however, was pervaded with a spirit of nationalism, imperial chauvinism, and mysticism, and should be vigorously opposed. The subsequent June 18, 1925, resolution of the Party Central Committee "On Party Policy in the Field of Imaginative Literature", was a setback to the Onguardists in that it prescribed a tactful and careful attitude toward fellow travelers, and an approach that would "guarantee all the conditions for their earliest possible movement in the direction of Communist ideology." [21] The resolution went on to state:

> While discouraging antiproletarian and anti-Revolutionary elements (now quite insignificant), and while fighting to expose the ideology of the new *bourgeoisie* which is taking form among a part of the fellow travelers — those of the "change-of-landmarks" stripe — the Party should have a patient attitude toward intermediate ideological formations, patiently aiding those inevitably numerous formations to develop in the process of ever closer comradely cooperation with the cultural forces of Communism.*

While condemning the Onguardists' excessive demands, including their hostility to the fellow travelers, the Party fully approved their ultimate objective — the creation of a hegemony of proletarian literature. Although the Party resolution obliged the Onguardists to change their tactics, it actually strengthened their position by affirming the very core of their program.†

The Federation of Soviet Writers' Organizations (FOSP) was set up at the request of the Onguardists in July 1925, in compliance with a provision in the Party resolution which called for the more extensive organization of literary forces, so that peasant writers and fellow travelers might be induced to accept a proletarian ideology. The more radical Onguardist leaders like Grigorij Lelevič (pseudonym of Laborij Kal'manson), Il. Vardin (pseudonym of I. V. Mgeladze), and Rodov opposed such a union, fearing that "close association with the fellow travelers would result in the ideological degeneration of proletarian litera-

* Edward J. Brown, *The Proletarian Episode in Russian Literature, 1928–1932*, [551], 237–238. Change of Landmarks was a movement among a comparatively few émigrés — scholars, writers, and journalists — who decided to accept the Revolution as a fact without subscribing to its Marxist ideology. Many of them, like the novelist Aleksej Tolstoj, returned to Russia.

† This interpretation varies from the more widely accepted view expressed by G. Struve, M. Slonim, and others who have considered the 1925 resolution as a complete rejection of the Onguardist position. For an extensive treatment of the Onguardists and the variant interpretation of the Party resolution, see H. Ermolaev, *Soviet Literary Theories, 1917–1934*, [794], chap. ii.

ture."* In the following year all three were expelled from the executive board of the All-Russian Association of Proletarian writers (Vserossijskaja associacija proletarskix pisatelej, VAPP), and the control of VAPP passed to the "young" Onguardists. The new leaders, headed by Leopol'd Averbax and Jurij Libedinskij, fully accepted the Party resolution and were willing to treat the majority of fellow travelers with tact in an effort to gain their cooperation and bring them closer to a Communist ideology. The general situation and plan of future attack were outlined later that year by Averbax, editor of *Na literaturnom postu* (*On Literary Guard*) and leader of VAPP (renamed RAPP in May 1928).

> What is our situation in the field of literary life? On the one hand, there is the [VAPP] together with the All-Russian Union of Peasant Writers [Vserossijskij sojuz krest'janskix pisatelej, VSKP]. They associate with an extremely limited number of revolutionary fellow travelers, such "fellow travelers" as Majakovskij and Aseev — men who have completely identified themselves with our Revolution! On the other hand, there is the All-Russian Union of Writers [Vserossijskij sojuz pisatelej, VSP], which consists of the entire mass of fellow travelers together with bourgeois inside-émigré writers. The *latter* play the leading role. *Our task is to tear away the masses of fellow travelers from the bourgeois writers and to create a unified block of fellow travelers and proletarian and peasant writers.*[22]

The plan of attack was clear. The influence of bourgeois writers, such as Zamjatin, had to be neutralized; they had to be stripped of their positions in the VSP, so that the majority of fellow travelers could be brought under the control of VAPP leadership. In 1926 Averbax lacked the power to do this, for the Party resolution of June 18, 1925, had stated that in "giving general leadership to literature, the Party cannot support any one faction in literature," and that "therefore the Party should declare itself in favor of the free competition of various groups and tenden-

* [794], 5, Zamjatin, who believed that FOSP could be a fine pedagogical tool, had favored its formation, but had warned against possible abuses: "There is one modest but indispensible requirement for the possibility of common work: to spit in your own handkerchief and not at your neighbors. Everyone joining the federation will have to fulfill this requirement whether he wants to or not" [155].

cies."[23] But by the end of 1928, the political scene was to have changed, and RAPP would be able to carry out in 1929 the plan which had been promulgated by Averbax some three years earlier.

Prior to the autumn of 1929, several skirmishes took place between Zamjatin and Communist critics. In 1927 the militant critic Gorbačev attacked Averbax's policy of uniting VSP and VAPP in a broad federation and reiterated the demands of Levič, Rodov, and others for the creation of a leftist federation of proletarian and fellow traveler writers that would oppose VSP.[24] Although his strategy differed, Gorbačev's aims were essentially the same: to separate the mass of vacillating, middle-of-the-road fellow travelers from right-wing, bourgeois writers like Èfros and Zamjatin. Gorbačev's article is of interest because it shows that Zamjatin enjoyed great popularity among the fellow travelers. Gorbačev revealed that the middle-of-the-road fellow travelers defended not only the contributors of *Rossija* (a "change-of-landmarks" literary journal edited by I. Ležnev) and *Russkij sovremennik*, but also the very journals themselves. He went on to say that "even the leftist fellow travelers are at times wont to speak good and 'pitying' words about the Zamjatins and Èfroses who are unjustly accused."[25] Appended to Gorbačev's attack was a brief diatribe by Zel. Štejnman attacking several of Zamjatin's post-Revolutionary works, as well as his participation in two discussions held by the VSP and chaired by Aleksandr Gizetti in June 1926.[26]

In September 1927 the first extensive analysis of Zamjatin's works by a radical Communist critic was published in *Na literaturnom postu*. According to the author Mašbic-Verov, Zamjatin's literary output was divisible into two periods, the pre-Revolutionary and the post-Revolutionary. As might be expected, the article stressed ideology. Zamjatin was branded a bourgeois writer and a "has-been" who was living on his past laurels. His pre-Revolutionary satires were called "inadequate" because he had not portrayed the proletariat and was limited by a petit bourgeois ideology, while his post-Revolutionary works were viewed as artistic expressions of his hatred for the October Revolution. Mašbic-Verov ended his article with an anachronistic reference to the nineteenth-century social critic Vissarion Belinskij: "And I think that at one time Belinskij had in mind such people as Zamjatin when he said: 'And you think that you are free men? You should all be placed on the same rack as tsars, priests, and plantation owners.' "[27]

The following year, in 1928, Zamjatin was involved in two incidents which indicated subtle changes in the literary climate. The first was in connection with the extreme shortage of grain. During 1928 the major economic problem faced by the Communist leadership was grain collection. Already apparent in January, the shortage had become acute by July when Stalin ordered the Party to "strike hard at the kulaks," whom he blamed for the situation. That same month several writers, including Zamjatin, Boris Pil'njak, Leonid Leonov, and Valentin Kataev, traveled to collective farms, with the ostensible aim of creating literary works depicting the problems of grain collection which would inspire the populace to greater efforts. This was one of the earliest attempts at "social order" in literature, if the term is interpreted in the narrower sense as a specific assignment to a writer. The writers were given a friendly send-off by the *Komsomol'skaja pravda* which, among other things, printed a short biography of Zamjatin that mentioned his anti-Revolutionary attitudes and a poem by Vladimir Majakovskij which began:

<table>
<tr><td>Čto poželat' vam,
  sèr Zamjatin?
Vaš trud
  zaranee zanjaten.
Kritikovat' vas
  ne berus',
Ne nam
  sudit'
    zanjat'e svetskoe,
No prosim
  pomnit',
    slavja Rus',
Čto Rus'
  — už desjat' let! —
    sovetskaja.[28]</td><td>What should we wish you,
  sir Zamjatin?
[We know] already that your work
  will be interesting.
I won't attempt
  to criticize you,
It is not for us
  to judge
    high society pursuits,
But we ask you
  to remember,
    in praising Russia,
That Russia
  for ten years past
    has been Soviet!</td></tr>
</table>

Zamjatin's summer excursion did not produce any literary works, and it is rather surprising that he even took part in such a program. He must have been conscripted into the program, perhaps as a representative of the Leningrad VSP.

The second incident concerned the staging of Zamjatin's

tragedy *Attila* and provided ample proof that literary censorship was gradually being tightened in 1928. On May 15, 1928, *Attila* was read at a meeting of the Artistic Soviet of the Leningrad Bol'šoj Dramatic Theater in the presence of eighteen factory directors and was warmly received by those present. The play was approved by the Central Repertory Committee (Glavreportkom) and was already being rehearsed when it was suddenly banned by order of the Leningrad Regional Administration of Literary and Publishing Affairs (Oblit). Evidently *Attila* was widely known and had been frequently discussed in connection with the dramatic repertory of 1928 at the meetings of various organizations. A Comrade Šapiro, at the fifth plenum of the Regional Union of Workers of Arts, (Oblrabis) complained of the contradictory evaluations of *Attila* and Mixail Bulgakov's *Beg* (*Flight*) that had been handed down by competent authorities.[29] And Comrade Sviderskij, presumably a member of the General Repertory Committee was caricatured in *Na literaturnom postu* for saying that the plays of Bulgakov and Zamjatin would be the best of the coming season.[30] In view of the play's generally favorable reception and its politically innocuous character, one may suppose that the ban imposed from above indicated increased hostility toward Zamjatin the writer and had not been provoked by the play itself. In any case, the death of *Attila* was indeed a tragedy for Zamjatin and represented an important incident among the many that culminated in his emigration from the Soviet Union.

By the end of 1928 there was a decisive change in the political situation of the U.S.S.R. Having overcome leftist opposition a year earlier, Stalin began a test of strength with the rightists by having the rightist N. Uglanov removed from his position as chief of the Moscow Party organization. Stalin was quick to follow up his advantage, and by the end of 1929 his victory over the rightists in both Party and governmental apparatus was secure. In connection with this, the Party and various sections of the government were subjected to a series of purges. The NEP line of compromise was discarded, and bourgeois elements were attacked and rooted out. In literature the change in attitude was already apparent in the Party Central Committee's formal resolution of December 28, 1928, on the needs of the mass reader, which was the result of an all-Union conference in the summer of 1928 on questions of agitation, propaganda, and cultural work.[31] Making no distinction between imaginative fiction on the one hand and propaganda brochures and educational writing on the other, the 1928 resolution marked a distinct departure from the tolerant policy of 1925. Addressed to publishing houses, the 1928 resolution dictated a policy for selecting books for publication and thereby determined the character of so-called Five Year Plan literature. The publication of imaginative fiction was to be increased, with an emphasis on works which developed contemporary political themes and opposed bourgeois influences, philistinism, and decadence.

With the formal adoption of the first Five Year Plan in April 1929, a new phase in Russian history was inaugurated. All of the nation's resources were directed toward socialist reconstruction, and state control was systematically extended to all branches of economic, social, and culural life. Literature was no exception. Discussion of "social order" had begun in 1928, and numerous articles on the subject appeared throughout the first half of 1929. In one article summarizing the results of the first All-Russian Congress of Peasant Writers (Vserossijskij s"ezd krest'janskix pisatelej), from June 3 to 8, the *Izvestija* correspondent A. Revjakin wrote that a strong front of proletarian-peasant literature now existed and could be used by the proletarian vanguard in its struggle for socialist reconstruction of all life and human relations.[32] In view of the political situation, the time was ripe for an assault on VSP, which was essentially an apolitical organization in which "bourgeois writers" such as Zamjatin were leaders. The VSP came under concentrated fire in August of 1929 and was brought down by the end of October. The method by which the VSP was discredited and subordinated to RAPP is of interest, not only because Zamjatin was prominently involved but because it provides an excellent insight into how the Communist conception of the writer and his social role was imposed on dissident Soviet authors. L. I. Timofeev aptly characterized that conception in the Academy of Sciences' *History of Soviet Russian Literature*: "The concept Soviet writer was by no means a geographical concept; it was from the very beginning a political concept, and herein lay its strength, value, and honor."[33]

The all-out campaign against Pil'njak, Zamjatin, and the VSP was preceded by a minor, but significant, incident. On May 2, 1929, a special Leningrad edition of the *Literaturnaja gazeta* (an organ of FOSP) was issued jointly by the Leningrad sections of FOSP and the State Publishing House (GIZ).[34] Included in this edition were eleven epigrams under the general title "Zlye èpigrammy" ("Malicious epigrams") written by Aleksandr Bezymenskij, a leader of RAPP's left wing. One, entitled "Spravka social'noj evgeniki" ("A Note on Social Eugenics"), was aimed at Zamjatin:

Tip: — Zamjatin.	Species: Zamjatin.
Rod: — Evgenij.	Genus: Eugene.
Klass: — buržuj.	Class: bourgeois.
V sele: — kulak.	In the village: a kulak.
Rezul'tat pererождenij.	The result of resuscitation.
Snoska:	Footnote:
vrag.[35]	an enemy.

There was nothing surprising in Bezymenskij's evaluation of Zamjatin, which was probably shared by most Onguardists and RAPP critics, but the events that followed were a prologue to the drama. Almost two months after Bezymenskij's epigrams were first published, the *Literaturnaja gazeta* published on June 25 an undated resolution issued by the executive committee of the Leningrad section of FOSP.[36] The resolution, which had been passed at the request of the VSP representatives to FOSP, rejected all responsibility for the publication of Bezymenskij's epigrams, which were described as "unacceptable material of a non-literary character," and censured Il'ja Sadof'ev and Leontij Rakovskij, who were the FOSP representatives on the editorial board of the Leningrad *Literaturnaja gazeta* of May 2, for their failure "to check and edit" this issue. The FOSP resolution was passed despite objections from RAPP representatives Libedinskij and Mixail Čumandrin. It elicited a lengthy response from Bezymenskij in which he convincingly identified it as essentially a defense of Zamjatin (of the eleven epigrams, only the one about Zamjatin could without qualification be considered non-literary).[37] Bezymenskij then quoted nine critical statements, each of which pointed out Zamjatin's hostility to the Revolution and the Soviet regime. After observing that his attitude toward Zamjatin was shared by "*all* Marxist criticism," Bezymenskij reiterated the well known fact that "within the ranks of the VSP there were writers close to the proletariat, writers that were vacillating, and writers whose works were hostile to October (Zamjatin, Bulgakov, Kljuev)." Appended in support of Bezymenskij's article was a brief resolution of the RAPP secretariat (signed by Vladimir Ermilov and Vladimir Sutyrin) attacking the FOSP resolution.[38] The FOSP resolution was significant in two respects: first, it showed that Zamjatin enjoyed firm support in the Leningrad VSP, and, second, the passage of the resolution over the protest of RAPP members indicated that the VSP faction in the Leningrad FOSP was the more powerful. In mid-1929 such a situation was intolerable to RAPP and the Soviet regime.

The final phase of the RAPP campaign against the VSP and the apolitical bourgeois writers was carried on in the *Literaturnaja gazeta* and began with an attack on the newspaper itself. From its beginning in late April 1929 as the sole rostrum for writers of all organizations, *Literaturnaja gazeta* had been under fire by RAPP and the Communist publications. At the insistence of RAPP representatives, the executive committee of the Moscow FOSP passed a resolution on August 5 (it was published August 12) recognizing the validity of the *Komsomol'skaja pravda's* criticism of the *Literaturnaja gazeta.*[39] *Literaturnaja gazeta* was accused of failing to carry out the theses of the December 1928 Party resolution on literature and of lacking a definite character (presumably, a political line). The faults were attributed primarily to the organizational structure of the editorial board. The rather vague accusations of the resolution were bluntly elucidated in an accompanying lead article by Boris Volin, a former editor of RAPP's *Na literaturnom postu* and director of the press division of the People's Commissariat of Foreign Affairs (Narkomindel) since 1927. The primary target of Volin's attack was the apolitical character of the paper, for which he blamed the VSP. After discussing the paper's errors, as identified by *Na literaturnom postu, Molodaja gvardija* (*The Young Guard*), and *Komsomol'skaja pravda*, Volin arrived at the following conclusions, which, as he admitted, were essentially those of the RAPP Secretariat:

> 1. The influence of the leading revolutionary detachments of Soviet writers has given way to the pressure of "bad fellow travelers," apoliticalism has taken the upper hand, and the newspaper has become a neutral rostrum for literary advertisements, scandals, and squabbles.
>
> 2. The clearest tendency in the paper has turned out to be the rightist tendency; the most audible voice — the voice of the [VSP]; the strongest emphasis — on apoliticalism come what may.
>
> 3. The result is obvious — the effacement of the class struggle in literature and art, the cultivation of literary philistinism.[40]

Volin's article, ostensibly a criticism of *Literaturnaja gazeta*, was in effect an attack on the VSP and its influential position on the newspaper's editorial board.

The next issue of *Literaturnaja gazeta* (No. 18, August 19) announced Efim Zozulja's resignation from the VSP. Zozulja, a leftist fellow traveler and member of the Moscow board, criticized the VSP for not having a guiding political platform and for the ideological diversity of its members ("from mystics to Communists"); and he accused the board of dealing "only with petty organizational questions."[41] Except for publicizing Zozulja's resignation, which repeated Volin's accusations, the *Literaturnaja gazeta* did not then follow up Volin's lead article of the previous week. Evidently, Volin and company were awaiting a reply from VSP before continuing their attack. That reply was published on August 26: "Acknowledging the truth of several isolated assertions expressed by comrade B. Volin in his article 'O *Literaturnoj gazete*,' . . . the presidium of the [VSP] nonetheless deems it necessary to disavow this article as a whole, for [the presidium] considers that [the article] in essence contradicts those bases on which the [FOSP] has been built.[42] This reply could be interpreted only as a refusal to adopt an "acceptable" political line and as an expression of satisfaction with the structure of FOSP and with the *Literaturnaja gazeta*. Since it had openly rejected RAPP criticism and political guidance, the VSP had to be humbled and brought into line. This was to be achieved by discrediting VSP leadership.*

* It should be remembered that at that time the Moscow and Leningrad sections of VSP functioned essentially as independent groups, al-

Volin's attack on the publication abroad of Pil'njak's *Krasnoe derevo* (*Mahogany*), Zamjatin's *My*, and Èrenburg's *Rvač* (*The Grabber*) appeared in the same issue as the VSP reply and reflected the tactical shift in RAPP's campaign against the VSP.[43] Although Volin was concerned with the alleged fact of deliberate publication abroad of these works, he emphasized that Pil'njak's novel had previously been rejected by Soviet magazines and that Zamjatin's novel had been "unacceptable to Soviet literature," thus implying that both writers had willfully violated the best interests of Soviet society. Since the article began with a discussion of the beneficial effects of public opinion on the literary production of rightist fellow travelers and concluded with the hope that all of Soviet society would uphold the condemnation, Volin's primary aim was to arouse public opinion against Pil'njak and Zamjatin.[44]

The September 2 issue of *Literaturnaja gazeta* (No. 20), which gave the entire front page to the Pil'njak and Zamjatin affair, revealed the strategy of the RAPP attack. The unsigned lead article, "The Writer and Politics", attacked Pil'njak not only for *Krasnoe derevo*, but for all of his recent works, which had shown a definite break with the Socialist Revolution. The essence of the article was contained in the following statement:

> The events which have taken place [presumably the publication abroad of *Krasnoe derevo* and *My*] pose concretely, rather than academically, the question of a Soviet writer's relationship to politics. The concept Soviet writer is not geographic, but social. Only he who ties himself and his work to socialist construction during the present period of reconstruction — a period when the proletariat attacks the remnants of capitalism, a period of frenzied resistance [on the part] of the class enemies of socialism — can call himself a Soviet writer.[45]

Evidently the transgressions of Pil'njak and Zamjatin had been introduced as concrete examples of the objectionable VSP apoliticalism. This contention is supported by an anonymous editorial comment appended to Pil'njak's explanatory letter: "We hope today, as well as in the future, that the public opinion of

---

though delegates from one section often attended meetings of the other. The same was true of FOSP, where the difference between sections was even greater because apparently the Moscow section was dominated by RAPP, while the Leningrad section was dominated by VSP.

men of letters and all Soviet society will force B. Pil'njak to consider the questions: what constitutes a Soviet writer, what his work should be like, and what his conduct should be within the Soviet Union and beyond its extensive borders." [46]

Although Volin's two articles and the FOSP resolution of August 5 were probably inspired by RAPP leadership, RAPP "officially" entered the fray only on September 2 with a resolution addressed to all members of the VSP. The resolution censured Pil'njak's anti-Soviet works and condemned the VSP leaders for having become the mainstay of bourgeois influence in Soviet literature. It also went so far as to claim that the VSP delegations to FOSP consisted of bourgeois writers who were "typical bureaucrats that had no direct relationship to literature." In fact, the RAPP resolution was a pointed restatement and extension of Volin's conclusions in his August 12 article. The resolution ended unequivocally: "Life has formulated the question facing the fellow travelers brusquely and directly: either in favor of Pil'njak and his defenders, or against them. There is no third choice." [47] A declaration in favor of Pil'njak would be tantamount to joining the ranks of anti-Soviet bourgeois writers, while the condemnation of Pil'njak implied the acceptance of a proper political tendency as basic to all literary works.

At first glance, it seems curious that Pil'njak bore the brunt of what had begun as an attack on Pil'njak, Zamjatin, and Èrenburg. But several reasons determined this strategy. First and most important, Pil'njak was the chairman of the Moscow section of VSP. Since the RAPP attack had been ostensibly aimed at the apolitical influence of the VSP in the *Literaturnaja gazeta*, a Moscow publication, it was only appropriate that the purge begin in that city. Second, RAPP's power was concentrated in Moscow, the capital and political center of the U.S.S.R. Once the Moscow section had been humbled, a much greater pressure could be brought to bear on Leningrad, where as subsequent events proved there was stronger resistance to RAPP policies. Therefore, Zamjatin was virtually ignored during the most violent phase of the attack on the VSP (September 2 and 9), while the case against Èrenburg was never developed since it was not essential to the discrediting of VSP leadership. Also, the case against Zamjatin's foreign publication was considerably weaker: *My* had been written nine years earlier, an English translation had appeared in 1924, a Czech version had come out in 1927, and the Russian excerpts which led to the charge of collaborating with the White émigré press had been published *more than two years earlier* in the spring of 1927.[48] In addition, although Zamjatin was still influential in the affairs of the Leningrad VSP, he was no longer its chairman.[49]

The Moscow VSP was quickly humbled, as was evidenced by two resolutions which were published in the September 9 *Literaturnaja gazeta* (No. 21). The title of the first resolution, "Not Only an Error, But a Crime!" indicates its contents: the publication abroad of *Krasnoe derevo* and Pil'njak's subsequent conduct were unequivocably censured, his resignation from the VSP directorate was accepted, and the participation, voluntary or involuntary, of any Soviet writer in the White émigré press was condemned. It is interesting that the Moscow VSP did *not* censure Zamjatin; it neutrally stated that "the board considers it imperative that the question concerning Zamjatin be investigated immediately." [50] A second resolution of the Moscow VSP, dated September 6, criticized the content of *Krasnoe derevo* and labeled it "a slander on the Soviet Union and its construction." [51] Zamjatin was not mentioned. The resolution of the Moscow FOSP appeared in the same issue and, due to the influence of RAPP representatives, was stronger than the VSP resolution. Aside from demanding that the "executive committee of the Leningrad section of FOSP immediately investigate the circumstances of the publication abroad of Zamjatin's *My* and reach a decision," it actually condemned the actions of Pil'njak *and* Zamjatin "in the name of all Soviet literature." [52] Zamjatin later commented on this resolution with justifiable irony: "So, first the sentence, then the investigation. In all probability, no court in the world has known of such a case. This was the action of the [FOSP]." [53]

At a general meeting on September 15, the Moscow VSP capitulated to the demands of RAPP critics. Among the major concessions was the admission that a writer could not be apolitical and that the VSP could not continue without social aims. The new board was given two weeks to work out a political platform, and a "purge of the Union's rank and file" was instigated. In addition, the "general meeting sharply censured the objectively slanderous attacks of B. Pil'njak and E. Zamjatin, their collaboration with White émigrés, and decisively rejected attempts to depict the disclosure of these anti-Soviet actions of B. Pil'njak and E. Zamjatin as the baiting or discrediting of the Union." [54] This was the first condemnation of Zamjatin by either Moscow or Leningrad sections of the VSP. In only three weeks the resistance expressed in the Moscow VSP's August 26 reply to Volin's first article had been reduced to abject surrender.

The submission of the Leningrad VSP was not achieved so easily and quickly. The September 2 RAPP resolution had included a special appeal to the Leningrad sections of the VSP and FOSP, as well as to all writers and literary groups, "to determine their attitude toward the actions of E. Zamjatin and B. Pil'njak and toward the situation within the VSP." This appeal indicates that, while progress had been made in Moscow, no concessions had been granted by the Leningrad VSP. This supposition is supported by an editorial which appeared two weeks later in the September 16 *Literaturnaja gazeta.* Entitled "Načalo pereloma" ("The Beginning of the Crisis"), the editorial welcomed the resolution of the Moscow VSP general meeting and the election of the new board, in accord with Soviet public opinion. The article went on: "The crisis in the Union of Writers has begun. It is necessary that it be reinforced and carried through to completion. It is necessary that it be fully reflected in the work of the Leningrad section of the VSP." [55]

A week later (September 23), ostensibly in answer to this, a resolution of the Leningrad FOSP, dated September 16, was published.[56] The Leningrad section accepted the undated resolution of the Moscow FOSP published on September 9 and approved the expulsion of Pil'njak from the Union of Playwrights (Dramsojuz); but they shelved the discussion of Zamjatin until representatives of the VSP and the Union of Playwrights had reported the results of their investigations to the executive committee of the Leningrad FOSP. The resolution went on to declare its dissatisfaction with the September 6 resolution of the Leningrad VSP (never published), "which had attempted by means of purely formal explanations to minimize the political significance of the Pil'njak issue." The FOSP resolution did approve a second resolution by the Leningrad VSP (dated September 10, but "due to the fault of the newspapers" not published then), declaring it to be "a significant step forward on the way to satisfying the demands of Soviet public opinion." This September 10 resolution was then (evidently for the first time) published with the September 16 FOSP resolution. It affirmed the Moscow VSP resolution of September 6 condemning Pil'-njak and the publication abroad of *Krasnoe derevo*. Zamjatin was not mentioned, and an excuse was even offered for so-called collaborators with the Whites: "The Leningrad section of the board considers it mandatory to point out that writers whose works were reprinted in the émigré press in most cases had not protested in good time simply because they were unaware of the fact of republication." [57]

A special general meeting of the Leningrad VSP on September 22 generated extraordinary interest in the Zamjatin affair. Many outsiders were turned away at the doors of the hall, which was barely large enough to house the membership. The two points of interest on the agenda were the situation within the Leningrad section and Zamjatin's explanation of the publication of *My*. After the Moscow delegation — Leonov, Vladimir Kirilov, a certain Šmidt, and Viktor Kin (pseudonym of Viktor Surovkin) — had reported on recent developments in their section, Zamjatin's explanation was read. The subsequent heated discussion included a vigorous defense of Zamjatin by Gizetti, whose speech was reported as having an "anti-Soviet and obscurantist character." The correspondent at the meeting for *Literaturnaja gazeta* continued: "The sympathy elicited by Gizetti's 'speech' left a somewhat depressing impression. This was simply another proof that the Leningrad section was in need of a serious purge." [58]

Although many writers accepted Zamjatin's explanations, "the majority found it safer to condemn [Zamjatin's] act" [59] and upheld the September 15 resolution of the Moscow VSP. In addition, the Leningrad VSP passed its own resolution about Zamjatin's explanations. Although dated September 22, the resolution was not mentioned in *Literaturnaja gazeta*'s report on the general meeting, and it was not published until three weeks later, on October 14.[60] This leads one to suspect that the resolution was drafted somewhat later, perhaps after the Leningrad opposition had been subdued. The resolution is of interest because it pinpoints the basis of Zamjatin's guilt. The facts as stated by Zamjatin were recognized as true, and he was therefore exonerated of collaboration with the White émigré press. However, the publication abroad of *My* in translation (with Zamjatin's consent) after the U.S.S.R. had banned it was acknowledged to be a political error. Furthermore, the resolution noted that Zamjatin's explanations contained neither "a confession of his error," nor "a repudiation of the ideas which were expressed in the novel and which were recognized as anti-Soviet by our public opinion." This resolution of the Leningrad VSP was seconded on October 11 by a resolution of the Moscow VSP which also denied that Soviet public opinion or the VSP had baited Zamjatin.[61] Evidently such accusations were widespread. The lead article of the October 14 paper also rejected all talk of baiting and asserted that "the attitude toward individuals in the politics of the working class is but a particular instance of the attitude toward [entire] social groups." [62]

The Leningrad section of the VSP offered considerably more resistance than did Moscow to the new line which subordinated the writer to definite political aims, namely, the struggle for socialist reconstruction. The general meeting of September 22 in Leningrad represented the final pitched battle in the defense of the VSP as an apolitical writers' organization. On September 30, the VSP was renamed the All-Russian Union of Soviet Writers (Vserossijskij sojuz sovetskix pisatelej, known as VSSP), and a purge, euphemistically called a reregistration of members, was begun in the Moscow section.[63] The new name was highly significant, for the addition of the term "Soviet" stressed the socio-political responsibility of the writer. This was seconded in the three criteria for admission to the VSSP: (1) the writer's literary ability, (2) his literary activity, and (3) his public character (*obščestvennoe lico*).

By October 23 the Moscow section was essentially purged: the membership had been reduced from 570 to 330. Of the 240 members who were dropped, 80 had not met the criteria; the others were translators for whom a separate union was being established.[64] At the same time the Leningrad section elected a new board and began its own purge.[65] By the end of November, the Leningrad purge was nearing completion: of the 96 members who had been examined, 16 had been dropped from the organization.[66] All told, 65 members were purged from the Leningrad section.[67] The subjugation of RAPP's major opponent was followed by an extensive critical discussion of FOSP activities.[68] A new editorial board for *Literaturnaja gazeta* was appointed, although Semen Kanatčikov was retained as chief editor.[69] By November 1929, the apolitical VSP had been destroyed and had been replaced by a new writers' organization, committed to support the socio-political aspirations of the Soviet regime.

Standing firm in his belief that "an unyielding, stubborn enemy was more worthy of admiration than a sudden Communist,"[70] Zamjatin (unlike Pil'njak) yielded neither to his attackers nor to the appeals of his friends throughout the campaign against him and the VSP.

Once the accusation of collaboration with the émigré White press had been made, he sent the Leningrad VSP a factual explanation which clearly documented his innocence. When the Leningrad section joined the Moscow VSP in censuring him, Zamjatin replied by reiterating the facts of his case and then demonstratively resigned from the VSP. He left declaring that it was impossible for him to belong to a literary organization which even indirectly took part in persecuting one of its members.[71]

Zamjatin's position during the next two years was unenviable. His "obituary" was prepared by A. Efremin (pseudonym of Aleksandr Frejman), a critic specializing in Dem'jan Bednyj's poetry. It appeared a few months after Zamjatin's denunciation. After enumerating Zamjatin's sins, Efremin concluded:

> A complete and unmitigated disbelief in the Revolution, a thorough and persistent skepticism, a departure from reality, an extreme individualism, a clearly hostile attitude to the Marxist-Leninist world view, the justification of any "heresy," of any protest in the name of that protest, a hostile attitude to the factors of class war — this is the complex of ideas within which Zamjatin revolves. Thrown out beyond the bounds of the Revolution by its centrifugal force, he, of necessity, is in the enemy's camp, in the ranks of the bourgeoisie. Decisive days have now arrived: every-

> one must look within himself and irrevocably say the final word, and Zamjatin will have to say his word louder and more distinctly than many others.[72]

Zamjatin chose not to compromise his principles and remained silent. This was interpreted as an expression of hostility to the regime, a view expressed unequivocally by the Communist writer Mixail Čumandrin two years later:

> Zamjatin's silence is extremely symptomatic. It undoubtedly signifies that this eminent writer scorns everything that could connect him with our revolutionary reality. By his silence Zamjatin strengthens his position of archbourgeois opposition to the working class that is building socialism and to those strata of the intelligentsia which are going along with the working class.[73]

Since Zamjatin refused to recant, his participation in literary activities became increasingly difficult. The Moscow publishing house, The Federation (Federacija), which had issued a four-volume collection of his works during the first third of 1929, received its share of criticism[74] and was closed to Zamjatin thereafter. His last outlet was the independent Writers' Publishing House in Leningrad (Izdatel'stvo pisatelej v Leningrade), which published his story "Navodnenie" in September 1930 as a separate volume illustrated by K. Rudakov. The following year they included his essay "Zakulisy" ("Backstage") in an interesting miscellany entitled *Kak my pišem* (*How We Write*).[75] The Writers' Publishing House not only published Zamjatin's works, but also retained him as stylistic editor until April 1931, when the Leningrad Association of Proletarian Writers (Leningradskaja associacija proletarskix pisatelej, known as LAPP) succeeded in having him removed from the editorial board. The LAPP attack was spearheaded by Libedinskij who condemned Zamjatin's "corrupting influence" and "gave a convincing analysis of Zamjatin's obviously hostile position" at the yearly meeting of shareholders. There it was decided to preserve the publishing house as a private organization, but "not for Zamjatins."[76] The last avenue for the publication of Zamjatin's works was then closed.

The extent of the repressions suffered by Zamjatin is well illustrated by the difficulties he experienced in editing a Russian translation of Richard Sheridan's *A School for Scandal* for the

Academia Publishing House. In addition to editing the text, Zamjatin also wrote an extensive introductory essay about Sheridan's life and works. In March 1931, the Leningrad Regional Administration of Literary and Publishing Affairs (Oblit) forbade the publication of his essay, and also refused to permit the mention of his name as editor of the text. Only after an appeal to Moscow did the central officials (Glavlit) reverse this decision, and *A School for Scandal*, with Zamjatin's introduction and full credits, finally did appear in September 1931.[77]

During the first half of that year, Zamjatin's essay "Zakulisy," the first new work to be published since his denunciation in 1929, was subjected to heavy criticism. And the miscellany *Kak my pišem*, in which the essay appeared, was deluged with negative reviews, some with such lurid titles as "The Disguised Raid of a Bourgeois Writer," "The Technology of the Unscrupulous," and "Something New in the Unmasking of Pil'njak and Zamjatin." [78] The essays of Zamjatin, Pil'njak, and, to a much lesser extent, Belyj bore the brunt of the attack against the "false" and "pernicious" bourgeois ideology which viewed the creative process as something "wondrous, elemental, involuntary and subconscious." [79] To some extent these reviews laid the foundations for extensive discussions of the "creative method" conducted in Leningrad in July and in Moscow in September. It is significant that the opening speeches of both the Leningrad and Moscow discussions, delivered by Zel. Štejnman and Aleksej Selivanovskij respectively, mentioned Zamjatin. He was, they said, a major proponent of pernicious theories concerning the writer's creative process, theories that were completely unacceptable to the Soviet writer and Soviet society.[80] In 1929 Zamjatin had been censured for committing a political error and for not repudiating the anti-Soviet ideology expressed in his novel *My*. Under attack now was his conception of the writer's creative process. Quite probably the persistent attacks on Zamjatin were spurred on by the closing paragraphs of "Zakulisy" which were essentially a defiant rejection of the criticism leveled at him in 1929 and a resolute assertion of his own integrity and independence:

> I spend much time [in rewriting], evidently much more than is necessary for the reader. But this is necessary for the critic, the

> most demanding and most caviling critic that I know of: for myself. I am never successful in deceiving this critic, and until he tells me that everything that is possible has been done — the final period cannot be placed.
>
> If I consider anybody else's opinion, then it is only the opinion of my friends, of whom I know that they know how a novel, a story, a play is made: they themselves have made them — and made them well. For me, there is no other criticism, and how it could exist, is incomprehensible to me. Just imagine that a smart young fellow who has never drafted a single blueprint of a ship were to show up at a factory, a shipbuilding pier, and begin to teach the engineer and workers how to build a ship: the young fellow would be quickly thrown out on his ear.
>
> Because of our kindheartedness we don't do this when such young people sometimes hinder our work no less than flies in the summertime.[81]

These words, and the tone of Zamjatin's letter of resignation from the VSP, stood in marked contrast to the numerous abject confessions and recantations that were voiced by others in 1930.

The banning of *Attila*, the public campaign against *My* and his subsequent resignation from VSP, the vociferous criticism of "Zakulisy," the difficulties in the publication of *A School for Scandal*, the withdrawal of his books from circulation and from the shelves of many libraries,[82] his removal from the editorial board of the Writers' Publishing House in Leningrad, the ever-increasing difficulty of publishing his works — all this finally led Zamjatin to compose his audacious "Pis'mo Stalinu" ("Letter to Stalin"), in which he described in detail the hopelessness of his situation in the Soviet Union. The general tone and frankness are strikingly illustrated in Zamjatin's summation:

> If I am not a criminal, I ask to be permitted to go abroad with my wife, temporarily, for at least a year with the right to return as soon as it becomes possible to serve great ideas in literature without fawning on small people, as soon as there is at least a partial change in the prevailing view of the literary artist. . . . I do not wish to conceal that the fundamental reason for my request for permission to go abroad together with my wife is my hopeless situation here as a writer, the death sentence which has been passed on me here as a writer.[83]

The letter, dated June 1931, was given to Stalin by Gor'kij, and it probably was through the intercession of the latter that Zamjatin and his wife were granted an exit permit and were allowed to go abroad for a year.[84] In November 1931 he left the Soviet Union, never to return.

Despite the difficulty of his situation during his last two years in the Soviet Union, Zamjatin continued his literary work. Although the full extent of his work will remain unknown until Soviet archives are made public, a few facts concerning this period are available. Zamjatin evidently continued to devote most of his energies to the theater. His translation of the play *The Front Page* by Ben Hecht and Charles MacArthur was accepted by the Vaxtangov Theater late in 1929, and the first performance of *Sensacija* (Zamjatin's translation) took place the following year on May 29.[85] During the next theatrical season (1930–1931), *Sensacija* was included in the Vaxtangov Theater's standard repertory, and it was performed by provincial theaters in such towns as Voronež and Bijsk.[86] Reviews of the play were mixed. Although most were not concerned with the quality of the translation, one critic did mention that the mild irony of the original was much intensified in Zamjatin's translation.[87] In addition to *Sensacija*, Zamjatin also worked on two original plays, *Afrikanskij gost'* (*The African Guest*) and *Roždenie Ivana* (*The Birth of Ivan*). *Afrikanskij gost'*, probably written during 1930 or 1931, was completed by December 1931, when Zamjatin stated:

> Lately I have been working mostly for the theater. Among my most recent works I would like to mention the Soviet farce *Afrikanskij gost'*, to which I have given the subtitle: an unbelievable incident in three hours. It is a satirical cut at people who think that they are Soviet but in reality are not and are only accommodating to Soviet ways. I have there three types of such people: an exdeacon, a secretary of the local "authorities," and a Soviet poet.[88]

Zamjatin's farce is well written and to the point, but it has never been staged and was published only recently.[89] In 1931 Zamjatin's other play, *Roždenie Ivana*, was also being written: "I have one play, *Roždenie Ivana*, written for MXAT-2, which is not quite completed. It is the history of a most common Russian Ivan, I would even say ivan with a small *i*; I am giving the play a background of Russian rites and songs."[90] *Roždenie*

Ivana, if written, has been lost, and all that remains is a six-page scenario.[91] The play was biographical: it was to have traced Ivan's life from his birth (around 1900) to the Revolution, at which time Ivan and thousands like him became the rulers of the nation. In this sense, the play was not to have been a biography of one Ivan, but a symbolic biography of all Russian Ivans, proletarians and peasants. The title was also doubly symbolic: the play began with the birth of the child and ended with the birth of the man — the moment when Ivan was freed from the horrors of war and was entrusted with the power of building his own future. The whole development was to be accompanied by folk rites (for birth, death, marriage), incantations, and traditional circle songs and games. The finished product would have been a highly original work that probably would have been quite acceptable to the Soviet regime ideologically.

Zamjatin did not completely give up writing prose. His short story "Mučeniki nauki" ("Martyrs of Learning"), which, like *Afrikanskij gost'*, poked fun at "superficially" Soviet people and continued in the light, satirical vein of such earlier stories as "Iks," was probably written in 1931, shortly before his departure from the Soviet Union. At about the same time Zamjatin's interest in prose apparently was shifting from the minor to the major genre, from the short story to the novel. He was still preoccupied with the figure of Attila, but work on the novel, which he had started in the autumn of 1924, had progressed very slowly: "In addition [to my plays] I am very much interested in the figure of Attila, which I have already treated in a drama and which is supposed to become the center of a large novel; as always, I see historical parallels and comparisons, but it is far from being completed."[92]

Work on the novel *Bič Božij* (*The Scourge of God*) continued slowly; it was not until four years later, in 1935, that the first part — one hundred pages — was at last completed. Concurrently, Zamjatin was working on "a novel of contemporary Russian life," which he first mentioned in 1931.[93] Judging from the rough drafts, the novel, which he tentatively called *Kolonny* (*Columns*), was to have been a large one.[94] Spanning a decade (1914 to the mid-twenties), it was set in Russia during

World War I, the Revolution, and the civil war. Some forty characters (including several commissars) were named and sketched. The plot centered around Prince Andrej Porfir'evič and his family of four sons and one daughter; several love intrigues were sketched; and the problem of adjustment to the new situation in Russia seemed to be of major importance. Among the materials for *Kolonny* were several pages of Old Russian words, folk songs and *častuški*; evidently Zamjatin intended to create a local, country flavor in some passages.

The striking feature about Zamjatin's works during 1930 and 1931 is the evidence of a renewed interest in the earth-shaking events of the decade after 1910, and an attempt to create a synthesized appraisal of the Revolution's effect on Russia and her people. In this respect, both *Roždenie Ivana* and *Kolonny* were conceived as serious, all-encompassing works whose tone was quite different from the gay, pointed irony of *Afrikanskij gost'*, "Mučeniki nauki," and his post-Revolution satires. Unfortunately Zamjatin did not develop this trend after his emigration.

CHAPTER FOUR

Exile and Death, 1931-1937

For five years of life abroad, he always was hurrying somewhere . . . or was it that his scenarios took up all his time? — movie scenarios! What relation have they to verbal mastery? . . . And Zamjatin's work of his last years — the idiotic cinema appeared to me to be so unnecessary; for his life's work, all those typically Russian verbal constructions — that's ours, Russian, that's our Russian literary treasure.

A. M. Remizov

The primary reason for Zamjatin's departure from the Soviet Union was his hopeless position there as a writer. Granted a year abroad by the Soviet authorities, he chose not to return, preferring to spend the last five years of his life in France. However, Zamjatin did not join the ranks of anti-Soviet White émigrés. With the exception of a few friends, such as the artists Boris Grigor'ev and Jurij Annenkov, the literary critic Marc Slonim, and the writer Aleksej Remizov, he generally avoided contact with émigré literary circles. During his years abroad Zamjatin did not publicly attack the Soviet regime, although he did criticize certain literary policies, especially those of RAPP.[1] In June 1934, he was elected to membership in the U.S.S.R.'s newly created Writer's Union, and some of his Soviet friends still were awaiting his return to the Soviet Union.[2] Because of his dire financial straits, Zamjatin turned his energies to writing film scenarios, the only literary activity that paid even a minimum. And because of this he wrote little else during this period. Aside from several articles for periodicals, he completed only four very short stories, "Časy" ("The Watch"), "Vstreča" ("The Encounter"), "Lev" ("The Lion"), and "Videnie" ("The Apparition"), and the first section of his long novel *Bič Božij*.

Zamjatin had left Russia with hopes of traveling to the United States, where he had planned to stage several plays and to work in the film studios of Cecil B. deMille. He had expressed his dreams of staging *Bloxa* in the United States as early as 1927,[3] and his intended collaboration with C. B. deMille was not simply wishful thinking. In August 1931, the two men had met in Moscow and had discussed various problems of the theater and the film industry at some length.[4] In February 1932, while applying for an American visa in Berlin, Zamjatin asked deMille for a letter of reference and received a warm and encouraging reply:

> I have this day written to the American Consulate, in Berlin, as you requested, and am hoping that we shall have the pleasure of seeing you in our part of the world. We are in need of good dramatic brains more than ever at the present time, for good dramatic fare is very scarce: and the "depression" makes it difficult for even good dramatic entertainment to produce good financial results.
>
> Looking forward to the pleasure of seeing you here with kindest regards from Mrs. deMille and myself. . . .[5]

The trip to America never did materialize, even though as late as 1935 Zamjatin still entertained hopes of getting there.[6]

Zamjatin's first stop upon leaving the Soviet Union was Riga. During his brief stay there, he visited the Theater of Russian Drama (Teatr russkoj dramy), met its actors, and, along with the celebrated Russian violinist Mischa Elman, attended a performance of M. N. Kuznecov's play *Kibicer-klub* (*The Kibitzer Club*).[7] Zamjatin, who was hailed as a visiting celebrity, had been well known in Riga before his arrival; rivaled only by Bulgakov's *Belaja gvardija* (*The White Guard*), his play *Bloxa* had enjoyed the greatest success, at the Theatre of Russian Drama for two seasons. The quality of production there was quite high. Zamjatin's *Obščestvo početnyx zvonarej*, which also played at that theater for several seasons, was performed so well there that Zamjatin later compared it favorably to the production at Leningrad's Mixajlovskij Theater.[8] He also began preliminary arrangements for staging his new plays (presumably *Afrikanskij gost'* and *Roždenie Ivana*), but it is highly doubtful that they were ever performed. This was the first in a series of setbacks in Zamjatin's attempts to stage his plays abroad.

From Riga he proceeded to Berlin where, late in November, he met the German playwright Karl Zuckmayer, who helped him rework and expand *Bloxa*.[9] Although the famous producer Max Reinhardt agreed to stage the play, the production failed to materialize because of the rapidly deteriorating political situation, which Zamjatin described ruefully in Russianized English:

> In Berlin now everybody is living as during some permanent earthquake, when one always could expect to be suddenly swallowed up by an abyss. This fate before my eyes experienced Max Reinhardt who was made to close up five of his six theatres in Berlin. And I should add that this occurred just on the eve of his decision to perform in German translation my play *The Flea*. So and I have made acquaintance with this abyss . . . No, there in Berlin is now quite impossible to do anything.[10]

While in Berlin, Zamjatin was invited by the Artists' Circle (Umělecká Beseda), a Prague literary and art society, to give a lecture in the Czech capital. Many years earlier, attracted by Czechoslovakia and its culture, he had expressed a desire to visit Prague, and he had even studied the language; so he accepted the engagement readily.[11] He arrived there in mid-December, and on the nineteenth he appeared at the circle's customary Saturday evening meeting. He read his short story "Desjatiminutnaja drama" in Russian, and then his translator Václav Koenig, editor of the newspaper *Lidové noviny*, read one of Zamjatin's fables and a chapter from "Navodnenie" in Czech. The reading was warmly applauded by an audience that included Prague's most prominent writers and artists. The following week both the *Prager Presse* and *Lidové noviny* carried extensive interviews with Zamjatin; another appeared somewhat later in the *Rozpravy Aventina*.[12] Zamjatin's public lecture, "Sovremennyj russkij teatr" ("The Contemporary Russian Theater"), was delivered in Russian on December 29. It was widely reviewed by the Prague press and was published in Czech translation the following month.

This lecture triggered a new attack on Zamjatin by Communist and Soviet critics. The Prague Communist newspaper *Rudé právo*, which published a highly distorted review of the lecture, attacked Zamjatin as a non-Soviet writer and claimed that he was in complete accord with his audience which it said consisted almost entirely of White émigrés. The reviewer failed to mention that Zamjatin had come to Prague and lectured as the guest of the Czech Artists' Circle, whose chairman Dr. Hlaváč had introduced him. And he ignored the fact that the audience had included the Soviet ambassador Arosev, representatives of the Soviet Trade Mission and the Czech Ministry of Foreign Affairs, Czech playwrights, directors, and writers, in addition — to be sure — to some White émigrés, and that a week earlier Zamjatin had been warmly greeted by V. Rabas, chairman of the Committee on Plastic Arts.[13] A second attack on Zamjatin appeared soon after in the Prague Communist magazine *Tvorba* (*Creative Work*), in an article reiterating many of the distortions in the *Rudé právo* article.[14] Word of the lecture soon reached the Soviet Union. A Russian translation of the slanted piece from *Rudé právo* was published in *Literaturnaja gazeta* with a commentary by a Mixail Skačkov which ended with a familiar appeal to public opinion: "This counter-revolutionary performance of a 'non-Soviet' writer cannot but evoke the indignation of Soviet writers. Widespread proletarian public opinion must brand Zamjatin's performance as the sally of a class enemy." [15]

Apparently it was still necessary to discredit Zamjatin in the eyes of sympathetic fellow-traveler writers, and if he could be branded a counterrevolutionary, so much the better. That many Soviet writers still did sympathize with Zamjatin was evident in several articles by proletarian writers in the last half of 1931. One July article claimed that the Zamjatin question was very topical in that a well known group of writers was still connected with him; two months later RAPP writer Čumandrin attacked the VSSP for remaining silent about the Zamjatin question, for not attacking Zamjatin "who is connected by a thousand threads to the [VSSP] and to individual writers who are even close to us." [16]

In response to Skačkov's article, Zamjatin's Czech translator and friend Koenig published a brief article denouncing the *Rudé právo* review as untrue, attacking Skačkov, and praising Zamjatin for doing more to strengthen Czecho-Russian cultural ties than any other cultural representative who had spoken in

Prague.[17] Skačkov retaliated with a second article in which he viciously attacked Koenig for an earlier "malicious essay in a nationalist-fascist magazine *Sobota* (*Saturday*) on Soviet literature." He then berated Zamjatin for association with such people, citing numerous distorted quotations taken out of context from Zamjatin's lecture.[18] When Zamjatin finally read Skačkov's two articles, he fired off a letter, dated March 30, 1932, to the editors of *Literaturnaja gazeta* in which he presented the facts and demonstrated with clever irony that the *Rudé právo* review was false and distorted. The letter was typical of Zamjatin in its straightforward denial of false accusations, in its refusal to compromise his principle of intellectual independence in the face of criticism, and in its somewhat haughty and biting tone. Beginning with the assertion that "I do not consider it superfluous to declare that I am still alive and that, consequently, abuse cannot be heaped on me as on a dead man," he went on to compare the false quotations with what he had actually said. The letter ended on the following note:

> Whether the "quotations" were taken out of the blue or from a free rendition of some foreign newspapers does not change the matter: I can answer only for what I publish under my own signature and not for the inventions of others, especially if they are unintelligent. Thomas Aquinas correctly considered stupidity to be the very last of mortal sins. I accept all other sins with pleasure, but it seems difficult to suspect me of this last sin: I assume that everyone except Skačkov knows me well enough for that.[19]

Although Zamjatin had written in March, his letter was not published until September 17; and when the RAPP leader Averbax was asked (presumably in April or May) whether Zamjatin's letter had been received, he answered: "It has been received, but shall not be published. Zamjatin writes about what he did not say. But he does not write about what he *did* say."[20]

Soon after, the Party Central Committee dissolved RAPP, and there was a partial reversal of Party policy in literature. During the flux, Zamjatin's letter finally appeared in print, five months after being received. Its publication must have been a great surprise to many Soviet writers, as it was to Konstantin Fedin:

> I am sending you [Zamjatin] a wonder of wonders: your letter published in the *Literaturnaja gazeta*! Without a commentary,

> without a remark, without footnotes, without marginal notes, without the editor's promise "to return" to the matter, without an "in general," without a "however," without a "but." And they say: "there is nothing mystical." Not on your life! Of course there is! In general, what can't happen?! Anything can happen! [21]

Fedin and Zamjatin had been good friends in Leningrad and had enjoyed playing poker in the same congenial group. During Zamjatin's first three years abroad (1932–1934), they carried on a sporadic but interesting correspondence.* One of Fedin's letters, written June 21, 1932, is especially interesting in that it aptly summarizes the rift between Zamjatin and his critics in both the 1929 and 1932 incidents:

> Your letter [of March 30 to the *Literaturnaja gazeta*] will not be published even now. The crux of the matter is that you fight against the distortion of facts, the reporters' falsifications, i.e., against *particulars*, but leave untouched the important question of the *general*. The goal and sense of the distortions and falsifications is to prove that you are a counterrevolutionary. Your task should consist in the converse. But you have always come forth catching your adversaries in dirtiness and lies, focusing your blow on the lowly means to which they have resorted. In this case, in attempting to dishonor you, they have begun to accuse you of almost outright "treason." It seems to me that you should have struck at this calumny with all your strength (*and at its essence*). The matter should not be reduced to counteraccusations against Smith, Jones and others, but to the routing of miserable intentions to make you a bugbear of insidious counterrevolution. And this time, too, just as before, you have left open the question—*how* you regard the Revolution—(obviously, the Revolution which is now taking place here and not revolution as an abstract phenomenon).
>
> I fear that this question, in the sphere of your individual being, belongs to the *eternal* questions. And you will never say anything decisive about this. But can you remain silent?

Zamjatin not only could, but did remain silent. He despised sycophancy and refused on principle to extol the Revolution and the wisdom of the Party at the demand of servile critics who unjustly accused him of counterrevolution. Because he believed in never-ending revolution, he refused to canonize October as

* Fedin's letters to Zamjatin have recently been published; see G. Ermolaev and A. Šejn, "Pis'ma Konstantina Fedina k Evgeniju Zamjatinu," *Novyj žurnal*, No. 92 (1968).

the final revolution. And because he considered satire to be the best means for elevating man above the level of animals and slaves, he categorically refused to repudiate his own satirical works. Zamjatin was an obstinate romantic; for him there could be no compromise, so he chose to remain abroad.*

After spending three weeks and very cheerful Christmas holidays in Prague, Zamjatin returned to Berlin. He remained there till late February 1932, when, thanks to the efforts of the writer Pierre Drieu La Rochelle,[22] he obtained a French visa and went on to Paris where he was cordially greeted by writers and the press. On March 4, Zamjatin, Henri Barbusse, Il'ja Èrenburg, and Ovadij Savič, were guests of honor at a dinner given by the Groupe des Ecrivains Prolétariens de Paris.[23] A month later several newspapers printed interviews with Zamjatin. He also began negotiating about the production of *Bloxa* and *Obščestvo početnyx zvonarej* with Jouvet, the director of the Comédie des Champs-Elysées.[24]

Zamjatin stayed in Paris about a month before traveling to the Riviera where he visited his old friend, the artist Boris Grigor'ev. Grigor'ev's cottage, the picturesque "Villa Borisella" which served as his studio and art school, was situated a mile from the sea near Cagnes-sur-Mer, a medieval Provençal town seven miles west of Nice. As soon as Grigor'ev had read of Zamjatin's arrival in Riga, he had sent an invitation which Zamjatin had accepted quickly. Zamjatin finally arrived there in early April 1932.[25] While resting, Zamjatin made plans toward four objectives: (1) the production of his plays, (2) a series of articles on Soviet theater and literature, (3) a new novel about

* Although I believe the term "romantic" to be most appropriate in describing Zamjatin's world view, his close friend Charles Malamuth argued in his letter to me of August 18, 1964: "Perhaps I don't understand your reference to him as a 'romantic' but he struck me as altogether too realistic for that sort of appellation. He was a man of great courage, great integrity; hence, uncompromising in his devotion to certain basic principles and standards. Does such a stance make one a romantic? Is the rotten compromiser, by comparison or contrast, the realist? I would challenge that. Surely, there is nothing sentimental or fanciful or unrealistic in being faithful to one's ideals, provided one faces the consequences with open eyes. There was no self-deception, no flight from reality in Zamyatin's stance on issues and principles. Hence, in my humble judgement, he was no romantic. That designation seems somehow out of tune with his personality, his awareness of the realities around him."

Attila, and (4) a lecture tour of the United States in October. Of the four projects, Zamjatin staked most on his plays, three of which had been translated into French by May 1932.[26] He returned to Paris in late May or early June to check on the progress of his various enterprises. On June 24 at a literary evening Zamjatin proved himself to be an excellent reader, as an appreciative audience listened to his rendition of "Navodnenie," an act from *Bloxa*, and two fables.[27] Unfortunately, his negotiations with Jouvet led nowhere, and his plans to stage his plays in Paris evidently were never realized.

Apparently all but one of Zamjatin's attempts to have his plays produced outside the U.S.S.R. proved unsuccessful. While in Czechoslovakia, Zamjatin had investigated the possibilities at the Prague National Theater and in Brno, but by March 1932, Koenig, his representative in Czechoslovakia, informed him that nothing had materialized.[28] Repeated attempts to stage the plays at the Bulgarian National Theater in Sofia were also unsuccessful.[29] An inquiry to Theodore Komisarjevsky, a Russian theatrical producer who had been active in London since the Revolution, also bore no fruit.[30] The sole ray of light was Paul Oettly's decision in August 1933 to stage Zamjatin's *Bloxa*, which he did in Brussels that same year.[31] The difficulty in staging his plays soon convinced Zamjatin that he should seek his fortune elsewhere, so he wrote no new plays after leaving Russia.

Zamjatin had considerably better success with the publication of about a dozen articles on theater, literature, and shipbuilding in the Soviet Union. The first of these writings, titled "Buduščee teatra" ("The Theater's Future"), appeared in the French journal *Le mois*. "Sovremennyj russkij teatr" ("The Contemporary Russian Theater"), a more extensive article which represented a polished version of Zamjatin's Prague lecture, was published somewhat later in German, French, and Serbo-Croatian translations. In December 1932, a short article entitled "Sovetskie deti" ("Soviet Children"), which depicted the psychological makeup of Soviet children in a series of conversations and anecdotes, appeared in the French weekly *Marianne*.[32] The following year he wrote his longest and most ambitious article, "Moskva-Peterburg," an extended comparison of the seven arts in Russia's two capitals.[33]

The Zamjatin Archive contains manuscripts of several other articles and reviews on Soviet literature, but the place of publication has not been ascertained in all cases. Written in Russian, many articles bear French titles, which would suggest that they were intended for French periodicals. They include: (1) "En l'URSS," a brief two-page essay on the effects of RAPP; (2) "Actualités soviétiques," a sketch on literary formalism and the "struggle against formalism;" (3) "Lettres russes," an essay on the historical novel including reviews of Aleksej Tolstoj's *Petr Pervyj* (*Peter the First*), Ol'ga Forš's *Jakobinskij zakvas* (*The Jacobin Leaven*), and Georgij Štorm's *Trudy i dni Mixaila Lomonosova* (*The Labors and Days of Mixail Lomonosov*); (4) "Lettres russes," an extensive review of Jurij German's *Naši znakomye* (*Our Friends*) and of Nikolaj Ostrovskij's *Kak zakaljalas' stal'* (*How the Steel Was Tempered*); and (5) an outline for an article entitled "Teatr i kino v sovetskoj Rossii" ("The Theater and Cinema in Soviet Russia"), which apparently was intended for *The Manchester Guardian*.[34] Two more articles titled "Lettres russes," the first with reviews of Aleksej Novikov-Priboj's *Cusima*, Aleksandr Lebedenko's *Tjaželyj division* (*The Heavy Division*), and Boris Lavrenev's *Sinee i beloe* (*The Blue and the White*), and the second of Prišvin's *Žen'-šen'* (*Ginseng*) and Jurij Janovskij's *Vsadniki* (*The Riders*), were published in the French weekly *Marianne*, but the Russian manuscripts are not in the Zamjatin Archive.[35]

Upon the death of Andrej Belyj on January 8, 1934,[36] and Maksim Gor'kij on June 18, 1936, Zamjatin wrote interesting recollections of both men. Since Zamjatin had known both personally, the memoirs not only sketched their lives (as was customary), but they also included personal observations which revealed something of them as human beings. During his years abroad Zamjatin did not completely ignore his first wife, shipbuilding. He wrote a very interesting essay entitled "O moix ženax, o ledokolax i o Rossii" ("About My Wives, Icebreakers, and Russia") in which he drew some amusing and astute parallels between icebreakers and the Russian people. In addition to his literary articles, three of his technical articles, which surveyed Russian shipbuilding during the years 1932–1934, were published in the *Glasgow Herald's* "Trade Review."[37]

Zamjatin's third project, a new novel about Attila, was realized only in part. The book had been conceived in 1924, and Zamjatin had worked on it in a desultory fashion since then. The first seven chapters about Attila's childhood in Rome were completed in 1935. The novel, *Bič Božij*, was to have had four sections: "Nakanune" ("On the Eve"), "Dnevnik Priska" ("Prisk's Diary"), "Meč" ("The Sword"), and "Nevesta" ("The Bride"). When compared to Zamjatin's synopsis of the novel,[38] it becomes apparent that the first seven chapters represented only half of the first section, or approximately one-eighth of the whole, as it was conceived. The seven chapters were published posthumously in 1939.*

Zamjatin's fourth project, a lecture trip to America, did not take place, even though he still entertained the idea as late as 1935. In June 1935 he did, however, undertake a brief lecture tour to Belgium and the Netherlands. In Amsterdam and Brussels he lectured on the crisis in European theaters, with special reference to the Soviet Union. Although the manuscript of his lecture "Teatral'nye paralleli" ("Theatrical Parallels") has been preserved, it apparently has never been published.[39] While in Brussels and Antwerp he also gave readings of his stories.[40]

It did not take long for Zamjatin to discover that the life of a Russian writer in France during the Depression was not easy. By July 1932, he undoubtedly realized that none of his four projects would earn him a living, so he turned to the film industry. Upon returning to the Riviera, Zamjatin settled at the "Villa Simple Abri" in Cros-de-Cagnes, wrote a synopsis of a film scenario for his novel *My*, and spent the summer making the rounds of film studios in search of a director.[41] He managed to arrange for the filming of a novel (presumably *My*) with Feature Productions, but unfortunately the project had fallen through by December.[42] After a brief stint with the Gaumont Productions, which proved to be "too inartistic" for his taste, Zamjatin wrote a scenario for Feodor Chaliapin about the folk

* [36]. The publication date is frequently and erroneously given as 1938. The *Bibliographie de la France*, No. 7–8 (Feb. 16–23, 1940), 1376, cites the date as May 3, 1939. This is corroborated by the appearance of reviews in mid-May and July of 1939 and by Mixail Osorgin's statement of March 10, that "in the near future a volume of unpublished works by E. I. Zamjatin, *Bič Božij*, will be published in Paris," [433].

hero Sten'ka Razin. The scenario, which he characterized as "a romantic, revolutionary affair, based on the folklore about the great robber chief of the Volga, and at the same time the hero of the first great peasant uprising," was sold to Vandor Films.[43] In March 1933, Zamjatin was commissioned to do a scenario of Lev Tolstoj's *Anna Karenina* for Pathé-Natan to be directed by Fédor Ozep.[44] Zamjatin made some interesting remarks in connection with this scenario:

> But my biggest cinema job since leaving Russia has been my scenario of *Anna Karenina* . . . I admit that the holy shade of Tolstoj was an awful bother. You see, in turning the novel into a film I simply had to cut out all the non-visual matter, and, naturally Levin, the Tolstoyan hero with his grasshopper philosophizing, had to be thrown overboard at once. I limited myself to the Karenin-Vronsky triangle. The dialogue had to be cut out, for both the dialogue and the psychology had to be translated into cinematic terms. The thing had to be visual and dynamic. The method of flash-presentation instead of narrative exposition was the method that you will find in all my books; so the medium was familiar enough to me. The dialogue is, naturally, also reduced to bare essentials, to mere significant flashes. . . . On the screen things have to be *shown*, not *told*. In a way, all my literary work has been cinematic; I never *explained*; I always *showed* and *suggested*.
>
> And after all (Zamjatin concluded, with a twinkle of self-satisfaction) you know where Soviet cinema learned its method and its basic idea. Was it not from the flashily obscure Soviet books of the early twenties? *Quorum pars magna fui.*[45]

Although similarities between Zamjatin's prose style and certain cinematic techniques may have helped stimulate his original interest in writing scenarios, his enthusiasm waned quickly. Necessity forced him to continue working in this new profession, but he resented the time lost to creative writing and became more and more dissatisfied:

> So as you see, I am alive. But, honestly speaking, I don't like the way I live. There is much good material in my head, but I waste it on *Ersatz*, on the writing of all sorts of scenarios — just because this is the only work here with a not-too-miserable compensation. And even this, by your American standards, is poor. I simply cannot manage "to get ahead" in my budget for — say — some six months in order to sit down and work on a novel.[46]

More than a dozen scenario synopses have been preserved,[47] but the full extent of Zamjatin's scenario work has not been determined. The scenario which undoubtedly gave Zamjatin the greatest satisfaction was his adaptation of Gor'kij's *Na dne* (*The Lower Depths*) for Jean Renoir's film *Les Bas-Fonds*. The Paris premiere was on December 10, 1936, and two weeks later the film was voted "the Best French Film of 1936."[48] In an interesting review, Georgij Adamovič pointed out that the film version was much altered from Gor'kij's original, but he did admit that "taken by itself, the scenario was artistically done."[49] Zamjatin's success as a scenarist did not, however, add to his stature as a master of Russian prose, and his readers, along with his good friend Remizov, may justifiably regret that his scenarios kept him from writing new prose works and from completing *Bič Božij*.

Zamjatin's last years were difficult. The VSSP refused to send him author's honorariums, and his ability to make a decent living was hindered by failing health.[50] When Zamjatin left the Soviet Union, he already had chronic colitis;[51] during the summer of 1932 he contracted the grippe;[52] and when Fedin visited him in the first week of 1934, he was suffering from sciatica. The severity of the attack may be judged from Fedin's letter of April 1934: "Why is it that Gene [Zamjatin] writes of feeling badly and of sleeping poorly? Is it his sciatica again? . . . But when I remember how Gene crawled and limped so that the attacks even stopped his movement when he made his way across the street, my heart is pierced by a really Christian compassion."[53] In the fall of 1936 Zamjatin's doctor pronounced him incurably ill. Suffering from angina pectoris, he was forced to stay in bed for weeks at a time.[54] His heart ailment was compounded by a stomach ulcer, and on March 10, 1937 at seven in the morning he died of a heart attack.[55] A small group of friends including Marc Slonim (who had made the final arrangements), Avgusta Damanskaja, Marina Cvetaeva, and Roman Gul', followed his coffin to the cemetery of Thiais near Paris, where he was buried on the wet and dismal morning of March 12.[56] His death went unnoticed by the Soviet press.

A month and a half after his death, a private evening gathering in commemoration of Zamjatin was given at a Mrs. Lowell's by his friends and admirers. Marc Slonim's introductory speech about Zamjatin's works was followed by readings of several stories — "Peščera" in French translation by V. Sirin (pseudonym of Vladimir Nabokov), "Drakon" in Russian by Ivan Bunin, and "Aprel' " in French by the actress Maria Reinhardt. Drieu La Rochelle recalled his meeting with Zamjatin, Oettly spoke of the Brussels performance of *Bloxa*, and the evening ended with Jean Renoir's reminiscences of Zamjatin's activity as a scenarist.[57]

So died one of Russia's most talented twentieth-century writers. To many he will remain the cool, reserved "Englishman" so aptly described by Slonim:

> He was lean, of medium height, clean shaven, with reddish-blond hair parted on the side. Then in his early fifties, he looked much younger, and the malicious twinkle of his gray eyes gave a boyish expression to his handsome face. Always wearing tweeds and with an "unextinguished" pipe in his wide, generous mouth, he resembled an Englishman. His whole appearance was neat and controlled. His manners were reserved, and to those who knew him but little he seemed all "buttoned up," a man who kept an "unmelting icicle" inside—some hard core of strong will, perfect self-mastery, and sharp intelligence.[58]

But to those who knew him well, Zamjatin possessed a ready sympathy and kindly disposition, even a hidden ardor.[59] In thought and deed Zamjatin was certainly a passionate lover of freedom, a romantic with uncompromising ideals, in short, an incurable heretic.

PART II

The Evolution of Zamjatin's Prose Fiction

All the complexities through which I passed turned out to be necessary in order to achieve simplicity.

Zamjatin, *Lica*

CHAPTER FIVE

Early Period, 1908-1917

During these years [1908–1910], amidst the blueprints and figures were several stories. I did not submit them for publication: in each still I felt something that was not quite "it." "It" turned up in 1911.

Zamjatin, *Autobiography*

Using such criteria as the date of writing, theme, structure, and style, Zamjatin's creative work can be divided into four periods. The first period (1908–1917), beginning with his maiden story "Odin" and terminating with the story "Pravda istinnaja," comprises his early works.* The setting for most of these is provincial Russia — the small town, the village, or the distant garrison. Local dialects and colloquialisms are abundant, and the *skaz* manner of narration is employed extensively. The second period (1917–1921) begins with the tale "Ostrovitjane" and culminates with Zamjatin's only complete novel, *My*. The works of this period depart from the folksy *skaz* and are characterized by the elaboration of a concise, elliptical style in which the role of imagery is highly intensified; several are set in great urban communities. The third period (1922–1927) shows a decided drop in the production of prose fiction (only seven stories were written in those years); these pieces are distinguished by much experimentation with form and a comic treatment of post-Revolutionary life, accompanied by new forms of *skaz* narrative. The major works of the final period (1928–1935) are simpler, have less elaborate imagery, lack *skaz*, and reflect the influence of the modern European novella

* For a chronological list of Zamjatin's prose fiction, see page 229.

in their plot dynamism and their use of surprise endings and false resolutions. These generalizations suggest considerable variety in Zamjatin's literary technique. Indeed, in Zamjatin's work the elaboration of one technique was followed by a search for a new and different technique — a search that reflected his philosophy of never-ending revolution in all spheres of life.

Zamjatin's belief that life is essentially tragic is expressed in all his early works. In "Odin" the imprisoned student-revolutionary commits suicide because his love is frustrated. In "Devuška" the heroine's needs for love remain unfulfilled. In "Uezdnoe" the rise of the ignorant, bestial Anfim Baryba to a powerful administrative position is in itself a tragic reflection of provincial life. The hero of "Neputevyj" dies uselessly on the Moscow barricades, and the heroine of "Črevo," thwarted in her irrepressible desire to have a child, murders her drunken husband whose beatings have caused her to miscarry. "Na kuličkax" depicts the spiritual bankruptcy of a distant army garrison and the destruction of a genuine love between Captain Šmit and his wife Marusja. In "Alatyr' " the dreams and aspirations of the central characters are thwarted, and in "Krjaži" the love between two strong personalities remains unrealized at the death of one. Konyč's inability to comprehend a situation ("Staršina") provides one more tragic example of provincial ignorance. Dar'ja ("Pis'menno"), overjoyed by the imprisonment of her hated husband, discovers a year later that she loves him. Fedor Volkov ("Afrika") abandons his shrewish wife in search of happiness, only to die. In "Pravda istinnaja" the letter of a country girl working as a servant in the city unintentionally betrays her unhappiness with her life there. The sole bright spot in Zamjatin's early stories is blossoming puppy love between two teen-agers in "Aprel'," but even there a tragic note is sounded when the uncomprehending adult world momentarily turns the emotion into a source of shame for the girl.

Despite the characteristically pessimistic endings of his early works, Zamjatin believed that life's tragedies could be surmounted either by religion or by irony. In contrast to the Symbolists, who had turned to religious mysticism, Zamjatin chose irony. It is ironic that Marusja ("Na kuličkax"), who loves Šmit so deeply, is not present at his funeral, while General Azančeev, the man who destroys Šmit and his love for Marusja, delivers an impassioned eulogy. It is ironic that Konyč, who in his ignorant zeal to serve the government has transgressed the law, is incapable of recognizing his error even after the trial. It is ironic that the meek and submissive Kostja Edytkin ("Alatyr'"), upon perceiving the hopelessness of pitiful Alatyr' life, is led off to prison surrounded by a clamoring mob that considers him a dangerous killer. Permeating all of the early works, irony underscores life's incongruities and illuminates the contradiction between truth and what people think to be true. Since the ironic rejection of the lives depicted is accompanied neither by solutions, nor by comments from the author, nor by an explicit ideology, the reader must make his own deductions which, hopefully, will stimulate him to seek a better life.

The apparent pessimism of the early stories is only a literary device; the critic Gizetti astutely observed that the indignation aroused by the denouement of "Uezdnoe," for example, was proof that beneath Zamjatin's artistic devices resided a firm faith in man's potential goodness.[1] Although Zamjatin once quipped that the Neorealists believed neither in God nor in man,[2] his critical essays left no doubt about his own deep-rooted belief in man's capacity for self-improvement on earth. His faith in the verbal whip of satire as the sole means of preventing man's reversion to lower, inhuman behavior underlay his early, essentially satiric works. On the other hand, Gizetti went too far in seeing "excellent opportunities for regeneration" in some of Zamjatin's early stories,[3] for within most of the stories themselves such hope is rare. The opportunity exists only for the reader.

Man's inhumanity, love, and revolution — set invariably in provincial Russia — are the central themes of Zamjatin's early period. The theme of man's inhumanity, which is basic to all three of Zamjatin's tales and the majority of his stories, is the keynote of the early period. It is first introduced in "Uezdnoe," Zamjatin's first extensive work in which he found "it" and which brought him widespread recognition.* Beginning with Anfim

* In [470], 48, Mark Slonim wrote that Zamjatin's "Uezdnoe" had received 300 reviews within two months, a claim that was reiterated in 1962 by D. J. Richards [454], 31.

Baryba's expulsion from school and home for laziness and stupidity, Zamjatin traces his activities over two years of theft, gluttony, sadism, rape, and professional perjury, until Baryba finally attains the position of town constable where, presumably, he can indulge his sadistic bullying unhindered. Although the adventures of Baryba are the organizing principle of the work, contemporary critics were correct in construing the author's aim to be the satiric depiction of the extremely negative aspects of provincial Russian life. As V. Polonskij put it:

> And when you have read to the end of the tale, it turns out that Anfim Baryba is of no importance, Anfim Baryba is simply an excuse, and the tale is not at all about Anfimka. One after another the little chapters flow together into one large chapter, they dissolve, drown in one general, unified picture, and the name of that picture is Russia, limited, dark, provincial Russia.[4]

Although Polonskij's conclusion is sound, one cannot agree that Baryba is simply a literary device, of no importance in himself. He is, after all, a product of his philistine environment and is neither better nor worse than the other characters of the tale. His crude, angular, and heavy features, especially his iron jaws, reflect the essence of his personality; and Zamjatin's frequent use of the epithet "stone" not only reinforces the basic picture of his heavy awkwardness but reveals the central problem of the tale: the petrification of human feelings within man.[5] Whatever human feelings Baryba may begin with (he yearns for human companionship while living among the dogs, and he is genuinely touched — if only momentarily — by Aprosja's care during his illness) are completely petrified by the tale's end, when he can neither bear the sound of human laughter nor recognize a momentary twinge of conscience. The final comparison — "as if it were not a man walking, but an old resurrected heathen idol, an absurd Russian stone idol" — endows the figure of Baryba with symbolic significance. It shows him as the embodiment of a cruel, stagnant, provincial Russia devoid of human compassion.

Resembling Baryba in their bestial, ignorant, and senseless existence, the other characters of "Uezdnoe" present variant expressions of inhumanity. Foremost among them is the well-to-do merchant's widow who owns the town bathhouse and leather factory, the incomparable Čebotarixa. A veritable mound of quivering, doughy flesh, she cannot resist the sight of young Baryba's tensed, firm, animal-like body, and, instead of punishing him for stealing her chickens, she takes him into her arms and her bed to feed her insatiable appetite. Timoša, the town tailor and philosopher who is aware of Baryba's lack of soul, nonetheless befriends him. A chronic alcoholic with consumption, Timoša forces his three children to eat from his plate in order to tempt God, in the tradition of the Dostoevskian rebels: Will He allow the suffering of innocent children? In a few instances Timoša serves as the author's ironic mouthpiece:

> It's nothing unusual [Baryba's being the 'companion' of a certain respected widow]. It's a matter of trade. Everything now, in accord with the times, is a matter of trade, that's how we make a living. The merchant sells herring, the gal sells her belly. Each has his own trade. And in what way is the belly any worse than herring, or the herring any worse than conscience? Everything is a commodity. (S.S. I, 86.)*

Timoša's words forecast all that follows: Baryba does indeed sell his conscience and even sends his friend Timoša to the gallows by perjuring himself for a hundred and fifty rubles and an appointment as town constable. The irony of Timoša's execution is purposely intensified: his intercession on behalf of one of the apprehended thieves, a slight lad who is being severely beaten by the tavern-keeper Čurilov, leads to his false conviction as an accessory to the crime: "Do you want to kill the kid because of a hundred rubles [the amount stolen]? Maybe you've already killed him? Look, he's not breathing. Devils, animals, isn't a man even worth a hundred rubles?" (S.S. I, 96.) The answer is an ironic negative, for this sole prominent humane impulse is rewarded by ostracism and death. This bleak picture is supplemented by a host of other grotesque characters: the fly-watching priest Father Evsej, the sensual and deceitful lawyer Morgunov, the presiding colonel at the military court whose upset stomach interests him more than justice, the prosecutor

* *Sobranie sočinenij,* I, [30], 86. Hereafter quotations from this four-volume edition of Zamjatin's collected works [30]–[33] will be identified in the text by the initials "S.S." plus volume and page numbers in roman and arabic numerals, respectively.

who wants a victim more than he wants the actual robber, and the district police officer who prefers pleasing his superiors to saving an innocent man.

Zamjatin's satire is not limited to any one group. In "Uezdnoe" he attacks small town inhabitants (Baryba, Čebotarixa, Aprosja, Timoša), the clergy (Evsej, Innokentij, d'jakonok, Savka), and the courts (the colonel, the prosecutor, the district police official, Morgunov). In "Na kuličkax," which further develops the main theme of "Uezdnoe," he shifts his attention to the military personnel of a remote Siberian garrison, but in this tale he endows some characters (Šmit, Marusja, Polovec, Tixmen') with human qualities which raise them above their environment. The tragedy is therefore all the more poignant when the three basic lines of action lead to the destruction of these four people. Polovec, ostensibly the central figure of the tale and a man of some capabilities and aspirations, cannot carry anything through to completion. Seeking love and fame, he decides to begin life anew out in the sticks, far away from his native Tambov. A dreamer and idealist, he resembles Lieutenant Romašov, the ill-fated hero of Aleksandr Kuprin's "Poedinok" ("The Duel"), to which "Na kuličkax" has frequently been compared. Both works give extremely negative pictures of garrison life, and they have similar plots: both heroes fall in love with married women, which forces them into duels; in both instances — for different reasons — the women request the heroes to play passive roles in order to ensure the husband's safety. The two women, however, differ greatly: Marusja has integrity and loves her husband, not the hero; Šuročka ("Poedinok") is a schemer who does not love her husband, but will sacrifice the hero Romašov's life for her own advancement. The outcome of the two works is quite different: Romašov is shot in cold blood, a victim of Šuročka's seduction, but Polovec, in despair at Marusja's enmity after her husband Šmit's suicide, is later drawn into the drunken, bestial revelry of the other officers: "Suddenly Andrej Ivanovič was swept up, whirled away by a drunken, hopeless revelry, by that very last revelry in which revels Russia, chased out into the sticks" (S.S. II, 129).

As in "Uezdnoe," the finale takes on symbolic proportions. The frenzied, hopeless revelry of the garrison out in the sticks engulfs not only Polovec, but all of Russia. This apocalyptic vision of impending catastrophe, which anticipated World War I, the Revolution, and the Civil War, stresses the need of a spiritual regeneration within Russia.

The love between Šmit and his wife Marusja represents the second line of action. Their two-year marriage is based on an unusually personal, human, faithful relationship which, envied and despised by the others,* stands in sharp contrast to "normal" garrison life. The tragic destruction of this unique love is effected by General Azančeev. In order to punish Šmit for mentioning his theft of government funds, Azančeev forces Marusja to submit to him. Unable to accept a profaned idol despite his continuing love, Šmit cruelly torments both Marusja and himself in a truly Dostoevskian love-hate relationship that culminates in his suicide.

The successful interweaving of three plot lines contributes a structural complexity to "Na kulickax" which reflects Zamjatin's increasing literary maturity. Joined by a traditional love triangle (Polovec-Marusja-Šmit), the two major plot lines are resolved by the dissolution of the triangle (Šmit's suicide and Marusja's departure). And the tale's structural integration is strengthened by an undeniable spiritual harmony between Marusja and Polovec. Established at their first meeting, this rapport is symbolized by a light golden web floating through the blue air (S.S. II, 21, 25). The central figure in the third plot line is Lieutenant Tixmen', who (like the tailor Timoša) is afflicted with a penchant for thought; he seeks to discover whether he is the father of Katjuška's ninth child. The subordinate plot is allied to the major triangle by a relationship both prognostic and contrastive: The suicide of Tixmen' in the face of an insoluble problem foreshadows that of Šmit, but Katjuška's behavior sets a garrison norm from which Marusja's is sharply differentiated. All lines of action are ultimately united by the central theme of man's inhumanity, expressed in the ignorance, spiritual bankruptcy, and utter boredom of Zamjatin's extensive gallery of negative characters: General Azan-

* Moločko and Katjuška speak enviously of it (S.S. II, 18) and Azančeev in a fit of rage lashes out at this relationship knowing it to be Šmit's only sensitive point (S.S. II, 35–36).

čeev, the froglike culinary artist, the Raphael of potatoes, who thrives on gluttony, embezzlement, and sex; the garrison cuckold Captain Nečesa whose favorite pastime is to skewer cockroaches with a needle; his round little wanton wife Katjuška; the garrison gossip and busybody, Lieutenant Moločko, who sleeps with the general's half-witted wife, with Katjuška and with anyone else who is available; the stupid, fish-eyed orderly Neprotošnov; the orderly Gusljakin whose predilection for keyholes furnishes the garrison with the details of each other's personal lives; the officers as a whole, flotsam of humanity who delight in howling endless songs at nightly drinking bouts and in shooting down passing coolies.

Although both tales depict the negative aspects of provincial life, there is a difference in their emphasis. In "Uezdnoe" Zamjatin focuses on the successful rise to power of an animal-like provincial amidst others like himself, while in "Na kuličkax" he shows the destruction of sensitive people amidst the animal-like inhabitants of a provincial garrison. The central tragedy of both works, however, is the same—man's inhuman behavior.

Love, the second major theme in Zamjatin's tales, is depicted in two aspects, the physical and the spiritual. For the negative characters of "Uezdnoe" there can be no question of a spiritual love. Baryba, for example, has liaisons with three women—Čebotarixa, her cook Pol'ka, and his landlady Aprosja. And in all three cases Baryba is merely satisfying a natural urge, without thought and without passion. The striking feature is Baryba's sexual indifference. Desire is aroused in him simply by the proximity of the woman, and, once gratified, it becomes an automatic daily function. The attitudes of the women vary. The sight of Baryba's body immediately arouses Čebotarixa, and, in showing him how to make the sign of the cross, she envelopes him in her doughy flesh. Baryba's reaction is instinctive: he turns, sinking his hands into her flesh, and later falls asleep contented. Čebotarixa's desire proves to be too demanding even for such a fine animal as Baryba, and one day, as he watches the cook Pol'ka tearfully run to the cellar to escape his sadistic bullying, the idea of possessing her occurs to him. In her master's hands Pol'ka becomes a rag doll, submitting fearfully and tearfully, which gratifies Baryba's sadistic nature. Pol'ka is not a source of sexual gratification to Baryba, but represents a chance to bully someone, to avenge himself for Čebotarixa's demands. This primitive trait of vengeance is the mainspring of Baryba's personality, and as the story ends he is bullying others because his father has again repudiated him. His third affair begins like the first, but unlike the others it is satisfactory to both parties. Every night, after completing her chores, the tired Aprosja, yawning, takes off her clothes, carries Baryba's freshly shined boots to him, and half an hour later, still yawning, returns to her own room, says her prayers, and falls fast asleep. Love has been reduced to a passionless, everyday, physical function that does nothing to dispel the boredom of provincial life.

The treatment of love is considerably more varied in "Na kuličkax." The automatic, instinctive, Baryba-like behavior is exemplified by Katjuška, who sleeps with any man. General Azančeev, like Katjuška, is interested only in physical love, and, like the lawyer Morgunov in "Uezdnoe," he has a jaded desire for a variety of mates. By contrast, Polovec's love for Marusja is that of an idealistic dreamer, spiritual in nature. And the relationship between Marusja and Šmit, portrayed only fragmentarily in Gusljakin's gossip, appears to be a healthy combination of the spiritual and physical aspects, which sets them apart from the rest of the garrison. Nevertheless, for the majority in "Na kuličkax" and in "Uezdnoe" love is a physical function which becomes an automatic part of their humdrum daily routine.

In Zamjatin's third tale, "Alatyr'," the love theme assumes central importance. The women of the provincial town of Alatyr', once famed for its fertility, have come upon barren times, with a dearth of eligible bachelors. In particular, Glafira, the daughter of the district police chief, is like succulent rye, ripe for harvest. Her dreams of a lover-general on a white stallion manifest her physiological need for fulfillment; and her ideal of ultimate happiness is exemplified by the police chief's cat Milka, who is contentedly suckling her four new kittens. The presentation of physical love in a positive, even lyrical, manner contrasts strongly with the negative treatment in "Uezdnoe" and "Na kuličkax." However, the archpriest's daughter Varavara, who is driven by the same physiological need and who is Glafira's chief rival for the affections of the new postmaster Prince Vadbol'skij, has a malicious character and is frequently likened to a dog, as her nickname Sobačeja (a derivation of the Russian word for dog) would indicate.

The masculine protagonists, both lacking this strong physiological urge, belong to the dreamer-thinker category and view Glafira as a godly embodiment of an ideal. In the third tale, however, the dreamer is not isolated amidst a mass of unthinking beings, since most inhabitants of Alatyr' are striving toward some particular dream or goal. It is true that their striving seems ridiculous and that, without exception, their aspirations are completely frustrated. Kostja Edytkin, a self-made peasant poet who is tutored by Glafira in preparation for civil-service examinations, seeks literary fame and aspires to Glafira's hand. Shy and timid, his romantic idolization of Glafira resembles Polovec's love for Marusja. His major work, *Vnutrennij ženskij dogmat božestva* (*The Inner Feminine Tenet of Godliness*), provokes the laughter of his whole audience, including Glafira, and his love is never reciprocated. Prince Vadbol'skij believes that all the problems of the world would be solved if everyone would speak one language. But his attempts to teach Esperanto to the townspeople fail miserably. Instead of establishing universal brotherhood and world peace, his efforts precipitate a pitched battle for his affection between his two best pupils, Glafira and Varvara. The police chief is always seeking to invent something beneficial to mankind, but all his attempts, including bread baked with bird droppings instead of yeast, are failures. Glafira's dreams of a general on a white stallion likewise remain unrealized. All of these dreams are needed to dispel the terrible tedium of the provinces, which is established in the first chapter: "All day in the police chief's home tedium loudly cuckoos like a cuckoo" (S.S. I, 116). And later, when Prince Vadbol'skij looks at the darkening sky, which appears "so terribly empty, so silent forever," there is a catch in his throat and he feels like howling (S.S. I, 145). In this environment all dreams are frustrated, and at the tale's end, in a moment of truth, Edytkin and the reader see how pitiful the people of Alatyr' are. There is prophecy in Edytkin's final cry of anguish, "We are doomed! Doomed, doomed . . . ," (S.S. I, 171) which recalls the symbolic finale of Zamjatin's other two tales.

Of the three tales, "Alatyr' " is the briefest and the most tightly structured. Centering on Glafira's need for a mate, the action develops quickly, with each of the eight chapters contributing to the forward movement of the plot. In integrating the motifs of frustration with the central love intrigue, Zamjatin displays great skill in attaining a remarkable unity of action. The police chief's frustrating experiment in bread baking introduces Edytkin into the narrative, thus altering the initial situation (suitorless Glafira). Edytkin's literary debacle not only foreshadows his failure in love, but makes him ridiculous in the eyes of his beloved, thus stimulating his envy and despair. The prince's Esperanto classes provide a field of rivalry for the two heroines and provoke the anonymous love notes which ultimately lead to the resolution of the love intrigue and the destruction of the prince's hopes for world peace through Esperanto. In comparison, the three plot lines of "Na kuličkax" provide less actional unity. Of the two central thrusts of action, Polovec's love is treated directly and fully, while the Marusja-Šmit relationship is seen primarily through secondary sources and consequently is somewhat blurred. The third line of action (Tixmen') is primarily used to retard the others, and the major unifying element is theme, rather than action. The purely episodic structure of "Uezdnoe" deemphasizes action, thereby stressing descriptive elements and bringing the theme into prominence as the central unity. Although divided into twenty-six very short chapters, the tale contains not tweny-six individual "vignettes" or "watercolors," as claimed by some critics,[6] but seven episodes in the life of Baryba: his failure in final examinations (Chapter 1), life with the dogs (Chapters 2–3), Čebotarixa (Chapters 4–9), the theft of Father Evsej's money (Chapters 10–12), life at Aprosja's (Chapters 13–16), professional perjury for Morgunov (Chapters 17–19), and his appointment with the police (Chapters 20–26). The unity of action resides solely in the person of Baryba, who, like Gogol's Čičikov, serves as a structural device which enables the author to depict many scenes and characters. In their structure Zamjatin's early tales show a definite progress toward greater actional unity, from an episodic to an internally cohesive plot structure. Greater actional unity tended to deemphasize the unifying role of theme and descriptive elements, which was one of the main factors contributing to the diminishing force with which the theme of ignorant, inhuman, provincial Russia struck the reader in "Uezdnoe," "Na kuličkax," and "Alatyr'."

In sheer volume, the three tales comprise more than half* of Zamjatin's output of imaginative prose for the years 1908 to 1917, and they are typical examples of the stylistic maturity he achieved prior to the Revolution. Significant structural features distinguish the tales from Zamjatin's stories, which exhibit much greater thematic and stylistic variety. This variety is more pronounced in the stories, especially the earliest ones, because the short form is better suited for experimentation. The size of the tales, which average ninety pages each, considerably exceeds that of his stories — six of the eleven stories number fewer than twenty pages each, and only three exceed thirty pages. The importance of brevity in the perfection of Zamjatin's literary technique, is clearly indicated by a significant decrease in the length of the later stories. In contrast to his first six stories (written from 1908 to 1913) which average thirty pages, the next five (written from 1914 to 1917) average only ten pages each. Although some of the stories ("Odin," "Neputevyj," "Čerevo," "Krjaži," "Afrika") contain numbered chapters, only in his tales does Zamjatin consistently use chapter titles which stress the central theme or event. Partly because of the greater length, each tale has eight to ten significant characters, while most of the stories, except "Neputevyj," have only one or two. The stories are comparatively static, often depicting only one or two events rather than a whole series, although "Neputevyj," "Čerevo," and "Afrika" are exceptions to this. These distinguishing features testify to Zamjatin's acceptance of the

* The figure is closer to two-thirds if "Odin" and "Devuska," his first two stories which he never allowed to be reprinted, are excluded. Zamjatin's prose of the early period covers 500 pages of the 1929 collected works (including projected equivalents for those two stories). Since each page holds about 165 words, Zamjatin's pre-Revolutionary output was only about 83,000 words.

established Russian genre differentiation between story and tale during the first decade of his literary career.

Although the love theme is central in Zamjatin's first four stories, which in many respects anticipate his tales, the treatment differs in that love is never reduced to the level of an automatic, daily physical function as in "Uezdnoe" and "Na kuličkax." Apparently the negative depiction was dictated by the choice of man's inhumanity as the major theme. The student Belov (in "Odin"), who is in solitary confinement because of his revolutionary activities, disdainfully rejects love on the basis of rationalistic argumentation, yet his solitude and his illicit correspondence with his friend Lel'ka combine to produce dreams of happiness and, ultimately, of love. Despite occasional lapses into sensual thoughts, Belov's love for Lel'ka is a spiritual feeling that alters his outlook on life by being a source of hope and joy for him. Learning of her marriage, he dies spiritually, cursing his sacred love; his subsequent suicide is merely the physical counterpart of his spiritual death. Belov's idealization of his beloved is echoed in Polovec's love for Marusja and in Edytkin's and the prince's love for Glafira. The motif of a destroyed idol recurs in "Na kuličkax," where Marusja's degradation results in Šmit's spiritual bankruptcy and ultimately in his suicide. In Zamjatin's second story, "Devuška," the heroine Vera experiences a strong desire for love, the product of daydreams stimulated by a strong physiological urge. In this respect Vera is the precursor of both Glafira and Varvara, and her behavior with the librarian on the park bench is remarkably similar to Varvara's behavior with the prince at the archpriest's home.* The presentation of the love theme in "Aprel'," Zamjatin's third story, remains unique in his work. Told in a light and fresh tone from the point of view of Nastja, a teen-age girl, the story describes her first kiss and the growth of her first love. Threatened by the action of adults (Nastja's kiss was observed and reported to her mother) and by her boyfriend's feigned indifference, her budding love is reasserted with renewed vigor at the story's end. Unlike the love of Vera or Glafira, hers has no overwhelming physiological desires, but only a wonderful innocence and purity. The fourth story, "Ne-

* Compare the two passages quoted on page 127–129.

putevyj," is an extended character sketch of a lovable, good-for-nothing Moscow student, Senja Babuškin, whose character is endowed with the softness of a warm summer day in the Kostroma Province and an irreconcilable duality: he reveres old Russian things, especially those connected with the Orthodox church, yet as a radical student he denies the existence of God. He expounds cynical theories about love, reducing it to physiological function, and at the same time he mawkishly cherishes sentimental ideas about it. Senja's vacillation on love echoes Belov's. However, unlike Belov who spends much time in self-examination and rationalization, Senja simply falls in love without thinking—and, in his typically ingenuous manner, with two girls at the same time. Unable to reconcile his two loves, Senja directs his energies to the revolutionary movement and, discontented with his lot, chooses a useless death on the barricades to a life without love. Senja, whose love, despite his theories, is spiritual rather than physical, represents an interesting variation of the frustrated dreamer; and his death on the barricades, so reminiscent of the death of Turgenev's Rudin, is a form of suicide like Belov's and Šmit's.

All of the remaining six stories of the early period were written after Zamjatin had established a stylistic and thematic norm. They differ from the tales, however, in that the protagonists are peasants rather than merchants, officials, priests, intelligentsia, or nobility. Vanjatka Konyč Tjurin (in "Staršina"), a huge bull-like peasant noted for his stupidity, is by chance elevated to being a village elder and is awarded a gold medal for his service to the tsar. Inspired by rumors, he takes it upon himself to appropriate the land of the local nobility in the name of the tsar and distributes it among the peasants of Lenivka (Lazyplace). He is tried and acquitted, for it is evident that his misdemeanor stemmed from ignorance rather than malicious intent. Konyč, however, never understands his error and glows with righteous self-satisfaction: "Well, there you are: acquitted, I'm going home. I know. I acted by decree, in the proper manner. You can't fool me!" (S.S. II, 280). Konyč, with his extreme ignorance and bullying abuse of power, is a peasant version of Baryba, and the story is just an appendix to "Uezdnoe." In describing Konyč's stupidity as a recruit, Zamjatin points out the incompatibility of the peasant with military order, a theme which he elaborates more directly in the peasant soldier Aržanoj in "Na kuličkax".

The treatments of love, dreams, and aspirations in "Črevo," "Krjaži," and "Afrika" represent variations on motifs in "Alatyr'." The heroine of "Črevo," like Glafira, has a strong physiological urge which dominates the entire work, motivating all action: she must bear a child. Married to the old widower Petra against her wishes (the motif of forced marriage to a repulsive mate recurs in "Pis'menno"), Afim'ja fails to become pregnant after more than a year of marriage and takes a lover, Van'ka Selifontov. After conception all her attention centers on her womb and the developing fetus, but one night after a merciless beating by Petra, she suffers a miscarriage. The loss of her child fills Afim'ja with a deep, primeval hatred for her husband, so one night, mechanically, she kills him with an axe. With Van'ka Selifontov's aid, she buries him. The murder of vengeance brings no relief, and during a late summer hot spell she begins imagining that the stench of Petra's decomposing body fills the air, permeating her hut. She retrieves the body and, mechanically again, cuts it into pieces, salts it, and stores it in her cellar. But she gains no inner peace until she at last confesses and is taken into custody. This powerful story, one of the most extreme examples of Zamjatin's primitivism, ends with an expression of the Russian peasant's typical compassion for criminals: "Farewell, Afim'juška. God will forgive you" (S.S. II, 193).

On the other hand, "Afrika," the first of three stories set in the distant north on the shores of the Arctic Ocean, shows a dreamer much in the fashion of "Alatyr'." Fedor Volkov, an Arctic boatman who ferries passengers from ships to shore, hears some gentry, including a lovely girl, speak a language that is not Russian. When he asks where they come from, they laughingly reply, "from Africa." Africa, the lovely girl, and Fedor's conception of ideal happiness merge into one illusory dream, quite different from his surrounding reality. The next spring Volkov attempts to realize his dream by earning passage to Africa as a harpoonist, but after missing the whale which would have brought his passage money, he falls dead. The author ironically comments: "There is an Africa. Fedor Volkov has reached it" (S.S. IV, 86). Unlike the dreamers of Alatyr', Volkov does not live to see his dreams and illusions frustrated. The author's message here seems to be that men should die striving for their goals, rather than live to discover them to be false illusions. This idea was to be stated explicitly two years later in the article "Skify-li?" A similar message can be extracted from the brief story "Pis'menno," where Dar'ja is forced by her mother to marry Eremej, a repulsive, heavy-handed widower. She wishes for his death and is overjoyed at her freedom when he is sent to Siberia for killing a man. She takes a lover, Savos'ka, and lives happily for a year, until she receives a humble letter from her husband begging forgiveness and describing his dire circumstances. After much thought, Dar'ja forsakes her lover and sets out to Siberia to help her husband. The narrator's comment, "What fools women are, oh what fools!," leaves the reader in a quandary which lends the tale its charm. Was the author, in contrast to the narrator, in favor of the humaneness of her sacrifice, or did he agree with the narrator in lamenting Dar'ja's denial of her happiness with Savos'ka?

The story "Krjaži" expresses Zamjatin's opinion that neither pride nor convention should stand in the way of the realization of love. Through stubborn pride, the strong physical attraction between Ivan and Mar'ja remains unrealized. The need to prove his worth results in Ivan's death, which is Mar'ja's loss, for, although she loves him, she has been too proud to encourage him. Zamjatin's final story of the early period, "Pravda istinnaja," is in the form of a peasant girl's letter to her mother. It reveals Dašutka's unhappiness as a domestic in town, despite her lip service to the happiness and the supposed benefits of town life. The letter, like many of Zamjatin's early works, discloses the negative aspects of provincial town life. Since the piece was written in England, one may speculate that it was inspired by a similar feeling on Zamjatin's part about his life in England.

It is rather surprising that the Revolution of 1905 to 1906 did not find a greater place in the works of Zamjatin, a onetime Bolshevik, exile, and student revolutionary. Discounting "Tri dnja," an impressionistic, first-person, eye-witness account of the "Potemkin" mutiny, this revolution only appears as a minor theme in "Odin" and "Neputevyj." In "Odin" Belov, like Zamjatin, has been imprisoned for revolutionary activity, and we find a brief two-page narrative by his imprisoned fellow revolutionary Tifleev, telling how a government agent has been murdered. The sensational element in Tifleev's account and its psychological effect on Belov are of much greater importance in the story, however, than the theme of the Revolution itself. The same is true in "Neputevyj," where Senja joins the movement of 1905 to fill an inner emptiness after losing Tanja and Vasilisa, and not because of political conviction: "I wouldn't set eyes on all those programs of theirs. Thank God, for the first time in ages we have overflowed the banks, and they want to put us back in them. I think that if it's flood time, then let it really flood, like the Volga. Right or not?" (S.S. II, 163). The revolutionary movement provides Senja with an opportunity to live, and the proximity of death makes life seem all the more valuable to him: "You queer fellow, it's gay, you understand, it's gay in the streets: life. I think that the people who are most alive are there now. A-ah, you say that they are close to death; that's why they are close to death, because they are most alive . . ." (S.S. II, 163). Never having been able to carry anything through to completion, Senja remains on the barricade after his comrades have wisely retreated. This does not indicate extraordinary bravery or extreme dedication to the Revolution; it is instead a tragic solution to his failures in life. For once, he finishes something.

The theme of revolution deserves fuller consideration here. It has been mentioned earlier that, under the influence of Robert Mayer, Zamjatin in 1920 and 1921 systematized his philosophic views, setting forth the thesis that energy (revolution) and entropy (stagnation) were the two cosmic forces governing the universe, man, and man's thought. The Communist critic Voronskij asserted that "all of the works published by Zamjatin . . . symbolize the struggle between these two principles," [7] but this generalization, valid for Zamjatin's major works of the second period (1917–1921), does not hold true for his early efforts. In works like the tale "Ostrovitjane" and the novel *My*, revolution represents a conscious rebellion against the accepted norm, and love is treated as a primitive physical passion that disrupts the regulatory mechanisms created by an automated society. This is not true, with minor exceptions, in Zamjatin's early works. In "Uezdnoe" love itself has been degraded to a tedious physical process. The strong physiological urge of Glafira and Varvara is indeed a primitive feeling, but it does not represent a rebellion against the status quo and the surrounding environment, for these women seek gratification and fulfillment within the existing social framework. Essentially the same is true of Anfim'ja's desire to have a child. Although her love might be considered a manifestation of energy in revolt against the forces of entropy (represented by her husband), D. J. Richards has embarked on rather risky speculation in attributing political significance to the story ("the conspiracy of Anfimya and her young lover against the old man represents the rebellion of young, politically revolutionary Russia against the decaying old order").[8]

It is true that elements of revolution can be detected in Zamjatin's dreamers insomuch as their dreams represent rejection of the existing order, but the aspirations of these dreamers are presented in a comic light and never are coupled with a primitive revolt of the passions symbolic of man's irrational impulses. In depicting a growing primitivism, the entropy of human thought and feeling, Zamjatin's early works fail to portray the disruptive force of energy (revolution). And the retroactive application of the entropy-energy dichotomy to these works is not really justifiable. At most, it can be said that the tedium shown in Zamjatin's early works "is but an unconscious demand for freedom, for struggle, for the conversion of 'entropy,' of rest, into 'energy,' revolution."[9] As such, it is the seed from which Zamjatin's later theories developed.

In 1915 Zamjatin started writing his fables. Of the twenty he published, only four appeared before the Revolution, although two others evidently had been written by then.[10] A *skaz* narrative in which the narrator speaks a colloquial Russian studded with regional and substandard lexical items prevails in these fables, whose protagonists are often animals. Frequently oblique in meaning, the fables center on themes of human frailty and ignorance. In "Bog" ("God") the carousing and bullying cockroach Sen'ka who does not believe in God is struck speechless with reverence for the poverty-stricken postman Mizjumin, a kind and omniscient diety who rescues him after a disastrous fall. The fable is probably aimed at ridiculing stupid people who ignorantly glorify or diefy the ordinary and commonplace.

A similar moral can be drawn from "D'jaček" (The Deacon") and "Pet'ka." A stupid boy Pet'ka, "too bright for his age," is given a beautiful talking doll with moving eyes. Curious to discover what makes it move and speak, he takes it apart with a knife, only to find uninteresting bearings, sawdust, a diaphragm, and a horn. His angry parents repair the toy, but it is no longer the same, so they punish the boy. Probably the doll represents the unquestionable "truths" and beliefs that ignorant men blindly accept. To question these false "truths," is to destroy or alter them; therefore ignorant men punish those who are either intelligent or naïve enough to question them, just as parents punish questioning children. Latent in this fable is Zamjatin's conception of philistinism and heresy. The third fable "D'jaček," tells of a deacon who, having won a 5,000 ruble lottery, decides to experience the vision of Moses, to look into the blue vault of the heavens from the top of Mt. Sinai. After forty days of fasting and climbing, he gains the mountaintop, only to discover that beautiful clouds are nothing but a damp, dark, autumnal, foggy drizzle. The moral is essentially that of "Pet'ka," and in this formulation we can discern the beginnings of Zamjatin's idea (expressed two years later in "Skify li?") that the attainment of an ideal philistinizes it. Zamjatin again returned to this image (beautiful distant clouds becoming damp, dismal fog at close quarters) in describing the Symbolists' disillusionment with their search for the beautiful ideal on earth.[11] The basic message in these fables would seem to be that man should not only be intelligent and curious enough to examine his own and others' conceptions and ideals, but he also should have the strength to recognize, accept, and apply any newly found truth in his life, without despair and disillusionment. The fables "Petr Petrovič" and "Angel Dormidon" ridicule ignorance more openly by showing that haste coupled with uncomprehending stupidity leads to disastrous results.

No survey of Zamjatin's works would be complete without a

discussion of style, perhaps the most distinctive aspect of his imaginative prose. A leading exponent of the Neorealist movement in Russian literature, Zamjatin was preoccupied with style and literary techniques as a direct consequence of his philosophy. As a firm believer in the Hegelian dialectic, Zamjatin considered Neorealism to be a synthesis of nineteenth-century Realism (thesis) and Symbolism (antithesis): "The symbolists did their part in the development of literature, and to replace them in the second decade of the twentieth century came the Neorealists, inheriting features of former Realists as well as features of the Symbolists."[12] The Realists were excellent mirrors — their stories attempted to depict a segment of life. The Symbolists sought to describe man's complex feelings and to depict the essence of man's spiritual being; in doing so, they rejected the "real" world. The Neorealists, like the Realists, depicted the real world, but they found their truth by focusing on a few, carefully chosen features, enlarging them to grotesque proportions. Zamjatin firmly believed that "apparent improbability — nightmarishness — reveals the true essence of a thing — its reality — more than probability does."

Quoting Dostoevskij's statement that "the real truth is always improbable," Zamjatin repeatedly utilized effective analogy to drive home his point.[13] Where the Realist saw only smooth skin covered with downy hair, the Neorealist with his cruel, ironic microscope saw gullies and mounds, thick stems of unknown plants (hair), and huge masses of earth and meteorites (dust particles).[14] In accordance with his aim, Zamjatin frequently used the grotesque in his early works. His depiction of life and people was exaggerated, deformed, and fantastic, which led some critics to protest Zamjatin's "excessively thickened paints" and moved some to contend that instead of depicting life, he caricatured it.[15] Others were more perceptive; in his review of Zamjatin's first collection of stories, A. Gvozdev made an excellent analysis of his technique:

> the author does not attempt to delineate the *byt** in detail, but is constantly drawn to a synthetic image, frequently resorting to the

* *Byt*: a peculiarly Russian term which indicates the general tenor of life, from customs and habits to social and economic conditions (usually of a particular social group).

> aid of comic grotesque. His art consists in the ability of imbuing exaggeratedly massive figures with a touch of some sort of bright truth of life. Isolating, in the characterization of his heroes, some one of their characteristics, E. Zamjatin imparts his character sketch with the extraordinary, sketches comic contours that border on the absurd, and widely utilizes exaggerated parody as a means of artistic embodiment. But angular contours, paradoxical situations, and the extraordinary harshness of the author's satirical inspiration do not keep the reader from the truth.[16]

In the characterization of Čebotarixa, for example, the primary, exaggerated feature was her excessive obesity, indicative of her unbridled gastronomic and sexual appetites. The reader's first glimpse of Čebotarixa comes through Baryba's eyes and immediately establishes her gluttony: "They finished eating, and Čebotarixa herself crawls out into the yard: red, settling, unable to walk because of overeating" (S.S. I, 29). When Čebotarixa is presented directly to the reader, the motif of not being able to walk recurs and is developed into an explicit presentation of the central characteristic:

> After the evening vespers or liturgy the priest of Pokrov Church would catch up with Čebotarixa, shake his head and say: "It's unseemly, mother. You must walk, take a promenade. Or before you know it, the flesh will completely conquer."
>
> But Čebotarixa would spread out like dough on her wagon and, knitting her lips, would say: "It's impossible, father, kintinual heart murmur." And Čebotarixa rolls onward through the dust, stuck to her wagon, inseparable from it, corpulent, flowing, springy. So no one had ever seen Čebotarixa in the street on her own feet without wheels. (S.S. I, 30.)

The impression of doughy obesity was maintained by the recurrent use of key words or new words which were associated with the original presentation: "The smell of her sweaty, *sticky* flesh" (S.S. I, 38). "Nonetheless, she *flowed* off, . . ." (S.S. I, 52). "Čebotarixa turned white and began shaking like *leavened dough* that had swollen to the very edges of the mixing bowl" (S.S. I, 52). " 'What's up, have you gone nuts?' said he, disentangling himself from her *flesh*. But she *stuck* to him like a spider" (S.S. I, 55). The last of these four examples is doubly effective in that it recalls another image associated with Čebotarixa's gluttony: "Her greedy mouth — a red wet hole" (S.S.

I, 38). This mouth image is repeated with a variation ("a greedy, gaping, sucking mouth") some six lines before the spider comparison, which, because of its proximity and the easy association with a spider sucking its prey, recalls the "greedy mouth" sequence and reinforces the idea of Čebotarixa's unbridled appetite.

Zamjatin's use of grotesque to underline a single basic characteristic was motivated by his own central subjective impression of a character, in which he trusted firmly and completely. Frequently originating as an explicit comparison or simile, his impression is usually continued in a recurrent implicit comparison — a metaphor: "Kipa, all in bows, frills, gathers, with a comb on her forehead — a Brahmaputra hen. As soon as Senja saw the Brahmaputra, he stuck at her side . . ." (S.S. II, 148). And later: "Petr Petrovič . . . looked at Senja and the Brahmaputra hen. They were alone in the room, Senja and Kipa-Brahmaputra, in a corner behind the plam tree" (S.S. II, 149).

External description and character depiction are kept to a minimum in Zamjatin's early work and usually consist of a basic impression which undergoes varying degrees of development depending upon the story, the importance of the character, and the felicity of the chosen impression. The impression is usually conveyed in one of three ways: The character can be compared to some animal, as above, in which case he assumes both the external features and the character traits of that animal. The girl Kipa ("Neputevyj") not only looks like a hen, but she is also a featherbrain. Pimen ("Afrika"), small and skinny and persistent, is compared to a mosquito: "Pimen . . . began to follow Fedor, hovering about him like a mosquito and biting him continually" (S.S. IV, 76). "Pimen hovered and hovered" (S.S. IV, 76). "Pimen sang, a caressing mosquito, and bit into Fedor Volkov's very ear" (S.S. IV, 77). "Pimen stretched forth his mosquito mug" (IV, 77). "Oh-ho! A mosquito soul?" (S.S. IV, 77). The same technique is used in characterizing General Azančeev as a frog ("Na kuličkax"); the tailor Timoša as a sparrow and the coachman Urvanka as a devil ("Uezdnoe"); Kostja Edytkin as a chicken, Varvara as a dog, Rodivon Rodivonovič as a rooster, the archpriest as a small, hairy sprite, and the county police chief's wife as an elephant ("Alatyr' "). In each case the physical and character similarities are equally important, and the numerous comparisons with animals are a major factor contributing to the central theme of animal-like provincial life.

A second technique for conveying the central impression consists in focusing attention on some physical characteristic associated with a basic character trait. The arctic fisherman Fedor Volkov is first described ("Afrika") as having huge shoulders, small ingenuous eyes, and a "crock-like head cropped like a kid's" (S.S. IV, 70). The crock-like head and ingenuous, inoffensive eyes are mentioned throughout the story in connection with his dreams of Africa; they symbolize his naïve simplicity:

> He shook his cropped crock: "And what if it ain't — Africa — that is?" (S.S. IV, 72.)
>
> . . . himself unseen, just a head, a cropped crock, rocking above the light sea. "What are you looking for, Fedor? Are you waiting for some guests from beyond the sea?" Fedor would glance with his ingenuous, inoffensive eyes and shake his crock-head. But whether he shook yes or no could not be fathomed. (S.S. IV, 75–76.)
>
> Fedor Volkov was silent: only his inoffensive eyes dumbly spoke to Jausta, but what they said could not be fathomed. (S.S. IV, 76.)
>
> And he tripped over something, began to cry woefully, put his cropped crock on the table. "I'll leave . . . I'll le-e-ave you all . . . Leave." (S.S. IV, 78.)
>
> He kept standing at the rail, hanging his cropped crock over the water, and kept smiling to himself. (S.S. IV, 80.)
>
> "Ugh!" Fedor only shook his crock, cropped like a kid's; only his small inoffensive eyes glimmered as a candle to God; and, really, what words could be found here? (S.S. IV, 84.)

The reader learns nothing more of Volkov's external appearance, nor does the author directly reveal any of Volkov's thoughts. There are no inner monologues, the narrator is not omniscient. The reader must deduce everything for himself from Volkov's actions and from the reported dialogues. The recurrent motifs of "cropped crock" and "ingenuous, inoffensive eyes" stress his most essential characteristic: a childlike simplicity which enables him to idolize distant Africa as the embodiment of all his dreams. The same technique is used with numerous other characters. Polovec's broad forehead, which contrasts sharply with the rest of his nondescript features, is symbolic of his intellectual and spiritual aspirations which are incapable of being realized. Marusja Šmit is characterized by a "hint of unchildish lines near her lips" which become marked and old-womanish after her relationship with Šmit has been destroyed by Azančeev. Prince Vadbol'skij's crafty nature ("Alatyr'") is indicated by his receding chin. Indrik's sad, unsmiling eyes ("Afrika") hint that he is aware of things forbidden to mortals, and they serve as a disquieting foreboding of the denouement, which imparts a genuinely tragic element to the story. Lieutenant Tixmen' ("Na kuličkax") is endowed with a long nose that not only indicates his predilection for serious thought but also causes his shyness with women. The orderly Neprotošnov's stupidity is reflected in his inhuman, "hopelessly fishy eyes," yet the one time he experiences a human feeling, his eyes become human and pour forth tears (S.S. II, 127).

The association of one or several attributives with a given personage is Zamjatin's third method of conveying his impression. The effect of the attributives is produced, as in the other two methods, by their frequent recurrence. But in this method the same attributive refers to all aspects of the person — sometimes to a physical feature, sometimes to an action, and sometimes directly to his character. Roundness, for example, is the basic attribute of the captain's wife Katjuška Nečesa; and, associated with her yearly pregnancies, it recurs in different environments:

> The captain's wife lay in bed, small and all round: a little round face, round quick eyes, round curls on her forehead, all of the captain's wife's charms were round. (S.S. II, 17.)
>
> She laughed roundly . . . (S.S. II, 18.)
>
> . . . she shook the round curls on her forehead. (S.S. II, 51.)
>
> Tixmen' kissed her round little hand. (S.S. II, 53.)
>
> The captain's wife's eyes, round as they were, became even rounder . . . (S.S. II, 54.)
>
> She laughed so roundly, so clearly. (S.S. II, 57.)

The same is true of Baryba's squareness and of Captain Šmit's hardness, although in these cases, because both characters are of central importance, a combination of all three methods is used.

The basic impression associated with a personage is often reinforced by the choice of an appropriate name, for Zamjatin claimed that: "Surnames, names, become attached to personages just as firmly as to living people. And that is understandable: if the name is felt, chosen correctly, then it indispensibly contains a phonic characterization of the personage."[17] In some instances the choices and significance are obvious. In "Uezdnoe" a lawyer's slyness is indicated by his blinking eyes, by his blinking gait, and by his name Morgunov (derived from the Russian verb *morgat'*, "to blink"). In other cases the choice is more subtle and depends on phonic features that evoke associations between the name and some physical feature or character trait. The surname Edytkin, used to designate a tall, lanky person with a pitiably thin neck, brings to mind — by means of the infrequent phonic combination *dytk* — the word for Adam's apple (*kadyk*), which reinforces the image of a thin neck. The ignorance of Polovec's orderly is exemplified by his recurrent mispronunciation of the phrase "exactly so, your excellency." And the mispronunciation *tak tošno, vaše-brodie*, which makes a significant play on the words "exactly" (*točno*) and "nauseating" (*tošno*), is echoed in the orderly's name Neprotošnov. Most frequently, however, the name of a personage is simply appropriate to his social position and psychological makeup. Čebotarixa is a typical, merchant-class name, and the suffix *-ixa* has an appropriate pejorative significance which the more usual suffix *-eva* lacks. The German name Šmit suits an unbending, honest military man whose severity borders on cruelty. In addition to using indicative and appropriate names, Zamjatin frequently employs such obvious nicknames as Sobačeja (a derivation of *sobaka*, "dog") for Varvara ("Alatyr' "), who is endowed with the characteristics and behavior of a dog.

The predominance of "a very strong, 90 proof *byt* that had been concentrated by centuries of aging"[18] was highly conducive to Zamjatin's grotesque imagery and would indicate that Zamjatin had utilized provincial Russia mainly as a stylistic device. The center of gravity in his treatment of bestial, ignorant, provincial life resided not in provincial life itself, but in bestiality and ignorance, which is in line with the humanism so basic to Zamjatin's world view and so dear to his lifelong heresy.

Furthermore, the provinces provided him with numerous colloquial and regional expressions to use in renovating the literary language. In all of his tales and in all but four of his earliest stories ("Odin," "Devuška," "Aprel'," and "Tri dnja") Zamjatin used *skaz,* a special mode of narrative prose in which a narrator manipulated by the author, but usually differing from the author in language, social position, and outlook, is introduced explicitly or implicitly as a stylistic device. Zamjatin's narrator speaks a Russian which grammatically is basically correct, but which contains numerous regional words and colloquial expressions that normally would not be considered appropriate to standard literary Russian. The peculiarities of the narrator's language are not only lexical; his speech also displays a highly stylized syntactical structure characterized by numerous inversions. The following sample, from "Uezdnoe," illustrates several typical features:

> Vstanet Baryba na utro smuryj i ves' den' kolobrodit. Zal'etsja do noči v monastyrskij les. Učilišče? A, da propadaj ono propadom!* (S.S. I, 24.)

The word *kolobrodit*, the expression *propadaj propadom*, and the use of *zal'etsja* with the meaning of "he set off" are all examples of colloquial speech; and the word *smuryj* is a substandard dialectal distortion of *xmuryj*. The inversion in the first sentences which places the verb in the initial position, the rhetorical question *Učilišče?*, and the use of the interjection *a* in the initial position followed by the emphatic particle *da* all contribute to the stylistically oral orientation of the narrative, so fundamental to *skaz*. In reported speech a few of Zamjatin's characters, unlike the narrator, use substandard phonetic and grammatical forms:

> "Gospodi, da pošli ž ty, štob učiliššа sgorela i mne ba tuda ne itit' . . ." (Konyč: S.S. II, 273.)
>
> "Tak tošno, vaše-brodie . . ." (Neprotošnov: S.S. II, 9.)

* "In the morning Baryba'd get up glumpy and fool around all day. He'd take off to the monastery woods till night. School? Aw, the hell with it!"

"Vaše prevosxoditel'stvo, už dozvol'te pojtit' vzjat'. Ved' naše takoe, znyčt', delo krest'janskoe, den'gi-to vot kak nadobny, podatja opjat' že . . ."* (Aržanoj: S.S. II, 69.)

Such grammatically substandard speech, however, is not widespread in Zamjatin's writing, where it is restricted to peasants. On the other hand, substandard literary speech in the form of regional words, colloquial expressions, and casual syntax is extremely frequent and typical of most of his characters, including the implicit narrator. When Zamjatin's first collection of stories appeared in 1916, most critics censured his style severely. A. Derman wrote that "all of the author's remarks, all descriptions are expressed . . . by this repulsive, half-dead, vulgar language, depressive in its monotony and hopeless grayness." [19] Another critic was appalled by the "depressive . . . characterless deterioration of the language." [20] Critics notwithstanding, the *skaz* narrative became a hallmark of Russian literature of the twenties and was immortalized in the stories of Mixail Zoščenko, a student of Zamjatin.

Another characteristic of Zamjatin's early prose was a concise, compressed style that he said was dictated by life itself, which had become more complex, more rapid, feverish, and Americanized—especially in the cities that were the cultural centers for which he intended his works.[21] The Neorealists learned to say in ten lines what would have taken a page before and to condense material suitable for a novel into a tale or a story. This may explain why none of Zamjatin's works, except the novel *My*, ever exceeded one hundred and twenty-five small pages. In this respect the main teacher of the Neorealists was Anton Čexov, "who had provided amazing examples of brevity in the art of writing." [22] Čexov's legacy was not limited to brevity, for he was the first Russian to employ "impressionism."†

* Lord, make the school burn down so I won't hab to goes there . . ." "Eksickly so, your beardship . . ." "Your excellency, let me go git it. You knows, it's us peasants' business, we needs the money, taxes again . . ."

† Zamjatin, "Čexov," [38], 48. One example Zamjatin cited of Čexov's impressionism was: "the district elder and district clerk had become imbued with falsehood to such a degree, that the very skin on their faces was knavish."

Directly related to his impressionistic imagery and his noted brevity was Zamjatin's tendency to demonstrate, rather than narrate. This was first pointed out by Ivanov-Razumnik early in 1914. In discussing L. Dobronravov's tale "Novaja bursa" ("The New Seminary"), he stated that "the young author knows how to observe and *to narrate* his observations. A. Terek and Evg. Zamjatin know how *to demonstrate*—that is the difference between them."[23] Seeking a greater economy of words and a more lively impression of life's activities, Zamjatin avoided static passages describing the hero and the setting. The external description and the character of a personage are indicated by a brief phrase or two, usually a recurrent motif, and any further information is demonstrated by the character's actions rather than being narrated by the author. Zamjatin himself cited his description of Morgunov's (Blinkman's) character as an example of demonstrating:

> "Semen Semenovič blinked continually: blink, blink, as if he were ashamed of his own eyes. And why speak of eyes: all of him blinked. When he would go along the street and begin to limp on his left leg, actually all of him, his entire being, would blink." Here there is no word of slyness, which comprised the essence of Morgunov's character; here action is given, and in the action, immediately, concisely, all of Morgunov, as if alive.[24]

Despite the importance of the Čexovian origins of Zamjatin's stylistic development, the latter's intense interest in verbal mastery was the result of much more immediate influences, namely the works of Aleksej Remizov and the Symbolists. In reviewing Zamjatin's first tale, Ivanov-Razumnik had written that: "The young author has not yet found himself; consciously or unconsciously there is much of Remizov in him, but already there is much of his own. If examples of how 'realism' can utilize the many technical achievements of 'modernism' are needed, then here is one of those examples, Evg. Zamjatin's tale."[25] Without a doubt, Zamjatin's great attention and interest in the style and form of his literary work was a legacy from the Symbolists, which Zamjatin himself freely admitted: "In the cultivation of the form of the work, in the perfection of the mastery of precisely the technique of writing, lies the greatest and fundamental service of the Symbolists."[26] Zamjatin did not, however, blindly ape Symbolist innovations; he adapted only those techniques that were congenial to his conception of art. Of specific importance to him were Sologub's *Melkij bes* (*The Petty Demon*), the novels and tales of Remizov, and to a lesser extent the prose works of Belyj. *Melkij bes* may justifiably be considered the forerunner of Russian Neorealism, for it was characterized by ironic laughter, by the depiction of provincial ignorance, by the grotesque, and by recurrent impressionistic imagery. Similar features frequently appeared in the early works of Remizov, who also developed a refined stylization of the *skaz* manner and showed a decided tendency toward colloquial and regional expressions. In respect to language, Remizov was the single most important influence on Zamjatin.

Considerably less discernible was the influence of Belyj, whose Neorealistic tendencies were most clearly expressed in his novel *Peterburg*, which first appeared in 1913 to 1914, well after Zamjatin had established his style.[27]

Traces of Zamjatin's interest in the rhythmic and musical qualities of prose were already manifest as early as 1914:

> Zabeleli utrenniki, zazjabla zemlja, ležala neujutnaja, žalas': snežku by. I na Mixajlov den' — sneg povalil. Kak xlynuli belye xlop'ja — tak i utixlo vse. Tixim kolobkom belym laj sobačij plyvet. Molča moljatsja za ljudej staricy-sosny v klobukax belyx.* (S.S. II, 267.)

Zamjatin attempted here to create the impression of falling, circling snowflakes by the repetition of the clusters *xl* and *kl*,[28] but this only begins to suggest the rich rhythmic and phonic qualities of this passage. Each sentence is endowed with a syntactic rhythm that is reinforced by stress distribution, word order, and alliteration. In the first sentence, three di-stress phrases were followed by two mono-stresses, a rhythm which is

* The frosts whitened, the earth froze, lying uncozily, shriveling: oh for some snow. And on Mixajlov Day snow fell. As white flakes flowed, all became quiet. In a silent white ball dogs' barking floats. In their silent white cowls the monk-pines pray for people."

further emphasized by the alliteration and assonance of *za, zazja, z, ža, ža,* and by the verb-noun contrast in the initial position. The next three sentences are each rythmically divided into equal halves emphasized twice by the dash (the stress distribution is two-two, three-three, three-three) and leads up to the final sentence, which has a three-two-two distribution reinforced by alliteration: *molč*a *mol*jatsja; *s*taric*y*-*s*osn*y*; k*l*o*b*uka*x* *be*l*yx*. The continuity between sentences stems not only from the central motif of falling snow and the use of *xl* and *kl*, but also from the frequent repetition of the liquid *l*; the recurrence of the key words *sneg, snežku, belyj* (three instances of the latter, twice in inverted order); *utixlo, tixim* (connected semantically with *molča*); and by the phonetic similarity of *kolobkom* and *klobukax*. Such rhythmical and musical organization reflects conscious manipulation by the author and goes far beyond the scope of normal *skaz* narrative. Despite his use of such instrumental features as alliteration and assonance in his prose, however, Zamjatin rejected the use of metrical feet in prose, which was so typical of Belyj at that time.[29]

The preceding discussion of stylistic features has been accompanied by examples from Zamjatin's early works. However, although all of the stylistic features enumerated are present in varying degrees in all three of Zamjatin's tales, they exist only in some of his stories. His first stories ("Odin," "Devuška," and "Aprel' ") seek neither to achieve a symbolic synthesis by means of grotesque, impressionistic, and recurrent images, nor do they utilize regional expressions and the *skaz* narrative. This is true also of the sketch "Tri dnja," although Zamjatin did attempt there to recreate the spirit and feelings of the time by means of an impressionistic pastiche of events. Lacking the later compressed brevity and differing in thematic treatment, the earliest stories aim at narrating, not demonstrating. Close scrutiny reveals an interesting stylistic evolution, which was essentially complete by the time Zamjatin had written "Alatyr'." A comparison of the following two texts will graphically illustrate this evolution: *

* Text *A* is from "Devuška" (*Novyj žurnal dlja vsex*, No. 25, Nov. 1910, 63–64), and Text *B* is from "Alatyr'," (*Russkaja mysl'*, No. 9, Sept. 1915, 25–26).

Text A

Beside them, nearby, the flowers smell pungently and sweetly. Vera inhales them and says: "Do you smell them? That's the flowers caressing each other and dying, and that's the scent of their caresses."

Vera feels his glance. Her heart pounds so that she wants to grab it with her hands and restrain it.

"How shameful, how shameful," Vera tells herself. "He's looking!"

And with terror she understands: she wants to grab and tear the lace on her breast and her dress, and give everything to him: look, here I am, for you alone . . . kiss me.

But he is silent. He has lowered his heavy head onto his arm.

Something was on the point of dying out and falling. She must grab it, hold it. She must quickly, quickly tell him something.

Vera's teeth rattle and she says: "Well, why do you sit like that? Amuse me."

And then she turns cold. Did she, did she say that? And it seems that she is on the verge of plunging into a hole, and, to keep from falling, she must grab the air with her hands.

Vera waves her arms and laughs loudly and strangely. He looks at her intently and says: "There you are laughing, Vera. But it seems to me that you are not at all gay.

Text B

"Father is visiting the parish," Varvara greeted the prince. She fingered the lamp in her hands, but for some reason did not light it.

Only then did the prince notice: why, it's rather late. Beyond the window the moon rose, waning, dull, narrow. And the sky appeared so terribly empty, so silent forever, that his throat gagged, and he felt like howling.

To remain silent was terrible. The prince forced himself to smile: "You know, I was coming to your place in a cab. And a pig gave a gru-u-unt at the horse. Your pigs are so fleet-footed!"

Varvara was silent, gazed out the window at the moon.

"And you've got all sorts of fences, empty lots, empty lots, the dogs howl . . ."

Varvara covered her face with her hands and strangely slipped from the chair to the floor. The prince got up startled.

"Don't leave . . . No! No!," cried Varvara convulsively.

Her eyes had such an expression, such pity began to ache in the prince, that he lacked the strength to leave. He sat down again on the chair.

"Well, I hope that soon . . . We will begin our work for the general good . . . ," muttered the prince turning away; he was embarrassed to look at Varvara, she had such eyes . . .

Text A (*continued*)

You have some sort of woe."

Vera again waves her hands and laughingly says: "Why, no. What sort of woe? You are such an interesting escort, I am gay with you."

Impatiently he stirs, and his voice is so strange: "I can't understand you. You are so . . . such a . . . It's difficult to talk to you."

He leans back, rustles in the grass behind the bench, looks for his cap. It's better to leave quickly, while this has passed. Why, even the musicians are leaving.

Vera screams to herself. I don't want to, I don't want to, and wrings her hands. Then she adjusts her hat and says: "Today the night is cold, you can catch a cold. It's time to go."

The distant lanterns die out. The flowers smell more furiously — they have but a minute to live. And it seems that the moon will move just once more and they will exhale the sickenly sweet breath of a corpse.

Vera inhales and speaks in a soundless voice, hidden by darkness: "Give me your hand."

She takes his hand and feels in it a scarcely perceptible caress. And suddenly, not knowing why, she slowly raises that hand to her lips. And at the end of the dark pathway stands the earlier Vera, waves her arms in mad terror and shouts at her:

Text B (*continued*)

It seemed that something was rubbing at his feet — the archpriest's dog. How did it get in from . . . He looked, but at his feet on the floor crept Sobačeja-Varvara. Caressingly she barred her canine teeth, pleaded with her eyes, pleaded: "Well, if you don't want to, then at least hit me, at least hit me," she rubbed against his legs . . .

The prince exclaimed, pushed away, jumped out onto the square without his hat. He broke into a run.

Text A (*continued*)

"What are you doing, what are you doing?"

She raises his hand to her lips and kisses it suddenly—quickly and greedily.

Then her whole body slips down from the bench onto the sand, she embraces his knees, presses to him with her breast and whispers, gasping: "I have never kissed, never kissed."

No, what is one to do with her? Bewildered, he grasps her head in his shaking hands. "Vera, I don't understand. Vera—forgive me. I'll go now. For God's sake."

He tears free his legs from her tenacious hands, the toe of his boot grazes something soft. Hurriedly he leaves, stumbling over tree roots crawling below. . . .

The situations in the two passages are essentially the same: a girl prompted by strong physiological drives throws herself at a man who does not reciprocate. But the styles differ. Zamjatin's progress toward a condensed style is reflected in the lengths of the passages: Text *A* is twice as long as Text *B*. Although Text *B* is not the best example of demonstrating, in comparison with the extensive description of the protagonist's thoughts in Text *A*, it definitely does indicate a tendency away from narrating. The extended use of an impressionistic image, absent in Text *A*, assumes central importance (Varvara—a dog) in Text *B*. In general, Text *A* contains several literary clichés left over from the decadents: the furious caresses of dying flowers, the smell of corpses, rattling teeth, pounding heart. The mature Zamjatin was careful to purge his style of the trite and banal. In Text *B* the waning moon, the sole item of external description, is well integrated into the action (both the prince and Varvara look at it and presumably experience the same feeling); and the moon has symbolic significance in evoking the major mood of the tale—silent, empty, provincial Russia.

Zamjatin's early works, then, represent the evolution of an original literary style which is equally distant from the unhurried narrative of the Realists and the abstractions of the Symbolists. Irony and satire were the tools Zamjatin chose for surmounting the essential tragedy he saw in life; and his early works, with their seemingly pessimistic denouements, rejected the life they depicted, in the hope if inspiring the reader to strive for a better one.

The underlying philosophy of these writings is humanistic, and their primary subjects are bestiality and ignorance, not provincial Russia as it might at first appear. Mankind's lack of human values is shown especially in Zamjatin's portrayal of love either as a physical necessity (negatively as an automatic function and positively as a lyric expression of physiological drives) or as a spiritual need that is frustrated by the inhuman environment of provincial Russia. The theme of revolution, aside from a few references to the Revolution of 1905, is not explicit in Zamjatin's works.

These works do not stem from abstract generalizations, as those of the Symbolists did, but are firmly rooted in *byt*. One obvious sign of this is the quantity of colloquial and regional expressions which permeate both dialogue and *skaz* narrative. Unlike the Realists, Zamjatin sought neither to depict the minutiae of this *byt* nor to analyze the spiritual tribulations of his heroes; he attempted to convey both to the reader by a seemingly fantastic grotesque which would underline the significant features and thereby create a synthesis which was symbolic not only of the individual character but of the universal human condition as well. In character depiction Zamjatin developed one central impression, relying heavily on animal imagery and the recurrence of select attributes and physical features having symbolic significance. Related to this technique, also, was his growth toward brevity and demonstration.

Inspired by a genuine humanism, Zamjatin's early works in many respects did represent a synthesis between the two divergent schools of Realism and Symbolism, and, as such, they played a significant role in the manifestation of Russian Neorealism during the second decade of the twentieth century.

CHAPTER SIX

Middle Period, 1917-1921

The philistine is growing, he is sprouting from all cracks like a weed, smothering man.
Zamjatin, *Lica*

The period when Zamjatin produced his greatest amount of imaginative prose began with the tale "Ostrovitjane," which was written in England, and ended with the completion of his novel *My* late in 1921. The novel, two tales, fourteen stories, four prose miniatures, one play, and a dozen fables were written during these four years. In addition, Zamjatin found time to pen more than a dozen essays, articles, and reviews, as well as a seventy-page biography of the German physicist Robert Mayer. His articles and the biography of Mayer reflected his formulation of the philosophical conceptions of man and society, which had been stimulated in him by the October Revolution and by his participation in the *Skify* group. As he elaborated his philosophical system of humanism, heresy, revolution, never-ending progress, and anti-philistinism, the influence of these key concepts became very apparent in Zamjatin's imaginative prose. As his system developed, new themes were introduced, and old themes were displaced or were treated in a different manner. Instances of intrusion by an "omniscient" author became frequent, and on occasion characters voiced ideas that clearly were the author's. In many respects the novel *My* was a culmination of these tendencies and represented an artistic synthesis of his prose fiction and his philosophical essays.

The tragic conception of life which underlies Zamjatin's

early works did not change in the middle period, and most of the middle stories end sadly. As in the early works, irony is used frequently to emphasize the incongruities of life's tragedies. The character Kemble's* stolid propriety, for example, obliges him to return a borrowed fountain pen to his friend before murdering him for seducing his betrothed ("Ostrovitjane"). The hero and heroine of "Zemlemer," too inhibited to declare their love, are assigned the same bedroom, but a servant's arrival ends forever their chances of establishing rapport. In the brief allegory "Glaza," a dog escapes from a detestable master, but returns in order to be fed. Marej ("Sever") becomes aware of the importance of life and love only a few minutes before being crushed to death. The gentle bibliophile Mamaj is driven to cruelty when he discovers that mice have eaten the money he has so painstakingly saved and hidden under the floor. While the blackmailer Craggs ("Lovec čelovekov") is searching out lovers in the park, his wife is being seduced by the church organist Bailey.[1] The monk Seliverst ("Znamenie") achieves a miracle, only to perish with profane thoughts. Having lost his wife at cards, Semen Semenyč ("Detskaja") becomes unable to distinguish dream from reality and is not even sure of his own identity. Although this does not exhaust the list of tragic situations in Zamjatin's stories of this period, it does indicate how Zamjatin's writings continued in the vein of his earlier works.

That the apparent pessimism in the stories is a literary device to spur the reader to thought and action becomes more obvious in some of Zamjatin's mature works, where he introduces optimistic elements supported by authorial intrusion. Despite the tragic conclusion of "Sever," the hero and heroine do experience one summer of beautiful love, which is depicted with lyric sympathy. The servile dog who rejects freedom for a bowl of rotten meat has beautiful eyes with a sad, "human" wisdom

* Since the transliteration of English names from their Russian renditions often leads to bizarre results, transliterated forms will be replaced by appropriate English names that closely correspond to the Russian: Kembl is given as Kemble (although Zamjatin may have intended the Scottish name Campbell), O'Kelli as O'Kelly, Mak-Intoš as MacIntosh, D'juli as Dewly, Džesmond as Jesmond, Kraggs as Craggs, Bejli as Bailey, and Missis Lori as Mrs. Laurie.

in their depths. In the face of imminent death in an air raid, Mrs. Laurie Craggs realizes that she lacks what is most important and finds it in the arms of Bailey. In depicting such moments, Zamjatin abandons the apparent neutrality of his earlier works and enters the stories with explicit statements of his own views. "Lovec celovekov" begins with his assertion that "delerium is the most wonderful thing in life, and the most wonderful delerium is being in love" (S.S. III, 95); and as the story approaches a climax, Zamjatin again inserts his own evaluation: "To live — five minutes more. The most important thing was needed" (S.S. III, 123). "Ostrovitjane," the major work of this period except for *My*, contains several passages, some with several paragraphs, where the author intrudes in order to describe sarcastically the philistine uniformity of the inhabitants of the town of Jesmond (S.S. III, 19, 37–38, 59–60). Although such intrusions occur but rarely in the shorter stories of this period, the reader nonetheless is frequently made aware of the author's judgments about the events being set forth.

The thematic differences between the early and middle works may at first glance seem rather pronounced. For example, provincial Russia recedes in importance, and the large city looms in the foreground: "Ostrovitjane" and "Lovec čelovekov" are set in urban England; "Mamaj," "Drakon," and "Peščera" occur in Petersburg; and the action of *My* takes place in a large city of the future. The difference, however, is primarily one of setting and not so much of theme, for the focus of Zamjatin's interest was on the people that inhabited these worlds. Whereas in his early tales Zamjatin had depicted the ignorance, bestiality, and spiritual bankruptcy of provincial inhabitants, in "Ostrovitjane" and "Lovec čelovekov" he displayed the smug self-satisfaction of the spiritually bankrupt urban bourgeoisie, which were neither more intelligent nor more human than the provincials. The depiction of philistinism, a central theme in most of Zamjatin's works, reflects his deep concern about the negation of the human personality and its free development. The consideration of provincial Russia and industrial Europe, as Jak. Braun has correctly pointed out, resulted in remarkable similarity in Zamjatin's works: on the one hand there is provincial philistine absurdity and darkness; and on the other, an inert philistine automation in the lifeless glitter of electric lamps.[2]

Unlike "Uezdnoe" where the actional unity (a series of episodes connected by the person of Baryba) is subordinate to thematic unity, "Ostrovitjane" is a well structured work in which the author achieves a fine balance between action and theme. The plot centers on Kemble, the son of an impoverished noble family who falls in love with Didi, a dance-hall entertainer. Upon discovering that his bethrothed has become his friend O'Kelly's mistress, he murders O'Kelly, is tried, and then executed. All of the characters are motivated by either of two forces—passionate love or philistine conformity. Both forces operate in Kemble, and his destruction is the result of philistinism's gaining the upper hand. Likened to a lumbering tractor and truck, Kemble is characterized by squareness, a family trait that symbolizes the philistine need for order, respectability, and conformity:

> And now everything was as it should be: a rug and a fireplace, and above the fireplace a portrait of the late Sir Harold (that same square chin of the Kembles'), and a mahogany table by the window, and a vase for Sunday carnations on the table. In all houses on the left side of the street could be seen green vases; on the right—blue ones. Lady Kemble lived on the right side, so she had a blue vase on her table. (S.S. III, 38–39.)

To the product of such an environment, passionate love is a disrupting influence. Despite his love for Didi, Kemble's respectability is so deeply ingrained that he will neither marry her nor consummate his love before it can be clad in the garments of respectability—the acquisition of one of the thousand identical homes, complete with furniture and all appliances, including a ten-shilling iron. This electric iron, a symbol of Jesmond philistinism, assumes gigantic proportions in his mind: "And Kemble dreamed of an electric iron: huge, glistening; it crawls and irons everything, and nothing remains, neither houses, nor trees, only something flat and smooth like a mirror. Kemble admired it and thought: 'And it's only ten shillings!'" (S.S. III, 64–65).

Zamjatin mocked this desire for a smoothly ironed, universal conformity through the words of O'Kelly:

> And by the way: have you heard that a bill has been introduced in Parliament, stating that all Britons must have noses of the same length? Well, it's the sole dissonance, which, of course, should be eliminated. And then — everyone will be the same, like . . . like buttons, like Ford automobiles, like ten thousand copies of the *Times*. Grandiose, to say the least. (S.S. III, 43.)

Love is presented as a natural physical passion in opposition to the man-made conventions which tend to atrophy the human personality. An anarchical element that makes itself felt at night in the Jesmond park, love is kin to the disorderly growth of new foliage and ultimately to the hot, life-giving sun under which Didi first succumbs to O'Kelly. Even the philistine Kemble is subject to its physical stimulus. He loses all propriety at ringside and challenges the champion because Didi brushes against him with her breasts (S.S. III, 47); and later a glimpse of her breasts sets off noisy, red waves in Kemble's head (S.S. III, 60).

Philistinism in its purest form is embodied in Lady Kemble, for whom the maintainance of the established order and its rules of conduct are the most essential thing, in Vicar Dewly, and in the other numerous but nameless ladies and gentlemen of Jesmond. The ultimate achievement in automated philistinism is Vicar Dewly's *Zavet prinuditel'nogo spasenija* (*The Testament of Compulsory Salvation*), a rational schedule for all human activities which would make of life a "well made machine that will lead us to the desired goal with a mechanical inevitability" (S.S. III, 8). The importance of the *Zavet* and the concurrent theme of philistinism is stressed by the very structure of the tale, which begins with a description of the *Zavet* and ends with Vicar Dewly's impassioned address pleading for its legislation. Vicar Dewly's role in the story is twofold: thematically he is an extreme expression of philistine conformity; in the action he precipitates the murder by informing Kemble of Didi's infidelity and showing him the scene of her trysts with O'Kelly. The ties between Dewly and Kemble are further strengthened through the Vicar's wife. Thematically Mrs. Dewly echoes the conflict between conformity and love that engulf Kemble (her slight transgressions of the *Zavet* show her to be capable of passion); and she contributes to the forward movement of the plot by spying on Didi (motivated by her own jealous love for Kemble) and discovering the infidelity with which her husband then confronts Kemble. The lawyer O'Kelly is also important on both levels. A bystander when Kemble is struck by a car, O'Kelly carries him into Vicar Dewly's home, gives him employment after his recovery (thereby enabling him to meet Didi), and then seduces Didi after her bethrothal to Kemble. Thematically the Irishman O'Kelly (a stock device in English literature) serves as a foil to English respectability and is allied with Didi (which is emphasized by his resemblance to her ugly porcelain pug). This duality of function, sustained in each of the main characters, creates a closer structural unity in both action and theme than is achieved in any other major work by Zamjatin.

It is not surprising that the same conflict between love and philistinism underlies "Lovec čelovekov," a discarded variant ending of "Ostrovitjane."[3] Mr. Craggs, who is an apostle of The Society Against Sin (Obščestvo bor'by s porokom) and a monumental model of philistine respectability, has something of Vicar Dewly in him. His home is a fine example of metallic order, where every item has its designated place—even each teaspoon has its own case. Unbeknown to his respectful neighbors and to his own wife Mrs. Laurie, Craggs makes his living by blackmailing lovers whom he hunts out in the public parks. Mrs. Laurie, like Vicar Dewly's wife, is not completely satisfied with her ordered existence, and it becomes progressively clearer that she desires passionate love and children. While Craggs is out hunting, Mrs. Laurie, threatened by falling bombs and thinking there may be only minutes to live, rushes into the yard and gives herself to her adoring neighbor, the church organist Bailey. The motivation is the same as in Didi's surrender to O'Kelly. The difference in emphasis stems from a difference in genre. In "Lovec čelovekov," a short story centered on the ironic juxtaposition of two simultaneous events (while Craggs is busy blackmailing a pair of lovers, Mrs. Laurie falls into Bailey's arms), primary emphasis is on the love theme: All of London swims in a delirium (S.S. III, 95), all of delirious London pours into the parks (S.S. III, 108), lovers drink the mad champagne of the sun (S.S. III, 110), and finally Mrs. Laurie realizes the overriding importance of love. In "Ostrovitjane," whose greater scope permits more characters and a fuller presentation of society and social interrelations, considerably more space is given to Jesmond's victorious philistine conformity than to the outbursts of passionate love.

Shortly after writing "Ostrovitjane" and concurrently with "Lovec čelovekov," Zamjatin wrote his first extensive philosophic article "Skify li?" in which he defined philistinism:

> And for any philistine the unsubmissive person who dares to think differently than he, the philistine, is the most hateful of all. Hatred of freedom is the surest symptom of this mortal disease: philistinism.
>
> To clip all thoughts to the same zero; to dress everyone in a prescribed uniform; to convert heretical lands to your own faith by means of artillery fire. That is how the Osmanlis converted the giaours to the true faith; that is how the Teutonic knights saved the pagans from the eternal fire by the sword and temporal fires; that is how in our Russia the Old Believers, Molokans, and Socialists were treated for their errors. And is it not the same now?[4]

The particular reference is to the events that followed the October Revolution. The thought is expressed again in the political fable "Poslednjaja skazka pro Fitu" ("The Last Fable About Fita"), where Fita's (clearly a caricature of Lenin) efforts to clip all thoughts to the same zero result in universal idiocy. The sentiments in the quoted passage, however, are applicable not only to the Revolution, but reflect Zamjatin's attitude toward Vicar Dewly's *Zavet prinuditel'nogo spasenija* and Mr. Craggs' Society Against Sin as well.

Written less than two years later, Zamjatin's first play, *Ogni svjatogo Dominika,* which is set in Seville in the second half of the sixteenth century, deals with the same problem. Although the Spanish Inquisition has come to stand for fanaticism, extreme cruelty, and efficiency in the philistine persecution of heresy, for Zamjatin it was just one more infamous example of "salvation" by fire and force. The protagonist Ruy de Santa-Cruz is betrayed to the Inquisition by his brother Baltasar for reading Juan Perez's translation of the New Testament, a work on the *Index librorum prohibitorum,*[5] and is burned unrepentant at the stake. As he is about to die, he momentarily breaks free and shouts: "You! Slaves! You look on calmly while those who dare to call themselves Christians . . ." (S.S. III, 323). Ruy's last words stress two of the basic themes—the fawning sycophancy of the people who do not protest their loss of freedom and the betrayal of truly Christian principles by the Inquisition. In ridiculing the Church's doctrine of infallibility, Zamjatin not only attacks the Catholic Church, but all philistine condemnation of those who dare to think independently. He also attacks the corollary that unselfish devotion to the Church is the sole criterion in all spheres of human endeavor:

> *Notarius:* I wanted to know: have you, your Reverence, read the poem written by Fra Sebastiano? So aptly: "the sword Tison with flashing fire"—notice the word fire. And your Reverence as the valorous Cid.
>
> *Munebraga:* Yes, he, of course, is not a Petrarch. But . . . (*he takes raisins from his pocket and puts them in his mouth*) the author does have an unselfish devotion to the Church, which makes him more valuable than Petrarch . . . Ah, by the way! Let me thank you, Fra Pedro, for the starling. Why, you perform absolute miracles with your birds! You understand, Señor Notarius—a starling whistles *Te Deum*.
>
> *Notarius: Te Deum*! To have used so wisely the natural inclination of birds to sing! *Te Deum*! How I'd like to hear it . . . (S.S. III, 283–284.)

Infusing his play with a fine ironic humor, Zamjatin attacks philistinism by artistically philistinizing the Grand Inquisitor Munebraga. Unlike Dostoevskij's Grand Inquisitor, who was an astute philosopher and a worthy opponent to Jesus Christ, Munebraga is a dimpled, rosy-cheeked gourmet who constantly munches raisins and who signs death decrees without interrupting his chatter about a delectable sauce for English lobsters.

Soviet critics interpreted the basically philosophical play as "a lying and insulting degradation of the Soviet system of proletarian dictatorship" and censured the "falsity of the basic idea and its analogy with Communists."[6] The objection of Efremin, who seemed particularly incensed that Zamjatin had "endeavored to depict matters in such a way as if we only valued starlings that could sing *Te Deum*,"[7] was not without foundation, for, of course, Zamjatin valued heresy above all things and was among the first to defend freedom of expression against orthodoxy and ideological regimentation. His answer to Efremin and other critics could well have been the ironic comment of the First Grandee as he watches one of the unrepentant heretics being gagged: "Ah, if only one could put a gag on all Spaniards at once! Just think, no one's hearing would be insulted by such . . . discomfiting words. It would be the surest means!" (S.S. III, 322).

The summation of Zamjatin's philosophy is contained in his novel *My*, which he once described as the "most jocular and most serious thing" that he had written. This paradoxical description is apt, in that *My* depicts a world of the future too fantastic to be true, yet the philosophical problems which underlie its conflicts were and still are of primary importance to mankind. The incompatibility of freedom and happiness, explicitly expressed in the legend of Adam and Eve as narrated by the poet R-13, is a transparent restatement of the philosophic kernel of Dostoevskij's "Legend of the Grand Inquisitor." [8]

> You see, the ancient legend about paradise . . . It was about us, about today. Yes, think it over. Those two in paradise were given a choice: either happiness without freedom or freedom without happiness. There is no other choice. They, the blockheads, chose freedom, and what happened? Naturally, for ages thereafter they longed for shackles. For shackles, you understand. That's what the world has been yearning for. For ages! And only we have again guessed how to regain happiness. . . . No, listen, listen further! God of the ancients and we, side by side, at one table. Yes! We have helped God to defeat the Devil once and for all, for it was he who urged people to transgress the interdiction and to taste pernicious freedom, he was the cunning serpent. But we placed a boot on his head and cr-runch! And we're all set: paradise again. And again we are simpleminded, innocent, like Adam and Eve. None of that jumble about good and evil: everything is very simple, paradisical, childishly simple. The Benefactor, the Machine, the Cube, the Gas Bell, the Guardians — all this is good, it's all majestic, beautiful, noble, exalted, crystal-pure, for it guards our unfreedom, that is, our happiness.*

* [37], 56. Future references to this novel will appear directly in the text. The pagination is identical in the 1967 Inter-Language Literary Associates' edition [40].

It has been stated quite justifiably that Zamjatin's *My* was the first major anti-utopia, "the first novel of literary importance that presented a relatively complete vision of the negative results involved in the realization of Utopia."* Although it was inspired by Zamjatin's acquaintance with the fantastic novels of H. G. Wells, the question of Wells's influence has not yet received extensive, systematic study.[9] Several features of Wells's novels attracted Zamjatin, among them the accuracy of numerous prognoses, but of prime importance for Zamjatin was the expression of a sincere humanism.[10] In attacking human cruelty and the destruction caused by war, Wells had dealt with problems that were of central importance in Zamjatin's essays written in the two years immediately after the October Revolution. Zamjatin's influence on anti-utopian novels written after *My* had appeared in English translation — in particular on Aldous Huxley's *Brave New World* and George Orwell's *1984* — has been extensively discussed in numerous articles, but it should be noted here that, while Zamjatin's influence on Orwell is beyond dispute, his influence on *Brave New World* has been categorically denied by Huxley ever since 1932, the year Huxley's novel was published.†

* [502], 90. Unlike many who have erroneously assumed that the novel is set in the twenty-sixth century, Woodcock places the action "almost a millenium ahead" (p. 86). In the Russian original and in the English translations of *My*, it is clearly stated on the first page that "a thousand years ago your heroic ancestors subjected the whole earth to the power of the Single State."

† The most extensive works on this subject are the articles of G. Struve [484], I. Deutscher, [348], G. Woodcock [502], and D. Richards [452]; and W. Browning's unpublished dissertation [339]. Orwell first learned of *My* in 1944 when he already was thinking of writing an anti-utopian novel (Orwell's unpublished letter of Feb. 17, 1944, to Gleb Struve). He immediately became interested in Zamjatin's novel, obtained the French translation late in 1945, and reviewed it in the *Tribune* (London), No. 471 (Jan. 4, 1946), 15–16. In an interview with Frédéric Lefèvre, Zamjatin stated that "Drieu La Rochelle told me the other day that in the course of a conversation with Huxley, he had asked him whether he had read *My*; he had not read it, which proves that these ideas are in the stormy air we breathe." [404], 1. In a conversation with me in 1959, Mme L. N. Zamiatine claimed that Huxley had repeated his denial to Zamjatin in person later in 1932. In view of this, Huxley's more recent statement (Oct. 25, 1962) that "Oddly enough I never heard of Zamjatin's book until three or four years ago . . ." is rather ironic (see [342], 351, fn. 1).

As a satire on rationalist, utilitarian, utopian collectivist ideas and ideals, the novel again reflected the Dostoevskian heritage, particularly the ideas of Šigalev and the revolt of the Underground Man. The influence of the latter on *My* was first pointed out by Braun and more recently has been examined at some length in Robert Jackson's study of the Underground Man.[11] Jackson was, of course, justified in seeing a satire on utopianism as one of the novel's "twin objectives," but one cannot agree with his assertion that the other objective was "to show that man is essentially an irrational being."[12] Although Zamjatin was very concerned with the preservation of the independent creative personality and was very aware of the dangers of rationalistic utopias, he did not reject rationality as did the Underground Man. This important difference is evident even in Zamjatin's choice of mathematical imagery. The essence of the Underground Man's rebellion, a desire to assert both himself as an individual and the supremacy of irrationality in human behavior, was symbolized by the equation $2 \times 2 = 5$, which is a renunciation of $2 \times 2 = 4$ and, consequently, of the entire real number system. The symbol of irrationality in Zamjatin's novel $\sqrt{-1}$ (the square root of minus one) is an integral part of the imaginary number system, which does not reject, but *includes* the real number system and the equation $2 \times 2 = 4$. By this Zamjatin implies that irrationality is inherent in man and, rather than being eliminated as the rulers of *My*'s Single State would wish, should be integrated with rationality in the complete man. The implicit is made explicit in the words of D-503 to I-330 when he (D-503) first learns from her of the existence of other men beyond the Green Wall:

> Aha! You won't leave yet! You won't leave until you have told me about them, for you love . . . them, and I don't even know who they are, where they come from. Who are they? The half that we have lost, H_2 and O, and in order to obtain H_2O, streams, seas, waterfalls, waves, storms—it is necessary that the halves unite. (*My*, 140–141.)

The small remnant of humanity that has been forgotten beyond the wall (irrationality) has reverted to an animal existence and has preserved primitive instinctive impulses and emotions, while life in the Single State has developed along rational lines with the suppression of instinct and feeling. Zamjatin's contention, as Edward J. Brown has observed, was that "only through the union of the two parts could a fully human being again develop." [13] The validity of this interpretation is confirmed in Zamjatin's own commentary about his novel in a letter to Annenkov: "There are two priceless fountainheads in man: brains and sex. From the first proceeds all science, from the second — all art. And to cut off all art from yourself or to force it into your brain would mean to cut off . . . well, yes; and to remain with only a pimple." [14]

The Faustian spirit of infinite development, expressed in the idea of unending revolution, represents another important component in the philsophical framework of *My*. I-330's eloquent assertion of an infinite number of revolutions (*My*, 149–150) and her metaphysic of energy and entropy (*My*, 142) are in one way simply new formulations (under the influence of Robert Mayer) of the Scythians' unending movement forward. However, the Faustian doctrine of always aspiring, but never attaining, is also an element in the Dostoevskian legacy, for it was articulated by the Underground Man in connection with the formula $2 \times 2 = 4$:

> But man is a frivolous and unseemly being and perhaps, like a chess player, he likes only the process of attaining a goal, and not the goal itself. And, who knows (one cannot vouch for it), perhaps the whole goal on earth toward which mankind strives, consists only in the continuity of the process of attaining, in other words — in life itself, and not at all in the goal which, to be sure, must be none other than two times two, that is, a formula; but two times two is no longer life, gentlemen, but the beginning of death. At least man has always been somewhat afraid of this two times two, and I fear it now. Let us suppose that the only thing man does is to search for this two times two; he surmounts oceans, sacrifices his life in this search, but of finding it, of really finding it — by God, he is somehow afraid. For he feels that when he finds it, then there won't be anything more to search for . . . He loves attaining, but not quite to attain . . .[15]

The influence of Dostoevskij, which is so great in the basic philosophical problems of *My*, is also perceptible in numerous incidents of lesser magnitude. The effect on D-503 by the recital of nineteenth-century music is significantly compared to an epileptic fit (*My*, 19). Before the seizure, in that moment of great clarity and brilliance which is familiar to all those who have read Dostoevskij's *Idiot*, D-503's inner self responds to the wild music before his conditioning rejects it. And, as is the case in Dostoevskij's novel, this brief illuminating flash must be regarded as a true insight into the real essence of things. The number who suddenly shouts "I am a genius, a genius above the law" clearly is a reference to Raskol'nikov, especially in view of D-503's comment that "fortunately the antideluvian times of all possible Shakespeares and Dostoevskijs — or however you called them — have passed" (*My*, 40), a statement infused with irony in the light of future events. Upon becoming aware of his own individual personality (his "I"), D-503 considers this awareness to be an alienating sickness and compares those who are so afflicted to thousands of microbes that have infested the city (*My*, 111). Is this not reminiscent of Raskol'nikov's dream about a world gone mad due to microbes which enlarge each man's ego to such a degree that he considers and understands only himself? It is all the more so since Zamjatin prefaced the passage with the asertion that "we" came from God, while "I" came from the devil, which recalls Dostoevskij's formulation of the Christian ethic in the epilogue to *Crime and Punishment*. This is not to imply that Zamjatin's views on Christianity were similar to those of Dostoevskij — quite the contrary. Grouping socialism, atheism, and Roman Catholicism together, Dostoevskij condemned them all for their rationalistic oppression of freedom and opposed them to genuine Christianity, represented by Jesus Christ and the Russian Orthodox church.[16] As a humanist Zamjatin believed that all men were brothers, and he abhorred senseless violence; but he rejected Christian pacifism, particularly meekness, humility, and salvation through suffering as championed by Dostoevskij. Zamjatin's attitude toward Christianity was no different from his attitude toward any other area of human experience: Since man's thought was subject to entropy, he welcomed new ideas, heresy, and revolution. Zamjatin admired Christ the heretic and sympathized with the early Christians because they had carried on an ideological struggle; but he condemned dogmatism, the Grand Inquisitor, the potbellied priest, and forcible salvation as expressions of universal philistinism. Significantly, the ancestors of the Single State in his novel were the Christians who had taught that "we" came from God and "I" from the devil and who had reverently deferred to entropy as to God (*My*, 111, 142). The revolutionaries from beyond the wall, on the other hand, are anti-Christians who symbolically bear the name Mefi (derived from Mephistopheles, whom Zamjatin elsewhere called "the world's greatest skeptic and . . . idealist").[17] In this respect Struve was correct in pointing out that Zamjatin's novel carried anti-Christian overtones, a contention borne out by Zamjatin's assertion that Neorealism had been an antireligious movement.[18]

Although the philosophic nucleus of the novel stems from Dostoevskij's works, there is much in it that had been foreshadowed by some of Zamjatin's own works during the years immediately preceding. The idea of unending movement forward expressed in "Skify li?" underlies I-330's conception of infinite revolution; and to the reader familiar with that article, the intentional irony in D-503's straightforward evaluation of life in the Single State, the antithesis of the Scythian's, is very apparent: "For it is clear: insofar as we know, all human history is a history of transition from nomadic to more settled forms of life. Does it not then follow that the most settled form of life (ours) is also the most perfect (ours)?" (*My*, 13).

The philistine idea of salvation by force and torture, which Zamjatin had first denounced in "Skify li?" and later satirized in the play *Ogni svjatogo Dominika*, is the means by which the Single State originally was established (*My*, 141). The related philistine idea that any torture can be justified if it serves a just cause is expressed in the Inquisition's justification of its use of instruments of torture and in D-503's approbation of the Single State's use of the Gas Bell (*My*, 71). However, the work most closely related to *My* is "Ostrovitjane." Vicar Dewly's *Zavet prenuditel'nogo spasenija*, with its mathematical regulations for all aspects of human life, including sex, clearly is the precursor of the Single State. O'Kelly's facetious reference to a bill in Parliament decreeing that all noses be of the same length reappears in *My*, but this time as a serious and potentially realizable goal of the Single State (*My*, 10–11). The depiction of a mathematical and a mechanical life yield identical metaphors: Both the introduction of Kemble into the Dewly household (S.S. III, 8) and the intrusion of I-330 into the thoughts of D-503 (*My*, 31) are compared with the insertion of a foreign body into a smoothly functioning machine; and both Kemble's and D-503's deviations from the prevailing norms of behavior are compared to the breakdown of a steering mechanism (*My*, 74; S.S. III, 44, 47–48).

Unlike numerous other writers of utopian and anti-utopian novels, Zamjatin does not depict a static society whose development is complete. Although the Single State is a thousand years old, many imperfections still exist: the personal hours are not yet completely regulated, the weather is not controlled, the world beyond the Green Wall has not been subjugated, and—most important—the inhabitants have not been purged of fantasy (irrationality). The use of the first-person narrative diary form indicates that Zamjatin was concerned not so much with a description of technological achievement as with the depiction of the growing psychological conflict within D-503 and the relationship of the individual with a completely rational, totalitarian system. On the level of individual psychology, the emergence of latent irrationality in D-503,[19] his failure to achieve a synthesis between the rational and irrational within himself, and his forced submission to the fantasiectomy (which creates a model citizen, happy in his non-freedom), are indeed tragic. The element of adventure in the plot is sustained by the Mefi's attempt to seize the spaceship and their destruction of the Green Wall. Final victory, however, seems to rest with the Single State; but this pessimistic denouement is the familiar literary device aimed at spurring the reader to action. Zamjatin stated in 1932 that "This novel is a warning against the twofold danger which threatens humanity: the hypertrophic power of the machines and the hypertrophic power of the State."[20] More than thirty-five years have elapsed since then, and the double danger has not been alleviated. On the contrary, in an age of computers and massive political states, it has greatly increased, and Zamjatin's novel remains pertinent today. In successfully integrating significant philosophical questions with a penetrating psychological study of the protagonist, a description of a satiric anti-utopia, elements of adventure, and love intrigue, Zamjatin created a literary work that has become a part of world — if not Soviet — literature.

In *My* love is a strong sexual attraction which, as in "Ostrovitjane" and "Lovec čelovekov," symbolizes revolution against an existing philistine order. A similar glorification of natural, passionate love, but without the development of a contrasting philistinism, is the central theme of Zamjatin's fifth and final tale, "Sever." The arctic setting of "Sever" and Marej's childlike simplicity recall "Afrika," while his fruitless efforts to build a beacon capable of dispelling the winter darkness continue the theme of frustrated dreamers from the early tales. Similarly, the rich, sensual merchant Kortoma continues the line of negative sensuality established by the lawyer Morgunov and General Azančeev. Despite such affinities with the early period, the lyric treatment of the love between Marej and the tempestuous Saami nomad Pel'ka endow the work with a new romantic admiration of the unspoiled primitive, recalling Zamjatin's appreciation of the northern stories of Jack London and Knut Hamsun.[21]

The stories of Zamjatin's middle period display several different thematic tendencies which do not reflect the attitude of his major works toward philistinism and love. The theme of love in "Zemlemer" is not at all typical of Zamjatin. One summer a Moscow land surveyor and Lizaveta Petrovna, a provincial landowner, fall in love; but the surveyor, self-conscious about his thin, flylike legs, effeminate shoes, and huge head, is afraid to reveal his feelings. Fleeing an outbreak of peasant unrest, they find temporary refuge in a crowded monastery, where they are assigned one room. As the surveyor gently embraces Lizaveta Petrovna, her servant, unaware of their emotions, arrives, makes up a bed for herself, and warns the surveyor not to miss his train. He departs meekly, presumably never to see Lizaveta Petrovna again. The minor key throughout the story, the muffled ending, and the inability of the two people to communicate lend this story a strong Čexovian flavor that is most unusual for Zamjatin.

"Detskaja," one of the finest stories of Zamjatin's middle period, is reminiscent of "Na kuličkax." Set in a distant seaport on the Pacific, the action occurs in the back room of a tavern where the thick tobacco smoke resembles the dense Pacific fog, in which everything seems like a dream — unreal, absurd, and simple. The gamblers are lost souls, much like the officers of "Na kuličkax," and to a great degree they too have lost all human feeling. The ruler of this kingdom is the imperturbable and unfathomable Captain Krug. Among the victims sucked into this vortex is Semen Semenovič, who loses his beloved wife Pavla to Krug at cards. Although passion — an intense desire to possess Pavla at any cost — is the motivating force behind Krug's actions, the central theme is the loss and perversion of basic human values.

Shortly after the Revolution, Zamjatin reported, "Man was dying. The proud *homo erectus* was getting down on all fours and growing fangs and fur; the beast was conquering man." [22] His humanism and concern for the increasing loss of human values is reflected in his stories about the Revolution. In "Peščera" post-Revolutionary Petersburg, besieged by famine, cold, and want, is likened to a wasteland of the distant glacial epochs when mammoths once roamed the earth. Focusing on the inhabitants of one of Petersburg's cave-like apartments, Zamjatin describes how Martin Martinyč and his sick wife Maša, surrounded by the remnants of culture and civilization, retreat before the invading cold. The deprivation of warmth and proper nourishment saps Maša's strength, and she no longer can leave her bed. In order to provide her with warmth on her name day, Martin Martinyč steals some logs. The fire momentarily restores some vitality in Maša, but soon it dies down. The theft is reported, and, unable to face the winter, Maša prepares to commit suicide, and Martin Martinyč goes out into the wintry street so that she may be alone. Essentially a tragedy about two ordinary human beings, "Peščera" was vehemently attacked by Communist critics for being hostile to the new regime. Accepting Zamjatin's depiction of conditions, they censured his "compassion for those disappearing people that were unfit for life" because they said the story had been intended to arouse malice against the Bolsheviks, who were responsible for those conditions (although in the story the Bolsheviks are not mentioned).[23] The critics missed the main point which was reflected in Martin Martinyč's struggle with himself at the moment of the theft:

> And on a line delineated by his scarcely perceptible punctuated breathing, two Martin Martinyčes grappled in a struggle to the death: the one, of old, of Scriabin, who knew he must not, and the new one, of the cave, who knew he must. He of the cave, with teeth grinding, trampled, strangled, the other . . . (S.S. III, 190.)

Man was getting down on all fours, and Zamjatin once again reminded him that he was *homo erectus*, that he should get up on his two feet. Although cavemen and animals live only for today, because " 'tomorrow' has no meaning in the cave" (S.S. III, 191), man should be man — he should love his fellow men and should look to the future, to tomorrow.

A similar concern for man's human elements is to be found in "Mamaj" and "Drakon." "Drakon" is merely a two-page sketch of a Bolshevik soldier standing on the platform of a thundering streetcar. After coolly commenting on how he has dispatched in cold blood some "intelligent mug" to the heavenly kingdom, the dragon-soldier bends over to pick up a sparrow and warms it with his breath. The contrast of his behavior toward man and bird represents the author's plea for brotherly love. Sharing certain features of "Peščera" and "Drakon," "Mamaj" contains an element of bitter humor which the other two stories lack. Petr Petrovič Mamaj, an ardent bibliophile modeled after Zamjatin's childhood friend Jakov Grebenščikov (also the prototype for Senja of "Neputevyj"),[24] has laboriously saved 4,200 rubles in order to buy rare books. He abhors violence and seems to be incapable of killing a fly. One day in fear of an impending search, he hides the money under a loose floorboard, only to have it eaten by a mouse. Unable to bear the loss with equanimity, he seizes a letter opener and mercilessly, like the Mamaj of the 1300's,* skewers the guilty mouse. Although the effect of Mamaj's tragedy — the tragedy of an ordinary little man — is mitigated by the warm humor with which Zamjatin describes the relationship between him and his wife (a balding little boy cared for by a grand, all-encompassing Buddha) and his discovery of a two-hundred-year-old book (likened to a

* A high Mongol army officer who ruled the Golden Horde west of the Volga River through a puppet khan, Mamaj was feared throughout Russia before he was routed in the Battle of Kulikovo Plain in 1380, Russia's first great victory against the Golden Horde.

voluptuous, enticing woman), the expression of Zamjatin's keen concern for human values is not dulled. It centers in Mamaj's conversation with Osip Malafeev as they stand guard one night at the house entryway:

> "I am a peaceful, natural man. It's difficult for me to live in such hate like this. Well, I thought, I'll go to my place in Ostaškov. I come there, and the international situation is simply impossible: everybody at everybody else's throat, no better than wolves. I can't live like that; I am a peaceful man . . ."
>
> In the peaceful man's hands was a revolver with six deaths compressed into cartridges.
>
> "How did you manage in the Japanese War, Osip? Did you kill?"
>
> "Well, in war! In war, of course."
>
> "Well, how was it with a bayonet?"
>
> "How . . . Its something like a watermelon: first it goes hard — the rind, and then nothing to it, very easy."
>
> The mention of the watermelon sent shivers down Mamaj's spine.
>
> "But I . . . If you were to kill me now, I could not do it for anything!"
>
> "Wait! The time will come, and you too . . ." (S.S. III, 175–176.)

But Mamaj is wrong, for in his own little world, the attack on the mouse bears the same weight as killing a man; and the final lines of the story clearly are intended to recall Mamaj's conversation with Osip: "And with his sword Mamaj bloodthirstily skewered his foe. A watermelon: for one second, hard — the rind; then easy — softness — and stop: the parquet square, the end" (S.S. III, 181). Under the proper circumstances, any man is capable of killing, and Zamjatin's story is a warning to those who believe they could not. Man, he urges, must make a special, conscious effort to rise above fratricide. Thus, again Zamjatin's main interest is the preservation of humanism at a time when the primitive and the elemental threaten to submerge it.

The brief allegory "Glaza" may be the clearest expression of Zamjatin's humanism. In the course of the author's direct address to a mangy cur, the reader learns of the dog's life: how it lives on a chain, licks the hand that feeds it, and how it gave up freedom in order to fill its belly with rotten meat. Yet a sad human wisdom in the depth of the dog's eyes causes Zamjatin to ask: "Perhaps you were once a human, and you will be a human again. But when?" (S.S. III, 203). The dog is a symbol of man, perhaps of the Russian people in particular. Its master is the ruling oligarchy, and its subservience to changing masters is a commentary on the fickleness of the masses. The dog's escape to freedom and its return to its new master might well be an allegory of the Revolution: the masses break free only to submit later to the hand that feeds them. Zamjatin is asking: When will man put aside things of the flesh and think of the spirit? And Zamjatin is optimistic, for he sees in the eyes of man the possibility of a spiritual regeneration that will overcome his primitivism in the name of humanity.

A somewhat different treatment of the Revolution appears in the story "Spodručnica grešnyx." Sikidin and his two men try to appropriate convent funds in order to aid the peasants of the village Manaenki, but at the most crucial moment the mother superior Nafanaila unwittingly disarms Sikidin with liqueur and solicitous attention to his bandaged hand. The story lacks the tragic element of "Peščera" and "Mamaj," because of its basic warmth and gentle irony. The rough peasants and the mother superior are from different worlds, yet, being human, they are susceptible to kindness and love. "Spodručnica grešnyx" was the precursor to a whole series of ironical anecdotes that Zamjatin wrote during the twenties, showing that people had remained essentially the same despite the upheaval of revolution.

"If I firmly believe in an image," wrote Zamjatin in 1930, "it invariably gives birth to a whole system of derivative images; it sends roots through paragraphs, pages. In a short story the image may become integral, extending throughout the entire work from beginning to end."[25] The prose of Zamjatin's middle period, which represents the zenith of his impressionistic techniques, can be distinguished stylistically from his earlier works despite many similarities. In the middle works, heightened impressionistic imagery is accompanied by the intensification of various related techniques common in the early works. The grotesque is still used in character depiction, with a focus on one or two characteristic features, and external depiction remains at a minimum. The difference in the middle works is an intensification of the early technique. For example, the basic impression is repeated more frequently than before, and central characters often are endowed with three or four such impressions. Lady Kemble is characterized by wriggling worms (her lips) and an unseen rein that pulls her head higher; and she is compared both to a mummy and to the carcass of a broken umbrella. The grotesque quality of such impressionistic characterizations is typical of both early and middle works, but their systematic use, the frequency of their occurrence, and the extension of their use to all characters are later developments. In discussing "Ostrovitjane," Viktor Šklovskij has pointed out quite correctly:

> The characteristic feature of this tale does not consist in its motivational banality, but in that Zamjatin for the first time has consistently applied his device. The device consists in the fact that a definite characteristic, something in the nature of an extended epithet, accompanies the hero throughout the entire work, and he is shown to the reader from this side only. If it is necessary to alter the hero, then the alteration is represented in the plane of that same original characteristic.
>
> For example, if the hero is defined as a tractor, then when aroused he will be compared to a tractor without a steering wheel.[26]

In his extensive analysis of Zamjatin's imagery, Šklovskij distinguishes between two types of images, the fixed and the actional. Fixed images (*proxodjaščie*) consist of unchanging attributes or characteristic depictions which accompany the character throughout a work, like Kemble's squareness and rigidity, Lady Kemble's worm lips, and Bailey's coltish lips ("Lovec čelovekov"). Actional images (*sjužetnye*) are not static; their change and development throughout a work represent changes in the character himself. Kemble's movements, which originally are compared to those of a tractor, are later likened to those of a tractor mired in mud, then to a stalled tractor, and finally to a tractor with a broken steering mechanism.[27] Adopting Šklovskij's distinction between fixed and actional images, the generalization can be made that actional images occur only rarely in Zamjatin's early work and are used primarily during his middle period.* Fixed images have been utilized during both periods, but much more systematically and more frequently during the middle period.

In the preceding chapter it has been pointed out that Zamjatin conveys his subjective impression by a comparison, by a physical characteristic, or by some general attributive. The same devices are employed in his middle works, but with considerably greater frequency, and often two or even all three devices are used with a single character. Not only is Kemble depicted as a tractor (comparison), but he also frequently wrinkles his forehead (physical characteristic), and he has a physical and mental squareness and rigidity (general attributives). Mr. Craggs is pictured as a cast-iron monument (comparison) and also is endowed with modestly lowered lids and crablike hands (physical characteristics, the latter being also a comparative).

In addition to the superimposition of several methods in the depiction of a single character, there are significant changes within each method. Whereas comparisons in the early works refer primarily to the animal kingdom (Brahmaputra hen, mosquito, chicken, dog, frog, elephant), the comparisons in the middle works are much more varied: Kemble is a tractor, Cecily an Easter lamb ("Ostrovitjane"); Mamaj is a forty-year-old bald-headed boy, his wife is a Buddha, and Elisej Eliseič is a gloomy Atlas ("Mamaj"); Kortoma is a copper samovar, his wife is a glove turned inside out, Babka Matrena is a Russian mother-stove ("Sever"); Mlle Žorž is a bird, Semen Semenyč is a dusty daguerreotype, Father Nikolaj is the image of Saint Nikolaj Mirlikijskij ("Detskaja"); and a Bolshevik soldier is a dragon ("Drakon"). In part the result of a greater variation of setting and theme, the more various comparisons represent an extension of Zamjatin's search for original and audacious images. The search for originality is also reflected in his choice of the particular physical characteristic (often com-

* An interesting and detailed analysis of another actional image (showing the correlation between the number of gold crowns displayed in Vicar Dewly's smile and the intensity of his mood) is given in Hongor Oulanoff's discussion of the metonymic representation of character in *The Serapion Brothers; Theory and Practice* [659], 116–119.

parative) which best reveals the hero's character or some basic aspect of it: for example, Marej's childlike eyes and huge shoulders (reminiscent of Fedor Volkov), Pel'ka's teeth, and Kortomixa's painfully gay smile ("Sever"); Captain Krug's eyebrows and the midshipman's dimples ("Detskaja"); O'Kelly's red hair and waving arms, Didi Lloyd's boyish bob and knitted brows, Vicar Dewly's gold teeth and raised brows, and Mrs. Dewly's pince-nez ("Ostrovitjane"); Osip's glasses and Mamaj's penguinlike arms ("Mamaj"); D-503's hairy hands, I-330's brows and sharp teeth, and S-4711's ears and bent body (*My*). The loss of a specific attribute is sometimes used to indicate a change in a person's character, the two outstanding examples being Mrs. Dewly's pince-nez and the rosy curtain that covers Mrs. Laurie's lips. With her pince-nez in place Mrs. Dewly is extremely cold in appearance; without them, she has a somewhat lost, blissful look. The presence or absence of the glasses not only accompanies a change in her character, but is even treated as the cause of the change. As the story develops, the presence of the pince-nez becomes a symbol of her jealousy of Kemble's interest in Didi, while its absence indicates her love for him (or at least her repentance for her jealousy).[28] Less tangible but equally real is the curtain of light, rosy silk that clings to Mrs. Laurie's lips. A symbol of Mrs. Laurie's suppressed instinctive desires for passionate love (the most important thing) and children, it disappears after she has fulfilled her desires with Bailey. Both these symbols also are examples of Šklovskij's actional images.

The intensification and systematization of Zamjatin's imagery sometimes results in an overemphasis on the image at the expense of plot, a tendency that was indicated by Šklovskij in the extended subtitle of his essay on Zamjatin: "The weakening of the plot as the consequence of the shift of attention to the image. The systematization of the image, the sham saturation of form mechanically by means of image building."[29] Although Šklovskij was not an admirer of Zamjatin, he did recognize the writer's "great and conscious skill" in the use and development of his images. The word "conscious" is of great importance here, for Zamjatin firmly believed in the conscious creation and repetition of images as an important literary device, claiming that the accidental image resulted from an author's inability to concentrate. In some of Zamjatin's shorter works the integrating image, or mother metaphor as D. Mirskij has called it,[30] becomes the major unifying principle, relegating the plot to a position of secondary importance. The two most extreme examples of this are the stories "Peščera" and "Mamaj," where the integrating images of a cave and a ship, respectively, have each determined an entire system of derivative images.

Zamjatin once wrote that "in words there is both color and sound: painting and music go farther together."[31] For him images were visual leitmotivs that helped fix impressions in the reader's mind. Another aspect of his "painting" in words was his use of color. The attentive reader may be struck by the paucity of color in Zamjatin's early works (except in "Odin"). This may be due in part to their brevity or the absence of external description, but nonetheless it is surprising that sometimes only a single color adjective appears in the space of two or three pages.[32] This is not so in the works of Zamjatin's middle period, where colors have great importance and are used with studied care. In describing a scene, the nineteenth-century realist would usually strive for an accurate rendition of the colors perceived, including their nuances. Zamjatin occasionally utilized color in such a fashion, but more often he used it impressionistically; that is, a particular color would be associated with one object or person and would convey the author's impression by repetition, much in the manner of a general attributive. Realizing that the overuse of this technique would destroy its effectiveness, Zamjatin used color primarily to intensify central images. An examination of the use of color in "Detskaja" will illustrate several distinct devices in Zamjatin's color technique. In this fifteen-page story, nine colors including gold and copper are mentioned thirty-four times. The dominant color is black, which is mentioned eleven times; white is second, with eight mentions; copper appears five times; and the remaining six colors occur only a total of ten times altogether. Black and copper are associated with the features of Captain Krug, the protagonist: "Of small height; a clean-shaven face, copper from the sea wind and closed forever by a lock. And suddenly brows; two harsh, straight, coal-black lines; and his face, among all others, would be remembered forever" (S.S. III, 149). The initial description of Krug consists of a cluster of images that reappear throughout the story. As the story develops, the color copper reinforces the image of a lock. Latent for the next seven pages, it is then discharged by four successive mentions: "A slight tremor appeared, it ran along the copper to the lips closed by a lock" (S.S. III, 156). And six lines later: "But copper was once again copper, and copper laughed" (S.S. III, 156). Here we have an excellent example of Zamjatin's masterful use of synecdoche: originally introduced as a modifying adjective, copper reappears as a noun standing first for Krug's face and then for Krug himself.

Different devices occur in the development of black. One of four leitmotivs associated with Krug's brows (harsh, straight, black, line), black remains dormant during the development of the other three until the climax of the story. Mentioned only once in the first ten pages, it reappears to reinforce the other motifs at the crucial point in the card game: "Semen Semenyč does not see, but clearly hears the harsh black line" (S.S. III, 159). The black line refers not only to Krug's brows, but also to the black line that Semen Semenyč must cross morally: he stakes his wife Pavla Petrovna and loses. Krug has him testify in writing to the loss of Pavla Petrovna in lieu of 9,500 rubles:

> Captain Krug slowly folded the sheet of paper. A face closed by a lock. The harsh, *black* line of his brows.
>
> It was like this very long ago in class: a blue sky cemented in the frame of the classroom window, shrill sparrows on the windowsill. And Semen Semenyč had written a class essay about spring, in verse. And then had stood at the lectern, and a goose quill [his teacher's] — scr-ratch! — a *black* line through spring.
>
> The *black* line of brows crossed out Semen Semenyč: "Well, there. Everything's in order. Tomorrow I'll go and collect my bill." (S.S. III, 161–162.)

By association, the black line of Krug's brows reminds Semen Semenyč of the childhood incident which then becomes symbolic of Semen Semenyč's present situation. By depriving him of Pavla Petrovna, Krug takes away the only thing of value in Semen Semenyč's life — love (easily associated with spring); metaphorically, Semen Semenyč ceases to exist — he is "crossed out." This conclusion is emphasized in Semen Semenyč's final thought: "Who am I? I do not exist. Nothing exists" (S.S. III, 163). The metaphoric symbolism of the climax is tied together by the use of black.

The color black also appears symbolically in other images: the sharp hateful black ace (S.S. III, 157) which Semen Semenyč is dealt three times in a row symbolizes death, and after his loss the black cross of the window frame that becomes visible as day breaks also is intended as a symbol of his death (S.S. III, 162). Elsewhere black is used with white just for sharp contrast: black bullet holes on white wallpaper (S.S. III, 150), rosy flesh between the black and the white (S.S. III, 151), and a lightning flash on a black background (S.S. III, 156).

Zamjatin also utilizes compound adjectives in which one component is a color and the other component is an object of that color, like foam-white (*belokipennyj*), coal-black (*ugol'no-černyj*), and gold-edged (*zolotoobreznyj*). Although in present-day English such compounds are not uncommon, the Russian forms used by Zamjatin were rather unusual and would have appeared so to the reader. The distribution of color in Zamjatin's middle works, whether in the form of compound adjectives, recurrent epithets, contrastive description, or symbol, is a deliberate and systematic stylistic device aimed at emphasizing the visual aspects of his images.

During the middle period, furthermore, especially in such works as "Lovec čelovekov," "Sever," and *My*, specific colors invariably accompany certain basic concepts. Human flesh—especially the breast which is one of Zamjatin's favorite leitmotivs—and human vivification are usually characterized by pink (often more felicitously rendered by *rosy* in English translation). In "Detskaja" Mlle Žorž's "flesh shows pink" (S.S. III, 151) and Semen Semenyč's "faded, daguerreotype smile turns rosy" with hope (S.S. III, 161). In "Lovec čelovekov," pink sets the general mood of the story, for all of London is caught up in a "pink milky mist" that symbolizes the delirium of love (S.S. III, 95). Mrs. Laurie succumbs to love and is depicted in pink: her lips are covered by a pink curtain (S.S. III, 98, 99, 121), her flesh is rosy (S.S. III, 97, 99, 120, 121), and her lingerie is pink and white (S.S. III, 99, 121). Raspberry, a variant shade of pink peculiar to this story, colors the parasol of lovers in the park and becomes the symbol of their blissful universe of love (S.S. III, 110–113), and also of Mrs. Laurie's one moment of love (S.S. III, 123). In *My* the coupons for sexual hours are pink, and 0-90, who loves D-503 and passionately desires to experience the joys of motherhood, is depicted in pink: she is round like a mouth, a pink *O* (My, 8); her own mouth is pink (*My*, 20, 69); her lips are a pink crescent (*My*, 17, 69); she laughs rosily (*My*, 38); and she smiles rosily in her happiness at being pregnant (*My*, 146).

In the same way that pink is the color of the flesh, yellow and gold are attributes of the sun and frequently are used to symbolize ardent passion, the life-giving force in man. In "Lovec čelovekov" the atmosphere of love is depicted as champagne, a light mist suffused with sharp, golden sparks (S.S. III, 110). I-330, the object of D-503's passion, has golden eyes, wears a saffron dress, and seduces D-503 in a room saturated with a golden-rosy sap (the life-force) as a smiling, golden Buddha looks on.[33] The pink of flesh and the gold of the life-giving sun are combined in the primitive world beyond the Green Wall:

> And if you too were ever as sick as I am now, you know the kind of sun there is — the kind of sun there can be in the morning — you know that rosy, transparent warm gold. And the very air is slightly rosy, and everything is saturated with the tender blood of the sun; everything is alive: the rocks are soft and alive; iron is warm and alive; people are alive, and every last one of them is smiling. It may happen that in an hour everything will disappear, in an hour the rosy blood will seep away, but in the meantime everything is alive. (*My*, 72.)

The warm golden sun beyond the Green Wall, quite different from the "light, blue sun" (*My*, 7) that shines on the rational Single State (blue and blue-gray symbolize rationality and order), is the source and symbol of the life-force in most of Zamjatin's middle works. In "Sever" Pel'ka and Marej consummate their love in a sunlit forest suffused with gold, and they are intoxicated by the sun the following spring (S.S. IV, 36). Didi and O'Kelly ("Ostrovitjane") are drawn together by the heat of the scorching sun (S.S. III, 68–70), and the final chapter of the tale is "The Triumphant Sun," an irony underscored by the author: "The sun was very bright. The sun was triumphant, that was clear to everyone, and there remained only the question, was it celebrating the triumph of justice and, consequently, of culture, or was it . . ." (S.S. III, 89). The implication is that the sun is celebrating the triumph of passion over philistine culture and justice. The representatives of philistinism abhor the sun: Lady Kemble finds "the bright summer sun to be shocking" (S.S. III, 38), and Vicar Dewly delights in the "comfortable, portable, pale suns" which filtered into his dining room through thick, cut glass (S.S. III, 66). Concomitant with the imagery of a golden, rosy life-force from the sun are red and green images of blood, flame, and vegetation. D-503 compares his passions to a crimson sea of fire within himself (*My*, 51–52); the people outside the Green Wall have preserved their hot red blood (*My*, 141); and in the depths of I-330's eyes there is a blazing fire (*My*, 27). Green, the color of the growing plants is but another expression of the life-force emanating from the sun. The Green Wall separates the inhabitants of the Single State from the wild, illogical growth of the plants beyond. O-90's rounded, pregnant contours are compared to green sprouts reaching toward the sun (*My*, 146); and Pel'ka, who wears fresh green wreaths throughout her summer of passionate happiness, sleeps with Marej ("Sever") on a bed of green moss (S.S. IV, 39).

The colors black and white have no recurrent symbolic values, as pink, yellow, red, and green do, yet they too are used systematically as attributives and to create vivid contrast. The night sky dissected by searchlights in "Lovec čelovekov" is repeatedly described in black and white (S.S. III, 116, 118, 122); I-330's black dress sharply accentuates her white flesh (*My*, 19); and in "Mamaj" the contrast between black and white underlies the expression "white flies," an unusual metaphor for snowflakes (S.S. III, 175, 176). Zamjatin was particularly fond of the contrast between white and pink, using it especially with his heroines. Their flesh, invariably pink, either is delineated by white cloth or shows rosily through white. A rather original treatment of a trite metaphor in "Ostrovitjane" will serve as a good example: "Didi would undo still another button on her blouse, and waves would rhythmically undulate in front of

Kemble: white—of cambric, and still others—pink, and still others, noisy and red—in Kemble's head" (S.S. III, 60). These examples do not begin to exhaust the relationships between color, imagery, idea, and symbol in Zamjatin's middle works.

Impressive as are Zamjatin's attempts to bring the elements of painting to his writing, no less significant are his achievements in endowing his prose with musical qualities. His interest in rhythmic and other musical effects is already apparent in some of his early works, but later it is self-evident in every story. Each sentence has been carefully honed, and the choice and order of words have attained paramount importance, as the following passage from "Sever" illustrates:

> V stanovišče nikogo net. Černye dyry v tumane—raskrytye okna pustyx izb. Vse—na tom beregu, za Tunežmoj. Tam, na poljane s pritoptannym belym mxom, ešče belee, žemčužnej tumana—dymnye stolby ot kostrov. Tixo tren'kaet trexstrunka, i kružatsja figury v tumane, prixodjat, uxodjat v tuman. Lopskie parni—s medlennymi, belymi zdešnimi devkami, zdešnie—s černymi lopkami, i sredi černyx—ryžee, bystroe—kak ot solnca na sosnovom stvole—pjatno. (S.S. IV, 17–18.)*

The rhythmic effects of the passage are deliberate. Three sentences consisting of short staccato phrases are followed by a long, flowing sentence. All four sentences are static and descriptive; and all four are without verbs, for Zamjatin has used a natural feature of the Russian language (the omission of *to be* in the present tense) to intensify the effect of ellipsis. In contrast the fifth sentence contains four verbs, emphasized by inver-

* "There is no one in the camp. Black gaps in the mist—the open windows of empty huts. All are on the other shore, across the Tunežma. There, in a glade with trampled white moss, still whiter, more pearly than the mist are the bonfires' smoky pillars. Softly strum the strings, and figures whirl in the mist, appearing, disappearing into the mist. Saami fellows with slow, towheaded local girls; local fellows with dark Saami girls; and amidst the dark ones, like sunlight on a pine trunk, a rapid, reddish spot." This passage is also typical of Zamjatin's use of color. Black and white are juxtaposed effectively, first contrasting the mist with open windows and then contrasting towheaded Russian and dark Saami girls. Pel'ka, represented by a reddish spot, is compared appropriately with sunlight on a pine trunk, for Pel'ka is filled with passion, with the life-force that stems from the sun.

sion and morphologic rhyme (*prixodjat, uxodjat*). The final sentence again lacks verbs (*prixodjat* and *uxodjat* are deleted from the first two clauses, and there is no verb in the third), and its long flow is emphasized by the parallel construction of its first two clauses.

The rhythmic effects are enhanced by the studied repetition of such key words as *tuman, belyj, černyj*, and *zdešnij* and also by alliteration and the repetition of certain consonant clusters (**p**oljane s **p**rito**p**tannym; **st**olby ot ko**st**rov; **t**ixo **tr**en'kaet **tr**exs**tr**unka; and **s**olnca na **s**o**s**novom **s**tvole). Stemming from Zamjatin's belief that consonants were the solid matter — the earth — of the language and were imbued with emotional overtones, instrumentation in the form of consonant repetition became particularly noticeable in his infrequent landscape depictions.[34] The depiction of fog in "Ostrovitjane" is enhanced by what Zamjatin considered to be the dull, dark *t*'s and *d*'s.

> Tuman, dušnyj, kak vata, i zakutannye stranno zvučat šagi — budto kto-to neotstupno idet szadi. (S.S. III, 71.)*

The rising wind is felt in series of *s*'s culminating in *c*; the birdlike cloud covers the sky with *k*'s; and darkness slowly falls in a series of *m*'s and *n*'s.

> Osennij veter besilsja, svistel, sek. S morja nasedala ogromnaja seraja ptica, zakryla kryl'jami polneba, nagibalas' vse bliže, neumolimaja, nemaja, medlennaja, i vse bolše temnelo. (S.S. III, 85.)†

Actually, the emotional overtones are not inherent in the consonants, but are skillfully determined by the initial instrumental environment of the image. The emotional overtones of darkness, oppression, and dullness are created by the semantic value of *tuman, dušnyj*, and *vata* (fog, stifling, and cotton), and become associated with *t* and *d* by the consonantal repetition in *tuman, dušnyj kak vata*. Although *s* does not occur in the Russian word for wind, its recurrence in all four words surrounding

* "The fog, stifling as cotton, and muffled steps sounding strangely, as if someone is persistently striding behind."

† "The autumn wind raged, whistled, whipped. From the sea a huge grey bird settled, its wings covering half the sky, stooping closer and closer, inexorable, mute, sluggish. It grew darker and darker."

veter, as well as the semantic value of the three verbs *besilsja, svistel,* and *sek* (raged, whistled, and whipped), immediately associate it with the wind's violence. The same technique is used in creating an external characterization of each character through the phonic qualities of the attributive images, many of which stem from the phonic qualities of the characters' names. Kemble is characterized by blunt, stubborn *b, l, r* ("Gromadnye, kvadratnye bašmaki, šagajuščie kak gruzovoj traktor" or "Verxnjaja guba Kembla obiženno, po-rebjač'i, navisla"); Lady Kemble by squirming, crawling *č, š, v* ("Guby . . . tončajšie i neobyčajno-dlinnye kak červi — izvivalis', ševelili vniz i vverx xvostikami . . ."); Craggs, by grasping *k, g* ("Mister Kraggs guljal, nesja vperedi, na živote, gromadnye krabovye klešni . . ."). Although Zamjatin had always taken pains to select appropriate names for his characters,* the consistent application of phonic characteristics in names and accompanying imagery represented an innovation of the middle period which suggests Belyj's influence.

The marked tendency of the early works toward brevity is continued in the elliptical prose and staccato rhythm of the middle period. Brevity and condensation, a consequence of Zamjatin's stress on the primacy of impressionistic imagery were, he thought, essential in establishing a creative rapport be-

* Even in *My* the letter-names (a significant mixture of Latin and Cyrillic letters in the Russian text) are appropriate, the most obvious being round, pregnant 0-90, slender and angular I-330, and the doubly bent secret-service man S-4711. Derivatives of *bryzgat'* (to splash) and *xlestat'* (to lash) characterize the speech of R-13 and are examples of consonantal phonics based on the expressive liquids *r* and *l.* In the case of the three cyrillic letters the link is associative: in Д-503, the name of the architect of the spaceship "Integral," Д stands for the mathematical symbol for increment △ as well as for the *d* of differential (Zamjatin once remarked that a "differential without an integral was a boiler without a manometer," [38], 239); Ф (I-330's lover) stands for *figa* (fico) and is most appropriate for Д-503's discovery of I-330's infidelity (*My,* 189); and Ю is a playful combination of the two women in Д's life, *I* plus *O.* On another level, the inclusion of R-13 and Д-503 in the same family triangle (*My,* 39, 41) indicates that Zamjatin perhaps envisioned R-13 as an archetypal shadow of Д-503 (*R* is the mirror image of Я, the Russian word for the first-person, singular, pronoun I), and further investigation of the letter symbolism would give support to Collins' archetypal analysis, [343].

tween author and reader which he considered to be the aim of Synthesism, a term which he used synonymously with Neo-realism:

> Not one secondary detail, not one extra line, not one word that could be crossed out: only the essence, an extract, a synthesis, which is revealed to the eyes for a hundredth of a second when all feelings are focused, compressed, sharpened . . . Today's reader and spectator will be able to complete the picture, to extend the word, and that which he extends, completes for himself, will be etched into him immeasurably more brightly and durably, will organically grow into him. Thus Synthesism opens the way to a joint creativity of the artist and the reader or spectator. In this lies its strength.[35]

One final characteristic of his middle works which distinguishes them from those of the preceding period is the marked modification of the *skaz* narrative. While all of Zamjatin's early works, except the four earliest stories, are written in the *skaz* manner, only four of his shorter middle stories utilize *skaz* in the narrower sense as defined on page 122. Of the four, only "Znamenie" is written in the *skaz* manner of his early works, and even there we see a slight difference in that regional and dialect expressions occur considerably less often. In "Spodručnica grešnyx" elements of Zamjatin's early *skaz* manner are combined with the staccato and elliptical style of "Mamaj" and "Peščera." The result is an interesting hybrid style in which elements of colloquial speech, purged of regional and dialectal expressions, blend with the author's own literary style. In "O tom, kak iscelen byl inok Erazm," a tale purportedly set down by the monk Innokentij, Zamjatin uses typically ecclesiastical elocution to create a parody of the genre of saints' lives in early Russian literature. His familiarity with ecclesiastical lexicon and syntax is especially evident in his use of coordinate independent clauses, in the length of his sentences, and in the absence of ellipsis — features not at all characteristic of Zamjatin's own literary style. "Tulumbas; poslanie smirennogo Zamutija, episkopa obez'janskogo," a brief, two-page oration written in the style of a sermon, presents an ironic commentary on contemporary conditions in Russia — namely, hunger, poverty, and fawning servility. Again, the distinguishing features are the selection of ecclesiastical lexicon, the use of exhortation, and the unusually long sentence structure. The style of both these works, although representative of one type of *skaz* narrative, has little in common with the *skaz* that became a hallmark of Zamjatin's early works. The modification of the first *skaz* probably was due to several considerations. First, the use of *skaz* had been determined in part by the theme and setting of Zamjatin's early works: the ignorance and bestiality of provincial Russia. The use of colloquial expressions, of regional dialect and expressions considered substandard to the literary norm, was suitable and effective in describing provincial Russia, but was not at all appropriate in describing England, the Russian capital, or an anti-utopia of the distant future. Second, Zamjatin had for all practical purposes reached the zenith of this technique in such works as "Na kuličkax" and "Alatyr' " and thereafter sought new directions.

Some critics may, with some justification, prefer to consider the style of the middle works to be only a more subtle form of *skaz* than that of the early works. Irwin Titunik has defined *skaz* as:

> a mode of narration in fiction brought about by the interpolation into the narrative structure of a reported-reporting text which is oriented toward the perceptibility of its speech event or, insomuch as the interpolated text is a text A [statements by author, i.e., reporting speech] in function, oriented toward the perceptibility of the speech event of the narration itself.[36]

This means that any form of narrative that makes itself perceptible to the reader can be defined as *skaz*. In this case, the rather unusual elliptical style of Zamjatin's mature works with its musical instrumentation and syntactical peculiarities, which certainly did aim at the perceptibility of the speech event, could be described as a *skaz* narrative. Such an interpretation, however, would make the term *skaz* almost meaningless by enlarging its scope to include all forms of literary stylization.

Boris Èjxenbaum defines *skaz* differently: "By *skaz* I mean that form of narrative prose which in its lexicon, syntax, and selection of intonations reveals an orientation toward the oral speech of the narrator . . . a form which fundamentally departs from written discourse and makes the narrator as such a real personage. . . ." [37] This more closely approximates the traditional meaning of the term and is still useful today if "an orientation toward the oral speech" is interpreted as the artistic use of oral speech, and if the distinction is made between orientation toward the oral speech of some fictitious narrator (who then becomes a character within the work) and toward the author's own oral speech.

By *skaz* narrative I refer to narratives where the presence of a narrator other than the author is indicated explicitly or implicitly to the reader. Most of Zoščenko's better known stories would be examples of *skaz* with an explicit narrator. Most of Zamjatin's early works are examples of *skaz* with an implicit narrator,* while his middle works are examples of stylized prose with a marked orientation toward conversational style and would not fall under this author's conception of *skaz*. Zamjatin's own definition of *skaz*, which he expressed in his essay on O. Henry, is not far removed from Èjxenbaum's:

> The type of O. Henry's stories is closest to that of the *skaz* form (till now still one of the favorite forms of the Russian story): an unconstrained dialogical language, authorial digressions, purely American words typical of the streetcar and sidewalk which cannot be unearthed in any dictionary. However, O. Henry has not carried the *skaz* form to completion, when there is no author, when the author is an actor, when even the authorial remarks are given in a language close to the language of the depicted environment.[38]

Like Èjxenbaum, Zamjatin stresses the need for a conversational narrative, the use of local and dialectal lexicon, and a perceptible narrator; but in demanding that the language of the narrator approximate that of the depicted environment, he goes a step further than the well known formalist critic. Zamjatin's conception of *skaz* was derived from three basic theses: the epic work (normal prose fiction) was a play in which the author was an actor; the language of prose fiction should be the language of the age and environment depicted; and the written

* The effect of implicit *skaz* was described by Kastorskij in his commentary on "Uezdnoe": "The narrator does not appear in person in the tale, but in the tone of the entire narrative it is felt that behind the author there is hidden some provincial man to whom the story has been entrusted." [396], 324.

language should approximate as closely as possible the unconstrained, conversational, living language. Comparing the author to an actor adhering to the Stanislavskij method (which Zamjatin labeled Neorealistic), Zamjatin claimed that the writer must think like his characters and experience their life. In demanding that the author's language be that of the depicted environment, Zamjatin rejected a literal rendition and argued for a *stylized artistic synthesis* of that language, while his insistence on narrowing the gap between the written and spoken languages echoed a basic premise of the Karamzinian reform a century earlier.[39] In accord with his theories, the language in all Zamjatin's works shows a decided orientation toward the oral idiom and in varying degree reflects the environment depicted. However, while an actor-narrator is indubitably present implicitly in the early works and explicitly in such stories of the twenties as "Iks," "Slovo predostavljaetsja tovarišču Čuryginu," and "Desjatiminutnaja drama," his presence in works of the middle and late periods is scarcely, if at all, perceptible. Although it can be argued (depending upon definition) that the middle and late works represent only a more subtle and refined *skaz* than those of the early and transitional periods, an obvious difference in narrator and narrative style must be admitted.

Zamjatin's literary works of both the early and the middle periods reflect his conception of life as tragic and his belief in irony as the best means of overcoming this tragedy. Basic to both periods is a broad humanism and a firm belief in man's capabilities and in human progress. Whereas the early works are essentially satires on non-human, provincial bestiality, the middle works attack the automated philistinism of the large city. In either case, what is at stake is the preservation of the individual personality. In the middle works passionate love became associated with the rebellion of the individual against the philistine conformity and dogmatism of society. The shift in thematics was reflected by changes in setting and style. Provincial Russia was replaced by population centers: England, Petersburg, the Single State. Correspondingly, the *skaz* narrative with its regional and dialectal expressions was modified in favor of a condensed, staccato, and elliptical narrative that nonetheless was based on a contemporary conversational style. The tendency to brevity, already apparent in the early works, was continued. The impressionistic imagery of the early works was systematically extended and developed to such an extent that in many instances it became a dominant organizing principle; in some short stories it even relegated plot and psychology to secondary positions. With the intensification and primacy of the image system, visual and acoustical elements assumed much greater importance: the rhythmic and musical qualities of prose were intensified, and a semi-symbolic color system relating to the central images was developed. Conceived as an expression of the new age with its tempestuous headlong rush forward, Zamjatin's elliptical, staccato prose aimed at conveying only the bare essence of his vision by using impressionistic images.

CHAPTER SEVEN

Transitional Period, 1922-1927

And therefore "socialist" or "bourgeois" realism is unrealistic: immeasurably closer to reality are projections onto speeding curved surfaces, that which new mathematics and new art do alike. Realism that is neither primitive, nor realia, *but* realiora, *consists in displacement, in distortion, in warping, in nonobjectivity.*

Zamjatin, *Lica*

The completion of Zamjatin's most extensive prose work, the novel *My*, was followed by a sharp decline in his output of prose fiction. The reasons for this decrease — Zamjatin's greater demands for stylistic perfection, his search for new literary forms, his extensive editorial activities, a growing interest in drama and cinema, the adverse criticism of Communist critics, and the increasing difficulty of having his work published — have already been discussed in the biographical chapters and need no further elaboration here. Whatever the reasons, only seven stories, amounting to about one hundred and twenty pages, were written and published during the six-years of 1922 to 1927. In some respects their basic themes represent a continuation of Zamjatin's previous works, but in their styles, these stories, unlike those of the early, middle, and late periods, are extremely varied.

The first of these, "Rus'," was inspired by a series of drawings by Boris Kustodiev entitled "Russkie tipy" ("Russian Types"), which the Akvilon Publishing House had sent Zamjatin for review in the autumn of 1922. Considering himself unqualified to write an essay on Kustodiev's painting technique, Zamjatin laid out the pictures as if they were on exhibit and then wrote the story "Rus'." In reminiscing about a Kustodiev painting that he had seen at a Petersburg exhibition when he was writing

"Uezdnoe," Zamjatin remarked that both he and Kustodiev had painted provincial Russia, but that "Kustodiev had seen Russia through eyes different from mine; his eyes had been much more affectionate and gentle, but there was only one Russia—she united us. . . ." Zamjatin went on to say that ten years later when the two men first met in person, "Magnificent, Kustodievan Old Russia already lay dead. One did not wish to speak about a dead person in the way one could talk about the living; the easy victory of booting a dead lion did not attract me. So it turned out that Kustodiev's Old Russia and mine could now be placed on canvas and paper in the same colors." [1]

Kustodiev's water colors were published together with Zamjatin's story by Akvilon in an attractive, brief brochure that appeared in two limited editions of a thousand copies each. The lyric three-page introduction, rich in musical and rhythmic effects, creates a eulogistic tone in the first paragraph which continues as the dominant mood for the entire work:

> A pine forest—dense, ancient, with bears' lairs, the pungent scent of mushrooms and pitch, with gray shaggy mosses. It has seen the iron helms of princes' martial retinues, and the monks' cowls of the old, true faith, and the torn hats of Stepan's freebooters, and the frozen plumes of Napoleon's Frenchies. And—it all passed, as if it never existed: and once again—blue winter days, the rustle of snowy hunks dropping down along the twigs, a vigorous frosty crackle, the woodpecker pecking; yellow summer days, wax candles in gnarled green hands, the transparent honeyed tears along firm, crusted trunks, the cuckoos counting the years. (S.S. IV, 121.)

An air of antiquity is created not only by the mention of historical events long past, but also by the choice of such archaic or infrequently used words as hardy (*kondovyj*), helms (*šelomy*), cowls (*kukoli*), and Stepan's freebooters (*stepanova vol'nica*).* The vividness of the description is enhanced by such original imagery as wax candles in gnarled green hands (sunlight in the foliage) and by the use of such stylistically expressive words as vigorous (*jadrenyj*), gnarled (*korjavyj*), and

* Stepan Razin (died, 1671), a Don Cossack (known as Sten'ka Razin) and freebooter on the shores of the Caspian Sea, led a peasant uprising along the Volga against the boyars and landlords in the late 1660's.

crusted (*zakoruzlyj*). But the seemingly indestructible and imperturbable Russian forest is, like all things, subject to the ravages of time and nature. Sadly comparing the passing of Old Russia (*Rus'*) to a pine forest which has been destroyed by flames, but which will live forever in the tales handed down from generation to generation, Zamjatin goes on to contrast Old Russia to Petrine Petersburg. And he culminates the imagery in the description of a genuine Russian beauty who, unlike the waspish Petersburg coquette, is rather like the Volga—"slow, imposing, broad, full-breasted, and . . . if you turn from the main channel toward shore, into the shadows, and look, backwaters . . ." (S.S. IV, 123). The undisguised hint at the old proverb "quiet backwaters breed devils" anticipates the denouement of the story. In shifting from general to particular (from true Russian, Volga-like beauties to the beauty Dar'ja Ivanovna), the author skillfully utilizes the eulogistic introduction to endow the story and its characters with a degree of universality.

The plot is extremely simple. Dar'ja, ripe for marriage, selects old Vaxramej as her husband, takes his virile coachman Pantelej as a lover, and then poisons Vaxramej and marries Pantelej. Following the cue of Kustodiev's "Russkie tipy," the theme of old provincial Russia is expressed both in the character-types of Zamjatin's story (Dar'ja, the full-bosomed Russian beauty; her aunt Felicata, the mother superior of a local nunnery; Sazykin, a self-willed, passionate merchant; Vaxramej, the town mayor; the trunk-maker Petrov, who provides the town's sole link with the outside world; and the young coachman Pantelej with his coal-black, gypsy eyes) and in the events described (Dar'ja's choice of her husband by drawing lots after praying to the Virgin Mary, her Venus-like excursion to the public baths, and even the "inadvertent" demise of Vaxramej from a poisonous mushroom "accidentally" hidden among the edible ones).

Continuing a theme from Zamjatin's middle works, love is depicted as a strong, deeply-rooted sexual urge which is activated by the coming of spring, by the blooming of flowers, by the heat of the sun. Desire is indicated by the tautness of Dar'ja's dress on her breasts, a recurrent image that marks the thematic intersection of full-blossomed Russian beauty and passionate love.

The apple imagery is first associated with Dar'ja before her marriage: "The bees hummed in the sun, and the scent of honey, or of apples, or of Dar'ja was in the air. 'Well, Dar'ja,' [said her aunt], 'Don't put off marriage. Apples should be picked when ready, or the birds will come and peck them; don't tempt fate!' " (S.S. IV, 124). It recurs at such other important instances in her life as after marriage (S.S. IV, 125–126) and just before she takes a lover: "Heat. Yellow days, heavy with that yellowness that is typical of apples that are already ripe and ready to fall—just slightly rock them, just look or blow on them" (S.S. IV, 132). The image stems from "Lovec čelovekov," where one of the characters, a woman ripe for love, not only is compared to an apple, but is known only by the recurrent appellation "Lady Apple": "She was all filled with the sweet amber juice of the sun: it was tormentingly necessary that someone sip just a bit of it. An apple on a windless, stifling evening: it is filled, becomes transparent, stifles—oh, the sooner to break free from the branch and fall to the earth." (S.S. III, 112). Basic to the apple image are the elements of fullness, the color yellow, and the sun's heat—all of which are symbolic of elemental, passionate love in Zamjatin's middle works. In "Rus'" Dar'ja's love, however, does not so much symbolize a rebellion against an existing philistine order as do the loves of Didi, Mrs. Laurie, and I-330. But Dar'ja's love is rather the expression of the essential life force, pure and simple, in the manner of "Sever." The author clearly sympathizes with Dar'ja's need for a young lover and even goes so far as to condone her actions in the highly lyrical concluding sentence:

> And in the evening, in the blue slits of forty belfrys, all the bells rock as one, and above the town, above the groves, above the water, above the fields, above the travelers on the roads, above the rich men and drunkards, above those who sin in a human way and those who are sinless like grass—above everyone spreads the copper velvet of the bells, and everything grows softer, more quiet, more settled, like the dust of warm dew on a summer evening. (S.S. IV, 135.)

Of paramount significance is the phrase, "above those who sin in a human way and those who are sinless like grass," for in it Zamjatin restates his thesis that for man to be man he must experience life and the full range of human passions — good and bad — and not hide behind lukewarm, vegetative conformity and philistinism. What begins as a eulogy to Old Russia turns out to be a eulogy to passionate human love as well. The same tone prevails in "Kuny," a brief, descriptive sketch of traditional mating games in the far north on Midsummer Eve, which very strongly recalls the style and setting of "Sever."

Zamjatin's longest and most elaborate prose work of the transitional period, "Rasskaz o samom glavnom," and the first issue of *Russkij sovremennik*, in which the story appeared, were met with hostility by Soviet critics. The journal's apolitical character was generally interpreted as an expression of inside-émigré sentiments, and Zamjatin's story was roundly censured for its glorification of sexual love and for its supposed hopelessness.[2] One of the more moderate critics, A. Ležnev, devoted a page and a half to a literary analysis of Zamjatin's story, but he found that it contained nothing new, that the connections between the two central plot lines were obscure, and that the author's intent remained unclarified. He concluded: "*Oh! l'amour c'est une belle chose!*"[3] Although the importance of sexual love should not be minimized, such a nearsighted interpretation overlooks the author's underlying, all-encompassing philosophy.

"Rasskaz o samom glavnom" depicts three worlds: the world of a yellowish-pink caterpillar named Rhopalocera, the world of the Kelbuj and Orel peasants who are fighting on opposite sides of the Russian Revolution, and the world of a distant dying star. The spacial intersection of the three worlds (Rhopalocera falls into Talja's lap as she converses with Kukoverov, leader of the anti-Bolshevik Kelbuj peasants, and the dying star finally collides with the Earth) is at best artificial. The basic unity of the story resides in the underlying philosophic conceptions and in the symbolic parallelism between events on Earth and on the dying star. Rhopalocera symbolizes one of the few indisputable truths known to man: sooner or later — tomorrow — all living things must die. The love latent in Kukoverov and

Talja, who have known each other only a week, is activated by the realization that the world is speeding a hundred times faster than before. At the moment of confession, Rhopalocera falls from a branch into Talja's lap, an event of double significance: Symbolic of tomorrow's death, it also serves as a literary device foretelling Kukoverov's fate. When he and Talja meet again that evening before the Orel attack, she still has Rhopalocera, and the theme of tomorrow's death throws open Kukoverov's heart to real love (S.S. III, 227). After Kukoverov is captured by the Bolsheviks, the dead cocoon of Rhopalocera makes Talja realize that Kukoverov will die, that something most important must be done quickly, that time is relative (S.S. III, 243); and she is stimulated to action, to the consummation of her love. Dorda, the Bolshevik leader who happens to have been Kukoverov's old friend, looks into his prisoner's eyes and cannot bear the thought that this living man, like Rhopalocera, will die tomorrow. The conflict between friendship and his firm dedication to a cause makes him waver, and he leaves his pistol within Kukoverov's reach. But Kukoverov has nothing to gain by the death of his friend, so the opportunity passes, and Kukoverov's execution remains a certainty. In allowing the young girl, Talja, to spend the night with the condemned man, Dorda is motivated by humanity—by love and respect for his fellow man and friend, themes that are also reflected in the fruitless efforts of the Orel peasants to end the rebellion with a minimum of bloodshed. In the final scene between Talja and Kukoverov, the recurrent image of drops falling on a stone creates an effect of timelessness which reinforces Zamjatin's thesis that time is relative.

The second line of action develops high above Earth on a dying star that has lost its atmosphere, where the four remaining persons of a great civilization are breathing the last reservoir of air. The drama on the star is not, as Ležnev put it, an "even weaker and more banal episode," but a symbolic mirror of events on Earth that emphasizes the universality of Zamjatin's vision. The symbolic function is underscored by Zamjatin's naming the four characters simply Mother, man, woman, and blind boy. As Dorda races across the bridge, thinking only of the most important thing (the defeat of the opposition), he does not know whether he will die. But on the distant star there is no doubt — today is the end. The need for air has become acute, and in order to live the man kills his brother, the blind boy, just as the Orel and Kelbuj peasants kill each other. The man, however, is unable to kill the Mother (who, like Rhopalocera, is ready to die), just as Kukoverov is unable to kill Dorda. Dorda's sympathy for Kukoverov, his friend and enemy, is reflected in the Mother's sympathy for her elder son who has murdered her younger son. The essence of the humanistic message here seems to be that only man can truly understand and pity his fellow man. And as Kukoverov's execution approaches, he embraces Talja and experiences love, just as man embraces woman on the distant star as it rushes toward earth and destruction. The importance of love is emphasized by the two parallel episodes, but love represents "the most important thing" only in the relationship between man and woman. The Soviet critics should remember that in this story Zamjatin also states that for flowers the most important thing is to bloom (S.S. III, 242), for Dorda the most important thing is to cross the bridge (S.S. III, 230), for Rhopalocera the most important thing is to die painfully in a cocoon (S.S. III, 211), and for man the most important thing is to live (S.S. III, 234). Zamjatin's basic philosophy here is comprehensive: life is truly life only when its basic function is being fulfilled. At such moments seconds become ages, and one moment of fulfillment is worth years of stunted existence. In essence this is a restatement of the maximalism that underlay his concept of the galloping Scythian.

"Rasskaz o samom glavnom," is the artistic embodiment of philosophical conceptions expressed earlier in several of Zamjatin's essays; it now stands out as a unique attempt to create a new literary form. In "O sintetizme" Zamjatin had pointed out that the extremely rapid tempo of the epoch was reflected in contemporary art and literature, that the dominant trend was toward a synthetism that sought to depict "only the essence, an extract, a synthesis that was revealed to the eye in a hundredth of a second when all feelings were sharpened, compressed, focused."[4] Zamjatin's story represents an attempt to create such a synthesis on the theme of "the most important thing," and Kukoverov's thoughts echo the author's own: "Has it never entered your head that now the earth is rotating a hundred times faster, and that all clocks — everything — is a hundred times faster, and that this is the only reason why no one notices it? And now, you understand, just one day, or a minute . . . Yes, a minute is enough to understand suddenly that for you another person is . . ." (S.S. III, 213–214).

In another article, written the same year as "Rasskaz o samom glavnom," Zamjatin states that contemporary literature should be imbued wih immense philosophic visions, like the view from a masthead or an airplane, that it should deal with ultimate questions like "why?" and "what further?" He points out that "for contemporary literature the plane of *byt* is the same as the earth for an airplane: simply a runway that enables flight upward, from *byt* to being, to philosophy, to the fantastic."[5] "Rasskaz o samom glavnom" represents a conscious attempt to apply such theoretical pronouncements. Zamjatin places his main emphasis on a moment of being (the realization of love) and seeks to endow it with philosophic significance by the symbolic use of the fantastic (the dying star). In the final paragraph, as well as in the introduction, Zamjatin expresses his belief in the birth of a wonderful new world through the collision and flaming destruction of the old worlds, a belief that reflects his central tenet of unending, cosmic revolution which creates new life through the destruction of existing life.

Another factor contributing to the unity and philosophic import of the story is Zamjatin's studied use of the first person singular in several crucial instances. The story is narrated in the third person by an omniscient author; there is no consistent attempt, as in most of Zamjatin's early works, to suggest the presence of an intermediate, earthy narrator by the use of *skaz* style. The occasional shifts to the first person in this later story represent the unmasked intrusion of Zamjatin himself; and, significantly, in such intrusions the author always identifies himself with his characters and their sensations. The effect is that of a fluid, omniscient entity who is a part of each and every living thing: the author is Rhopalocera, and his body is racked with pain (S.S. III, 211); he is both an Orel and a Kelbuj peasant, shooting at himself as he runs across the bridge and falls

(S.S. III, 211); he is a corpse with naked, icy flesh on a distant star (S.S. III, 211–212); he is also the last living man on that same star, wanting to live, killing his brother (S.S. III, 221), and loving the woman (S.S. III, 234); and he is Dorda and every man charging across the bridge into the hail of machine-gun fire (S.S. III, 219). This technique, which apparently has been overlooked by critics, creates a transtructural unity of plot lines by identifying all the sensations depicted with a single person, the all-encompassing spirit of the author himself. It is an unusual attempt to combine the lyric form (the revelation of the author's personality) with that of the epic (a narration about others in which the author is an actor).[6]

"Iks" is the most extensive and successful of Zamjatin's anecdotal stories in which ironic humor is combined with literary parody. Love, gullibility, and the Revolution's effect on the ignorant population are the major themes. The story centers on ex-deacon Indikoplev, whose public recantation of the Orthodox faith, inspired by Marfism — not Marxism, is used ironically to illuminate human gullibility: "Deacon Indikoplev, having publicly repented for having deceived the people for ten years, naturally now enjoyed the confidence of both the people and the authorities" (S.S. IV, 140). The superficial philistine adaptation to the new environment is not only developed in the conduct of Indikoplev and others, but is suggested also in numerous incongruous juxtapositions such as the corner of Pancake and Rosa Luxemburg streets. The heroine Marfa, a buxom Russian beauty of easy virtue, with pearly teeth and rich, ripe, golden tresses, is drawn with the same Kustodievan brush that created Dar'ja; and at the moment of the deacon's conversion to Marfism (when he observes Marfa naked by the stream), Zamjatin deliberately recalls "Rus'" and Kustodiev's Russian beauties with the phrase, "Oh, if only the deacon were able to draw like Kustodiev!" (S.S. IV, 147). Passionate desire is associated with spring, the surge of nature, and the growth of vegetation — in this particular case, the bloom of fragrant lilac. The center of all love intrigue, Marfa bestows her favors under the blooming lilac in her backyard to all comers — to the telegraph operator Aleška, to the Communist Xaskin, to the exdeacon, and to the fugitive Socialist Revolutionary Perepečko. "Cursed with that heritage of capitalism — the proprietary instinct" (an excellent example of Zamjatin's frequent play on Communist jargon), Indikoplev jealously guards Marfa's back yard, only to be mistaken for Perepečko by the authorities. He is apprehended after a comic chase by agents dressed in white straw hats, which prove to be the mysterious "special clothes," that unknown "x" (hence the title "Iks") which the citizens have been eagerly anticipating since the story's beginning.

Zamjatin's conscious play with literary form is the other major comic element. The story opens with an original metaphor in which the thematic content is equated to a spectrum whose major colors are gold, red, and lilac. Gold, the color of church cupolas, represents religious elements; red stands for the Revolution, the local authorities, and the new, post-revolutionary environment; lilac, the color of the blossoming bushes, symbolizes love. Having established the lines of the story's color spectrum, Zamjatin repeatedly and humorously refers to them:

> On the corner of Pancake and Rosa Luxemburg there appears a procession, evidently a religious one: eight clergymen, well known to the entire town. But the clergymen are waving brooms, not censers, which transfers all action from the religious plane to the plane of Revolution: it is simply the non-working element fulfilling its work obligation for the benefit of the people. Instead of prayers, golden clouds of dust rise to the sky. (S.S. IV, 139.)

And a few pages later: "A catastrophe was in the making there: the collision of two antogonistic lines of the spectrum — the red and the gold, the revolutionary and the cupolic — in a certain human point" (S.S. IV, 144).

Zamjatin's play with thematic lines, however, is only part of an extensive parody of literary forms. The narrator's refusal to reveal what Aleška sees in Marfa's garden ("very likely, it's not worth tearing sleeves and climbing fences after the poet: it's all the same — sooner or later we will find out what Aleška saw there" (S.S. IV, 143) is a transparent parody of retardation. The rainstorm that "discharges" the emotional tension of the people on the street (S.S. IV, 146) probably parodies Viktor Šklovskij's conception of a "false resolution," and the extended description of events on Rosa Luxemburg Street in the manner of a theatrical performance (S.S. IV, 151–153) is intended as a parody of *ostranenie* (the device of making strange).* The final scene at the Cheka headquarters parodies the ageless motif of mistaken identity (everyone in town knows who Indikoplev is); and the figure of Comrade Papalagi with his huge, black moustache is undoubtedly a spoof on Stalin. Although much of his previous work is essentially satirical, the extensive parody of literary devices in "Iks" represents an innovation in Zamjatin's work that had no precedent, with the possible exception of "O tom, kak iscelen byl inok Erazm," the clever parody of the genre of saints' lives. But even that differs stylistically from "Iks" and lacks the element of self-parody.

The theme of philistinism, which had receded to the background since *My*, reappears again here in a new form—the superficial acceptance of the Soviet Revolution by ignorant philistines who do not really understand it. This theme is further developed in the story "Slovo predostavljaetsja tovarišču Čuryginu" and in *Afrikanskij gost'*, a three-act farce which is "a satirical cut at people who think that they are Soviet, but in reality are only accommodating to Soviet ways."[7] In "Slovo predostavljaetsja tovarišču Čuryginu," Zamjatin directs his irony at the ignorance of the peasants who, upon hearing rumors of unrest in the capital, attack the local landowner in the names of Grigorij Efimyč (Rasputin) and Mars, and of the narrator Čurygin, who believes himself enlightened, yet whose speech and actions show him still to be an ignorant peasant who has been affected only superficially by the Revolution. Religious faith is depicted as merely another expression of philistine habit. The deacon's renunciation of Orthodoxy is dictated by social and sexual expediency, but old habits (making the sign of the cross and invoking God) persist, causing him no small discomfiture. The same is true of Čurygin who thanks the Lord that he no longer believes in God. In both cases Zamjatin points out that philistinism has only been converted from the religious

* Zamjatin knew Formalist methodology and must have been acquainted with Šklovskij's essay "Iskusstvo kak priem," *Poètika; sborniki po teorii poètičeskogo jazyka* (Petrograd, 1919), which included a discussion of the "device of making strange."

to the Revolutionary plane. In this respect, the humorous anecdotes of Zamjatin's transitional period continue the line of his fables, which also are aimed primarily at gullibility, ignorance, and other human failings.

The remaining two stories of Zamjatin's transitional period, "O čude proisšedšem v Pepel'nuju Sredu" and "Žitie Bloxi . . . ," are both anecdotal parodies centered on one impossible situation: a humble, cloistered monk gives birth to a child. In the first story, the presence of the Mephistophelian Dr. Vojček, with his green, goatlike eyes and red hair that sticks up like horns on his forehead, combined with Archbishop Benedikt's caressing kindness to the dimpled, womanish canon Simplicij (Zamjatin hints at a homosexual relationship), permits the reader to believe with the canon in the miraculous birth of his son Feliks. On the other hand, if one considers the smiles that continually crawl about Vojček's face, his laughter through tears as the dying Simplicij reveals the secret to Feliks, and the death of a pregnant woman just prior to Feliks' miraculous birth, then a more earthly answer becomes apparent. In all probability a parody of some ribald medieval Czech tale about the evil powers of the Devil, the story has modern significance in that it mocks the gullibility of the simple, ignorant people who are all too ready to accept the improbable.

A parodistic history of Zamjatin's play *Bloxa*, the story "Žitie Bloxi . . ." originally was intended only for a small group of friends, the members of the Physio-Geocentric Association, which held numerous evenings of parody at the House of Arts during the winter of 1926–1927.[8] The monk's name is a legacy from Remizov's mock literary society the House of Apes (Obez'janskaja palata), where Zamjatin had been dubbed "Zamutij, Bishop of the Apes", a title he previously used in "Tulumbas . . . ." After a visit from the turbulent Dikij, Zamutij begins to swell, just as Simplicij does after his evening with the archbishop, and finally gives birth to a strange, promiscuous creature named Bloxa. The rest of the story is a comic account of Bloxa's trials and tribulations during 1925 and 1926. Although the basic situation of "Zitie Bloxi . . ." undoubtedly was inspired by "O čude, proisšedšem v Pepel'nuju

Sredu," its pseudo-ecclesiastical style also continues the tradition of "O tom, kak iscelen byl inok Erazm" and "Tulumbas. . . ."

While the style of Zamjatin's early works is generally characterized by a form of *skaz* narrative which utilizes colloquial and regional expressions, the technique of demonstrating, exaggerated grotesque, animal imagery, and the repetition of synthetic attributes, the style of his mature period is distinguished by greater brevity and frequent ellipsis, the intensification of imagery, and the creation of derivational image systems, the semisymbolic use of color, and a departure from *skaz* narrative. No similar generalization can be made about the few transitional works. Their styles are greatly dissimilar, especially since parody occurs frequently in these pieces. The eulogistic styles of "Rus' " and "Kuny" come closest to the *skaz* of Zamjatin's early works, but differed in that the implicit narrator's speech is generally free from dialect. "Rasskaz o samom glavnom" is written more in the style of Zamjatin's middle works, particularly in its use of ellipsis in the passages dealing with the star hurtling through space. The absence from this story of an intermediate narrator and the presence of the author in first-person intrusions clearly indicate new development in Zamjatin's style. "Iks" and "Slovo predostavljaetsja tovarišču Čuryginu" are fine examples of a *skaz* narrative quite different from that of the early works. The narrative style in "Iks" is definitely oriented toward stylized oral speech, and the narrator, a Soviet citizen of good education with a literary bent, frequently resorts to addressing the reader directly. His discussion of the three lines of the story's spectrum may very well be intended as a self-parody of the middle period's color symbolism. "Slovo predostavljaetsja tovarišču Čuryginu" stands out as the purest example of Zamjatin's *skaz* narrative. Consisting of a speech delivered by Čurygin at a meeting discussing the Revolution, the story is a masterpiece of sustained *skaz* oratory. At the time of the Revolution Čurygin was an uneducated peasant living in the village of Kujmani, but since then has acquired a vague knowledge of Marxist theory and a smattering of Soviet jargon that he manages to misuse in unbelievable syntactic periods:

> But since all this exists in a minute of Capitalism, there was likewise an opposite class at a distance of three versts, but more precisely an ex-spider, that is the landowner Tarantaev, who, of course, sucked our blood and brought back from abroad all sorts of objects in the guise of naked statues, and these statues were set every which way, especially one with a spear, like God—of course, not our Orthodox God, but just a god. (S.S. IV, 172.)

Of the other two stories, the ecclesiastical style of "Žitie Bloxi . . ." has already been mentioned. The *skaz* narrative of "O čude, proisšedšem v Pepel'nuju Sredu," although initiated by the narrator in direct address to the reader, is sustained only by infrequent authorial intrusion, such as "Yes, it's strange, but, then, it seems right. Figures: there's no arguing with them" (S.S. IV, 245), which is scarcely perceptible in what otherwise is a third-person, highly stylized narrative. There are no dialectal or regional expressions, no Soviet or ecclesiastical jargon.

The transitional period began with "Rus'" and "Kuny," a nostalgic return to the provincial Russia satirized in the early works. Then came "Rasskaz o samom glavnom," which, following Zamjatin's theories on literature, was an attempt to create a new style and technique in accord with the new age. This attempt failed, perhaps because, for once, Zamjatin created a plot by deduction rather than induction (he first posed an abstract idea and then embodied it in images, events, and people).* Whatever was Zamjatin's evaluation of this story, he subsequently turned to new directions. Despite the differences characterizing the remaining transitional works, they reveal a definite trend toward the anecdote, the narration of a story in which the action assumes a much greater importance than the complex of images accompanying it. There is a tendency for the elliptical prose of these works to be smoother—still concise, but more like normal elocution. Images are still used, but the extensive derivational systems of such works as "Peščera" and "Mamaj" were a thing of the past. There is also a definite turn to a *skaz* narrative in which a narrator other than

* Zamjatin himself had warned apprentice writers against the deductive technique, for "plots created by this method rarely were molded in an irreproachably artistic form" and were readily susceptible to scholasticism. [168], 149–150.

the author is readily apparent. But perhaps most significant of all is a decided predilection for parody—"most significant" because parody of others precluded Zamjatin's working out a distinctive style of his own. Zamjatin's new style, the style of his late works, finally crystallized in 1928 when he forsook literary parody and once again took up writing prose fiction in earnest.

CHAPTER EIGHT

Late Period, 1928-1935

The philistine is like mold. For a moment it seemed that the Revolution had burned him to the ground, but here he is again, smirking, crawling out from under still-warm ashes — cowardly, narrow-minded, dull, self-assured, all-knowing. And satire's whip must whistle over him again . . .

Zamjatin, *Lica*

Zamjatin's late works, beginning with "Desjatiminutnaja drama" and "Ela," represent the final crystallization of his artistic techniques. Taken as a whole, the works of this final period stand out structurally, stylistically, and thematically from those of his early and middle periods. In some respects, they represent the final expression of tendencies manifested in several stories of the transitional period. The tragic conception of life, evident throughout Zamjatin's career, finds its most powerful expression in "Ela" and "Navodnenie," the two major stories of his final period, and it was to have been a central theme in his unfinished novel *Bič Božij*. The themes of love and human ignorance, despite a somewhat different treatment, remain basic in his late works. The tendency toward literary parody, so striking in his transitional stories, continues and, under the influence of Western models, gives rise to a new form of the story. But, although many such stylistic features of the preceding periods are retained, there is a marked movement toward general linguistic simplicity and the use of a simple, albeit syncretistic, spoken language in the narrative.

Of the various changes in Zamjatin's late works, perhaps the greatest is in the structure of his stories. Throughout his early and middle works, he maintained a distinction between the tale and the story: as a general rule, the tale was considerably longer, was subdivided into numerous chapters (many with titles which indicate their themes), and depicted many characters and events; the briefer story depicted only a few characters and one or two central events. After "Sever," written in 1918, Zamjatin wrote no more tales. The story "Rasskaz o samom glavnom," almost as long as the shorter tales (fifty pages), is nonetheless a story; for, despite its multilevel structure, it has a definite unity of time (twenty-four hours) and of action (although several events are shown, they are closely linked thematically, symbolically, temporally, and spacially). Of the eight stories written in the late period, two are quite long ("Ela" and "Navodnenie") and have no structural innovations.* The remaining six stories ("Desjatiminutnaja drama," "Mučeniki nauki," "Videnie," "Časy," "Vstreča," and "Lev"), however, do introduce a new form in Zamjatin's prose work — the ironic novella.

Zamjatin's six novelle are all brief (four are no longer than nine pages each), and all have well developed action. The major actional stress in them is on the denouement, usually a surprise ending which gives the novella an ironic or parodic character. In "Desjatiminutnaja drama" a drunken workman informs a young dandy in no uncertain terms what the working class will do to the capitalists. Threatening words and gestures build a dramatic tension, which is unexpectedly discharged by a moist kiss from drunk to dandy, rather than a heavy blow. In "Videnie" two drunken friends, haunted by an apparition of a white elephant, begin to fear for their sanity, until they suddenly learn that the elephant is real. In "Časy" the meek Semen Zajcer is spurred by his love for Veročka to resist a man whom he believes to be stealing his precious watch, but his bravery backfires: his watch has not been stolen, and it is he who inadvertently has taken the watch of a passerby. In order to im-

* The stories are thirty and forty-four pages, respectively. (Length in pages is cited according to the 1929 collected works [30]–[33]. If a work was not in that collection, its length has been calculated here at the rate of that edition — 165 words per page.) Although they have chapters, these two stories are not tales, for they center on a single situation and have very few characters. At first publication they were designated as stories; they were called tales only once, posthumously, in *Grani*, No. 51 (1962), 1, 43.

press his girlfriend Katja, the timid Petja Žerebjakin ("Lev") becomes an extra in a ballet. In the role of a lion that is shot and falls from a cliff, Petja hesitates at the crucial moment and — to the merriment of Katja and the rest of the audience — fearfully makes the sign of the Cross before plummeting downward. In "Vstreča" a pre-Revolutionary colonel encounters Popov, a political prisoner whose chessboard he once took. Remembering Popov's vow of vengeance, the colonel blanches with fear when he sees Popov recognize him and then reach into his pocket. The colonel closes his eyes in fright, but, instead of a gun, Popov pulls out a pocket chess set and asks him to play. The longest of the novelle, "Mučeniki nauki," actually has two surprise endings. The widow Varvara Stolpakova, a doting mother who will do anything to ensure her son's college education, goes to the civil registrar's office with her suitor Miša, but unexpectedly marries her coachman Jakov instead. This surprise is followed by another upon her return home: the hitherto silent and submissive Jakov makes Stolpakova serve *him*, now that she is his wife.

The irony of the surprise endings is supported by further irony throughout these novelle, frequently attained by the parody of literary convention and the revelation of literary devices — a technique that had appeared in some of his transitional stories. The very title, "Desjatiminutnaja drama," for example, reflects Zamjatin's play with the dramatic form: he speaks of the passengers as "actors in my story"; the conductor's cry is described as "a prologue to the drama; in it were evident the essential factors for a tragic conflict"; the arrival of the drunken workman is heralded as "the appearance of a second element, indispensible for dramatic conflict"; and when the workman approaches the young dandy and takes his hand out of his pocket, Zamjatin interrupts the story with, "here, according to the laws of dramatic composition, a pause is necessary so that the audience's nerves would be drawn taut, like strings" (BB, 112–114).* Elements of literary parody are also

* Textual references to "Desjatiminutnaja drama" and "Časy" will be cited from *Bič Božij* [36], abbreviated BB; references to "Lev," "Vstreča," and "Navodnenie" will be cited from *Povesti i rasskazy* [39], abbreviated

present in "Časy," where Zajcer "in terror awaited that laughter, as the heroes of Tolstoj's novels await the explosion of a revolving bomb" (BB, 99), where a happy, banal ending is falsely predicted by the narrator (BB, 102), and where the emotions of the newly declared lovers are merely hinted at, in coy imitation of the usual banal descriptions: "It is not known whether Comrade Zajcer slept that snowy spring night (probably not). It is not known whether Veročka slept (perhaps)" (BB, 102). Although there is no obvious literary parody in "Lev," the play with literary form begins with the initial description of a drunken lion (it is not revealed till the second paragraph that the "lion" is only a man in costume) and is sustained by authorial remarks which reveal literary convention. For example, "the secret was known only to Petja Žerebjakin and, to be sure, the author of this story" (PiR, 243). And "however, all this was a thing of the past: now he is speeding through the autumn rain to Glinka Street. Luckily, it was near the theater and, luckily, he found the militiaman Katja at home"(PiR, 245). "Vstreča" and "Videnie" are narrated without explicit authorial intrusion or literary parody, although the device of beginning *ex abrupto*, used with comic effect in "Lev," appears again in "Vstreča," but at much greater length and with the intent of confusing the reader with seeming fantasy.

It is highly probable that Zamjatin's turn to literary parody and to the composition of short, actional novelle was due to Western influences, particularly O. Henry. Zamjatin's interest in English literature, first stimulated by his stay in England during World War I, was developed further by his editorial activities for World Literature. His anti-utopian novel *My*, for instance, was inspired by his work with the fantasies of H. G. Wells. Zamjatin's greatest exposure to the short story probably came between 1922 and 1924, when he was an editor of *Sovremennyj zapad*, an interesting journal devoted to Western literature. Among that journal's translations were some of O. Henry; furthermore, in 1923 Zamjatin edited a volume of O. Henry's short stories, which he supplied with an introductory

PiR; "Videnie," from *Mosty* [92], abbreviated M; "Mučeniki nauki," from *Novyj žurnal* [90], abbreviated NŽ.

essay. This essay is of considerable interest because it reveals his great sympathy for O. Henry, as well as his admiration for the style and structure of his stories. Glossing over O. Henry's two major faults — sentimentality and didacticism (which, according to Èjxenbaum, were responses to the demands of the myopic American reading public)[1] — Zamjatin examined O. Henry's philosophy. He found it to be the philosophy of Charlie Chaplin, millions of New Yorkers, and, implicitly, Evgenij Zamjatin and the Russian Neorealists. "Perhaps his sole philosophy," wrote Zamjatin, "is that life must be conquered by a smile."[2] Zamjatin's commentary on O. Henry's style could well have been a self-evaluation. He praised O. Henry's "biting language, which sparkled with eccentric and unexpected symbolism" (a reference to O. Henry's use of imagery that was internally connected to the characters); his use of "integrating" images (images that appear throughout a story, frequently undergoing development); and his use of *skaz* style (conversational language, authorial digressions, and colloquial slang). However, no claim of O. Henry's influencing Zamjatin in these areas can be supported. Quite the contrary — it can be said that Zamjatin saw and valued in O. Henry only those stylistic features which he had already valued and developed in his own prose. Zamjatin did, however, adopt one aspect of O. Henry's prose which was not typical of his own works before 1922: the dynamism of O. Henry's plots, with their surprise endings, sometimes achieved by means of false resolutions — that is, when the reader's conclusions are suddenly proved to be mistaken.[3] A new stress on plot dynamism and on actional elements, which soon appeared in such transitional works as "Iks" and "O čude proisšedšem v Pepel'nuju Sredu," assumes central importance in Zamjatin's late novelle, whose chief aim is the artistic narration of an incident. The turn to plot dynamism, the recurrence of surprise endings, and occasional false resolutions (the reader's assumption that Zajcer is robbed, for example, or that the elephant in "Videnie" is real) all suggest O. Henry's influence.

The element of literary parody was also partly a legacy from O. Henry. Èjxenbaum spoke at length on the extensive "literariness" of O. Henry's stories in their unmasking of literary convention, their play with motivation, their authorial intrusion, their ironic treatment of the banal, and their conscious underlining of constructive devices.[4] Most of his observations applied equally to Zamjatin's novelle and some of his transitional works. Zamjatin's use of O. Henry's techniques was not a haphazard appropriation of foreign material, but was a natural development of his own literary style and a reflection of the development of Russian literature during the 1920's. In commenting on O. Henry's "A Night in New Arabia," Èjxenbaum remarked that "the entire novella is constructed on a continuous ironizing and underlining of devices, just as if O. Henry had passed through the 'formal method' in Russia and frequently had had discussions with Viktor Šklovskij."[5] It is therefore not surprising that Zamjatin, who was very sympathetic to the Formalists and whose style already had much in common with O. Henry's, should have assimilated his literary parody and certain structural devices.

As much of the humor stemmed from Zamjatin's treatment of thematic material (the incongruity of old habits after the Revolution) as from his play with literary form and the unexpected endings, however. In this respect, the novelle are a direct continuation of the transitional stories "Iks" and "Slovo predostavljaetsja tovarišču Čuryginu." There, the object of Zamjatin's satire — the common, everyday citizen who is interested primarily in promoting his personal interests — is treated with ironic affection. Zamjatin believed, as did Anatole France, that "the irony which I recognize is not cruel; it does not mock love nor beauty: it teaches us to laugh at malicious and stupid people, whom we would have had the weakness to hate without it." * Zamjatin's bent for satire may have found further stimulation in the works of France, for whom he had great respect; and the question of France's influence, particularly the relationship of such novels as *L'ile des Pingouins* and *La révolte des anges* to *My*, certainly deserves investigation.

Although the novelle are essentially actional stories in which attention is focused on the denouement, the Soviet Russian setting is successfully integrated in them as an indispensible, ironic

* [38], 102. Zamjatin's enthusiastic appraisal of France's satire, especially in this respect, was understandable. Significantly, he considered France to be a literary heretic of the same magnitude as Lev Tolstoj.

element. This is especially true in "Časy" and "Mučeniki nauki," where the unusually extensive treatment of central figures requires an uncommonly detailed depiction of their social environment. Through the vicissitudes of the Revolution a tailor's apprentice, Semen Zajcer ("Časy"), becomes the director of wood-fuel distribution in Petersburg. The modest hero gives way to a "capitalistic" inclination and procures an exceptional gold pocket watch in order to impress his secretary. Environment, meekness, love for Veročka, and great affection for the watch combine to bring about his ignominious downfall. Zajcer, despite the Revolution, has remained a petty philistine who needs a gold watch to win himself a wife. The traditional Communist-bureaucrat conflict is parodied in Zajcer's confrontation with his rival Kubas, the leader of the local Communist cell and editor of the departmental newspaper.

The widow Stolpakova ("Mučeniki nauki") is the best example of Zamjatin's kindly but ironical treatment of superficial adaptation to the new environment. Unlike Indikoplev, Zajcer, and the accommodating philistines of *Afrikanskij gost'* who seek only personal gain, Stolpakova desires only the well-being of her son. Deprived of her sugar beet factory by the Revolution, her imperious attitude toward her ex-coachman Jakov nevertheless remains unchanged, just as his ignorance and ingrained peasant psychology do. The ironic reversal of fortunes at the story's end, after Stolpakova marries her coachman to give her son the desirable working-class status, illustrates the basic unchangeability of certain human traits. Zamjatin's irony, however, is not directed only at failings in his characters, but also at aspects of the Soviet regime, such as discrimination according to a person's socio-economic heritage ("Varvara Sergeevna Stolpakova's first error was that she had chosen her parents most improvidently," NŽ, 12).

Religious vestiges are a recurrent source of humor in many of the novelle. Reflected in the title of "Mučeniki nauki" ("Martyrs of Learning"), this theme is developed in the initial paragraph of the story and reappears at a decisive moment in Varvara Sergeevna's life:

> At last the word had been said: "professor". . . . She now knew the name of the god for whom she would sacrifice herself.

> The mention of god, even without a capital letter, is really out of place here. Life itself in those years had led everyone to a firm, scientifically materialistic world view. (NŽ, 16.)

The same theme is of central, comic importance in "Desjatiminutnaja drama," where it is combined with parody on dramatic form:

> The conductor's invocation began the action: "Annunciation Square, newly called the Square of Labor!"
>
> This invocation was the prologue to a drama. In it were evident the essential factors for a tragic conflict: on the one hand, labor; on the other hand, a non-labor element in the form of the archangel Gabriel appearing before the Virgin Mary. (BB, 112.)

Embodied in a young dandy traveling to Vasil'evskij Island to visit a "half-virgin" Mary, the "non-labor" religious element becomes associated with the capitalistic element; and the connection is sustained throughout the story by references to "his Mary" and "Christian obligation." In "Lev" a religious vestige is the crucial element in the surprise ending: During the war Petja Žerebjakin used to cross himself ("according to a country custom") before attacking, so it is only natural for this ingrained habit to crop up in his moment of extreme stress. Of the many other aspects of post-Revolutionary *byt* in Zamjatin's novelle, some (like the men's strong reaction to Katja, the first militia-woman on the Nevskij Prospect, in "Lev") give an opportunity to narrate a humorous incident peculiar to the period; others (like the pock-marked Red Army guard who escorts the tsar's white elephant to the Moscow zoo in "Videnie") are not in themselves comic, but serve to establish a post-Revolutionary setting.

Thus, Zamjatin's comic portrayal of the post-Revolutionary philistine, which began in the transitional story "Iks," found expression in a series of ironic novelle which were very different structurally and thematically from the rest of his later works. Lacking the intensity of a Gogolean "laughter through tears," Zamjatin's mildly ironic presentation of the human comedy in these novelle differed significantly from the stark and poignant depiction of human tragedy in "Ela" and "Navodnenie."

A sense of tragic fate, heightened by its inexorability, pervades the two major stories of Zamjatin's late period. Human aspirations and emotions are of central importance in these stories, where they are expressed tersely, but powerfully, in his straightforward presentation of simple plots. Unlike the unexpected endings of the novelle, the denouements of both "Ela" and "Navodnenie" are the logical consequences of what has occurred, for which the reader is well prepared and of which he has been symbolically forewarned. The tragic mood is unrelieved by comic moments, the action is not based on an anecdotal incident, and there is no play with literary forms or conventions. The narration, unlike that in the early and middle works, has a simple, unobtrusive literary style; there is no intermediate narrator, and the author himself is almost totally inconspicuous.

Numerous features of "Ela" recall Zamjatin's two earlier works about the distant North, "Afrika" and "Sever," and all three are appropriately grouped together in the fourth volume of his collected works. The protagonist of "Ela," a fisherman named Cybin who lives on Deer Island near the Murmansk Coast, has one ambition: to possess his own fishing boat. For almost three years he and his wife direct all their efforts toward amassing enough money for a Norwegian yawl, the symbol of a wonderful new life. As a hired hand for Klaus Ostrand, Cybin finally earns enough to purchase his boat in Murmansk. However, as Klaus tows Cybin's unballasted yawl home to Deer Island, a storm breaks, and the men are forced to cut the towline and abandon it. At the final moment Cybin leaps onto his new yawl and perishes with it. Like Volkov ("Afrika") and Marej ("Sever"), Cybin is a dreamer who seeks a better life. For each of the dreamers, the vision is embodied in a concrete object — for Volkov, distant Africa; for Marej, a huge beacon; for Cybin, a graceful yawl. Each of the dreamers meets with defeat: Volkov dies before attaining his goal and discovering it to be an illusion; Marej's beacon is also an illusion, and he loses his wife Pel'ka in his pursuit of it; and Cybin, too, in the quest for a yawl, loses first his wife Anna (her health is broken) and ultimately his own life. In all three instances the hero rejects the present in the pursuit of future happiness and finds only death. Zamjatin does not deny human aspiration to an ideal, but he does reject the naïve hope that the attainment of a simple, material goal will automatically lead to a new and wonderful life. In espousing progress (unending movement forward) and in assailing all manifestations of philistinism, Zamjatin does not forget that man is human, that man is mortal, and that he should live to his fullest capacity. And a very important part of life for Zamjatin is, as we have seen, the consummation of a love rooted in strong, physical desire. In this respect, the dreamers of Zamjatin's northern stories have failed: Childless Anna's withered breasts, once filled to brimming, are mute testimony of a lack of love that cannot be set right by the purchase of a yawl; passionate Pel'ka's infidelity is a direct consequence of Marej's disinterest in her; and Volkov's disillusionment with Jausta stems from her philistine attitude that a clean floor is of more immediate importance than warm love (S.S. IV, 75).

Thematic parallels and similarities in the northern stories indicate that Zamjatin's world view did not change significantly in the decade following the Revolution. Stylistic and structural differences in the three works (even though "Afrika" and "Sever" are not quite typical of their periods) are significant in themselves, as well as being illustrative of Zamjatin's literary evolution. Common to all three is the author's use of subjective impressions in his imagery and characterizations. The protagonists are described simply and laconically: Volkov has huge shoulders, ingenuous eyes, and a crocklike cropped head; Marej is huge and broad, with the blue eyes of a child; and Cybin is solid and swarthy, with white teeth and hands like weights. The basic, impressionistic characterization accompanies the protagonist in varying forms throughout the work. The use of imagery, however, is considerably more extensive in "Sever" than in the early and late works; and in combination with ellipsis the imagery creates a staccato effect that is typical primarily of Zamjatin's middle period:

> Na Ivana-Kupalu — žaryn'. Bereg, krasnyj kamen' granit, stal gorjačij, snizu podnimalas' temnaja zemljanaja krov'. Ostryj, nesterpimyj zapax ptic, treski, gnijuščix zelenyx morskix kosm. Skvoz' tuman — ogromnoe rumjanoe solnce, vse bliže. I navstreču — nalivaetsja more temnoj krov'ju, navstreču — v more nabuxajut, dybjatsja belye grudi.
>
> Noč'. Vyxod iz buxty meždu dvux skal — okoško. Ot ljubopyt-

> nogo glaza okoško zavešeno beloj štoroj — belyj, šerstjanoj tuman. I tol'ko vidno: tam, za štoroj, proisxodit krasnoe.* (S.S. IV, 17.)

Compare the profusion of impressionistic images, the frequency of ellipsis, the paucity of active verbs, and the staccato rhythm in the above passage with the opening lines of "Ela," written twelve years later:

> Dvuxnedel'nye tuči vdrug rasporolo kak nožom, i iz prorexi aršinami, saženjami polezlo sinee. K polnoči solnce uže bilo nad Olen'im ostrovom vovsju, tjaželo, medlenno blestel okean, kričali čajki. Oni padali v vodu, vzletali, padali, ix stanovilos' vse bol'še, oni sklikali vsex, otovsjudu.† (S.S. IV, 89.)

The second passage reads much more smoothly, and it has many active verbs. The initial audacious image of blue issuing forth from a tear in the clouds is enhanced by the smooth flow of the rest of the passage and by the absence of other distracting images. The more sparing use of impressionistic imagery, which sets off the individual image by placing it amid relatively neutral prose, is a hallmark of Zamjatin's major prose works of the late period. To cite another example, this time from his novel *Bič Božij*:

> It was already the end of winter; the snow no longer squeaked; vapor rose from the horses. They made their way to a river, which was Atil; it was also called Ra, and still later — the Volga. Daybreak was near. The dawn hung in the sky in shreds, like pieces of raw meat, and dropped red drops on the snow. Mud'jug's wife began to scream so much that everyone stopped. (PiR, 261.)

* "On the day of Ivan Kupala — a heat wave. The shore, red granite rock, became hot; from below dark, earthy blood was rising. The pungent, unbearable odor of birds, of cod, of rotting, green, matted sea-hair. Through the fog — a huge, ruddy sun, closer and closer. And in greeting — dark blood suffuses the sea, in greeting — white breasts swell and rear up from the sea.

"Night. The mouth of the bay between two cliffs — a window. The window is curtained to the curious eye by a white shade — white, woolly fog. And one can see: there, behind the shade, something red is happening."

† "The two-week-old overcast was suddenly ripped as by a knife, and from the tear began to crawl yards and yards of blue. By midnight the sun was already blazing away above Deer Island; the ocean shone heavily, slowly; the gulls cried. They fell into the water, flew up, fell, they became more and more numerous, they beckoned everyone, from everywhere."

Impressionistic imagery was perhaps the major distinguishing feature of Zamjatin's prose throughout his career. Laconic characterization of his personages by means of epithetic, fixed images is as typical of *Bič Božij* (Attila's lowered brow and coarse forelocks protruding like horns) as it is of his early and middle works. However, Zamjatin's use of this device varied; it became more consistent and widespread only toward the end of the early period ("Afrika"); and in such middle works as "Ostrovitjane," "Lovec čelovekov," and *My*, the number of fixed images associated with a single personage is greater and each image recurs more often than in the works of the early and late periods. Consider, for example, the rich imagery associated with Mr. Craggs ("Lovec čelovekov"), who is characterized by the fixed images of a cast-iron monument on a pedestal, lowered lids, piercing eyes, a rat, and padding paws. The use of actional images, whether as comparison (Kemble-tractor) or as attribute (Mrs. Dewly's pince-nez, Mrs. Laurie's veil), is characteristic primarily of the middle works and occurs only sporadically in the early works (Marusja's wrinkles near her lips) and rarely in the late works. The same is true of his large, derivational image systems which assume paramount importance at the expense of actional elements in the middle period: for example, the Petersburg building that is a ship at sea ("Mamaj") and the Petersburg apartment that is a cave ("Peščera"). On the other hand, the appearance of audacious isolated images, like those from "Ela" and *Bič Božij* cited above, is an innovation in Zamjatin's use of imagery which distinguishes his late works.

The use of symbolism also underwent considerable modification during Zamjatin's literary evolution. In his early works there is no symbolism, in the strict sense of the word, although Zamjatin did attempt to use the grotesque to create a symbolic synthesis of the significant features in his characters. In addition, the closing paragraphs of his early tales are generalizations about the preceding action, which attempt to endow the works with some symbolic significance. A different form of symbolism is introduced in the middle works, where certain objects and colors symbolize specific elements in the author's world view. Thus, the sun repeatedly serves as a source of energy, revolution, and passion, while natural vegetation, as a recipient of this life-giving energy, symbolizes free, natural, unrestricted growth and serves as a background for the development of natural, passionate love, the antipode of philistine rationality. Red is frequently symbolic of passion and revolution; golds and yellows, of the life-giving force, of passion, of the sun; pinks, of human flesh, of human warmth; green, of vegetation, of disorderly natural growth, of life. Sometimes blue, the color of eyes and of the sky, is associated with clarity and ingenuousness, yet it also symbolizes coldness, rationality, and lack of passion. And white and black are used primarily as visual contrast. Applied consistently in the major works of the middle period ("Ostrovitjane," "Lovec čelovekov," "Sever," and *My*), only remnants of this type of symbolism can be seen in the late works. There, on the whole, it has been superseded by a primarily aesthetic symbolism which, lacking the philosophical implications of the symbolism of the middle period, is subservient to the plot.

Symbolic of Cybin's hopes for a new and better life, the yawl (significantly painted bright yellow) is likened to a smartly dressed bride (S.S. IV, 102). The owner of the yawl, an attractive blonde, blue-eyed Norwegian widow, has two features — dark summer shadows beneath her eyes (S.S. IV, 102) and cold hands (S.S. IV, 103) — which hint that she is a death symbol. After Cybin throws another would-be purchaser off the yawl, the woman looks at him, "perhaps sees everything," (S.S. IV, 107), and agrees to sell it to him:

> Then everyone drank again in the crew's quarters, and Cybin drank too. It seemed to him that he understood everything that the woman said in Norwegian. Klaus said: "She tells you that now the yawl is yours, and that in exchange she will take you."
>
> The Norwegian laughed and touched Cybin's cheek with her hand. Her hand was cold, like a corpse's; Cybin moved away, got up. (S.S. IV, 107.)

The previous implicit hint of death now becomes explicit, and, as Cybin leaves the yawl, the woman stands outlined against a clear, bright sky that has a slightly noticeable line on the horizon. That evening, as Cybin and his fellow fishermen sail away with the yawl in tow, he sees a dog nuzzle the woman's hand, only to tuck its tail suddenly between its legs and run off barking, which reminds him of her cold hands (S.S. IV, 109). At the same time he notices that the yawl has no ballast (a bad thing, should the wind arise); and, as they put out to sea, the wind shifts, and the scarcely noticeable line on the horizon rapidly and fatefully grows into a storm. As the clouds gather, Cybin once again remembers the woman with her cold hands (S.S. IV, 112), and when the yawl is cut loose, he imagines that she is calling to him from it. His leap aboard brings him together forever with his yawl — his bride — and death. Throughout the story, the woman with the cold hands symbolizes death and projects a grim foreboding of the story's tragic ending.

In "Navodnenie" Zamjatin returns to a theme he treated sixteen years earlier in "Črevo": a woman's basic, physiological need to bear a child. Both the similarities and the differences in the two treatments are striking. Motivated by the instinctual desire to conceive a child, both heroines, without premeditation, commit axe murders and bury their victims in the earth. Neither heroine is able to find peace until she confesses her crime. In other respects, the stories differ considerably. Although Petra discovers his wife Afim'ja's infidelity ("Črevo"), she continues her trysts until she becomes pregnant and then gives way to introspection and dreams of suckling her child. When Petra's beatings cause a miscarriage, she kills him. The murder is an act of vengeance unleashed by his frustration of her need to bear a child. In "Navodnenie" Trofim Ivanyč and Sof'ja are still childless after thirteen years of marriage, but in this case the fault is with the wife, Sof'ja, who cannot fully unfold. To fill the void in their lives, they take in an orphan girl, Gan'ka. When she matures, Trofim Ivanyč openly leaves his wife at night to stay in the kitchen with Gan'ka. This situation continues all summer, until at last Sof'ja murders Gan'ka. The murder is motivated not so much by vengeance as by Sof'ja's desperate, subconscious hope that Gan'ka's death will bring Trofim Ivanyč back to her. The murder effects a psychological catharsis which enables Sof'ja to conceive a child. After the birth of her baby girl, she no longer can bear her guilt, and, half-delirious from a postnatal fever, she confesses her crime.

In some respects, these two stories examine the problem posed by Dostoevskij in *Crime and Punishment*, for in them all the punishment is the mental anguish that follows the crime. Like Raskol'nikov, Afim'ja is cut off from humanity and beset by hallucinations. Her confession is complete, and her suffering is recognized and respected by the villagers and the author (who likens her face to that of a holy icon). For both Afim'ja and Sof'ja, neither reason nor pride has marred the pacifying confession, as had been the case with Raskol'nikov. There is also a striking similarity between the murder scenes in "Navodnenie" and *Crime and Punishment*: having dispatched their victims with axes, both Sof'ja and Raskol'nikov stand with bated breath and watch the latch jiggling as somebody attempts to enter.[6] The similarity in detail is too great to have been accidental: quite probably Zamjatin borrowed this incident from Dostoevskij in order to intensify an extreme moment of tension.

The theme of death begetting life, which is the axis of "Navodnenie," is an artistic embodiment of Zamjatin's belief in permanent revolution. That idea had been applied by Zamjatin most frequently to human intellectual endeavor. In "Rasskaz o samom glavnom," however, Zamjatin applied the concept to life itself: the collision of a star with a planet destroys all existing life at the same time as the seeds of a new life are being sown (S.S. III, 260). And in "Navodnenie" the same philosophical concept underlies the story of a personal tragedy: the seed of new life — which is implanted in Sof'ja — is the direct result of the destruction of existing life — the murder of Gan'ka.

In stressing basic, instinctual human desires, "Črevo" and "Navodnenie" may be the most extreme expressions of Zamjatin's tendency toward primitivism. In dealing with the theme of conception, Zamjatin utilizes similar basic metaphors in both stories. In "Crevo" the womb is compared to the earth several times: "For her womb — like parched earth — awaits rain in order to give birth" (S.S. II, 175). And later, when Afim'ja returns to consciousness and learns of her miscarriage: "Afim'ja leaped from the bench, howled, not with her own womanish voice, but with that of an animal. And from her womb, empty, like a field pelted by hail on the eve of harvest, from her womb gushed blood" (S.S. II, 182).

The same is true in "Navodnenie," where Sof'ja's desire for

fertility is underlined by a symbolic description of the landscape at the outset of the story: "By day unceasingly the sun sped around the earth in birdlike circles. The earth lay bare. In the twilight the entire Smolensk Field steamed with vapor like a heated horse" (PiR, 216).

After the murder of Gan'ka, the earth image assumes double significance in that it also refers to Gan'ka's buried remains: "Her stomach was round, it was the earth. In the earth, deep down, visible to none, lay Gan'ka, and in the earth, visible to none, burrowed the white roots of seeds" (PiR, 235). It is as if the burial of Gan'ka results in the planting of a seed in Sof'ja's womb—from death comes life. And after her delivery, when Sof'ja first suckles her child: "Sof'ja felt how warm tears, warm milk, warm blood flowed from her; all of her unfolded and from her flowed juices. She lay warm, blissful, moist, restful, like the earth—all her life she had lived for the sake of this moment; everything had been for this" (PiR, 237). This image restates the thesis previously developed in "Rasskaz o samom glavnom": that everything has its purpose, and that life is the fulfillment of this purpose, whatever it may be.

The image of Smolensk Field steaming like a heated horse initiates the paragraph in which Gan'ka is introduced. The neighbor boys have been chasing Gan'ka around the yard, and as she runs up to Sof'ja, "Gan'ka exuded heat, she was breathing quickly, and you could see how her upper lip with a small black mole was quivering" (PiR, 217). Sof'ja realizes that Gan'ka is young enough to be her daughter, yet she feels an instinctive hatred for her: "Suddenly something contracted in her stomach, it rose up to her heart; Gan'ka's scent and her scarcely quivering lip with the black mole became hateful to Sof'ja" (PiR, 217).* From the very beginning there is a dual relationship between Sof'ja and Gan'ka. By taking in the orphan girl, Sof'ja sublimates her mother instinct; but she also introduces a potential sexual rival into the household, one who possesses youth and

* The image of revulsion as a primordial sensation arising from the depths of her viscera occurred three times: when she first met Gan'ka in the yard, when she first learned of her intimacy with Trofim Ivanyč, and when she killed her (PiR, 217, 222, 227–228).

warmth. Sof'ja's instinctive, primitive hatred of Gan'ka, suggested by the image of something rising from her stomach, stems from her subconscious recognition that Gan'ka has the ardor which she lacks (symbolized by Gan'ka's scent and the steaming vapor of the earth). Sof'ja's revulsion at Gan'ka's scent is of paramount importance, for it triggers the murder:

> Gan'ka became heated from [cutting kindling]; Sof'ja was enveloped by the hot, sweet scent of her sweat — she must smell just like this at night.
>
> No sooner had Sof'ja inhaled this scent, than something rose up in her, from below, from her stomach. It poured over her heart, flooding her. She wanted to clutch at something, but she was carried along just as the logs and cat on the table had been carried along the street during the flood. (PiR, 227–228.)

Both the murder and Sof'ja's hatred are shown without mitigation as the products of raw, primitive emotion. Herein lies the artistic strength of the story and the reason for its disfavor among Soviet critics. They objected vehemently to Zamjatin's primitivism and called "Navodnenie" an attack on man himself and — since Trofim Ivanyč belongs to the working class — "a most vile lampoon on the socialist epoch and its creators." [7]

Whatever the thematic similarities between "Čerevo" and "Navodnenie," stylistic differences reflect the years that separate the two stories. As is the case with most of the early stories, "Čerevo" lacks developed symbolism, having only an embryonic fixed-image system (drooling Vasjatka; the dark, icon face of Petrovna). By comparison, "Navodnenie" displays a well developed system of images that frequently are symbolic. Each central character is accompanied by a set of fixed, descriptive images. Trofim Ivanyč's swarthy features and white teeth (like the keys of an accordion) resemble those of a gypsy, and his broad build and short legs give the impression that he is deeply rooted in the ground. Continually compared to a cat, Gan'ka is appropriately endowed with green cat-eyes, as well as with blonde bangs and a black mole on her lip. The cat comparison is strengthened by the subconscious awareness of the similarity by some of the characters in the story: "Turning slowly, somebody's table floated by [in the flood]. On it sat a white cat with red spots; her mouth was open — she must have been mewing.

Not calling Gan'ka by name, Sof'ja thought of her; her heart began to pound" (PiR, 224).

Sof'ja, her movements, and the movements of her heart are continually compared to a bird. The choice of bird and cat motifs underlines the hostile relationship between Gan'ka and Sof'ja:

> Only sometimes [Gan'ka] would slowly, fixedly turn her green eyes on Sof'ja, obviously thinking about her, but what? Staring into your face like this, cats look and think about something all their own—and suddenly you become terrified of their green eyes, of their incomprehensible, alien, cat thoughts. Sof'ja would don an overblouse, a thick kerchief, and go somewhere—to the store, to church, or simply into the darkness of Malyj Prospect—only to escape being alone with Gan'ka. (PiR, 219.)

Her lips, pressed together tightly as if forever, represent the second major leitmotiv accompanying Sof'ja throughout the story. Sof'ja's lips are indicative of her unsuccessful sexual relationships with her husband and her inability to conceive a child. With Gan'ka's murder and her great emotional relief, Sof'ja's lips—all of her—open for the first time in her life (PiR, 232). Shortly after, however, a change occurs: At night Sof'ja sleeps poorly, her eyes become shadowed and sunken, and she grows absentminded and clumsy. These symptoms and her parted lips are given a dual interpretation—pregnancy and her need to confess her crime:

> "Over the edge . . . ," Sof'ja repeated in confusion; her lips, which were always compressed, were open as at night. She looked at Trofim Ivanyč; it seemed that she wanted to say something. "Well, what?" he asked. She turned away. "Is it something . . . about her . . . about Gan'ka?" She heard his voice, forced through white, gypsy teeth. She did not answer. (PiR, 234.)

In answer to Trofim Ivanyč's urging, Sof'ja reveals that she is pregnant, thus confirming one of the two possible interpretations. The other still remains and is realized only in the closing sentence of the story after Sof'ja has confessed: "She slept breathing evenly, quietly, blissfully; her lips were widely parted" (PiR, 241).

The image of the lips is closely bound with the story's symbolic structure; at the beginning, the author describes a dream:

> At night . . . Sof'ja ran out into the street. She knew that it was the end, that she could not go back. Sobbing violently and loudly, she ran to Smolensk Field where someone was lighting matches in the darkness. She tripped, fell, her hands touched something wet. It grew light, she saw that her hands were bloody. (PiR, 216.)

At first this dream is accompanied by her menses and represents a monthly trial at which she is found guilty. But later, every time Trofim Ivanyč feigns sleep in response to her advances, "Sof'ja again dreamed that in the darkness she ran alone to Smolensk Field; she screamed aloud, and in the morning her lips were compressed even more tightly" (PiR, 216). The recurrent nightmare then becomes reality:

> She was alone on Smolensk Field; it was growing dark rapidly. She dug a hole and dumped everything there that was in her bag.
>
> When it was completely dark, she brought a full bag again, covered the hole, and went home. Under her feet was black, uneven, swollen earth; the wind lashed her legs with cold, taut towels. Sof'ja tripped. She fell, stuck her hand in something wet, and went on with her wet hand—she feared wiping it. Far away, perhaps on the shore, a light kept going on and off, but perhaps it was very close — someone lighting a cigarette in the wind. (PiR, 229.)

All of the essential elements of the dream recur in reality: the place (Smolensk Field), darkness, tripping and falling, hands sticking in something wet (blood in the dream, the fear of blood in reality), and winking lights. The symbolic connection between Sof'ja's conception and Gan'ka's murder is indicated in the earth-womb imagery discussed earlier and by the circumstances of the confession (in Sof'ja's postnatal delirium, the confession symbolically becomes a second birth) (PiR, 239).

The old, deserted house on Malyj Prospect is another example of Zamjatin's prophetic symbolism, which foretells Sof'ja's pregnancy. The empty house reminds Sof'ja of her barrenness, and she always passes it with averted eyes. Yet, one day childrens' voices resound in the house, and Sof'ja sees a gypsy boy inside, who resembles Trofim Ivanyč. The house has come alive and with it, Sof'ja's hopes of bearing a child.

As the title indicates the central image is the flood, occurring on two planes. On one level, it is literally the rise and fall of the Neva River. On another, it symbolizes the ebb and flow of human passions, which rise and fall with the Neva. Having learned of Trofim Ivanyč's intimacy with Gan'ka, Sof'ja lives through the long, hot summer in a somnambulistic trance. With the first severe autumn rainstorm, Sof'ja, her husband, and Gan'ka are forced by the flooding waters of the Neva to live upstairs in Pelageja's apartment for three weeks. The proximity of others forces Trofim Ivanyč to discontinue his liaison, and tension mounts. When the waters recede, they return to their old quarters. That night another storm strikes, the river floods, and Sof'ja kills Gan'ka. With Gan'ka's disappearance, Trofim Ivanyč's lust, pent up for three weeks, has no release other than Sof'ja; to spite Gan'ka, he turns to his wife. Emotions and flood waters subside until spring. As Sof'ja's confinement draws near, the Neva again begins to flood, reminding her of that fateful autumn night. In her postnatal delirium, Sof'ja suffers from hallucinations in which she sees Gan'ka and, hearing the howling wind and the booming cannon warning of the spring flood, she hysterically confesses her crime. Zamjatin considered the flood to be an integrating image like the cave ("Peščera") and the ship ("Mamaj").[8] The imagery of "Navodnenie," however, differs from that of "Peščera" and "Mamaj" in two important respects: First, it is more subtle, as it exists on both the real and the symbolic planes. Second, the image of the flood, although it is central to the work, does not generate a vast system of derivative images which overwhelms the plot and the psychological conflicts, as the cave and the ship did. In "Navodnenie" the psychological conflict and the actional elements are clearly delineated, and the integrating image emphasizes, rather than detracts from them.

In editing and polishing his writings for his four-volume 1929 *Collected Works*, Zamjatin looked back over his literary evolution, and he wrote:

> All the complexities through which I had passed turned out to be necessary in order to achieve simplicity ("Ela," "Navodnenie"). Simplicity of form is natural for our epoch, but the right to this simplicity must be earned. Any other simplicity is worse than thievery; it contains disrespect for the reader: "Why should I waste time, subtilize — they'll swallow it as is."[9]

By complexities Zamjatin probably was referring to the elaborate imagery and stylistic instrumentation of his middle works. Although the prolific alliteration and consonance, so striking in such middle works as "Lovec čelovekov," and "Ostrovitjane," is not as obvious later, Zamjatin still was very much concerned with subtle instrumentation and sought to correlate vowel phonic patterns with phrasal semantics. Adopting Belyj's term of "phrasal breathing," Zamjatin defined inhalation as an increase in vowel height (*u-o-e-a-y-i*) and exhalation as the drop in height from *i* to the closed, dull *u*.[10] Zamjatin was not a linguist, and his suggested vowel arrangement was patterned according to the place of articulation horizontally (from back to front with the reversal of *e* and *a*) and not vertically (low to high) as he had implied, although it was significant that his pattern also reflected a shift from rounded to unrounded vowels. In a phrase such as "Sof'ja č*u*vstvovala, kak iz nee tek*u*t t*e*plye sl*e*zy, t*e*plaja kr*o*v' . . . ona lež*a*la t*e*plaja, blažennaja, vl*a*žnaja kak zemlj*a* . . . ," the general phonic shift from the rounded back vowel /*u*/ through /*o*/ to the broad open /*a*/ correspond to Sof'ja's inner unfolding, her psychological liberation.

In comparison with the middle works, the style of "Ela," "Navodnenie," and *Bič Božij* indeed seems lucidly simple and represents, to use a term coined by Mirsky, the most transparent prose written by Zamjatin. The highly polished, unconstrained, conversational narrative marks the successful fulfillment of Zamjatin's thesis that the prose narrative should be a stylized approximation of the living, spoken idiom. Unlike most of the early works, these works do not suggest the presence of a narrator other than the author; and, unlike most of the transitional works they do not contain passages where the author himself enters as a narrator. Zamjatin's late prose is characterized by lexical purity and syntactical simplicity. Although he approximated a conversational language, Zamjatin was careful to exclude words that were dialectal, archaic, substandard, or too colloquial; and therefore his final lexicon contrasted sharply with that of his early works, which abounded in dialectal and substandard expressions. The narrative in "Afrika," for example, contains many dialectal expressions, such as *kolguška*, *ražyj, zakomariny, and plemjaš*; archaic forms that may have been preserved in particular regions, such as *načetnik* and *ljasy* (fishnets); and such substandard words as *ixnij, inda*, and *ètak*. By contrast, the language in "Ela" has been purged of all such expressions. The feeling of the specific region — Russia's arctic shore — is created in "Ela" by the description of fishing activities and by the use of specific terms, such as *ela, bot, karabas, šljupka*, and *murmanka*, which are perfectly acceptable in the literary Russian language. Although such colloquial expressions as *vovsju* and *kuda men'še* do appear occasionally, they are typical of conversational Russian and would not be considered substandard. Sentences in these late works are short and frequently are strung together with commas or the conjunction *and*:

> From the steppes came the ground squirrels. There was a multitude of them, they were fat, they were roasted over open fires and eaten. Then the people, one after another, began to swell, to turn black, to die. Then Mud'jug understood that they must abandon everything and leave this place, so that everyone would not die. (PiR, 261.) (For other examples, see passages on p. 192.)

Unlike the syntax of the early works, which is modeled after a folksy, provincial narrative characterized by diminutives, inversions (noun-adjective, verb in first position), repetition, and parallelism, and unlike the staccato, elliptical syntax of the middle period, the syntax of the late period resembles the conversational narrative of a literary Russian. As such, the emphasis is not on the verbal technique itself (as was the case — in differing ways — in the early and middle works), but toward the narration of events in a highly polished narrative prose, rather than a striking *skaz*.[11]

The unfinished novel *Bič Božij*, Zamjatin's major prose work of the late period, was conceived as a massive canvas depicting the struggle between a dying Rome and the barbaric hordes of the East. Zamjatin began work on the novel, originally planned as a tale, in the autumn of 1924; but then he decided to write a play on the subject, which he completed in 1927.[12] In 1928, if one can rely on the dates in the posthumous editions, he resumed work on the novel in earnest, but by 1935 he had completed only the first seven chapters. In 1936 he spoke of how clearly he visualized the next section of the novel and how quickly he hoped to write it, but death cut the project short.[13] A ten-page summary of the novel (about one hundred and seventy-five lines), preserved among his papers, indicates that Zamjatin had not only conceived the next section clearly, but had thought the whole novel through to the end.[14] The first twenty lines summarize the action of the seven completed chapters, which indicates that the novel was to have been by far the most ambitious and extensive of Zamjatin's works.

The novel opens with two pages describing the frenzy that has seized Europe in the wake of widespread natural disasters like earthquakes and tidal waves. The description is essentially timeless, for nothing in it indicates whether the events took place last year or centuries ago. Thus, Zamjatin sought to emphasize the universality of human response to a given situation and to underline the importance of historical parallels; for, in the struggle between Attila and Rome, Zamjatin saw a similarity to the twentieth-century conflict between Russia and the West.[15] The natural tidal wave in the novel presages the human tidal wave that is to flood in from the East and engulf Rome. Having shifted to the particular, Zamjatin stresses the softness of Rome and its legions, and then begins the narrative proper on the eve of the entry of Uld (prince of the Huns) into Rome on April 12, 405. The decay of the Romans, symbolized by the softness of their language (they say "Ul'd" instead of "Uld"), is also reflected in the resistance of the hungry masses to the government agents, by the absence of the emperor, and by the empty ceremonial pomp which greets the triumphant Uld. In sharp contrast stands the rough barbarian Uld, who reeks of sweat and leather and prefers his horse to a gilded triumphal chariot. His entry into the city is marred by a strange incident: when he speaks to a young hostage prince from his own country and places his hand on him, the youth savagely bites Uld, drawing blood. That youth is Attila. The onlookers, as well as the reader, wonder about the meaning of the event. The remaining six chapters are a flashback showing Attila's birth, several childhood incidents, and his tutelage in Rome up to the day of Uld's arrival. Having returned to the point of the narrative, Zamjatin laconically tells of Attila's brief confinement in prison, his release, and his return home. Interwoven with the description of Attila's Roman tutelage is the story of a young Byzantine student, Priscus of Panium (?–471),* who eventually becomes the historiographer of the struggle between Rome and Attila. The unwritten portion of the novel was to alternate between entries from Priscus' diary and the third-person, authorial narrative used in the first seven chapters.

The central theme, the conflict between the Roman Empire and the barbarian hordes, is clearly set forth in the novel's first chapter and is sustained throughout the work, right up to Priscus' closing words: "For our hands already resemble the hands of old men that have lost their strength, and other nations hold our fate in their hands" (PiR, 316). The emperor Honorius Flavius (384–423) is a weak, spineless man who is concerned more about the fate of his pet rooster than the fate of Rome; and the reins of the government are held by his strong-willed, fiery sister Aelia Galla Placidia (?–450). In some respects, Placidia resembles the passionate heroines of Zamjatin's middle works (golden-red hair, green eyes, sharp teeth, and a need for sensual gratification). But, unlike them, she has a definite air of decadence: she is her brother's mistress and seeks out entertainment amongst the dregs of society in Rome's dingiest pubs. Not a rebellion against the philistine environment, her behavior represents the moral decline which is, in part, a consequence of the recent natural disasters that augured Rome's fall. Philosophically, the conflict between Rome and the Huns is one more expression of Zamjatin's conception of never-ending revolution, whose universal nature is emphasized by the historical parallelism.

The novel reveals no new tendencies in Zamjatin's artistic techniques. The style is essentially that of "Ela" and "Navodnenie," as has been indicated. The continued use of prognostic symbolism is, perhaps, especially appropriate to this work, which deals with the Roman Empire where augury was highly esteemed. For example, the transparent symbolism of a caged

* English forms of Latin names, in preference to Russian forms, have been used here in discussing *Bič Božij*: Prisk is rendered as Priscus, Gonorij as Honorius, Placidija as Placidia, Evzapij as Eusebius, and Atilla as Attila.

wolf (*volčij* is one of Attila's recurrent attributes) that dies attacking the Emperor's retinue is probably intended as a fore-warning of Attila's own fate, as is Placidia's momentary thought as the wolf leaps out, "better this, than to be killed sometime by your soldiers" (PiR, 301). The broad scope of the work calls for certain formal features that are not typical of Zamjatin's shorter works, like the chronological displacement of the narrative (the extensive flashback) and the greater development of characters by descriptions of incidents from Attila's childhood and of Priscus' tutelage under Eusebius and Bass. In this respect, the novel shows a return to features of nineteenth-century Russian Realism. The extensive use of the "device of making strange" in young Attila's first impressions of Rome is more in the manner of Lev Tolstoj's *War and Peace* and lacks the parodistic elements that accompany it in some of Zamjatin's transitional stories.

Although Zamjatin's late works include two distinct genres — the story and the novel — major structural, thematic, and stylistic considerations require a threefold distinction — novelle (or short stories), longer stories, and the unfinished novel. The novelle, essentially anecdotal in nature, are characterized by brevity, actional stress, surprise endings, sustained irony (often based on the incongruity of old habits in the new environment), and the parody of literary conventions. The tendency toward dynamic plots and literary parody continues a trend already apparent in the transitional works, which probably shows the influence of the works of O. Henry and other Western writers. The two longer stories "Ela" and "Navodnenie" lack the elements of parody, comedy, and incongruity and are essentially psychological studies of human tragedy. They present variations on themes already treated in the early and middle works: never-ending revolution, the dreamer's search for a better life, and the importance of sexual fulfillment and procreation. The theme of never-ending revolution, of course, also is central to *Bič Božij*. Stylistically the prose of the late works shows a turn to simplicity. The late style is distinct from that of the preceding periods in its use of fixed, impressionistic imagery which does not spawn the extensive derivate systems typical of the middle works; in its use of isolated images; in its prognostic symbolism; and in its simple, conversational narrative. But perhaps the most significant distinction of all is the polarization of human comedy and human tragedy, the former residing in the novelle and the latter in the three major works.

Notes

Notes

INTRODUCTION

[1] [592], 15.

[2] [590], 76, 300.

[3] [396] and [611], respectively.

[4] [427].

[5] See, for example, [513], 62; [687], 212; and [611], 232.

[6] M. Kuznecov, [611], 232–233.

[7] [502], 83.

[8] [226].

[9] [227].

[10] There seems to be an increased interest about Zamjatin among Czech scholars, which in time could lead to his partial rehabilitation. In [334], 36, František Bráblík has pointed out the error of calling Zamjatin a White émigré, while more recently Miroslav Drozda, who edited the Czech translation of the three-volume Soviet *History of Soviet Russian Literature*, has called for the publication of Zamjatin's *My* (see [356]).

CHAPTER 1 / EARLY YEARS, 1884–1917

Epigraph: [177a], 15.

[1] "Dlja sbornika o knige," [38], 257.

[2] "Zakulisy," [38], 267.

[3] "L. Andreev," [38], 53–56.

[4] [166], 21. The rather free rendering of the Russian word *texnika* by "shipbuilding" was dictated both by style (the English words technics and technology are amorphous and reduce the sharpness of

the contrast) and by reference to Zamjatin's own English paraphrase of this same idea when interviewed in 1932 [434].

[5] Although "Odin" [41] was dated 1907 when published in *Obrazovanie*, No. 11 (Nov. 1908), 17–48, in two autobiographies, [177] and [179], 15, Zamjatin stated that it was written in 1908.

[6] In *Tjur'my i ssylki* [597], 42, Ivanov-Razumnik stated that Zamjatin had been a Party member "during his student years." In a letter to me dated December 9, 1962, Mme L. N. Zamiatine cited 1907 to 1908 as the time when Zamjatin had "ceased being a Bolshevik."

[7] In [166], 25, Zamjatin lists ten icebreakers and claims that "there were traces of my work in each of them," but in two different interviews in 1932 ([434], 9, and [404], 1), he claimed credit for only six.

[8] "Postanovlenie SPB Komiteta po delam pečati o naloženii aresta na povest' 'Na kuklíčkax' (žurnal *Zavety* No. 3, 1914 g.)," quoted in [300], 74.

[9] [626], 236. No. 3 is available at the New York Public Library, while the British Museum has a copy of No. 3a.

[10] All twenty of Zamjatin's fables were published in [17], but most had appeared earlier (1916–1918) in newspapers and journals. The 1929 four-volume edition of Zamjatin's collected works indicated that six fables ("Bog," "D'jaček," "Drjan'-mal'čiška," "Kartinki," "Angel Dormidon," "Petr Petrovič") were written in 1915–1916. Of these, the first four were published in 1916, and "Angel Dormidon" in 1918; I have been unable to determine the place of first publication for "Petr Petrovič." See [93]–[112].

[11] [777a].

CHAPTER 2 / MAN OF LETTERS, 1917–1929

Epigraph: A sentence from Ivanov-Razumnik's foreword in *Skify*, I (Petrograd, 1917), used as an epigraph to Zamjatin's polemical article "Skify-li?" [123], 285.

[1] See [762e], 3, and [574], 237.

[2] [632], 117–118.

[3] [123], 285–293. Zamjatin's use of this pseudonym has been attested by three sources: I. F. Masonov, *Slovar' psevdonimov russkix pisatelej, učenyx i obščestvennyx dejatelej*, II (Moskva, 1957), 366; Mme L. N. Zamiatine in her letter to me, of March 12, 1963; and Jak. Braun, [335], 232.

[4] [123], 285.

[5] [123], 286.

[6] "L. Andreev," [38], 53.

[7] "Novaja russkaja proza," [38], 195–196.

[8] [597], 41–42.

[9] "Xudožnik i obščestvennost': k xudožestvennoj proze," ZA 4:176. One of Zamjatin's unpublished lectures, probably written in 1919.

[10] "Zavtra," [38], 173. According to the bibliography in *Lica* this essay first appeared in 1919 in the pamphlet *V zaščitu čeloveka* (Peterburg), yet the date of writing is given as 1919–1920! I cannot verify the publication, but the date of writing was, in all probability, 1919.

[11] "O literature, revoljucii, èntropii [i o pročem]," [38], 253.

[12] "Alexsandr Blok," [38], 16.

[13] "Zemlemer" was first published in January 1918 [57]. Although dated 1918 in later collections, it must have been written late in 1917, especially since Zamjatin claims to have rewritten it five times. See "Zakulisy," [38], 272.

[14] The complete lecture [164] was published in *Grani* from October to December 1956. Zamjatin's presence in Lebedjan' at that time was acknowledged in a report on the Second Congress on Education in the Tambov Province [684].

[15] [451], 430.

[16] Anon., "Utro pisatelej o Rossii," *Novaja žizn'*, No. 80 (Apr. 30, 1918), 4. The other information on the SDXL is from P. P. Širmakov's highly informative article "K istorii literaturno-xudožestvennyx ob'edinenij pervyx let sovetskoj vlasti; Sojuz dejatelej xudožestvennoj literatury (1918–1919 gody)," [694]. Although Širmakov cites N. Gumilev as the third organizing member of the SDXL, this could not have been true, since Gumilev left London for Russia only in April 1918, a month after the SDXL was formed (from Gleb Struve's Gumilev Archive).

[17] "Alexsandr Blok," [38], 18.

[18] Most of the information in this paragraph was taken from original documents of the period (especially Nos. 1, 2, 6, 9, 15, 19, and 21), edited by A. Mjasnikov [647].

[19] At first World Literature adopted six authors (Zamjatin, Gumilev, Šiškov, Grin, Čapygin, Mujžel') of SDXL's first series, three from its second series (Merežkovskij, Blok, Gippius), and added one of its own (Čukovskij). Compare [647], 80, with [694], 465.

[20] The titles and dates of publication are given in [647], 85–86. The fact that Zamjatin was the editor of these volumes was gleaned from *Knižnaja letopis'*, reviews, and from the catalog *Vsemirnaja literatura; katalog knig* (Moskva-Leningrad, 1927). For full information on works edited by Zamjatin, see [201]–[223].

[21] Apparently the studio's program (subjects, perhaps even lecture titles) was listed in Document No. 9, but unfortunately Mjasnikov chose to delete this portion in his publication, [647], 80.

[22] "Ja bojus'," [38], 188.

[23] [583], 108–110.

[24] [583], 108–110. Also see S. D. Baluxatyj's commentary to Gor'kij's article [537], and Zamjatin's essay "Aleksandr Blok," [38], 20–21.

[25] Baluxatyj states only that "the play was written later," implying that it was written after the Section of Historical Pageants had ceased to function. At least two sources indicate that the play was written in 1920. In *Russkaja kniga*, No. 1 (Jan. 1921), 22, it was stated that Zamjatin "had written a play, set in the time of the Spanish Inquisition, *Ogni svjatogo Dominika*, which, according to reports, was significant in thought and execution." In "Gor'kij sredi nas," [569], 158, Fedin quotes Gor'kij as saying: "Other plays have been written. For example, by Evgenij Zamjatin. Interesting, significant. His play will take its place in the cycle . . ." Judging from the context of the rest of the memoirs, this statement was made between March and July 1920 (see pp. 145, 179, and the intervening material).

[26] [38], 23.

[27] The activities of the House of Arts were chronicled in three anonymous articles: "Dom iskusstv," *Dom iskusstv*, No. 1 (1921), 68–69; "Dom iskusstv," *Dom iskusstv*, No. 2 (1921), 120; and "V Dome iskusstv," *Letopis' Doma literatorov*, No. 1/2 (Jan. 15, 1922), 6.

[28] The date is given incorrectly as December 13 in the "Xronika literaturnoj žizni," [592], 561. The opening date cited in *Dom iskusstv*, No. 1 (1921), 68, was December 19.

[29] Edited by A. E. Kaufman, the magazine appeared monthly for three years (1919–1921). It ceased publication with No. 3 (1922), a few months after the editor's death.

[30] *Periodičeskaja pečat' SSSR, 1917–1949*; *bibliografičeskij ukazatel'*: *žurnaly, trudy i bjulleteni po jazykoznaniju, literaturovedeniju, xudožestvennoj literature i iskusstvu* (Moskva, 1958), 21.

[31] Anon., "Dom literatorov," *Dom iskusstv*, No. 1 (1921), 71.

[32] Anon., "V sovetskoj Rossii; v Peterburge," *Rul'*, No. 315 (Nov. 30, 1921), 4. The evening was held in late October 1921.

[33] "Literaturnyj konkurs 'Doma literatorov'," *Vestnik literatury*, No. 9 (1920), 15, and [547].

[34] Anon., "V Dome literatorov," *Letopis' Doma literatorov*, No. 5/6 (Jan. 15, 1922), 6.

[35] The provisional directorate was chaired by Volynskij and included Čukovskij, A. Ganzen, Gor'kij, Ljubov' Gurevič, Valentin Ireckij, Evtixij Karpov, Nikolaj Volkovysskij, and Zamjatin. Anon., "Literaturnaja žizn'," *Kniga i revoljucija*, No. 1 (July 1920), 59–60. The permanent directorate elected in October consisted of eleven members (Karpov was removed, while Blok, Šiškov, and A. Tixonov were added). Anon., "Sojuz pisatelej," *Dom iskusstv*, No. 1 (1921),

73–74, and Anon., "Po Rossii; v Peterburge," *Pečat' i revoljucija*, No. 1 (May–July 1921), 180–181. The second issue of *Dom iskusstv* (1921), 121, reported that the directorate consisted of fourteen members, which included P. K. Guber, V. A. Mazurkevič, and V. B. Šklovskij in addition to the eleven mentioned above.

36 Anon., "V sovetskoj Rossii; v Sojuze pisatelej," *Rul'*, No. 351 (Jan. 12, 1922), 4. This article was reprinted (perhaps condensed) from a report in an issue of the *Letopis' Doma literatorov* which was unavailable to me.

37 [579], 183.

38 Anon., "Leningradskaja Federacija sovetskix pisatelej," *Na Literaturnom Postu*, No. 11/12 (June 1927), 111.

39 "E. Zamjatin [ešče] nedavno vozglavljal ego [VSP's] Leningradskij otdel." Taken from the lead article of the *Literaturnaja gazeta*, [522].

40 [582], 19.

41 Anon., "Literaturnaja studija Doma iskusstv," *Dom iskusstv*, No. 1 (1921), 70–71.

42 V. Šklovskij specifically mentions Nikitin and Zoščenko as Zamjatin's students at the House of Arts studio. See [697], 377. Kaverin was mentioned as a studio student in *Dom iskusstv*, No. 2 (1921), 120. Some of Zamjatin's lectures have been published in émigré journals; see [165], [168], and [169].

43 Fedin's "Sad" won the competition; Nikitin's "Podval" was second; and Kaverin's "Odinnadcataja aksioma," Lunc's "Vrata rajskie," B. Terleckij's "Step'," and Tixonov's "Sila" were third. The jury was V. A. Azov, A. V. Amfiteatrov, A. L. Volynskij, E. I. Zamjatin, V. Ja. Ireckij, A. M. Red'ko, and B. M. Èjxenbaum. See "Xronika literaturnoj žizni," [592], 581, and Anon., "Dom literatorov," *Dom iskusstv*, No. 2 (1921), 121.

44 Although no published version of this work is known to me, the story "Pirog" was mentioned as having been completed in Anon., "Sud'ba i raboty russkix pisatelej, učenyx i žurnalistov za 1918–1921 g.," *Russkaja kniga*, No. 4 (Apr. 1921), 16, and in A. Damanskaja's article [345], 19, where she stated that " 'Pirog' resurrects the somewhat crude, rich strokes of 'Uezdnoe,' but the theme is developed in a new manner and the device of unfolding the plot solely through dialogue is new."

45 "M. Gor'kij," [38], 88–89.

46 Nine of his books were published in 1922; eight more appeared in 1923.

47 Although the story was dated 1924 in Zamjatin's *Sobranie sočinenij*, it apparently was written during the summer of 1923, as the following reference to an "indecorous story" could not refer to any other known work: "During the summer and autumn I wrote two

stories. One is long . . . 'Rasskaz o samom glavnom.' The other is short but indecorous, similar to 'Erazm' (it was written in the summer, and, as is well known, the lecherous devil is powerful during hot spells)." Zamjatin's letter of November 13, 1923, to L. Lunc [181], 185.

[48] For a more detailed treatment of this mass deportation see G. Struve, [714], 18.

[49] N. Ocup's version was incorrect [430], 101: Zamjatin *was not* given a choice between remaining in or leaving the Soviet Union. At Mme L. N. Zamiatine's request both Ju. Terapiano and Ju. Annenkov published corrections of Ocup's version—the former in [490], 7, and the latter in [300], 76–77. It seems that Annenkov, however, embellished the truth by stating that Zamjatin, on the day of his release, was informed by Pil'njak of the abrogation of his exile. Mme Zamiatine has presented the facts in her letter to me of March 12, 1963: "Evgenij Ivanovič" learned from me of his reprieve from exile when I visited him in prison. When he was arrested, and for a short time thereafter, I unfortunately was not in Petersburg. I, of course, would not have permitted the 'reprieve.'"

[50] "My innocence and morality are guarded extremely well, and therefore I do not receive letters from abroad with regularity; I did not receive your first letter." Zamjatin's letter of November 13, 1923, to L. Lunc, [181], 185.

[51] Anon., "Literaturnye obščestva; Institut živogo slova v Petrograde," *Nakanune*; *literaturnaja nedelja*, No. 52 (Mar. 2, 1924), 5.

[52] Gržebin's idea of establishing World Literature abroad was presented by M. Gor'kij to V. V. Vorovskij, director of the RSFSR Gosizdat, in a letter dated May 21, 1919. On April 27, 1920, the Council of People's Commissars sanctioned in principle the publication of Russian books abroad, and Gržebin spent the summer making arrangements to establish a publishing house bearing his name. (Documents No. 8, 13, 14, and 19, [647].) The date of founding was taken from Anon., "Izdatel'stvo Z. I Gržebina," *Dom iskusstv*, No. 1 (1921), 73. Gržebin's first publications appeared late in 1921. Anon., "Izdatel'stvo Gržebina," *Russkaja kniga*, No. 1 (Jan. 1921), 9–10.

[53] Anon., "Sud'ba i rabota russkix pisatelej, učenyx i žurnalistov za 1918–1920 g.," *Russkaja kniga*, No. 1 (Jan. 1921), 22.

[54] Anon., "Izdatel'stvo 'Alkonost'," *Novaja russkaja kniga*, No. 6 (June 1922), 29–30.

[55] Anon., "Izdatel'stvo 'Epoxa'," *Novaja russkaja kniga*, No. 1 (Jan. 1922), 35.

[56] A list of the twelve titles appeared in [26], 95. See [220].

[57] The address of the editorial offices of *Russkij sovremennik* was given in No. 1 as Moxovaja, 36 (in the next three issues it was Moxo-

vaja, 37, but the telephone number remained the same). Zamjatin moved to Moxovaja, 36, in the summer of 1922 (*Novaja russkaja kniga*, No. 8 [Aug. 1922], 36), although he could have moved as early as 1921, which was the date cited by Mme L. N. Zamiatine in a letter of December 9, 1962, to me.

58 [34], 35–36.

59 [643], 440.

60 [26], 4 and 91.

61 Anon., "Po literaturnym kružkam," *Izvestija*, No. 34 (Feb. 11, 1925), 6.

62 [186].

63 [186]. A prose work titled "Bič Božij" was actually announced in *Russkij sovremennik*, No. 4 (1924), 288, as forthcoming in No. 5.

64 The date of writing "Attila" is subject to question. In A. III [179a], 19, Zamjatin said that he had completed it in 1928, but in an interview with a Czech journalist in October 1927, he said that the play was completed and had been accepted by the Petrograd [sic] Bolšoj Dramatic Theater. See [421]. A draft of the play probably had been completed and was circulated among literary acquaintances as early as 1926, since in [731] A. Zonin said that "Zamjatin has noticeably shifted to the left in his new play *Attila*," and the play was announced as completed in Anon., "Literaturnaja žizn' Leningrada," *Na literaturnom postu*, No. 3 (Feb. 5, 1927), 76.

65 [583], 110. The entire first act of Zamjatin's four-act tragedy concerns Attila's reception of the Roman envoys Vigila, Maksimin, and Prisk.

66 [421]. *Istorija goroda Glupova* was, presumably, first staged by Mejerhol'd and later played in several provincial theaters, among them, the Bakinskij rabočij teatr during the 1928–1929 season [624].

67 *Krasnaja gazeta* (večernij vypusk), July 31, 1928, *ZA* 6:167.

68 [434], 161.

69 [499], 102.

70 [527] and an unidentified Leningrad newspaper clipping "Moskva; slučaj na s"emke", in *ZA* 6:170.

71 A. Radakov, "Medved' ne vyderzal," *Smexač*, No. 30 (1927), 4, in *ZA* 6:174.

72 See the announcement of the premiere of *Severnaja ljubov'* in *Pravda*, No. 47 (Feb. 24, 1928), 6.

73 [187].

74 [499], 102.

75 See the announcement of the premiere of *Dom v sugrobax* in *Pravda*, No. 70 (Mar. 23, 1928), 6.

76 [12], 5–7.

77 [12], 56.

78 [12]. The italics are mine. Zamjatin obviously preferred Mayer's philosophic definition of entropy to the one used currently in twentieth-century thermodynamics, namely, a quantity that is the measure of the amount of energy in a system not available for doing work.

79 [37], 142. The quoted passage occurs in the final third of the novel, which was written in late 1920–1921 see note on p. 38). Published in 1922 in Gržebin's series "Biografii zamečatel'nyx ljudej," *Robert Majer* [12] was probably written in 1920 when Gržebin was actively soliciting manuscripts and setting up his publishing house. In the second half of 1921, in an unpublished essay intended for *Zapiski mečtatelej*, Zamjatin enumerated Galileo, Leonardo da Vinci, Fulton, and Mayer as dreamers (*ZA* 4:179). The inclusion of Mayer among such universally acclaimed men indicates considerable admiration for Mayer and familiarity with his achievements.

80 When originally published [149], the essay was dated "X. 1923."

81 The Russian translation of Eve's essay, "In the Beginning; An Interpretation of Sunlight Energy," which was first published in the *Atlantic Monthly*, Vol. 131 (May 1923), 664–677, appeared in *Sovremennyj zapad*, No. 4 (1923), under the title "O solnečnoj ènergii." An anonymous eleven-line introduction drew attention to Eve's original commentary on entropy and could have been written by Zamjatin, an editor of the magazine.

82 "O literature, revoljucii, èntropii [i o pročem]," [38], 249.

83 [38], 250.

84 [38], 250.

85 "Nabrosok k stat'e," *ZA* 4:172. A draft of a rebuttal, probably written late in 1921, to those who attacked his essay "Ja bojus'."

86 Unpublished draft of an essay "Po povodu stat'i Fedina," *ZA* 4:184–185.

87 [384], 167. The comparison was reiterated by D. J. Richards in [454], 107.

88 "Zavtra," [38], 173–174.

89 [658].

90 "Zavtra," [38], 174.

91 "Cel'," [38], 177.

92 [123], 290–291.

93 "Fedor Sologub" (titled "Belaja ljubov' " at first publication), [38], 37.

94 "Anatol' Frans," [38], 101–102.

95 "Ja bojus'," [38], 189.

96 "Po povodu stat'i Fedina," *ZA* 4:184–185.

97 "Tezisy," *ZA* 4:168.

98 "O sovremennoj kritike," *ZA* 4:173, 175.

99 "Tezisy," *ZA* 4:168.

100 "O segodnjašnem i o sovremennom," [38], 213–214.
101 "Cel'," [38], 180–181.

CHAPTER 3 / DENUNCIATION AND DEFAMATION, 1929–1931

Epigraph: "Cel'," [38], 178.

1 [533], 78.
2 [564], 2.
3 [496].
4 [496], 314.
5 [496], 321.
6 [669], 144. He wrote an identical evaluation [670] two years later.
7 [668], 156.
8 [667], 301.
9 [670], 226.
10 [666], 208.
11 [679], 74. The article is dated November, 1922.
12 [335], 238.
13 [464]. The article was apparently written about three years before its publication, for Šklovskij speaks of the English translation of *My* as "soon forthcoming" (p. 66), which indicates that it was written in 1924.
14 [696], 98.
15 [721].
16 [607], 3.
17 [678], 308.
18 [529].
19 [765a], 215.
20 [580], 36 (Zamjatin's name also appears on pp. 24, 26, 70, 90, 96, 174, and 183).
21 The resolution was published in *Pravda*, No. 147 (July 1, 1925), 1. The English translation is from [551], 237.
22 [535], 196–197.
23 [551], 239.
24 [579]. Although published in 1927, the article was dated July 1, 1926.
25 [579], 186.
26 [476].
27 [420]. This was only the fourth extensive Soviet article about Zamjatin.
28 [415]. See also a caricature on this theme in *Čitatel' i pisatel'*, No. 29 (1928), in *ZA* 6:76.
29 [553].
30 Kukryniksy, "V Glavrepertkome," *Na literaturnom postu*, No. 20/21 (1928), 137 in *ZA* 6:75.

[31] For a more detailed discussion of the 1928 resolution ("*Ob obsluživanii knigoj massovogo čitatelja*") and for an English translation of the text, see [551], 88–89, 241–242.

[32] [798].

[33] [592], 15.

[34] [788]. See also the Leningrad *Literaturnaja gazeta* of May 2, 1929 in *ZA* 6:72.

[35] The text of the epigram is from Bezymenskij's article "Za pravo na èpigrammu" [328] (written in response to the FOSP Resolution of June 25) and differs slightly from the original version of May 2 in its punctuation and by the substitution in line 5 of *pererožd̆enij* for the misprint *pererožd̆ennyj*.

[36] [788].

[37] [328].

[38] "V redakciju *Literaturnoj gazety*." *Literaturnaja gazeta*, No. 12 (July 8, 1929), 2.

[39] [779]. The *Komsomol'skaja pravda* criticism had been expressed a few weeks earlier in an extensive article [796] by I. Lomov, who ended his attack with a demand for the reorganization of *Literaturnaja gazeta*.

[40] [799].

[41] [800].

[42] [791].

[43] [725].

[44] In the early 1930's Max Eastman gave a good account of Zamjatin's case in his book *Artists in Uniform* [357], while in a more recent article [386], Max Hayward has analyzed the campaign against Pil'njak and Zamjatin in considerably greater depth and detail. However, several minor inaccuracies in Hayward's account should be mentioned: (1) Zamjatin was not the head of the Leningrad VSP, as stated on p. 85 (*see* fn. 49); (2) Semen I. Kanatčikov was the editor of *Literaturnaja gazeta*, not B. Volin, as stated on p. 86; (3) The date of the first "unsatisfactory" resolution issued by the Leningrad VSP was September 6, not September 8, as stated on p. 90; and, (4) Zamjatin was not mentioned, let alone condemned (p. 90), in the September 10 resolution of the Leningrad VSP.

[45] [787].

[46] [786].

[47] [691].

[48] *Volja Rossii* (Prague), Nos. 2, 3, and 4 (February through April, 1927). The magazine's editor M. Slonim had prefaced the excerpts with a claim that that they were a Russian translation from the Czech version. See [469] and [471] for Slonim's account of the incident.

[49] The September 9, 1929, lead article of the *Literaturnaja gazeta* [522] stated that Zamjatin *had recently been* the chairman of the Leningrad section of the VSP. The RAPP resolution published on

September 2 [691] had attacked "B. Pil'njak, chairman of the Union's Moscow section, and E. Zamjatin—a member of the Union." Had Zamjatin been chairman of the Leningrad section at the time, it certainly would have been mentioned. In addition, Mme L. N. Zamiatine has stated in a letter of March 12, 1963: "No, I do not remember during which years Evg. Iv. [Zamjatin] headed the Leningrad Union of Writers (I do not even remember that he ever did). But I can definitely state that in 1929 he did not head [the union]."

50 [520]. The resolution was not dated.

51 [789].

52 [526].

53 [188].

54 [528].

55 [783].

56 [517].

57 [784].

58 [518].

59 [188].

60 [525].

61 [524].

62 [530].

63 [792].

64 [781].

65 [782].

66 [790].

67 [797].

68 See *Literaturnaja gazeta*, Nos. 24 through 28 (Sept. 30 to Oct. 28, 1929).

69 [785].

70 "Cel'," [38], 178.

71 [188].

72 [358], 235. Efremin was also the author of "Rokovoj put'" ("The Fatal Path") [360], a shorter article to the same effect in *Učitel'skaja gazeta*, and of an extensive negative review of Zamatin's four-volume collected works, which was published under the title "Na grani" ("On the Borderline") [359] in *Komsomol'skaja pravda.*

73 [558].

74 [795].

75 [156]. Originally untitled, Zamjatin's essay was reprinted with some omissions as "Zakulisy" in *Lica* [38], 259–274.

76 [676]. See also Zamjatin, "Pis'mo Stalinu," [38], 280.

77 R. B. Šeridan, *Škola zloslovija* (Moskva-Leningrad, 1931), recorded in *Knižnaja letopis'*, No. 54 (Sept. 1931), item 22697. See Zamjatin's account in "Pis'mo Stalinu," [38], 278.

78 [744c], [744e], and [744b].

[79] [744a].

[80] [675] and [692].

[81] [38], 274.

[82] See [608]; "Pis'mo Stalinu," [38], 280; and [527A].

[83] [38], 281–282. An English translation of the entire letter appears in [226], xiii–xviii.

[84] [38], 96–97, and [451], 430.

[85] Anon., "Teatr im. Vaxtangova," *Literaturnaja gazeta*, No. 36 (Dec. 23, 1929), 3, and an advertisement in *Pravda*, No. 146 (May 29, 1930), 8.

[86] [767c] and [767a].

[87] [767b].

[88] [399].

[89] A typed manuscript with the author's corrections has been preserved in the Zamjatin Archive, Folio 2: 77–134, but the last two or three pages of the final section are missing. In 1963, presumably from another manuscript, the play was published in an émigré journal [120].

[90] [399].

[91] "Roždenie Ivana," *ZA* 2:59–65.

[92] [423], 126.

[93] [399].

[94] "Nabroski k romanu," *ZA* 4:38–59.

CHAPTER 4 / EXILE AND DEATH

Epigraph: [451], 425, 426.

[1] [434].

[2] Fedin's letter of April 16, 1934, and postcard of June 21, 1934, to Mr. and Mrs. Zamjatin, *ZA* 5:71–74.

[3] [421].

[4] [280a], 145.

[5] Cecil B. deMille's letter of March 22, 1932, to Zamjatin, *ZA* 5:110.

[6] [198] and [200].

[7] [431]. See also the notice "Segodnja v gostjax u Russkoj dramy — tri russkix znamenitosti," from an unidentified newspaper in *ZA* 6:146.

[8] [404], 8.

[9] [514] and [347].

[10] [191].

[11] [421]. For an interesting first-hand description of Zamjatin and his visit to the First German Society of Slavicists in Prague, see R. Pletnev, [437].

[12] [323], [399], and [423].

[13] [323], [773f], and [192].

[14] [773k].

[15] [462].

[16] [540] and [558].

[17] [400].

[18] [463].

[19] [192], *Literaturnaja gazeta*, No. 42 (Sept. 17, 1932). The letter was undated, but when reprinted the next day in *Izvestija*, No. 259 (Sept. 18, 1932), 4, it bore the date: "Paris, March 30, 1932."

[20] Konstantin Fedin's letter of June 21, 1932, to Zamjatin, *ZA* 5:46. The critic I. Gruzdev's letter to Gor'kij, which contained an even more cryptic account of Averbax's reaction as well as a copy of Zamjatin's letter, would indicate that the interest among Soviet writers in Zamjatin was considerable at this time. Gruzdev's undated letter was erroneously dated November 1931, rather than May 1932, by the editors of *Arxiv A. M. Gor'kogo* [531 A], 281–282.

[21] Fedin's letter of September 27, 1932, to Zamjatin, *ZA* 5:48.

[22] [495].

[23] [515].

[24] [340] and [404]. See also, Anon., "Auteur dramatique et ingénieur," *Carnet de la semaine*, April 17, 1932, *ZA* 6:20.

[25] E. Grigor'eva's letters of December 3 and December 10, 1932, to Evgenij and Ljudmila Zamjatin, *ZA* 5:77–84, and [191].

[26] [191]. Apparently none of these translations was ever published.

[27] [290] and [378].

[28] Koenig's letters of January 18 and March 1932 to Zamjatin, *ZA* 5:31–34.

[29] N. Ma—'s letter (signature illegible) of April 26, 1934, to Zamjatin, *ZA* 5:23–24.

[30] T. Komisarjevsky's letter of September 30, 1933, to Zamjatin *ZA* 5:17–18.

[31] Letter of August 28, 1933, to Zamjatin, *ZA* 5:21–22, and [300], 90–91.

[32] [279a].

[33] The Russian manuscript of the first section was dated July 1933 (*ZA* 3:171), while that of the second section (dealing exclusively with literature) was dated December, 1933 (*ZA* 3:145). The editor's note on the publication of this essay in the original Russian in *Novyj žurnal*, No. 72 (1963), 115, indicated that it had been written for a French magazine. The French version is unknown to me, although German and Serbo-Croatian translations have been published, [256].

[34] (1) Written after RAPP's dissolution in April 1932, *ZA* 3:240–241; (2) written after the Writers' Congress in Moscow, *ZA* 3:249–253; (3) *ZA* 3:254–261, published in *Marianne* [271b];

(4) written in 1935, *ZA* 3:262–268; and (5) *ZA* 3:235–239. I am indebted to D. J. Richards for information on Zamjatin's publications in *Marianne*.

35 [271a] and [271c].

36 Belyj's obituary was supposedly published in *Les nouvelles littéraires* in 1936 (see *Lica*, 283), but I have not found the French version.

37 "Russian Shipbuilding: Problems Following the Revolution," *The Glasgow Herald Trade Review*, December 31, 1932, p. 66; "Russian Shipbuilding: 'Higher Production at Any Price,'" *The Glasgow Herald*, June 30, 1934, p. 4; "Shipbuilding in Soviet Russia: Efforts Toward Better Production," *The Glasgow Herald Trade Review*, December 29, 1934, p. 45. I am indebted to Richard Hallett for locating these articles.

38 *ZA* 2:49–58.

39 *ZA* 3:173–182.

40 [198].

41 [193]. The synopsis was entitled "D-503," and the Russian version was dated July 15, 1932, *ZA* 2:20–29.

42 [196].

43 [499], 102. A synopsis of the scenario and other materials pertaining to "Sten'ka Razin" have been preserved, *ZA* 2:484–536.

44 Anon., "Fédor Ozep 'découpe' 'Anna Karenine' qu'il réalisera pour Pathé-Natan," *Comoedia*, March 13, 1933, in *ZA* 6:30. According to Annenkov, the film was never made. [300], 92.

45 [499], 103. The Latin is from Vergil's *Aeneid*, II, 6: "Of which things I was a great part."

46 [194].

47 The synopses are in Folio 2 of the Zamjatin Archive and include "Car' v plenu," "Le grand amour de Goya," "Attila," "Pikovaja dama," "Mazepa," "Vojna i mir," "Vešnie vody," "Žizn' načinaetsja snova," "Dezdemona," "Nos," "Vladyka Azii," and "Čingis-xan."

48 Anon., "'Na dne'," *Poslednie novosti*, No. 5739 (Dec. 10, 1936), 5; Anon., "Premirovanie fil'ma 'Na dne'," *Poslednie novosti*, No. 5752 (Dec. 23, 1936), 3; and Anon., "Premirovannyj fil'm," *Poslednie novosti*, No. 5754 (Dec. 25, 1936), 4. Two drafts of the scenario have been preserved: "Na dne," *ZA* 2:160–189, and "Le bas fond," *ZA* 2:190–216. Both are in Russian.

49 [511].

50 [432].

51 [189].

52 [193], 87.

53 Fedin's letter of April 16, 1934, to Zamjatin and his wife, *ZA* 5:71–72.

54 [471], xxv.

55 [316A].

[56] I am grateful to Professor Simon Karlinsky for bringing to my attention Cvetaeva's account of the funeral, which is at odds with the account of Gul', [602], 113–114.

[57] [495]. The gathering was on Monday, April 26.

[58] [471], xxiii.

[59] [503].

CHAPTER 5 / EARLY PERIOD, 1908–1917

Epigraph: [179a], 16.

[1] [575], 309.

[2] [164], 95.

[3] [777n], 246.

[4] [442], 260.

[5] The idea of the gradual petrification of human feelings within Baryba was first discussed by Ju. Ajxenval'd in [777a].

[6] [454], 30, and [442], 264.

[7] [496], 310.

[8] [454], 33.

[9] [335], 229.

[10] The date of writing for both "Petr Petrovič" (date of first publication not known) and "Angel Dormidon" (published in *Novaja žizn'*, No. 83 [May 4, 1918], 1) was given as 1916 in [33], 263, 270. See [93]–[112] for publication data on the other fables.

[11] [164], 92, 94.

[12] [164], 93.

[13] [164], 95.

[14] [164], 95, and "O sintetizme," [38], 234–235.

[15] [577], 690.

[16] [777p], 137.

[17] "Zakulisy," [38], 267.

[18] [164], 97.

[19] [777l].

[20] [777h], 304.

[21] [164], 98.

[22] [164], 98.

[23] [595], 96.

[24] [164], 98.

[25] [595], 95.

[26] [164], 93.

[27] In 1914 Zamjatin had written an extremely negative review of *Peterburg*, comparing Belyj to an unfortunate contortionist [171]. (Although Zamjatin's authorship of this review is a surmise, the style of the review, the initialed signature "Evg. Z.," and his association with the journal at the time support the conjecture strongly.) But four years later in 1918, Zamjatin cited *Peterburg* several times as an

example of certain Neorealistic features, refraining from negative pronouncements about the novel itself ([164], 93, 95–96, 97, 99). Sixteen years later in his obituary of Belyj, Zamjatin spoke of *Peterburg* in glowing terms: "In this book, the best of everything written by Belyj, Petersburg has found its true artist for the first time since Gogol' and Dostoevskij" ("Andrej Belyj," [38], 78). Although the rather different evaluations in part reflect the very nature of the articles, they also indicate a gradual but definite change in Zamjatin's opinion, which may have been influenced by personal friendship.

[28] [164], 99.

[29] [169], 97.

CHAPTER 6 / MIDDLE PERIOD, 1917–1921

Epigraph: [38], 230.

[1] An obvious reference to Christ's words to Simon and Andrew (Matthew 4:19, Mark 1:17, and Luke 5:10), the appellation *lovec čelovekov* (fisher of men) ironically applies to Bailey, who "catches" women with his music, as well as to the blackmailer Craggs, who "catches" lovers in the park. [464], 65.

[2] [335], 231.

[3] The genetic relationship of the two works was explained in Zamjatin's untitled contribution to *Kak my pišem* [156], 34, but the highly interesting appendix (pp. 44–47) containing Zamjatin's original character sketches and plot outlines for "Ostrovitjane," which gave considerable insight into his creative process, was unfortunately deleted in the condensed version included in *Lica* [38] under the title "Zakulisy."

[4] [123], 286–287.

[5] Any Spanish translation of the Bible was automatically prohibited without being listed in the *Index*. Juan Pérez de Pineda, the author of several religious tracts, published his Castilian translations of the Psalms of David, the New Testament (from the Greek), and the first Spanish Calvinist Catechism in the 1550's. His name and some of his works were recorded in the "Index auctorum et librorum prohibitorum," *Index librorum prohibitorum et expurgatorum* (Madrid, 1612), 68, and were retained in the *Indexes* of 1640 and 1667.

[6] [358], 235, and [420], 64.

[7] [360].

[8] The Dostoevskian heritage in *My* has been examined at length by Struve [484], Richards [452], and Jackson [391].

[9] E. J. Brown has touched on the Wellsian legacy in [338], 37–39, while C. Collins has devoted a brief article to the same question, [342], 351–360.

[10] See Zamjatin's "Gerbert Uèlls," [38], 110–114, 117–118, and his "Predislovie" in [127], 10–12.

[11] [335], 234, and [391].

[12] [391], 151. For a discussion of Zamjatin's use of $\sqrt{-1}$ as a symbol of irrationality, infinity as a mathematical idea in relation to life, and the idea of having a soul, see [500].

[13] [337], 76.

[14] [180], 70.

[15] Dostoevskij, "Zapiski iz podpol'ja," *Sobranie sočinenij*, IV (Moskva, 1956), 160–161.

[16] [452], 222–223.

[17] "Answer to Fedin," *ZA* 4:184.

[18] [484], 162, and [164], 95, 99.

[19] For an unusual analysis of D-503's alienation in terms of archetypal images in myth, see C. Collins [343].

[20] [404], 1.

[21] See Zamjatin's introduction to [126] and his own characterization of "Sever" as a "bit Knut Hamsunish" [499], 102.

[22] "Zavtra," [38], 174.

[23] [763a] and [496], 315.

[24] [451], 429.

[25] "Zakulisy," [38], 270.

[26] [464], 50.

[27] See [464], 53–54, for a detailed account of this image.

[28] [464], 55–56.

[29] [464], 43.

[30] [426], 298.

[31] [156], 37.

[32] The first chapter of "Uezdnoe," for example, is four pages long, but contains only one color adjective: *belyj listok bileta.*

[33] For a detailed study of the golden imagery in *My*, see [446].

[34] The artistic use of consonantal phonics was first pointed out by Zamjatin himself in his untitled contribution to *Kak my pišem*, [156], 39.

[35] Originally applied to the works of Zamjatin's friend, the artist Jurij Annenkov, and first published in Annenkov's *Portrety* (Peterburg, 1922), 36, this passage was later quoted with minor changes by Zamjatin in relation to his own work ([156], 40–41).

[36] Irwin Titunik, "The Problem of *Skaz* in Russian Literature" (unpublished Ph.D. dissertation, Department of Slavic Languages and Literatures, University of California at Berkeley, 1963), 45.

[37] Quoted by Titunik (*ibid.*, 9), the definition appeared in B. Èjxenbaum's "Leskov i sovremennaja proza," *Literatura • Teorija • Kritika • Polemika* (Leningrad, 1927), 214–215.

[38] [38], 153.

[39] Zamjatin's pronouncements on language theory and the writing of prose fiction were presented in the article "O jazyke," [169].

CHAPTER 7 / TRANSITIONAL PERIOD, 1922–1927

Epigraph: [38], 255.

1 [38], 59–60.

2 See [765b] and [765a].

3 [765c], 306.

4 [38], 240–241.

5 [38], 252, 254.

6 [169], 97–98.

7 [399].

8 [34], 35.

CHAPTER 8 / LATE PERIOD, 1928–1935

Epigraph: [38], 35.

1 B. Èjxenbaum, "O. Genri i teorija novelly," *Zvezda*, No. 6 (June, 1925), 294.

2 "Predislovie" [144], 8, reprinted in [38], 150. Compare this with his statement that "there are two means of surmounting life's tragedy: religion or irony. The Neorealists have chosen the second means." [164], 95.

3 [38], 153.

4 Èjxenbaum, "O. Genri i teorija novelly," 297–298.

5 *Ibid.*, 301.

6 Compare the murder scene in Dostoevskij's *Prestuplenie i nakazanie, Sobranie sočinenij*, V (Moskva, 1957), 89, and in "Navodnenie," [39], 229.

7 [336], 115, 116.

8 [38], 270–271.

9 [156], 43.

10 [156], 38. The interesting passage on the *dyxanie frazy* was omitted in the *Lica* reprint.

11 In view of the above discussion, E. J. Brown's statement that "the stories 'Afrika' and 'Ela' contrive an impression of the dialect spoken in the fishing villages of the far north" was highly misleading in its implication that Zamjatin had used the same stylistic techniques all through his career. See [338], 33.

12 [186] and [421], dated "Moskva, říjen [October] 1927."

13 [468], 8.

14 "Bič Božij (exposé romana)," *ZA* 2:49–58.

15 [421].

A Chronology of Zamjatin's Prose Fiction

A Chronology of Zamjatin's Prose Fiction (excluding fables)

	WRITTEN	FIRST PUBLISHED IN RUSSIAN
EARLY PERIOD, 1908–1917		
1. Odin	1908	1908
2. Devuška	1910	1910
3. Uezdnoe; povest'	1911–12	1913
4. Aprel'	1912	1915
5. Neputevyj	1913	1914
6. Tri dnja; očerk	1913	1914
7. Črevo	1913	1915
8. Na kuličkax; povest'	1913–14	1914
9. Staršina	1914	1915
10. Alatyr'; povest'	1914	1915
11. Krjaži	1915	1916
12. Pis'menno	1916	1916
13. Afrika	1916	1916
14. Pravda istinnaja	1917	1917
MIDDLE PERIOD, 1917–1921		
15. Ostrovitjane; povest'	1917	1918
16. O svjatom grexe Zenicy-devy	1917	1917
17. Zemlemer	1917	1918
18. Lovec čelovekov	1917–18	1922
19. Drakon	1918	1918
20. Glaza	1918	1918
21. Znamenie	1918	1918
22. Na divane	1918	1918
23. Sneg	1918	1918
24. Tramvaj	1918	1918

MIDDLE PERIOD, 1917–1921–(Cont'd.)	WRITTEN	FIRST PUBLISHED IN RUSSIAN
25. Zverjata	1918	1918
26. Kolumb; dve glavy iz povesti	1918	1918
27. Spodručnica grešnyx	1918	1922
28. Sever; povest'	1918	1922
29. Detskaja	1920	1922
30. Mamaj	1920	1921
31. Tulumbas. Poslanie smirennogo Zamutija	1920	1921
32. Peščera	1920	1922
33. O tom, kak iscelen byl inok Erazm	1920	1922
34. My; roman	1920–21	1927
TRANSITIONAL PERIOD, 1922–1927		
35. Vse; otryvok iz povesti	1922	1922
36. Rus'	1922	1923
37. Kuny	1922	1923
38. Rasskaz o samom glavnom	1923	1924
39. O čude, proisšedšem v Pepel'nuju Sredu	1923–24	1926
40. Iks	1926	1926
41. Slovo predostavljaetsja tovarišču Čuryginu	1926	1927
42. Žitie Bloxi . . .	1926	1929
43. Privetstvie ot Mestkoma pokojnyx . . .	1927	1962
LATE PERIOD, 1928–1935		
44. Ela	1928	1928
45. Desjatiminutnaja drama	1928	1928
46. Navodnenie	1929	1929
47. Mučeniki nauki	1931	1962
48. Časy	1934	1939
49. Lev	1935	1939
50. Vstreča	1935	1939
51. Videnie	mid-1930's	1962
52. Bič Božij; roman	1924–35	1939

A Bibliography of Zamjatiana

No adequate bibliography of Zamjatin's works and relevant secondary literature has previously been published. The few items included in K. D. Muratova's *Istorija russkoj literatury konca XIX-načala XX veka; bibliografičeskij ukazatel'* (Moskva-Leningrad, 1963) are woefully inadequate, and the exclusion of a section on Zamjatin from the current six-volume *Russkie sovetskie pisateli prozaiki; bibliografičeskij ukazatel'* (Leningrad, 1959–) indicates that no bibliography from Soviet sources will be forthcoming soon. Although the four-volume *Sobranie sočinenij* (Moskva, 1929) contains much of Zamjatin's prose fiction, it is far from complete. The critical investigator must search out materials on his own by referring to a myriad of literary histories and general bibliographies, many of which are outdated or highly selective. The following is an attempt to remedy this situation and, while making no claim to completeness except in Section I, is the single most extensive bibliography of Zamjatiana published to date.

Section I, which comprises all of Zamjatin's published works, as well as his unpublished plays and some letters, has been subdivided into archives, monographs, prose fiction, fables, plays, essays, reviews, autobiographies, letters, and edited works. The month of publication has been determined by consulting *Knižnaja letopis'*, review literature, and advertisements. Although the resultant chronological order is admittedly approximate, the reader can reasonably assume that the works were already in circulation by the date indicated.

Section II, which comprises published translations of Zamjatin's works, is intended as a guide for persons who do not read Russian, future translators, and comparativists interested in Zamjatin's reception and influence abroad.

The secondary materials listed in Section III include works on Zamjatin, general works which mention him, reviews, and a list of other works cited in my discussion of the campaign against the VSP. Although articles on Zamjatin in Western encyclopedias have been plagued by factual inaccuracies, they may prove of use to comparativists' reception studies and therefore are included in Section III. Introductions to all Russian-language editions of Zamjatin's works are listed, but brief translators' introductions are not, unless they are of special interest. Even the most cursory mentions of Zamjatin in Soviet sources are included because of their value in determining Zamjatin's position in Russian letters and the critical attitudes toward him, but most cursory mentions in Western sources are excluded. Some one hundred anonymous announcements and factual references in literary chronicles have been omitted, but they are listed in the bibliography of my dissertation [460]. Among the general works in Section III, page references are provided for the Russian books, which usually lack indexes, but they are not given for indexed Western scholarly studies. Titles of review articles are cited only when they differ from the work reviewed (many reviews of essays and stories bear the titles of the journals in which Zamjatin's works originally appeared). The code *ZA* is explained in [1]. Items which I have been unable to examine are marked with asterisks, as in [2]*.

I. THE WORKS OF EVGENIJ IVANOVIČ ZAMJATIN

Archival Materials

[1] Archive of Russian and East European History and Culture, Columbia University, New York City. Zamjatin Collection (1923–1936). References in the footnotes and bibliography are to materials on microfilm and are identified by the code *ZA*, followed by the folio number and then the frame number (folio title page has been counted as zero).

[2]* Central'nyj gosudarstvennyj arxiv literatury i iskusstva SSSR (CGALI), Moskva, fond 1776, 10 edinic xranenija (1920–1927).

[3]* Gosudarstvennaja publičnaja biblioteka imeni M. E. Saltykova-Ščedrina (GPB), Leningrad, fond 292, 25 edinic xranenija (1892–1931).

[4]* Institut mirovoj literatury imeni M. Gor'kogo Akademii nauk SSSR (IMLI), Moskva, fond 47, 625 edinic xranenija (1903–1932).

Monographs listed chronologically by date of publication

[5] *Uezdnoe*; *povest'*. Moskva: Sovremennye problemy, 1916. 145 pp. [Pub. Oct. 1915.]

[6] *Uezdnoe*; *povesti i rasskazy*, Tom I. Petrograd: M. V. Popov, 1916. 197 pp. [Pub. Feb.] Contents: Uezdnoe, Neputevyj, Črevo, Alatyr', Staršina, Krjaži.

[7] *Vereški*. Petrograd: Artel' xudožnikov Segodnja, [1918]. 7 pp. [Pub. June.] Contents: Na divane, Zverjata, Tramvaj, Sneg.

[8]* *Krjaži*. Petrograd: Kolos (*Korobejnik*. Čtenie dlja goroda i derevni, No. 8), 1918. 31 pp. [Pub. Sept.]

[9] *Gerbert Uèlls*. Peterburg: Èpoxa, 1922. 47 pp. [Pub. Jan.] Contents: Gerbert Uèlls, Genealogičeskoe derevo Uèllsa.

[10]* *Črevo*; *rasskaz*. *Zemlemer*; *rasskaz*. Peterburg: Èpoxa, 1922. 48 pp. [Pub. May.]

[11] *Ostrovitjane*; *povesti i rasskazy*. Peterburg-Berlin: Z. I. Gržebin, 1922. 168 pp. [Pub. June.] Contents: Ostrovitjane, Lovec čelovekov, Sever, Zemlemer, Drakon, Mamaj, Peščera, Glaza.

[12] *Robert Majer*. Berlin-Peterburg-Moskva: Z. I. Gržebin, 1922. 72 pp. [Pub. Aug.]

[13] *Tri dnja*. Petrograd: Byloe, 1922. 27 pp. [Pub. Aug.]

[14]* *Tri dnja*; *očerk*. Kursk: Knigoizdatel'skoe tovariščestvo pri Kurskom Gubkome R.K.P.(B), 1922. 32 pp. [Pub. Nov.–Dec.]

[15] *Ogni svjatogo Dominika*. Berlin: Slovo, 1922. 59 pp. [Pub. Dec.]

[16] *O tom kak iscelen byl inok Erazm*. [*Otrok* replaces *inok* on cover.] Berlin: Petropolis, 1922. 46 pp. [Pub. Jan. 1923.]

[17] *Bol'šim detjam skazki*. Berlin-Peterburg-Moskva: Z. I. Gržebin, 1922. 47 pp. [Pub. 1923.] Contents: twenty fables (*see* Fables, [93]–[112]).

[18] *Rus'*. 1st ed. Petrograd: Akvilon, 1923. 23 pp. plus 23 plates. [Pub. March.] 2nd ed. [Petrograd: Akvilon, 1923]. 38 pp. Pod redakciej i so vstupleniem V. Zavališina.

[19] *Ostrovitjane*; *povesti i rasskazy*. Berlin-Peterburg-Moskva: Z. I. Gržebin, 1923. 190 pp. [Pub. April.] Contents: same as [11].

[20]* *Mamaj*. *Zemlemer*. Petrograd: [Izd. Frenkelja], 1923. 32 pp. [Pub. May.]

[21] *Ogni svjatogo Dominika*; *p'esa v četyrex dejstvijax*. Petrograd: Mysl', 1923. 46 pp. [Pub. June.]

[22] *Uezdnoe*; *povesti i rasskazy*. Tom I. 2nd ed. Moskva-Peterburg: Krug, 1923. 170 pp. [Pub. July.] Contents: same as [6].

[23] *Na kuličkax*; *povesti i rasskazy*. Petrograd-Moskva: Petrograd, 1923. 152 pp. [Pub. Sept.] Contents: Na kuličkax, Znamenie, Afrika, Detskaja, Pis'menno, Aprel', Pravda istinnaja.

[24] *Na kuličkax*; *rasskazy*. Berlin: Z. I. Gržebin, 1923. 143 pp. [Pub. Dec.] Contents: Na kuličkax, Znamenie, Detskaja, Spodručnica grešnyx, Pravda istinnaja (entitled * * *), Afrika, Pis'menno.

[25] *Bloxa*; *igra v četyrex dejstvijax*. Leningrad: Mysl', 1926. 98 pp. [Pub. Nov. 1925.] Contents: Predislovie [Zamjatina], Bloxa, Priloženie [Programma Bloxi v MXAT 2-m].

[26] *Obščestvo početnyx zvonarej*; *tragikomedija v 4-x dejstvijax*. Leningrad: Mysl', 1926. 91 pp. [Pub. Feb.]

[27]* *Na kuličkax*; *povest'*. Moskva-Leningrad: Gos. izd. (Universal'naja biblioteka No. 39–40), 1926. 128 pp. [Pub. March.]

[28] *Fonar'*; *rasskaz*. Moskva-Leningrad: Gos. izd. (Universal'naja biblioteka No. 115), 1926. 64 pp. [Pub. Aug.] Contents: Sever.

[29] *Nečestivye rasskazy*. Moskva: Krug, 1927. 179 pp. [Pub. May.] Contents: Rasskaz o samom glavnom; Iks; Spodručnica grešnyx; Rus'; O tom, kak iscelen byl inok Erazm; O čude, proisšedšem v Pepel'nuju Sredu; D'jačok; Bog.

[30] *Uezdnoe*; *povesti, teatr*. (*Sobranie sočinenij*, Tom I.) Moskva: Federacija, 1929. 256 pp. [Pub. Jan.] Contents: Avtobiografija [1929], Uezdnoe, Alatyr', [novoe] Predislovie [k Bloxe], Bloxa, Priloženie k "Bloxe."

[31] *Na kuličkax*; *povesti, rasskazy*. (*Sobranie sočinenij*, Tom II.) Moskva: Federacija, 1929. 286 pp. [Pub. Feb.] Contents: Na kuličkax, Neputevyj, Črevo, Znamenie, Aprel', Spodručnica grešnyx, Pis'menno, Krjaži, Staršina, Pravda istinnaja.

[32] *Ostrovitjane; povesti, rasskazy, teatr*. (*Sobranie sočinenij*, Tom III.) Moskva: Federacija, 1929. 324 pp. [Pub. Mar.] Contents: Ostrovitjane, Lovec čelovekov, Zemlemer, Detskaja, Mamaj, Peščera, Glaza, Rasskaz o samom glavnom, Ogni svjatogo Dominika.

[33] *Sever; povesti, rasskazy, skazki*. (*Sobranie sočinenij*, Tom IV.) Moskva: Federacija, 1929. 287 pp. [Pub. Apr.] Contents: Sever; Afrika; Ela; Rus'; Iks; Slovo predostavljaetsja tovarišču Čuryginu; Tri dnja; O tom, kak iscelen byl inok Erazm; O čude, proisšedšem v Pepel'nuju Sredu; Bog; Petr Petrovič; D'jaček; Angel Dormidon; Èlektričestvo; Kartinki; Drjan'-mal'čiška; Xeruvimy; Bibliografija.

[34] *Žitie Bloxi ot dnja čudesnogo ee roždenija i do dnja priskorbnoj končiny*. Leningrad: Knigoizdatel'stvo pisatelej, 1929. 37 pp. [Pub. Oct.]

[35] *Navodnenie*. Leningrad: Knigoizdatel'stvo pisatelej, 1930. 68 pp. [Pub. Aug.]

[36] *Bič Božij*; *roman*. Pariž: Dom knigi; n.d. 125 pp. [Pub. May 1939.] Contents: Anon., "[Biografija]"; Bič Božij; Časy; Lev; Desjatiminutnaja drama; Vstreča.

[37] *My*. N'ju-Jork: Izdatel'stvo imeni Čexova, 1952. 200 pp. Contents: V. Aleksandrova, "Evgenij Zamjatin"; My.

[38] *Lica*. N'ju-Jork; Izdatel'stvo imeni Čexova, 1955. 285 pp. Contents: Ot izdatel'stva, Aleksandr Blok, Fedor Sologub, Čexov, L. Andreev, Vstreči s B. M. Kustodievym, Andrej Belyj, M. Gor'kij, Anatol' France (Nekrolog), Gerbert Uèlls, Genealogičeskoe derevo Uèllsa, O'Genri, Ričard Brinsli Šeridan, Zavtra, Cel', Ja bojus', Novaja russkaja proza, O segodnjašnem i o sovremennom, O sintetizme, O literature, revoljucii i èntropii, Dlja sbornika o knige, Zakulisy, Pis'mo Stalinu.

[39] *Povesti i rasskazy*. Mjunxen: Central'noe ob"edinenie političeskix èmigrantov iz SSSR (COPÈ), 1963. 320 pp. Contents: M. Slonim, "Pisatel' i ego tvorčestvo"; Avtobiografija [1929], Uezdnoe, Spodručnica grešnyx, Sever, Lovec čelovekov, Peščera, Mamaj, Rus', Russkaz o samom glavnom, Iks, Navodnenie, Lev, Vstreča, Bič Božij, Knigi Zamjatina.

[40] *My*; *roman*. N'ju-Jork: Meždunarodnoe literaturnoe sodružestvo, 1967. 225 pp. Contents: Evgenija Žiglevič, "*My* i my"; My; Vladimir Bondarenko, "Veka i desjatiletija."

[40A] *Lica*. N'ju-Jork: Meždunarodnoe literaturnoe sodružestvo, 1967. 311 pp. Contents: same as [38] with the omission of "Ot izdatel'stva" and the addition of essays by M. Korjakov, "Lica i xari," and V. Bondarenko, "Evgenij Zamjatin i sovetskij period russkoj literatury."

Prose fiction (očerki, povesti, rasskazy, romany), **excluding fables** (skazki), **listed chronologically by date of first publication (genre is** rasskaz **unless indicated otherwise). Reprinting in monographs already listed are cited only by bracketed number; other reprintings are cited in full. See page 229 for a chronological list by date of writing.**

[41] "Odin." *Obrazovanie*. No. 11 (November 1908), 17–48.

[42] "Devuška." *Novyj žurnal dlja vsex*. No. 25 (November 1910), 55–68.

[43] "Uezdnoe; povest'." *Zavety*. No. 5 (May 1913), 46–99. Reprinted in [5], [6], [22], [30], [39].
  a. Excerpts entitled "Komu na Rusi žit' xorošo." *Bjulleteni literatury i žizni*. No. 1 (September 1913), 10–16.

[44] "Neputevyj." *Ežemesjačnyj žurnal*. No. 1 (January 1914), 8–16. Reprinted in [6], [22], [31].
  a. Excerpts entitled "Senja." *Bjulleteni literatury i žizni*. No. 12 (February 1914), 714–719.

[45] "Tri dnja; iz prošlogo [očerk]." *Ežemesjačnyj žurnal*. No. 2 (February 1914), 37–46. Reprinted in [13], [14], [33].

[46] "Na kuličkax; povest'." *Zavety*. No. 3 (March 1914), 35–109. Reprinted in [23], [24], [27], [31].

a. *Al'manax arteli pisatelej Krug*. I. Moskva-Peterburg: Krug, 1923, 55–133. [Pub. Jan.]
b. Excerpt entitled "Božij zevok." *Volja Rossii*. No. 15 (September 15, 1923), 1–3.

[47] "Staršina." *Ežemesjačnyj žurnal*. No. 1 (January 1915), 36–38. Reprinted in [6], [22], [31].

[48] "Aprel'." *Sovremennik*. No. 4 (April 1915), 12–19. Reprinted in [23], [31].

[49] "Črevo." *Russkie zapiski*. No. 4 (April 1915), 158–170. Reprinted in [6], [10], [22], [31].
a.* *Nedelja* [sbornik]. Petrograd: Vestnik znanija, 1916.

[50] "Alatyr'; povest'." *Russkaja mysl'*. No. 9 (September 1915), 9–38. Reprinted in [6], [22], [30].

[51] "Krjaži." Zamjatin. *Uezdnoe*. Petrograd: M. V. Popov, 1916, 185–195. [Pub. Feb.] Reprinted in [8], [22], [31].
a. *Reč'*. No. 99 (April 10, 1916), 4.

[52] "Pis'menno." *Birževye vedomosti* (utrennij vypusk). No. 15,454 (March 21, 1916), 2. Reprinted in [23], [24], [31].
a.* *Korobejnik* [sbornik]. Petrograd, 1918.
b. *Volja Rossii*. No. 15 (September 15, 1923), 3–6.

[53] "Afrika." *Severnye zapiski*. No. 4/5 (April–May 1916), 1–10. Reprinted in [23], [24], [33].

[54] "O svjatom grexe Zenicy-devy. Slovo poxval'noe." *Delo naroda*. No. 181 (October 15, 1917), 5.

[55] "Pravda istinnaja." *Novaja žizn'*. No. 210 (December 24, 1917), 5. Reprinted in [23], [24], [31].

[56] "Ostrovitjane; povest'." *Skify*, II. S.-Peterburg: Skify, 1918, 119–163. [Pub. Jan.] Reprinted in [11], [19], [32].

[57] "Zemlemer." *Ežemesjačnyj žurnal*. No. 1 (January 1918), 65–74. Reprinted in [10], [11], [19], [20], [32].

[58] "Glaza." *Novaja žizn'*. No. 39 (March 10, 1918), 2. Reprinted in [11], [19], [32].
a. *Sobač'ja dolja; peterburgskij sbornik rasskazov*. Berlin: Slovo, 1922, 9–15. [Pub. Jan.]

[59] "Drakon." *Delo naroda*.* [Spring] 1918. Reprinted in [11], [19].
a. *Modern Russian Short Stories*. Edited by G. Gibian and M. Samilov. New York, Evanston, and London: Harper and Row, 1965, 125–126.

[60] "Znamenie." *Mysl'*, I. Petrograd: Revoljucionnaja mysl', 1918, 78–89. [Pub. May.] Reprinted in [23], [24], [31].

[61] "Na divane." Zamjatin. *Vereški*. Petrograd: Artel' xudožnikov Segodnja, [1918] 3. [Pub. June.]

[62] "Zverjata." *Ibid.*, 4.

[63] "Tramvaj." *Ibid.*, 5.

[64] "Sneg." *Ibid.*, 6.

[65] "Kolumb; dve glavy iz povesti." *Pred rassvetom; sbornik dlja naroda*. Petrograd: Kul'tura i svoboda, 1918, 26–30. [Pub. Sept.]

[66] "Mamaj." *Dom iskusstv*. No. 1 (1921), 7–11. [Pub. Jan.] Reprinted in [11], [19], [20], [32], [39].

a. *Modern Russian Short Stories*. Edited by G. Gibian and M. Samilov. New York, Evanston, and London: Harper and Row, 1965, 127–135.

[67] "Tulumbas; poslanie smirennogo Zamutija, episkopa obez'janskogo." *Zapiski mečtatelej*. No. 2/3 (1921), 177–179. [Pub. June]

[68] Lovec čelovekov." *Dom iskusstv*. No. 2 (1921), 3–14. [Pub. Feb. 1922] Reprinted in [11], [19], [32], [39].

[69] "Peščera." *Zapiski mečtatelej*. No. 5 (1922), 82–89. [Pub. Feb.] Reprinted in [11], [19], [32], [39].

a.* *Golos Rossii* (Berlin). July 23, 1922.

b. *Literaturnaja Rossija*. Edited by V. Lidin. Moskva: Novye vexi, 1924, 72–83. [Pub. Aug.]

c. *Russian Stories*. Edited by G. Struve. New York: Bantam Books, 1961, 292–312.

[70] "Vse; otryvok iz povesti." *Vestnik literatury*. No. 2/3 (1922), 15–16.

[71] "Spodručnica grešnyx." *Peresvet*, II. Moskva: N. V. Vasil'ev, 1922, 25–30. [Pub. Apr.] Reprinted in [24], [29], [31], [39].

[72] "Sever; povest'." *Peterburgskij al'manax*, I. Peterburg-Berlin: Z. I. Gržebin, 1922, 73–121. [Pub. by July.] Reprinted in [11], [19], [28], [33], [39].

[73] "Detskaja." *Sovremennye zapiski*. No. 12 (September 30, 1922), 42–52. Reprinted in [23], [24], [32].

a.* *Petrograd; literaturnyj al'manax*, I. Petrograd-Moskva: Petrograd, 1923, 6–15. [Pub. Sept.]

[74] "O tom, kak iscelen byl inok Erazm." Zamjatin. *O tom, kak iscelen byl inok Erazm*. Berlin: Petropolis, 1922, 5–46. [Pub. Jan. 1923.] Reprinted in [29], [33].

a. *Russkij sovremennik*. No. 4 (1924), 43–55.

[75] "Kuny." *Rossija*. No. 5 (January 1923), 1–3.

[76] "Rus'." Zamjatin. *Rus'*. 1st ed. Petrograd: Akvilon, 1923, 7–23. [Pub. Mar.] Reprinted in [29], [33], [39].

[77] "Rasskaz o samom glavnom." *Russkij sovremennik*. No. 1 (1924), 11–39. Reprinted in [29], [32], [39].

[78] "O čude, proisšedšem v Pepel'nuju Sredu." *Novaja Rossija*. No. 1 (January 1926), 57–62. Reprinted in [29], [33].

[79] "Iks." *Novaja Rossija*. No. 2 (February 1926), 49–62. Reprinted in [29], [33], [39].

a. *Volja Rossii*. No. 8/9 (1926), 3–21.

[80] "My; roman." *Volja Rossii.* No. 2 (February 1927), 3–33; No. 3 (March 1927), 3–32; No. 4 (April 1927), 3–28. [Many alterations, chapter 14 omitted.] Reprinted in [37], [40].

[81] "Slovo predostavljaetsja tovarišču Čuryginu." *Al'manax arteli pisatelej Krug,* VI. Moskva-Leningrad: Krug, 1927, 145–154. [Pub. July.] Reprinted in [33].

[82] "Ela." *Pisateli Krymu; literaturnyj al'manax.* Moskva: Komitet sodejstvija bor'be s posledstvijami zemletrjasenija v Krymu pri Narkomzdrave RSFSR, 1928, 9–34. [Pub. May.] Reprinted in [33].
a. *Grani.* No. 51 (1962), 43–59.

[83] "Desjatiminutnaja drama." *Dni* (Paris). No. 1459 (June 24, 1928), 2. Reprinted in [36].
a.* *Gul zemli; literaturno-naučnyj i xudožestvennyj sbornik.* Leningrad: Krasnaja gazeta, 1928. [Pub. Oct.]

[84] "Navodnenie." *Al'manax Zemlja i fabrika,* IV. Moskva: ZIF, 1929, 217–250. [Pub. Mar.] Reprinted in [35], [39].
a. *Grani.* No. 32 (October–December 1956), 71–89.

[85] "Žitie Bloxi." Zamjatin. *Žitie Bloxi . . .* Leningrad: Knigoizdatel'stvo pisatelej, 1929, 11–32. [Pub. Oct.]

[86] "Bič Božij; roman." Zamjatin. *Bič Božij; roman.* Pariž: Dom knigi, n.d. [pub. May 1939], 13–93. Reprinted in [39].

[87] "Časy." *Ibid.*, 94–104.

[88] "Lev." *Ibid.*, 105–111. Reprinted in [39].
a. *Russian Short Stories.* Edited by J. Iwanik. Boston: D. C. Heath, 1962, 101–107.

[89] "Vstreča." Zamjatin. *Bič Božij,* 117–123. Reprinted in [39].

[90] "Mučeniki nauki." *Novyj žurnal.* No. 67 (March 1962), 12–25.

[91] "Privetstvie ot Mestkoma pokojnyx pisatelej [excerpts]." *Grani.* No. 51 (1962), 81 [written in collaboration with Mixail Zoščenko].

[92] "Videnie." *Mosty.* No. 9 (1962), 17–20.

Fables (skazki), **listed alphabetically with date of writing and of first publication, if known. All twenty fables were published in the book** Bol'šim detjam skazki **(Berlin-Petrograd-Moskva: Z. I. Gržebin, 1922), which was in Gržebin's hands in manuscript form by 1920.**

[93] "Angel Dormidon." *Novaja žizn'.* No. 83 (May 4, 1918), 1. [Written 1916.] Reprinted in [33].

[94] "Arapy." *Peterburgskij sbornik; poèty i belletristy.* Peterburg: Letopis' Doma literatorov, 1922, 43. [Pub. Apr.]

[95] "Bjaka i Kaka."

[96] "Bog." *Letopis'.* No. 4 (April 1916), 46–47. [Written 1915.] Reprinted in [29], [33].

[97] "Cerkov' Božija." *Peterburgskij sbornik; poèty i belletristy.*

Peterburg: Letopis' Doma literatorov, 1922, 41–42. [Pub. Apr.]

[98] "Četverg." *Gazeta-Protest Sojuza russkix pisatelej* [odnodnevnaja petrogradskaja gazeta]. November 26, 1917, 2.

[99] "D'jaček." *Letopis'*. No. 4 (April 1916), 48–49. [Written 1915.] Reprinted in [29], [33].

[100] "Drjan'-mal'čiška." Originally published as "Pet'ka." *Letopis'*. No. 4 (April 1916), 50. [Written 1915.] Reprinted in [33].

[101] "Èlektričestvo." *Delo naroda.** 1918. [Written 1917.] Reprinted in [33].

[102] "Ivany."

[103] "Kartinki." *Prjanik osirotevšim detjam*. Petrograd: A. D. Baranovskaja, 1916, 72. [Written 1916.] Reprinted in [33].

[104] "Ognennoe A." *Novaja žizn'*. No. 106 (June 2, 1918), 2.

[105] "Pervaja skazka pro Fitu." Originally published as "Fita." *Delo naroda.* No. 198 (November 3, 1917), 2.

[106] "Petr Petrovič." [Written 1916.] Reprinted in [33].

[107] "Poslednjaja skazka pro Fitu."

[108] "Tret'ja skazka pro Fitu." Originally published as "Malen'kij fel'eton; dejanija Fity." *Delo naroda.* No. 218 (November 24, 1917), 2–3.

[109] "Vtoraja skazka pro Fitu." Originally published as "Dejanija Fity." *Delo naroda.* No. 206 (November 11, 1917), 1.

[110] "Xaldej."

[111] "Xeruvimy." *Delo naroda.* No. 232 (December 14, 1917), 1. [Written 1917; much shortened in later versions.] Reprinted in [33].

[112] "Xrjapalo."

Plays, listed chronologically by date of writing, with dates of first publication and first performance, if known.

[113] "Ogni svjatogo Dominika; p'esa v četyrex dejstvijax." *Literaturnaja mysl'*; *al'manax*, I. Peterburg: Mysl', 1922 ["1923" on cover], 37–61. Reprinted in [15], [21], [32]. Written 1920, not performed.

[114] "Bloxa; igra v četyrex dejstvijax." Zamjatin. *Bloxa.* Leningrad: Mysl', 1926, 7–94. Reprinted in [30]. Written in 1924 as an adaptation of N. Leskov's story "Levša." First performed by MXAT 2-j on February 11, 1925.

[115] "Obščestvo početnyx zvonarej; tragikomedija v četyrex dejstvijax." Zamjatin. *Obščestvo početnyx zvonarej*. Leningrad: Mysl', 1926, 5–90. Written in 1924 as an adaptation of Zamjatin's tale "Ostrovitjane." First performed by the Mixajlovskij Theater on November 21, 1925.

[116] "Atilla; tragedija v četyrex dejstvijax." *Novyj žurnal.* No. 24 (1950), 7–70. Written in 1925–1927, not performed.

[117]* "Peščera." Unpublished. Written in 1927 as an adaptation of Zamjatin's story "Peščera." First performed by the Vaxtangov Theater in 1927–1928[?].

[118]* "Istorija goroda Glupova." Unpublished. Written in 1927 as an adaptation of M. Saltykov-Ščedrin's novel of the same name. First performed by the Mejerhol'd Theater in 1927–1928[?] and then by the Baku People's Theater in 1928–1929.

[119]* "Sensacija." Unpublished. Written in 1929 as an adaptation of Ben Hecht and Charles MacArthur's *The Front Page*. First performed by the Vaxtangov Theater on May 29, 1930.

[120] "Afrikanskij gost'; neverojatnoe proisšestvie v trex časax." *Novyj žurnal*. No. 73 (1963), 38–95. Written in 1929-1930, not performed.

Essays (stat'i, predislovija), **listed chronologically by date of first publication, with date of writing, if known. The posthumous collection** Lica **[38] included twenty-one of these essays, five of which apparently were being published for the first time. The pagination of Zamjatin's articles in the new edition of** Lica **[40A], published after this biography was compiled, is identical to that in [38].**

[121] "Elizaveta Anglijskaja." *Novaja žizn'*. No. 7 (January 11, 1918), 1.

[122] "O belom ugle" (signed: Inž. Ev. Z.). *Novaja žizn'*. No. 103 (May 30, 1918), 1.

[123] "Skify li?" (signed: Mix. Platonov). *Mysl'*, I. Petrograd: Revoljucionnaja mysl', 1918, 285–293.

[124]* "[Title unknown]" (signed: Mix. Platonov). In the collection *Iz nedavnego prošlogo*. Peterburg, 1919.

[125] "Zavtra." In the collection* *V zaščitu čeloveka*. Peterburg, 1919. Reprinted in *Lica* [38], 171–174.

[126] "Predislovie." In Džek London. *Syn volka i drugie rasskazy*. Peterburg: Vsemirnaja literatura, 1919, 5–9. [Pub. Sept. 25.]

[127] "Predislovie." In Gerbert Uèlls. *Vojna v vozduxe* (*Izbrannye sočinenija*, IX). Peterburg: Vsemirnaja literatura, 1919, 7–13. [Pub. Sept. 28.]

[128] "G. D. Uèlls." In G. D. Uèlls. *Mašina vremeni*. Peterburg: Vsemirnaja literatura, 1920, 5–14. [Pub. Feb. 5.]

[129] "O romane *Mašina vremeni*." *Ibid*., 15–20.

[130] "Uèlls." *Vestnik literatury*. No. 11 (1920), 16–17.

[131] "Ja bojus'." *Dom iskusstv*. No. 1 (1921), 43–45. [Pub. Jan. 1921; "1920" on cover.] Reprinted in *Lica* [38], 183–190.

[132] "Končina A. A. Bloka." *Zapiski mečtatelej*. No. 4 (1921), 11. [Pub. Aug.]

[133] "Gerbert Uèlls." In Zamjatin. *Gerbert Uèlls*. Peterburg:

Èpoxa, 1922, 5–40. [Pub. Jan.] Reprinted in G. Uèlls. *Armageddon* [220a], 7–35, and in *Lica* [38], 103–138.

[134] "Genealogičeskoe derevo Uèllsa." In Zamjatin, *Gerbert Uèlls*, 41–47. Reprinted in G. Uèlls. *Armageddon* [220a], 35–41, and in *Lica* [38], 139–146.

[135] "Serapionovy brat'ja." *Literaturnye zapiski*. No. 1 (May 25, 1922), 7–8.

[136] "Predislovie." In Gerbert Uèlls. *Neugasimyj ogon'*. Peterburg: Gos. izd. Vsemirnaja literatura, 1922, 7–12. [Pub. July.]

[137] "Predislovie." In Gerbert Uèlls. *Nevidimka*. Peterburg: Gos. izd. Vsemirnaja literatura, 1922, 5–8. [Pub. July.]

[138] "A. P. Čexov." In A. P. Čexov. *Izbrannye sočinenija*, I. Berlin-Peterburg-Moskva: Z. I. Gržebin, 1922, v–xxiii. [Pub. Sept.]

[139] "L. Andreev." [Written 1919.] *Kniga o Leonide Andreeve*. Berlin-Peterburg-Moskva: Z. I. Gržebin, 1922, 105–109. [Pub. Sept.] Reprinted in the second expanded edition in 1922, 167–173, and in *Lica* [38], 51–56.

[140] "Robert Majer." In E. Zamjatin. *Robert Majer*. Berlin-Peterburg-Moskva: Z. I. Gržebin, 1922, 5–72. [Pub. Sept.]

[141] "O sintetizme." In Ju. P. Annenkov. *Portrety*. Tekst E. Zamjatina, M. Kuzmina, M. Babenčikova. Peterburg: Petropolis, 1922, 19–40. Reprinted in *Lica* [38], 231–243, and Ju. Annenkov. *Dnevnik moix vstreč*, II. N'ju-Jork: Meždunarodnoe literaturnoe sodružestvo, 1966, 12–19.

[142] "Predislovie k rasskazu 'Kirasir Kjuvel'e' Ž. Djuamelja" (signed: E. Z.). *Sovremennyj zapad*. No. 1 (1922), 6.

[143] "Predislovie k rasskazu 'Igra cikad' G. Mejrinka" (signed: E. Z.). *Sovremennyj zapad*. No. 1 (1922), 54.

[144] "Predislovie." In O. Genri. *Rasskazy*. Peterburg-Moskva: Vsemirnaja literatura, 1923, 7–12. [Pub. Jan.] Entitled "O'Genri" in *Lica* [38], 147–154.

[145] "Predislovie k novelle 'Gercoginja' K. Edšmida" (signed: E. Z.). *Sovremennyj zapad*. No. 2 (1923), 4.

[146] "Predislovie k p'ese 'Načinaetsja' B. Šo" (signed: E. Z.). *Sovremennyj zapad*. No. 2 (1923), 75–76.

[147] "Èrenburg." *Rossija*. No. 8 (April, 1923), 28. A condensed version was included in [148].

[148] "Novaja russkaja proza." *Russkoe iskusstvo*. No. 2/3 (1923), 57–67. Reprinted in *Lica* [38], 191–210.

[149] "O literature, revoljucii, èntropii i o pročem." [Written Oct., 1923.] *Pisateli ob iskusstve i o sebe*; *sbornik statej*. No. 1. Moskva-Leningrad: Krug, 1924, 65–75. Reprinted in *Lica* [38], 245–256.

[150] "Anatol' Frans." *Sovremennyj zapad.* No. 2 (6) (1924), 202–203. Reprinted in *Lica* [38], 99–102.

[151] "O segodnjašnem i o sovremennom." *Russkij sovremennik.* No. 2 (1924), 263–272. Reprinted in *Lica* [38], 211–230.

[152] "Vospominanija o Bloke." *Russkij sovremennik.* No. 3 (1924), 187–194. Entitled "Aleksandr Blok" in *Lica* [38], 13–28.

[153] "Belaja ljubov'." *Sovremennaja literatura; sbornik statej.* Leningrad: Mysl', 1925, 76–81. Originally a speech given February 11, 1924, at the celebration of the fortieth anniversary of Sologub's literary activity. Entitled "Fedor Sologub" in *Lica* [38], 29–37.

[154] "Predislovie." In E. Zamjatin. *Bloxa.* Leningrad, 1926, 5–6. Much revised in *Uezdnoe* [30], 175–176.

[155] "Ko vsem pisateljam SSSR [otvet na anketu]". *Žizn' iskusstva.* No. 45 (1926), 17.

[156] "[Untitled article]." *Kak my pišem; teorija literatury.* Leningrad: Izdatel'stvo pisatelej, 1930, 29–47. [Pub. Jan. 1931.] Reprinted with several significant deletions in *Lica* [38], 259–274, under the title "Zakulisy."

[157] "Ričard Brinsli Šeridan, 1751–1816." In R. B. Šeridan. *Škola zloslovija.* Moskva-Leningrad: Academia, 1931, 18–29. Reprinted in *Lica* [38], 155–170.

[158] "Vstreči s B. M. Kustodievym." [Written 1928.] *Novyj žurnal.* No. 26 (1951), 183–192. Reprinted in *Lica* [38], 57–72.

[159] "Čexov." *Lica* [38], 39–49. A speech given in February 1925 at an evening in memory of Čexov, under the auspices of MXAT.

[160] "Cel'." [c. 1926.] *Lica* [38], 175–181.

[161] "Dlja sbornika o knige." [Written Dec. 23, 1928.] *Lica* [38], 257.

[162] "Andrej Belyj." [Written 1934.] *Lica* [38], 73–80.

[163] "M. Gor'kij." [Written 1936.] *Lica* [38], 81–98.

[164] "Sovremennaja russkaja literatura." *Grani.* No. 32 (October–December 1956), 90–101. A public lecture at the *Lebedjanskij narodnyj universitet* on September 8, 1918.

[165] "Psixologija tvorčestva." [Written 1919–1920.] *Grani.* No. 32 (October–December 1956), 102–106.

[166] "O moix ženax, o ledokolax i o Rossii." [Written 1932.] *Mosty.* No. 9 (1962), 21–25.

[167] "Moskva-Peterburg." [Written 1933.] *Novyj žurnal.* No. 72 (June 1963), 115–137.

[168] "O sjužete i fabule." [Written 1919–1920.] *Novyj žurnal.* No. 75 (March 1964), 148–156.

[169] "O jazyke." [Written 1919–1920.] *Novyj žurnal.* No. 77 (September 1964), 97–113.

Reviews (recenzii), **listed chronologically.**

[170] "*Ènergija.* Sbornik pervyj i vtoroj" (signed: Evg. Z.). *Ežemesjačnyj žurnal.* No. 3 (March 1914), 156–157.

[171] "*Sirin.* Sbornik pervyj vtoroj" (signed: Evg. Z.). *Ežemesjačnyj žurnal.* No. 4 (April 1914), 157–158.

[172] "Berngard Kellerman. *Sočinenija,* Tom I–IV" (signed: Evg. Z.). *Ežemesjačnyj žurnal.* No. 5 (May 1914), 154.

[173] "Raj" (signed: Mix. Platonov). *Dom iskusstv.* No. 2 (1921), 91–94.

[174] "*Grjaduščaja Rossija* (Berlin)" (signed: Mix Platonov). *Dom iskusstv.* No. 2 (1921), 94–96.

[175] "Anglija i Amerika [review of James Joyce's *Ulysses*]" (signed: E. Z.). *Sovremennyj zapad.* No. 2 (1923), 229.

[176] "Nik. Nikitin. *Sejčas na zapade.*" *Russkij sovremennik.* No. 2 (1924), 287–288.

Autobiographies, listed by date of publication, with subsequent reprintings.

[177] "Avtobiografija [1922]," published under various titles.

a. "Molodaja Rossija: Avtobiografija E. Zamjatina." *Vestnik literatury.* No. 2/3 (1922), 15.

b. "Pisateli o sebe: Evg. I. Zamjatin." *Novaja russkaja kniga.* No. 3 (March 1922), 42–43.

c. "E. I. Zamjatin o sebe." *Rul'.* No. 426 (April 9, 1922), 9.

[178] "Avtobiografija [1924]."

a. *Literaturnaja Rossija.* Edited by V. Lidin. Moskva: Novye vexi, 1924, 69–71.

b. *Pisateli; avtobiografii i portrety sovremennikov; sbornik.* Edited by V. Lidin. Moskva: Sovremennye problemy, 1926, 109–111. Second edition, 1928, 129–132.

c. Condensed version, E. F. Nikitina. *Russkaja literatura ot simvolizma do našix dnej.* Moskva: Nikitinskie subbotniki, 1926, 318–319.

[179] "Avtobiografija [1929]."

a. *Uezdnoe* [30], 1929, 5–19.

b. *Povesti i rasskazy* [39], 1963, 9–16.

Letters, listed by date of writing. Addressees' names are cited in the language in which each letter is written.

[180] "Juriju Annenkovu," [1921]. **Socialističeskij vestnik* (New York). June, 1954. Reprinted with [188], [193], [194], [195], [197], and [199] in *Grani.* No. 51 (1962), 69–71, 82–84, 87–91, and in Ju. Annenkov. *Dnevnik moix vstreč,*

I. N'ju-Jork: Meždunarodnoe literaturnoe sodružestvo, 1966, 258–260, 270–273, 276–280.
[181] "L'vu Luncu," November 13, 1923. *Novyj žurnal.* No. 82 (1966), 184–186.
[182] "L'vu Luncu," February 1, 1924. *Novyj žurnal.* No. 83 (1966), 158.
[183] "L'vu Luncu," February 21, 1924. *Novyj žurnal.* No. 83 (1966), 167–168.
[184] "L'vu Luncu," May 7, 1924. *Novyj žurnal.* No. 83 (1966), 176–177.
[185] "Avraamu Jarmolinskomu," [December 1924]. Unpublished. *ZA* 5:124.
[186] "Avraamu Jarmolinskomu," March 11, 1925. Unpublished. *ZA* 5:130–131.
[187] "Pis'mo v redakciju," [March 1928]. *Žizn' iskusstva.* No. 11 (1928), 22.
[188] "Pis'mo v redakciju," September 24, 1929. *Literaturnaja gazeta.* No. 25 (October 7, 1929), 4. Reprinted in *Volja Rossii.* No. 10/11 (October–November 1929), 190–192. See [180].
[189] "Pis'mo Stalinu," June 1931. *Lica* [38], [40A], 276–282.
[190] "To Cecil B. De Mille," February 12, 1932. Unpublished. Cecil B. De Mille Trust files.
[191] "To Avrahm Yarmolinsky," May 11, 1932. Unpublished. *ZA* 5:125–128.
[192] "Pis'mo v redakciju," March 30, 1932. *Literaturnaja gazeta.* No. 42 (September 17, 1932), 4. Reprinted in *Izvestija.* No. 259 (September 18, 1932), 4, and in *Poslednie novosti.* No. 4199 (September 20, 1932), 5.
[193] "Juriju Annenkovu," September 30, 1932. See [180].
[194] "Juriju Annenkovu," October 14, 1932. See [180].
[195] "Juriju Annenkovu," October 24, 1932. See [180].
[196] "To Joan London Malamuth," December 29, 1932. Unpublished. *ZA* 5:115–116.
[197] "Juriju Annenkovu," November 6, 1933. See [180].
[198] "Čarlzu Malamutu," May 14, 1935. Unpublished. *ZA* 5:117–120.
[199] "Juriju Annenkovu," August 12, 1935. See [180].
[200] "To Charles Malamuth," September 11, 1935. Unpublished. *ZA* 5:122–123.

Works edited by Zamjatin.

Periodicals.

[201] *Dom iskusstv.* Peterburg, 1921 (2 issues).
[202] *Russkij sovremennik.* Leningrad-Moskva, 1924 (4 issues).

[203] *Sovremennyj zapad.* Peterburg-Moskva, 1922–1924 (6 issues).

Books, arranged alphabetically by author.

[204] Čexov, Anton P. *Izbrannye sočinenija v trex tomax.* Redakcija, vstupitel'naja stat'ja [138] i primečanija Evg. Zamjatina. Tom I. Berlin-Peterburg-Moskva: Z. I. Gržebin, 1922. 375 pp. [Pub. Sept.]

[205] Genri, O. *Rasskazy.* Pod redakciej i s predisloviem [144] Evg. Zamjatina. Peterburg-Moskva: Gos. izd. Vsemirnaja literatura, 1923. 251 pp. [Pub. Jan.]

[206] London, Džek. *Ljubov' k žizni i drugie rasskazy.* Pod redakciej i s primečanijami Evg. Zamjatina. Peterburg: Gos. izd. Vsemirnaja literatura (Narodnaja biblioteka, vyp. no. 48), 1922. 124 pp. [Pub. Oct.–Dec.]

[207] London, Džek. *Put' moroznyx solnc.* Pod redakciej Evg. Zamjatina. Peterburg: Izd. Vsemirnaja literatura pri Gos. izd. (Narodnaja biblioteka, vyp. no. 43), 1920. 103 pp. [Pub. May 24.]

[208] London, Džek. *Syn volka i drugie rasskazy.* Pod redakciej i s predisloviem [126] Evg. Zamjatina. Peterburg: Izd. Vsemirnaja literatura pri Narodnom komissariate po prosveščeniju (Narodnaja biblioteka, vyp. no. 13), 1919. 119 pp. [Pub. Sept. 25.]

[209] London, Džek. *Zakon belogo čeloveka i drugie rasskazy.* Pod redakciej E. I. Zamjatina. Peterburg: Izd. Vsemirnaja literatura pri Narodnom komissariate po prosveščeniju (Narodnaja biblioteka, vyp. no. 22), 1919. 87 pp. [Pub. February 5, 1920.]

[210] Rollan, Romèn. *Teatr revoljucii.* Redakcija E. Zamjatina. Peterburg: Gos. izd. Vsemirnaja literatura, 1922. 218 pp. [Pub. Aug.]

[211] Šeridan, Ričard. *Škola zloslovija; komedija v pjati dejstvijax.* Redakcija i vstupitel'naja stat'ja [157] Evg. Zamjatina. Predislovie P. S. Kogana. Moskva-Leningrad: Academia, 1931. 176 pp. [Pub. Sept.]

[212] Sinklèr, Èpton. *Ad.* Pod redakciej M. Lozinskogo i Evg. Zamjatina. Moskva-Petrograd: Gos. izd. Vsemirnaja literatura, 1923. 165 pp. [Pub. Sept.]

[213] Šo, Bernard. *Nazad k Mafusailu.* Pod redakciej Evg. Zamjatina. Predislovie A. P. Pinkevič. Moskva-Petrograd: Gos. izd. Vsemirnaja literatura, 1924. 347 pp. [Pub. Jan.]

[214] Šo, Bernard. *P'esy.* Pod redakciej Evg. Zamjatina i K. Čukovskogo. Predislovie K. Čukovskogo. Peterburg-Moskva: Gos. izd. Vsemirnaja literatura, 1922. 388 pp. [Pub. Oct.–Dec.]

[215] Uèlls, Gerbert. *Ljubov' i mister L'juišem.* Redakcija Evg. Zamjatina. Moskva-Petrograd: Gos. izd. Vsemirnaja literatura, 1923. 196 pp. [Pub. Nov.]

[216] Uèlls, Gerbert. *Mašina vremeni.* Pod redakciej i so stat'jami [128], [129] Evg. Zamjatina. Peterburg: Izd. Vsemirnaja literatura pri Gos. izd. (Narodnaja biblioteka, vyp. no. 36), 1920. 192 pp. [Pub. Feb. 5.]

[217] Uèlls, Gerbert. *Neugasimyj ogon'.* Pod redakciej i s predisloviem [136] E. I. Zamjatina. Peterburg: Gos. izd. Vsemirnaja literatura, 1922. 179 pp. [Pub. July.]

[218] Uèlls, Gerbert. *Nevidimka.* Pod redakciej i s predisloviem [137] Evg. Zamjatina. Peterburg: Gos. izd. Vsemirnaja literatura (Narodnaja biblioteka, vyp. no. 41), 1922. 264 pp. [Pub. July.]

[219] Uèlls, Gerbert. *Rasskazy o vremeni i prostranstve.* Pod redakciej E. I. Zamjatina. Moskva-Petrograd: Gos. izd. Vsemirnaja literatura, 1923. 201 pp. [Pub. Oct.]

[220] Uèlls, Gerbert. *Sobranie sočinenij v dvenadcati tomax.* Pod redakciej i s predisloviem Evg. Zamjatina. Leningrad: Mysl', 1924–1926. Although only ten series volumes were listed in *Argameddon* [p. 232], subsequent lists consistently included twelve volumes, in the order given below. None of the books bore a volume number, except *Morskaja deva*, which, despite its designation as Volume II, was listed in the sixth position.

a. *Armageddon; rasskazy (1).* So stat'jami [133], [134] Evg. Zamjatina. 1924, 231 pp. [Pub. Dec.]

b. *Džoana i Piter; roman (2).* 1924 (on cover, 1925). 295 pp. [Pub. Jan. 1925.]

c. *Mister Polli; roman (3).* 1924. 234 pp. [Pub. Sept.]

d. *Novyj Makkiavelli; roman (4).* 1926, on cover. 311 pp. [Pub. Apr.]

e. *Tajniki serdca; roman (5).* 1925 (on cover, 1924). 187 pp. [Pub. Oct., 1924].

f. *Morskaja deva; roman (6).* 1924. 129 pp. [Pub. June.]

g. *Velikie iskanija; roman (7).* 1926, on cover. 264 pp. [Pub. Apr.]

h. *Anna-Veronika; roman (8).* 1926, on cover. 264 pp. [Pub. June.]

i. *Ljudi kak bogi (9).* Predislovie D. O. Zaslavskogo. 1925. 287 pp.

j. *Žena sèra Ajzèka Xarmana; roman (10).* 1925. 321 + 3 pp.

k. *Škola žizni* (Prodolženie romana *Džoana i Piter) (11).* 1925. 376 pp.

l.* *Rasskazy* (12).

[221] Uèlls, Gerbert. *Spjaščij probuždaetsja.* Pod redakciej E. I. Zamjatina s predisloviem Raf. Grigor'eva. Peterburg: Izd. Vsemirnaja literatura pri Narodnom komissariate po prosveščeniju (Narodnaja biblioteka, vyp. no. 14), 1919. 345 pp. [Pub. Aug. 20.]

[222] Uèlls, Gerbert. *Vojna v vozduxe* (*Izbrannye sočinenija*, IX). Pod redakciej i s predisloviem [127] E. I. Zamjatina. Peterburg: Izd. Vsemirnaja literatura pri Narodnom komissariate po prosveščeniju, 1919. 319 pp. [Pub. Sept. 28.]

[223] *Zavtra; literaturno-kritičeskij sbornik.* Pod redakciej Evg. Zamjatina, M. Kuzmina i M. Lozinskogo. Berlin: Petropolis, 1923. 137 pp.

II. TRANSLATIONS OF ZAMJATIN'S WORKS

Collections, listed chronologically.

[224] Zamiatin, Eugenio. *El farol y otros cuentos.* Tr. by Tatiana Enco de Valero. Madrid: Revista de Occidente, 1927. 189 pp.

[225] Zamjatin, Jevgenij. *Sever*; *pripovetke.* Tr. by Mira Lalić. Beograd: Nolit, 1963. 219 pp.

[226] Zamyatin, Yevgeny. *The Dragon*; *Fifteen Stories.* Tr. and ed. by Mirra Ginsburg. New York: Random House, 1966. 291 pp.

[227] Zamyatin, Yevgeny. *Essays.* Tr. and ed. by Mirra Ginsburg. University of Chicago Press (forthcoming in 1969). [The translated essays in this book are not listed separately in this Bibliography.]

Works published as monographs or in journals, anthologies, and collections, listed chronologically under the original Russian titles.

[228] *Afrika*
- a. "L'Afrique." Tr. O. Pertzov and M. Benoist de Beaulieve. *Marianne.* No. 299 (July 13, 1938), 10.

[228A] *Andrej Belyj*
- a. "Andrej Belyj (1880–1934)." *Slavische Rundschau.* Vol. 6, No. 2 (1934), 108–111.
- b. "Andrej Bjelij." Tr. I[rina] A[leksander]-K[unina]. *Književnik.* Vol. 7, No. 3 (March 1934), 124–126.
- c.* "[Andrej Belyj]." *Narodní osvobození.* [Before April 14] 1936.
- d.* "[Andrej Belyj]." *Les nouvelles littéraires.* 1936.

[229] *Angel Dormidon*
- a. "El ángel Dormilón." [224], 155–162.
- b. "Andjeo Dormidon." [225], 204–207.

[230] *Arapy*
a. "Los negros." [224], 163–166.
b.* "Arapi; bajka." *Jugoslovenski rasvit.* Vol. 3, No. 3 (June 1935).

[231] *Avtobiografija* [1922]
a. "[Autobiography]." In Eugene Zamiatin, *We.* Tr. Gregory Zilboorg. New York: Dutton, 1924, xvi–xviii. Paperback reprint, 1959.
b. "[Excerpts]." *Twentieth Century Authors.* Ed. by S.J. Kunitz and H. Haycroft. New York, 1942, 1567–68.

[232] *Avtbiografija* [1924]
a. "Autobiografija Evgenija Zamjatina." *Ruski arxiv.* No. 40/42 (1937), 228–230.

[233] *Bič Božij*
a. Samjatin, Jewgenij. *Die Geissel Gottes: Attila.* Tr. Xaver Schaffgotsch. Hamburg und München: Ellerman, 1965 (Pub. 1966), 119 pp.

[234] *Bjaka i Kaka*
a. "Biaka y Tiaka." [224], 181–184.

[235] *Bloxa*
a.* "La pulce." *Teatro russo.* Milano, 1955.
b. Samjatin, Jewgenij and Nikolai Lesskow. *Der Floh. Der Linkshänder.* Tr. Johannes von Guenther. Hamburg und München: Ellerman, 1962, 10–94.

[236] *Bog*
a. "El Dios." [224], 139–145.
b. "God." *New Russian Stories.* Ed. and tr. by Bernard G. Guerney. [Norfolk, Conn.:] New Directions, n.d., and London: Peter Owen Ltd., 1953, 190–192.

[237] *Buduščee teatra*
a. "L'avenir du théâtre." *Le Mois.* No. 17 (May 1932), 145–150.

[238] *Časy*
a. "La montre." *Les nouvelles littéraires.* No. 641 (January 26, 1935), 1–2.
b. "The Watch." Tr. Jaques Le Clercq. *Fiction Parade.* Vol. 1, No. 1 (May 1935), 117–122.

[239] *Cerkov' Božija*
a. "El templo." [224], 147–153.
b. "The Church of God." [226], 83–85.

[240] *Četverg*
a. "Četvrtak." [225], 212–213.

[241] *Črevo*
a. "Utroba." [225], 95–118.

[242] *Desjatiminutnaja drama*
a. "Ein Zehnminutendrama." Tr. Maxim Hekter. "Dichtung und Welt," Beilage *Prager Presse*. July 15, 1928, 2.
b. "Una tragedia in dieci minuti." Tr. Giovanni Comisso and Susanna Campaux. *Convegno*. Vol. 10, No. 3 (March 25, 1929), 132–136.

[243] *Detskaja*
a. "La 'Camera dei bambini'." Tr. Ettore Lo Gatto. *Narratori russi*. Ed. by Tommaso Landolfi. Milano: Bompiani, 1948, 952–962.

[244] *Drakon*
a. "Smok." Tr. Binom. *Ludzie jaskiniowi*. Warszawa: Rój, 1927, 25–26.
b. "Der Drache." *Russland erzählt*; *zwanzig Erzählungen*. Ed. and tr. by Johannes von Guenther. Frankfurt am Main und Hamburg: Fischer Bücherei, 1959, 97–98.
c. "The Dragon." [226], 70–72.

[245] *Ela*
a. "Jola." Tr. M. Pešić. *Ruski arxiv*. No. 20/21 (1932), 5–18.

[246] *Električestvo*
a. "Elektrika." [225], 208–209.

[247] *Fita*
a. "Fita: I, II, III, IV." [224], 115–138.
b.* "Bouffe-papier." *Noir et blanc*. 1934.

[248] *Glaza*
a. "Oči." *Preporod*. No. 58 (May 1923).
b.* "Die Hundeaugen." Tr. D. Umansky. *Das neue Ufer*. 1925.
c. "Oczy." Tr. Binom. *Ludzie jaskinowie*. Warszawa: Rój, 1927, 41–45.
d. "Les yeux." *Voix paysanne*. No. 5 (1933).
e.* "Oči." [225], 131–138.

[249] *Iks*
a.* "L'aventure du Diacre Indikopleff." *Le monde*. No. 6 (June 1932).
b. "X." [226], 218–238.

[250] *Ivany*
a. "Los Ivanes." [224], 167–173.
b. "Ivani." [225], 201–203.
c. "The Ivans." [226], 85–88.

[251] *Krjaži.*
a.* "Die starke Menschen." *Das asiatische Gesicht Russlands*. Augsburg: Orplid Verlag, 1928.

[252] *Lev*
a.* "Le lion." *Paris soir*. No. 12 (1935).

b. "Lion." Tr. Mirra Ginsburg. *Saturday Evening Post*. Vol. 239, No. 22 (October 22, 1966), 72–74. Reprinted in [226], 285–291.

[253] *Lovec čelovekov*.

a. "Le chasseur d'hommes." *Anthologie de la prose russe contemporaine*. Ed. and tr. by Vladimir Pozner. 2nd ed.; Paris: Hazan, 1929, 268–292.

b. "El cazador de hombres." *Revista de occidente*. Vol. 28, No. 82 (April 1930), 45–75.

c. "Il cacciatore d'uomini." Tr. Renato Poggioli. *Convegno*. Vol. 11, No. 7/8 (August 25, 1930), 263–285.

[254] *M. Gor'kij*

a. "Maxime Gorki." *La revue de France*. Vol. 16, No. 15 (August 1, 1936), 509–526.

b. "Maksim Gorki." Tr. B. Kovačević. *Ruski arxiv*. No. 38/39 (1936), 23–31.

[255] *Mamaj*

a. "Mamaj." Tr. Binom. *Ludzie jaskiniowi*. Warszawa: Rój, 1927, 27–39.

b. "Mamaj." Tr. Arthur Luther. *Dreissig neue Erzähler des neun Russland*; *junge russische proza*. 1st ed.; Berlin: Malik Verlag, 1928. 3rd ed., 1931, 281–298.

c. "Mamaj." Tr. B. Vračarević. *Književnik*. Vol. 3, No. 10 (October 1930), 445–450. Reprinted in **1000 najlepšix novela 1000 svetskix pisaca*. No. 25. Ed. by Ljubo Wiesner. Zagreb, 1931.

d. "Mamai." *Soviet Literature*; *an Anthology*. Ed. and tr. by George Reavey and Marc Slonim. London: Wishart, 1933, 72–81. 2nd ed.; New York: Covici Friede, 1934, 72–81. Reprinted in *14 Great Short Stories by Soviet Authors*. Ed. by George Reavey. New York: Avon Books, 1959, 95–104, and in *Modern Soviet Short Stories*. Ed. by George Reavey. New York: Universal Library, 1961, 15–24.

e. "Mamaj." Tr. Stevan Janić. *Srpski književni glasnik*. New Series, Vol. 50, No. 7 (April 1, 1937), 497–504. Reprinted in *Savremene ruske pripovetke*. Ed. and tr. by Stevan Janić. Beograd: Izdanje Profesorske zadruge, 1940, 55–66.

f. "Mamaj." [225], 169–184.

[256] *Moskva-Peterburg*

a. "Moskva-Ljenjingrad" (Part I only). Tr. I. K. A. *Nova Evropa*, Vol. 26, No. 10 (October 26, 1933), 472–481.

b. "Moskau-Leningrad." *Slavische Rundschau*. Vol. 5, No. 5 (1933), 298–310.

c. "Moskau-Leningrad; II. Die Literatur." *Slavische Rundschau.* Vol. 6, No. 3 (1934), 174–187.

[257] *Mučeniki nauki*

a.* "Une martyre de la science." *Lu.* July 1, 1932.

b.* "The Turning of Another Worm." *Hearst's International — Cosmopolitan.* Vol. 90, No. 3 (March 1931), 22–23, 184–188.

[258] *My*

a. *We.* Tr. Gregory Zilboorg. New York: Dutton, 1924, 286 pp. 2nd ed. (paperback), 1959, 218 pp.

b. *My.* Tr. V. Koenig. Praha: Lidová knihovna Aventina, 1927, 173 pp.

c. *Nous autres.* Tr. B. Cauvet-Duhamel. 2nd ed., Paris: Librairie Gallimard, 1929, 236 pp.

d. *Noi; romanzo.* Tr. Ettore Lo Gatto. Bergamo-Milano: Minerva Italica, 1955, 272 pp. Reprinted, *Milano: Feltrinelli, 1963.

e. *Wir: Roman.* Tr. Gisela Drohla. Köln-Berlin: Kiepenheuer und Witsch, 1958, 254 pp. Reprinted: "Eintragungen" (Chapters 1–5). *Russische Erzähler des XX. Jahrhunderts.* Ed. by Eugen Gagarin. München: Lucas Cranach, 1960, 202–213. And "Wir; Roman" (complete). *Gemordete Literatur; Dichter der russischen Revolution.* Ed. by Milo Dor and Reinhard Federmann. Salzburg: Otto Müller, 1963, 597–747.

f. *Me; romaani.* Tr. Juhani Konkka. Jyväskylä: K.J. Gummerus, 1959, 304 pp.

g. *Vi.* Tr. Noemi Eskul-Jensen. København: C. A. Reitzel, 1959, 167 pp.

h. *Vi.* Tr. Alf Biem. Oslo: Tiden, 1959, 199 pp.

i. *Vi.* Tr. Sven Vallmark. Stockholm: A. Bonnier, 1959, 238 pp.

j. "We." *An Anthology of Russian Literature in the Soviet Period from Gorki to Pasternak.* Ed. and tr. by Bernard G. Guerney. New York: Random House, 1960, 167–353.

k.* *A muralha verde.* Tr. José Sanz. Rio de Janeiro: GRD, 1963, 174 pp.

[259] *Na kuličkax*

a.* *Tamo gde je Bog rekao laku noć; roman.* Tr. M. N. Zagreb, 1925.

b. *Tamo gdje je vrag rekao laku noć.* Tr. Irina Aleksander. Zagreb: Socijalna Misao, 1931, 112 pp.

[260] *Navodnenie*

a. "L'inondation." Tr. B. de Schloezer. *La revue de France.* Vol. 12, No. 20 (October 15, 1932), 628–665.

b. "Poplava." Tr. Branka Kovačević. *Ruski arxiv*. No. 32/33 (1935), 28–47.
c. "The Flood." [226], 251–284.

[261] *O čude, proisšedšem v Pepel'nuju Sredu*
a. "Le miracle du mercredi des cendres ou le chanoine Simplice et le Dr Voitchek." Tr. S. Mandel and René Lebourg. *Europe*. Vol. 33, No. 143 (November 15, 1933), 336–344.
b. "The Miracle of Ash Wednesday." Tr. Mirra Ginsburg. *Kenyon Review*. Vol. 28, No. 5 (November 1966), 640–649. Reprinted in [226], 209–217.

[262] *O literature, revoljucii, èntropii i o pročem*
a. "Ueber Literatur, Revolution, Entropie und anderes." *Russische Rundschau*. No. 1 (October–November 1925), 59–64.
b. "O književnosti, revoljuciji i entropiji." *Ruski arxiv*. No. 38/39 (1936), 77–82.
c. "On Literature, Revolution, and Entropy." Tr. Walter Vickery. *Partisan Review*. Vol. 28, No. 3/4 (May–June 1961), 372–378. Reprinted in *Dissonant Voices in Soviet Literature*. Ed. by Patricia Blake and Max Hayward. New York: Pantheon Books, 1962, 12–19.
d. "O književnosti, revoluciji i entropiji." [225], 25–36.

[262A] *O moix zenax, o ledokolax i o Rossii*
a. "Brise-glaces." [Condensed.] *Marianne*. No. 11 (January 4, 1933), 13.

[263] *O tom, kak iscelen byl inok Erazm*
a. *Del bienaventurado anciano Fray Pamva Neresta, de su prodigiosa sabiduría, de muchas milagrosas revelaciones acaecidas y de como fué curado el monje Erasmo* [on cover, *De como se curó el doncel Erasmo*]. Madrid: Revista de Occidente, n.d.[1927], 46 pp.
b. *Vyléčený mnich*. Tr. Miroslav Heřman. Praha: Miroslav Heřman, 1934, 28 pp.
c. "The Healing of the Novice Erasmus." [226], 146–160.

[264] *Obščestvo početnyx zvonarej*
a. *Mister Kemble. La società degli onorevoli campanari. Tragicommedia in quattro atti*. Tr. C. Perris. Roma: Anonima Romana Editoriale, 1930, 156 pp.

[265] *Ognennoe A*
a. "La A de fuego." [224], 175–180.
b. "Vatreno A." [225], 215–216.

[266] *Ogni svjatogo Dominika*
a. *Ognie św. Dominika*. Warszawa: Ksiazka, 1924, 71 pp.
b.* *Feuer des heiligen Dominikus*. München: K. Desch, 1965.

[267] *Ostrovitjane*

a.* *Die Insulaner.* Tr. and adapted to the stage by E. Boehme. Wien: Internationale Theaterverlag Gesellschaft, 1927.

b. "Les insularies." Tr. O. Pertzoff. *Europe.* Vol. 50, No. 198 (June 15, 1939), 173–197.

[268] *Peščera*

a. "The Cave." Tr. D. S. Mirsky. *The Slavonic Review.* Vol. 2, No. 4 (June 1923), 145–153. Reprinted in *Bonfire; Stories Out of Soviet Russia.* Ed. by S. Konovalov. London: Ernest Benn, 1932, 299–310.

b. "Die Höhle." Tr. Dmitrij Umanskij. *Die neue Rundschau.* No. 1 (January 1925), 49–58.

c.* "[The Cave]." Tr. Yonekawa. [*Ten Stories by Soviet Writers*]. Yokohama, 1925.

d. "Ludzie jaskiniowi." Tr. Binom. In the collection *Ludzie jaskiniowi.* Warszawa: Rój, 1927, 11–23.

e. "La caverna." Tr. Marc Slonim and Giovanni Comisso. *Convegno.* Vol. 9, No. 3 (March 25, 1928), 143–152.

f. "Pećina." Tr. R. Živadinović. *Srpski književni glasnik.* New Series, Vol. 28, No. 8 (December 16, 1929), 577–584.

g. "Pećina." Tr. Mira Čehova. *Nova ruska proza.* Beograd: Nolit, 1933, 283–295.

h. "La caverne." Tr. Jacque Sabry. *Marianne.* No. 10 (October 9, 1935), 13. Reprinted in *Anthologie de la littérature soviétique 1918–1934.* Ed. by Marc Slonim and George Reavey. Paris: Gallimard, 1935, 60–69.

i.* "La caverna." Tr. Tito A. Spagnol and Marc Slonim, *Scrittori sovietici.* Milano, 1935.

j. "The Cave." Tr. M. Partridge. *A Second Series of Representative Russian Stories: Leskov to Andreyev.* Ed. by Janko Lavrin. London: Westhouse, 1946, 127–136.

k. "The Cave." *The Heritage of European Literature,* Vol. II. Ed. by E. H. Weatherly. Boston: Ginn, 1949, 714–718.

l. "The Cave." Tr. Alex M. Shane. *Occident* (Berkeley) Spring 1958, 33–39. Reprinted in *Russian Stories.* Ed. by Gleb Struve. New York: Bantam Books, 1961, 293–313.

m. "Die Höhle." *Russland erzählt; zwanzig Erzählungen.* Ed. and tr. by Johannes von Guenther. Frankfurt am Main und Hamburg: Fischer, 1959, 99–107. Reprinted in *Heilig-unheiliges Russland; Meistererzählung aus zwei Jahrhundert.* Ed. and tr. by Guenther. Düsseldorf: Droste, 1960, 983–994.

n. "The Cave." *Soviet Short Stories*. Ed. and tr. by Avrahm Yarmolinsky. New York: Doubleday, 1960, 1–11.
o. "The Cave." Tr. Richard Ravenal. *Great Soviet Short Stories*. Ed. by Franklin D. Reeve. New York: Laurel Editions, 1962, 422–432.
p. "Pećina." [225], 153–168.
q. "The Cave." [226], 135–145.

[269] *Pet'ka*
a. "Pećka." [225], 210–211.

[270] *Petr Petrovič*
a. "El gallo." [224], 185–189.

[271] [*Pis'ma o russkoj literature*]
a. "Lettres russes" (1). *Marianne* No. 74 (March 21, 1934), 4.
b. "Lettres russes" (2). *Marianne* No. 127 (March 27, 1935), 4.
c. "Lettres russes" (3). *Marianne* No. 182 (April 15, 1936), 4.

[272] *Pis'mo Stalinu*
a. "Lettre a Staline." *Le contrat social*. March–April 1962, 104–106.
b. "A Letter to Stalin." *Dissent*. Vol. 9, No. 3 (Summer 1962), 287–290. (Translated from the French.)
c. "Letter to Stalin." [226], xiii–xviii.

[273] *Pis'mo v redakciju* Literaturnoj Gazety, September 24, 1929
a. "Letter to the Literary Gazette." Tr. by Max Eastman in his *Artists in Uniform: A Study of Literature and Bureaucratism*. New York: A. A. Knopf, 1934, 87–91.

[274] *Predislovie k* BLOXE [1929]
a. "Vorwort des Verfassers." Tr. Johannes von Guenther. J. Samjatin and N. Lesskow. *Der Floh. Der Linkshänder*. Hamburg und München: H. Ellermann, 1962, 8–9.

[275] *Rasskaz o samom glavnom*
a. "A Story About the Most Important Thing." [226], 173–208.

[276] *Rus'*
a. "Russj." Tr. Arthur Luther. *Russische Erzähler des XX. Jahrhunderts*. Ed. by Eugen Gagarin. 1st ed.; München: Federmann, 1948, 146–158. Reprinted in 2nd ed., München: L. Cranach, 1960, 101–110.
b. "In Old Russia." [226], 161–172.

[277] *Sever*
a. "El farol." [224], 9–113. An excerpt entitled *"El ciervo de oro" was published in *Gaceta literaria*. No. 6 (1927).

b.* *Za bozjim ledama.* Tr. I. Aleksander. Zagreb: Zabavna biblioteka, 1928.
c. "Sever." [225], 37–94.
d. "The North." [226], 89–134.

[278] *Slovo predostavljaetsja tovarišču Čuryginu*
a. "La parole est au camarade Tchourigine." Tr. V. Soukhomline. *La revue de France.* Vol. 13, No. 24 (December 15, 1933), 603–617.
b. "Ima reč drug Čurygin." [225], 185–200.
c. "Comrade Churygin Has the Floor." Tr. Bernard G. Guerney. *Russians*: Then *and Now*. Ed. by Avrahm Yarmolinsky. New York: Macmillan, 1963, 239–249.
d. "Comrade Churygin Has the Floor." *The Fatal Eggs and Other Soviet Satire.* Ed. and tr. by Mirra Ginsburg. New York: Macmillan, 1964, 193–203. Reprinted in [226], 239–250.

[279] *Sovetskie deti*
a. "Enfants soviétiques." *Marianne.* No. 9 (December 21, 1932), 7.

[280] *Sovremennyj russkij teatr*
a. "Soudobé ruské divadlo." Tr. V. Koenig. *Rospravy Aventina.* Vol. 7, No. 18 (1932), 145–146, 154, in *ZA* 6:196–198.
b. "Il teatro sovietico: attori, poeti, registi." Tr. Renato Poggioli. *Scenario.* May 1932, 17–24.
c. "Das russische Theater der Gegenwart." Tr. M. Gorlin. *Osteuropa.* Vol. 8, No. 1 (October 1932), 10–25.
d. "Le théatre russe contemporain." *Le mercure de France.* Vol. 40, No. 826 (November 15, 1932), 50–71. Reprinted in *Cahiers du monde russe et soviétique.* Vol. 5, No. 4 (October–December 1964), 489–501.
e. "Moderno rusko pozorište." *Ruski arxiv.* No. 22/23 (1933), 37–45.

[281] *Spodručnica grešnyx*
a. "Notre-Dame de Bon-Secours des Pécheurs." Tr. B. de Schloezer. *Les nouvelles littéraires.* No. 589 (January 27, 1934), 7.
b. "Zaštitnica grešnih." [225], 139–152.
c. "The Protectress of Sinners." [226], 73–82.

[282] *Tri dnja*
a. "Les trois jours." Tr. N. Mandel. *Marianne.* No. 100 (September 9, 1934) 13–14.

[283] *Uezdnoe*
a. "A Provincial Tale." [226], 3–69.

[284] *Vospominanija o Bloke*
a. "A. A. Blok." Tr. E. Zaharov. *Ruski arxiv*. No. 30/31 (1935), 14–22.

[285] *Vstreča*
a. "Recontre." Tr. D. Ergas. *Vendredi*. No. 29 (May 22, 1936), 10.

[286] *Xeruvimy*
a. "Heruvimi." [225], 214.

[287] *Zakulisy*
a. "Iza kulisa." Tr. Lj[udmila] Mih[ajlović]. *Ruski arxiv*. No. 18/19 (1932), 9–17.

[288] *Znamenie*
a. "Znamenje." [225], 119–130.

III. SECONDARY SOURCES

Works on Zamjatin, including articles, separate sections in books, and introductions to his works, arranged alphabetically by author.

[289] Adamovič, G. "Literaturnaja nedelja; *My* i *Krasnoe derevo*." *Illjustrirovannaja Rossija*. No. 41 (October 5, 1929), 12.

[290] A[damovič], G. "Večer Evg. Zamjatina." *Poslednie novosti*. No. 4113 (June 26, 1932), 3.

[291] Aleksander, I. "Evgenije Ivanovič Zamjatin." *Književnik*. Vol. 3, No. 10 (October, 1930), 451–457.

[292] Aleksander, I. "Mjesto predgovora." In J. Zamjatin, *Tamo gdje je vrag rekao laku noć*. Zagreb, 1931, 5–8.

[293] Aleksandrova, Vera. "Evgenij Zamjatin." In E. Zamjatin. *My*. N'ju-Jork, 1952, i–xiii.

[294] Aleksandrova, Vera. "Umro Evgenij Zamjatin." *Nova Evropa*. Vol. 30, No. 5 (April 26, 1937), 169–174.

[295] Alexandrova, Vera. *A History of Soviet Literature*. Garden City, N.Y., 1963, 84–96.

[296] Altauzen, D. "*My* i vy." *Komsomol'skaja pravda*. No. 196 (August 29, 1929), 4. Reprinted in *Rul'*. No. 2666 (September 3, 1929), 4.

[297] Andreev, N. "E. I. Zamjatin." *Russkaja mysl'*. No. 1027 (March 9, 1957), 2–3.

[298] Andreev, N. "'Eres'' Zamjatina." *Grani*. No. 32 (October–December 1956), 118–126.

[299] Annenkov, Ju. "E. I. Zamjatin." *Vozroždenie*. No. 124 (April 1962), 113–115.

[300] Annenkov, Ju. "Evgenij Zamjatin." *Grani*. No. 51 (1962), 60–96. Reprinted in Ju. Annenkov. *Dnevnik moix vstreč* (Vol. I). N'ju-Jork, 1966, 246–286.

[301] Anon. "Beseda s E. I. Zamjatinym." *Poslednie novosti*. No. 4039 (April 13, 1932), in *ZA* 6:153.

[302] Anon. "Čtenie E. I. Zamjatina." *Poslednie novosti*. No. 5110 (March 21, 1935), 3.

[303] Anon. "Delo Pil'njaka i Zamjatina." *Volja Rossii*. No. 10/11 (October–November 1929), 189–193.

[304] Anon. "E. I. Zamjatin v Rige." [*Poslednie novosti*. November 1931] in *ZA* 6:147.

[305] Anon. "Eugen Samjatin." *Berliner Zeitung am Mittag*. No. 294 (December 17, 1931) in *ZA* 6:178.

[306] Anon. "Eugène Zamiatine." *Le mois*. No. 75 (March 1937), 233.

[307] Anon. "Evgenij Zamjatin." *Komsomol'skaja pravda*. No. 152 (July 3, 1928) in *ZA* 6:77.

[308] Anon. "Evgenij Zamjatin umro kao emigrant u Parizu, posle dvomesečnog bolovanja." *Politika* (Beograd). Vol. 34, No. 10350 (March 17, 1937), 8.

[309] Anon. "Gallereja sovremennyx pisatelej: E. Zamjatin." *Literaturnaja nedelja* (priloženie k *Krasnoj gazete*, No. 158), No. 27 (July 11, 1928), 1, in *ZA* 6:131.

[310] Anon. "M. Eugène Zamiatine et la jeune Russie." *Le mois*. No. 17 (May 1932), 178–182.

[311] Anon. "Molodaja Rossija. II. E. I. Zamjatin." *Vestnik literatury*. No. 2/3 (1922), 14–15.

[312] Anon. "Novoe v samorazoblačenii Pil'njaka i Zamjatina." *Na literaturnom postu*. No. 5 (1931), 33, in *ZA* 6:44.

[313] Anon. "O tom, o sem . . ." *Vozroždenie*. No. 2672 (September 25, 1932), in *ZA* 6:149.

[314] Anon. "[Ot izdatel'stva]." In E. Zamjatin, *Bič Božij*. Pariž, [1939], 7–12.

[315] Anon. "Ot izdatel'stva." In E. Zamjatin, *Lica*. N'ju-Jork, 1955, 7–11.

[316] Anon. "Pisatel'skie organizacii o pis'me E. Zamjatina." *Literaturnaja gazeta*. No. 26 (October 14, 1929), 1.

[316A] Anon. "Skončalsja E. I. Zamjatin." *Poslednie novosti*. No. 5830 (March 11, 1937), 1.

[317] Anon. "Skončalsja E. I. Zamjatin." *Meč* (Varšava). No. 11 (March 21, 1937), 6.

[318] Anon. "Smrt Evgenija Zamjatina." *Književnik*. Vol. 10, No. 3/4 (March–April, 1937), 175.

[319] Anon. "Travlja Pil'njaka i Zamjatina." *Rul'*. No. 2666 (September 3, 1929), 4.

[320] Anon. "Travlja Zamjatina i Pil'njaka." *Volja Rossii*. No. 8/9 (August–September 1929), 198–200.

[321] Anon. "Večer Evg. Zamjatina." *Poslednie novosti*. No. 4103 (June 16, 1932), 2.

[322] B., I. "*Krasnoe derevo* s beloj serdcevinoj; antiobščestvennyj

postupok pisatelej B. Pil'njaka i E. Zamjatina." *Komsomol'skaja pravda.* No. 196 (August 29, 1929), 4.

[323] B., K. "Fünfjahrplan und Kunst; eine Unterredung mit Evg. Zamjatin: Atempause in der russischen Literatur." *Prager Presse.* December 22, 1931, 4, in *ZA* 6:179.

[324] B., O. "Nachrufe; Evgenij Ivanovič Zam'atin." *Slavische Rundschau.* Vol. 9, No. 3 (1937), 210.

[325] Balika, D. *V laboratorii poèta (F. Sologub, A. Belyj, E. Zamjatin).* Belebej, 1917, 16–20.

[326] Bem, A. "Pis'ma o literature; o Evgenii Zamjatine." *Meč* (Varšava). No. 19 (May 23, 1937), 6.

[327] Benét, W. "Zamyatin." *The Reader's Encyclopedia* (2nd ed.). London, 1965, 1113–1114.

[328] Bezymenskij, A. "Tribuna pisatelja; za pravo na èpigrammu." *Literaturnaja gazeta.* No. 12 (July 8, 1929), 2.

[329] Bezymenskij, A. "Zlye èpigrammy. Spravka social'noj evgeniki." *Literaturnaja gazeta* [odnodnevnaja leningradskaja gazeta]. May 2, 1929, in *ZA* 6:72.

[330] Bodurtha, Helen. "Eugene Zamiatin: His Philosophy and Its Presentation in His Creative Writings." (Unpublished M.A. thesis, Slavic Department, Columbia University, New York, 1961). 68 pp.

[331] *Bol'šaja sovetskaja ènciklopedija* (1st ed.). Vol. XXVI. Moskva, 1933, Article, "Zamjatin," 154–155. (Deleted from 2nd edition.)

[331A] Bondarenko, V. "Evgenij Zamjatin i sovetskij period russkoj literatury." In E. Zamjatin, *Lica.* N'ju-Jork, 1967, 283–308.

[332] Bondarenko, V. "Veka i desjatiletija; Evgenij Zamjatin i Džordž Orvell — dva puteševstvennika vo mrak buduščego i buduščij mrak." *Grani.* No. 56 (1964), 188–204. Reprinted in [40], 203–223.

[333]* *Bonniers Lexikon.* Vol. XII. Stockholm, 1967. Article, "Zamjatin."

[334] Bráblík, F. "Poznámky k medailónu Jevgenije Zamjatina." *Československá rusistika.* Vol. 10, No. 1 (1965), 35–40.

[335] Braun, Ja. "Vzyskujuščij čeloveka; tvorčestvo Evgenija Zamjatina." *Sibirskie ogni.* No. 5/6 (September–December 1923), 225–240.

[336] Brovman, G. "Reakcionnaja literatura i ee tvorčeskij metod." *Molodaja gvardija.* No. 15/16 (August 1931), 113–118.

[336A] Brown, Edward J. "Eugene Zamjatin as a Critic." *To Honor Roman Jakobson. Essays on the Occasion of His Seventieth Birthday, 11 October 1966* (Vol. I). The Hague, 1967, 402–411. (Janua linguarum, Vol. 31.)

[337] Brown, Edward J. *Russian Literature Since the Revolution.* New York, 1963, 69–83.

[338] Brown, Edward J. "Zamjatin and English Literature." *American Contributions to the Fifth International Congress of Slavists; Sofia, 1963.* Vol. II, Literary Contributions. The Hague, 1964, 21–40.

[339] Browning, William. "Anti-Utopian Fiction: Definition and Standards for Evaluation." (Unpublished Ph.D. dissertation, Louisiana State University, 1966). 146 pp. Summarized in *Dissertation Abstracts*, Vol 27, No. 5 (November 1966), 1360A–1361A.

[340] Cardinne-Petit, R. "En U.R.S.S.: M. Zamiatine auteur et ingénieur nous dit les résultats obtenus à Moscou par le théâtre soviétique." *Comoedia.* No. 7005 (April 12, 1932), 1–2, in *ZA* 6:23.

[341]* Collins, Christopher. "Expressionism and Myth: An Approach to the Major Works of Evgenij Zamjatin. (Unpublished Ph.D. dissertation, Department of Slavic Languages and Literatures, Indiana University, in progress).

[342] Collins, C. "Zamyatin, Wells and the Utopian Literary Tradition." *Slavonic and East European Review.* Vol. 44, No. 103 (July 1966), 351–360.

[343] Collins, C. "Zamjatin's *We* as Myth." *Slavic and East European Journal.* Vol. 10, No. 2 (Summer 1966), 125–133.

[344] *The Concise Encyclopaedia of Modern World Literature.* Ed. by Geoffrey Grison. London, 1963. Article, "Zamiatin," 494–495.

[345] Damanskaja, A. "Evg. Ivan. Zamjatin." *Russkaja kniga.* No. 3 (March 1921), 18–19.

[346] Damiani, E. "Zamjatin." *Grande dizionario enciclopedico* (2nd ed.). Vol. XII. Torino, 1962, 1274.

[347] Despotuli, V. "U Evg. Zamjatina." *Poslednie novosti.* No. 3938 (January 3, 1932), 2.

[348] Deutscher, I. "*1984* — The Mysticism of Cruelty." In Isaac Deutscher, *Heretics and Renegades.* London, 1955, 35–50. Reprinted in I. Deutscher, *Russia in Transition.* New York, 1957, 230–245; revised ed., New York, 1960, 250–265.

[349] *Diccionario enciclopédico Salvat.* Vol. XII. Barcelona, 1964. Article, "Zamiatin," 772.

[350] *Diccionario enciclopédico U.T.E.H.A.* Vol. X. Mexico City, 1952. Article, "Zamiatin," 1184.

[351] *Dictionary of Russian Literature.* Ed. by William Harkins. New York, 1956. Article, "Zamyatin," 430–432.

[352] *Dictionnaire biographique des auteurs de tous les temps et de tous les pays.* Vol. II. Ed. by Lafont and V. Bompiani. Paris, 1958. Article, "Zamiatine," 724.

[353] *Dizionario enciclopedico italiano.* Vol. XII. Roma, 1961. Article, "Zamjatin," 972.

[354] *Dizionario universale della letteratura contemporanea.* Vol. IV. Ed. by O. Bernardi. Milano, 1962. Article, "Zamjatin," 1220–1221.

[355] D[mitriev], Ju. "Zamjatin." *Teatral'naja enciklopedija.* Vol. II. Moskva, 1963, 737.

[356] Drozda, M. "Pilát v krédu?" *Literární noviny.* Vol. 15, No. 47 (November 19, 1966), 5.

[357] Eastman, M. "The Framing of Eugene Zamyatin." In Max Eastman *Artists in Uniform; A Study of Literature and Bureaucratism.* New York, 1934, 82–93.

[358] Efremin, A. "Evgenij Zamjatin." *Krasnaja nov'.* No. 1 (January 1930), 228–235.

[359] Efremin, A. "Na grani." *Komsomol'skaja pravda.* December 11, 1929, in *ZA* 6:65.

[360] Efremin, A. "Rokovoj put'." *Učitel'skaja gazeta.* January 4, 1930, in *ZA* 6:62–63.

[361] Ehre, M. "Studies in the Prose of Yevgeni Zamyatin." (Unpublished M.A. thesis, Slavic Department, Columbia University, New York, 1966). 70 pp.

[362]* Ehre, M. "Zamjatin's Aesthetics and Some Examples of Their Application." *Slavic and East European Journal.* (Forthcoming.)

[363] Elovson, H. "Zamjatin." *Svensk uppslagsbok.* Vol. XXXII. Malmo, 1955, 225.

[364] *Enciclopedia Motta.* Vol. V. Milano, 1945. Article, "Zamjatin," 995–996.

[365] *Enciclopedia universal ilustrada evropeo-americana.* Vol. X (Apéndice). Madrid-Barcelona, 1933. Article, "Zamiatine," 1302.

[366] *Ensayo de un diccionario de la literatura (*2nd ed.). Vol. III. Ed. by F. Sainz de Robles. Madrid, 1956. Article, "Zamyatin," 1219.

[367] *Ensiklopedia Indonesia.* Vol. III. Bandung-'s-Gravenhage, [1955]. Article, "Zamjatin," 1441.

[368] Eskul-Jensen, N. "Forord." In J. Samjatin, *Vi.* [København], 1959, 5–7.

[369] F[edorov], N. "Evgenij Zamjatin. U spomen talentiranom ruskom piscu." *Jutarnji list.* Vol. 26, No. 9030 (1937), 19.

[370] Fischer, Peter. "A Tentative New Critique of E. I. Zamjatin." (Unpublished Ph.D. dissertation, Department of Slavic Languages and Literatures, Harvard University, 1967). 275 pp.

[371] Forgues, P. "Le théâtre russe vers 1930." *Cahiers du monde*

russe et soviétique. Vol. 5, No. 4 (October–December 1964), 479–488.

[372] Gibian, G. and M. Samilov. "Evgeny Zamiatin." In *Modern Russian Short Stories*. Ed. by George Gibian and Michael Samilov. New York, Evanston, and London, 1965, 123–125.

[373] Ginsburg, M. "Yevgeny Zamyatin (1884–1937)." In [226], v–xi.

[374]* Glebov, K. "Kleveta na Zamjatina." *Posev*. September 9, 1955.

[375] Goleniščev-Kutuzov, I. "Evgenij Zamjatin." *Vozroždenie*. February 17, 1932, in *ZA* 6:161–162.

[376]* Goleniščev-Kutuzov, I. "Evgenije Zamjatin." *Jugoslovenski rasvit*. Vol. 3, No. 3 (1935), 41–44.

[377] Goleniščev-Kutuzov, I. "Evgenije Zamjatin." *Srpski književni glasnik*. New Series. Vol. 49, No. 8 (December 16, 1936), 607–616.

[378] G[oleniščev]-K[utuzov], I. "Večer Evgenija Zamjatina." [*Vozroždenie*. June 1932] in *ZA* 6:144.

[379] Gregg, R. "Two Adams and Eve in a Crystal Palace: Dostoevsky, the Bible, and *We*." *Slavic Review*. Vol. 24, No. 4 (December 1965), 680–687.

[380] Grigor'ev, R. "Novyj talant." *Ežemesjačnyj žurnal*. No. 12 (December 1914), 82–85.

[381] *Der grosse Brockhaus*. Vol. X. Wiesbaden, 1956. Article, "Samjatin," 240.

[382] *Der grosse Herder*. Vol. VIII. Freiburg, 1956. Article, "Samjatin," 64.

[383] Guenther, J. v. "Nachwort." In J. Samjatin and N. Lesskow. *Der Floh. Der Linkshänder*. Hamburg und München, 1962, 155–161.

[384] Guerney, B. "Evgenii Zamiatin." In *An Anthology of Russian Literature in the Soviet Period from Gorki to Pasternak*. Ed. by Bernard G. Guerney. New York, 1960, 163–167.

[385] Gullón, R. "El totalitarismo no es irreversible." *Insula. Vol.* 20, No. 222 (May 1965), 1, 10.

[386] Hayward, M. "Pilnyak and Zamyatin; Two Tragedies of the Twenties." *Survey*. No. 36 (April–June 1961), 85–91.

[387] Holthusen, Johannes. *Russische Gegenwarts Literatur*. Vol. I (1890–1940). Bern und München, 1963, 106–110.

[388] Hooning, T. "Een vergeten anti-utopist: E. Zamjatin." *Tirade*. Vol. 8 (1964), 549–560.

[389] *The International Who's Who* (1935). Article, "Zamiatin," 1116. Reprinted in the 1937 ed., 1160.

[390] Iwanik, J. "E. I. Zamyatin, 1884–1937." *Russian Short Stories*. Ed. by John Iwanik. Boston, 1962, 100–101.

[391] Jackson, R. "Zamiatin's *We*." In Robert L. Jackson, *Dostoevskij's Underground Man in Russian Literature*. 'S-Gravenhage, 1958, 150–157.

[392] Janjić, S. "Jevgenjij Zamjatjin." *Srpski književni glasnik*. New Series. Vol. 50, No. 7 (April 1, 1937), 514–522.

[393] J[ovanović], Ž. "Evgenij Ivanović Zamjatin (1884–1937)." *Srpski književni glasnik*. New Series. Vol. 50, No. 7 (April 1, 1937), 574–576.

[394] Kaschin, A. "Moskaus grössere Orwell: Denkmal für einen totgeschwiegenen Schriftsteller." *Antikommunist*. No. 14 (1957), 41–45.

[395] Kašin, A. "Xudožnik i čelovek." *Grani*. No. 32 (October–December 1956), 107–117.

[396] Kastorskij, S. "*Gorodok Okurov* i povest' E. Zamjatina *Uezdnoe*." In S. V. Kastorskij, *Povesti M. Gor'kogo* Gorodok Okurov, Žizn' Matveja Kožemjakina. Leningrad, 1960, 323–329.

[397] *Kleine slavische Biographie*. Wiesbaden, 1958. Article, "Zamjatin," 790–791.

[398] *Kleines literarisches Lexikon*. München, 1961. Article, "Samjatin," 352–353.

[399] Koenig, V. "Jevgenij Zamjatin vypravuje; ruský spisovatel a dramatik o sobě, o své tvorbě a ruské literatuře." *Lidové noviny*. December 22, 1931, in *ZA* 6:186.

[400] Koenig, V. "Kulturní kronika; néco o denunciacích a kulturním sblíženi s SSSR." *Lidové noviny*. February 25, 1932, in *ZA* 6:182.

[400A] Korjakov, M. "Lica i xari." In E. Zamjatin, *Lica*. N'ju-Jork, 1967, 1–11.

[401] Kubka, F. "Russland; Jevgenij Ivanovič Zamjatin." *Prager Presse*. October 17, 1926, in *ZA* 6:180.

[402] Lalić, M. "Jevgenij Zamjatin." In J. Zamjatin, *Sever; pripovetke*. Beograd, 1963, 9–24.

[403] Lavrin, J. "Zamiatin." *Cassell's Encyclopedia of Literature*. Vol. II. Ed. by S. H. Steinberg. London, 1953, 2082.

[404] Lefèvre, F. "Une heure avec Zamiatine." *Les nouvelles littéraires*. No. 497 (April 23, 1932), 1, 8.

[405] Levinson, A. "Džentl'men; zametki o proze E. I. Zamjatina." *Poslednie novosti*. [March 1923] in *ZA* 6:139.

[406] *Lexikon der Weltliteratur*. Ed. by Gero von Wilpert. Stuttgart, 1963. Article, "Zamjatin," 1456–1457.

[407] Lo Gatto, Ettore. "Introduzione. Evgénij Ivànovič Zamjàtin e il romanzo *Noi*." In E. Zamjatin, *Noi; romanzo*. Bergamo-Milano, 1955, 5–27.

[408] Lo Gatto, Ettore. "Prefazione." In E. Zamjatin, *Mister*

Kemble. La società degli onorevoli campanari. Roma, 1930, v–ix.

[409] Lo Gatto, Ettore. *Storia della letteratura russa contemporanea.* Milano, 1958, 383–392.

[410] Lo Gatto, Ettore. "Zamjatin." *Dizionario letterario Bompiani degli autori di tutti i tempi e di tutte le letterature.* Vol. III. Milano, 1957, 935.

[411] Lo Gatto, Ettore. "Zamjatin." *Enciclopedia dello spettacolo.* Vol. IX. Roma, 1962, 2084–2085.

[412] Lo Gatto, Ettore. "Zamjatin." *Enciclopedia italiana di scienze, lettere ed arti.* Vol. XXXV. Roma, 1937, 877.

[413] Luckyj, G. "Zamjatin." *Lexikon der Weltliteratur im 20. Jahrhundert.* Vol. II. Freiburg-Basel-Wien, 1961, 1302–1303.

[414] Lunin, È. "Zamjatin." *Literaturnaja ènciklopedija.* Vol. IV. Moskva, 1930, 302–310.

[415] Majakovskij, V. "Rabotnikam stixa i prozy, na leto eduščim v kolxozy." *Komsomol'skaja pravda.* No. 152 (July 3, 1928) in *ZA* 6:77. Reprinted in V. Majakovskij, *Sobranie sočinenij.* Vol. IX. Moskva, 1958, 148–151.

[416] *Malaja sovetskaja ènciklopedija* (1st ed.). Vol. III. Moskva, 1929. Article, "Zamjatin," 233. (Deleted from 2nd and 3rd editions.)

[417] Malozemova, E. "Evgenij Zamjatin, 1884–1937." *Novoe russkoe slovo.* March 10, 1962, 4.

[418]* M[andel'štam], Ju. "[Nekrolog]." *Vozroždenie.* March 1937.

[419] Mandelstamm, I. "Lettres russes: Eugène Zamiatine." *La revue de France.* Vol. 17, No. 8 (April 15, 1937), 751–757.

[420] Mašbic-Verov, I. "Evgenij Zamjatin." *Na literaturnom postu.* No. 17/18 (September 1927), 56–65. Reprinted with minor changes in I. Mašbic-Verov, *Pisatel' i sovremennost'; stat'i.* Moskva, 1931, 7–28.

[421] Melniková-Papoušková, N. "Má setkání se spisovateli v Sovětském Rusku; II. E. Zamjatin." *Rozpravy Aventina.* (1927), 81, in *ZA* 6:195.

[422] Melniková-Papoušková, N. "Spisovatel ze SSSR; Jevgenij Zamjatin i jeho tvorba." *Přítomnost.* January 20, 1932, 41–44, in *ZA* 6:201–204.

[423] Melniková-Papoušková, N. "Z mých setkání a rozmluv s Jevgenijem Zamjatinem." *Rozpravy Aventina.* Vol. 7, No. 16 [December 1931], 126, in *ZA* 6:199–200.

[424] Meyer, Ruth. "Zamjatin's Revolution." (Unpublished B.A. thesis, Division of Letters and Arts, Reed College, 1966), 1–26. Includes translations of "Mamaj," 27–40; "Lev," 41–49; and *Bič Božij,* 50–150.

[425] *Meyers Handbuch über die Literatur*. Mannheim, 1964. Article, "Samjatin," 732.

[426] Mirsky, Dmitry. *Contemporary Russian Literature, 1881–1925*. New York, 1926, 296–299.

[427] Mixajlov, O. "Zamjatin." *Kratkaja literaturnaja ènciklopedija*. Vol. II. Moskva, 1964, 987.

[428] Moriturus (pseud. of V. A. Zorgenfrej). "Literaturnyj nekropol'; Evg. Zamjatin." *Krasnaja nov'*. No. 10 (December 1925), 279.

[429] *The New Century Cyclopedia of Names*. Vol. III. Ed. by C. L. Barnhart and W. D. Halsey. New York, 1954. Article, "Zamyatin," 4210.

[430] Ocup, N. "Evgenij Zamjatin." *Poslednie novosti*. No. 2780 (November 1, 1928), 2. Reprinted in Nikolaj Ocup, *Sovremenniki*. Pariž, 1961, 95–101.

[431] Or., B. "Evgenij Zamjatin v Rige." *Segodnja*. No. 319 [November 1931], 10, in *ZA* 6:148.

[432] Osorgin, M. "E. I. Zamjatin." *Poslednie novosti*. No. 5830 (March 11, 1937), 2.

[433] Osorgin, M. "Evgenij Ivanovič Zamjatin." *Poslednie novosti*. No. 6556 (March 10, 1939), 3.

[434] Paris Correspondent (pseud. of A. Werth). "Literature in Soviet Russia; An Interview with Eugene Zamiatin; The Proletarians." *Manchester Guardian*. No. 26808 (August 9, 1932), 9–10. Reprinted as "A New Soviet Novelist." *The Living Age*. Vol. 343 (October 1932), 160–163.

[435] Pierre, A. "L'écrivain russe Zamiatine est mort." *Les nouvelles littéraires*. No. 753 (March 20, 1937), 4.

[436] *Pisateli sovremennoj èpoxi; bio-biografičeskij slovar' russkix pisatelej XX veka*. Vol. I. Ed. by B. P. Koz'min. Moskva, 1928. Article, "Zamjatin," 131–133.

[437] Pletnev, R. "O E. Zamjatine." *Novoe russkoe slovo*. April 28, 1957, 8.

[438] Poggioli, R. "Antinomie di Zamjatin." In Renato Poggioli, *Pietre di paragone*. Firenze, 1939, 107–112.

[439] Poggioli, R. "Eugenio Zamjatin, l'ultimo dei nihilisti." *Nuova antologia*. Vol. 392 (August 1, 1937), 358–360.

[440] Poggioli, R. "Nota sullo stile di Zamjatin." *Convegno*. Vol. 9, No. 7/8 (August 25, 1930), 257–262.

[441] Poljanskij, V. "Geršenson i Zamjatin. (Sovremennye literaturnye nastroenija)." *Sovremennik*. No. 1 (1922), 148–154. Reprinted in Valer'jan Poljanskij, *Na literaturnom fronte; sbornik statej*. Moskva, 1924, 164–172.

[442] Polonskij, V. "Zametki o molodyx; Čapygin, Nikandrov, Zamjatin." *Letopis'*. No. 3 (March 1916), 253–265.

[443] Pottecher, H. " 'Les Bas-Fonds' de Gorki inspirent à l'écran

français une oeuvre respectueuse, populaire, profunde avec la collaboration de Jean Renoir, Mary Glory, Jean Gabin et E. Zamiatine." *Comoedia.* No. 8570 (July 29, 1936), 1, in *ZA* 6:26.

[444] Pottecher, H. "Trois heures à Bellevue avec l'écrivain russe Evguéni Zamiatine." *Comoedia.* No. 7870 (August 27, 1934), 1, in *ZA* 6:1–2.

[445] Pozner, M. "Književni značaj dela Evgenija Zamjatina; posle smrti ruskog pisca." *Politika* (Beograd). Vol. 34, No. 10356 (March 1937), 10.

[446] Proffer, C. "Notes on the Imagery in Zamjatin's *We.*" *Slavic and East European Journal.* Vol. 7, No. 3 (Fall 1963), 269–278.

[447] *Reader's Adviser and Bookman's Manual* (9th ed.). Ed. by Hester R. Hoffman. New York, 1960. Article, "Zamyatin," 733–734.

[448] Redakcija. "[Predislovie k 'Atille']." *Novyj žurnal.* No. 24 (1950), 7–8.

[449] Redakcija. "Uspomeni E. I. Zamjatina, 1884–1937 g." *Ruski arxiv.* No. 40/42 (1937), 228.

[450] Remizov, A. "Ni za njux tabaku." In Aleksej Remizov, *Krašennye ryla. Teatr i kniga.* Berlin, 1922, 91–95.

[451] Remizov, A. "Stojat' — negasimuju sveču pamjati Evgenija Ivanoviča Zamjatina, 1884–1937." *Sovremennye zapiski.* No. 64 (1937), 424–430. Reprinted with editorial notes in *S-Peterburgskij politexničeskij institut.* Sbornik No. 2. Pariž-N'ju-Jork, 1958, 91–97. Translated into Serbo-Croatian in *Ruski arxiv.* No. 40/42 (1937), 231–237.

[452] Richards, D. "Four Utopias." *Slavonic and East European Review.* Vol. 40, No. 94 (December 1961), 220–228.

[453] Richards, D. "Zamyatin; Life and Works." (Unpublished B. Litt. dissertation, Magdalen College, Oxford University, 1960). 227 pp.

[454] Richards, D. J. *Zamyatin; A Soviet Heretic.* London, 1962. 112 pp. Reviewed by E. J. Brown, *Slavic Review,* Vol. 23, No. 2 (June 1964), 389–390, and C. Collins, *Slavic and East European Journal,* Vol. 7, No. 1 (Spring 1963), 68–69.

[455] Rudy, P. "Introduction." In E. Zamiatin, *We.* New York, 1959, v–xi.

[456] Rühle, J. "Nachwort." In J. Samjatin, *Wir; Roman.* Köln-Berlin, 1958, 241–254. Reprinted as "Die erste Vision der totalitären Welt" in Jurgen Rühle, *Literatur und Revolution; Die Schriftsteller und der Kommunismus.* Köln-Berlin, 1960, 46–54.

[457]* Schneider, Phillip. "*We* by Evgeny Zamyatin and Its Place among Russian and Foreign Literary Works Concerning the

Possibility of the Realization of a Utopian Society." (Unpublished M.A. thesis, Dept. of Graduate Studies in Russian, Monterey Institute of Foreign Studies, 1968) 158 pp.

[458] *Schweizer Lexikon.* Vol. VI. Zürich, 1948. Article, "Samjatin," 797.

[459] Shane, Alex M. "An Analysis of Zamiatin's *We* Including a Study of Its Influence on Huxley's *Brave New World* and Orwell's *1984*." (Unpublished M.A. essay, Department of Linguistics, University of Chicago, 1955), 59 pp.

[460] Shane, Alex M. "Evgenij Zamjatin; A Critical Study." (Unpublished Ph.D. dissertation, Department of Slavic Languages and Literatures, University of California at Berkeley, 1965), 382 pp. Summarized in *Dissertation Abstracts*, Vol. 26, No. 2 (August 1965), 1049–1050.

[461] Shane, Alex M. "Zamjatin's Prose Fiction." *Slavic and East European Journal.* Vol. 12, No. 1 (Spring 1968), 14–26.

[462] Skačkov, M. "Gastroli Evgenija Zamjatina." *Literaturnaja gazeta.* No. 6 (February 4, 1932), 1.

[463] Skačkov, M. "Pražskie zaščitniki E. Zamjatina." *Literaturnaja gazeta.* No. 12 (March 11, 1932), 1.

[464] Šklovskij, V. "Potolok Evgenija Zamjatina." In Viktor Šklovskij, *Pjat' čelovek znakomyx.* [Tiflis] 1927, 43–67.

[465] Slonim, Mark. "E. I. Zamjatin." *Novoe ruskoe slovo.* March 10, 1957, 8.

[466] Slonim, Mark. "Literaturnye otkliki; Evg. Zamjatin." *Volja Rossii.* No. 8/9 (May 1923), 89–95.

[467] Slonim, Marc. *Modern Russian Literature from Chekhov to the Present.* New York, 1953, 289–293.

[468] Slonim, Mark. "Pisatel' i ego tvorčestvo." In E. Zamjatin, *Povesti i rasskazy.* Mjunxen, 1963, 5–8.

[469] Slonim, Mark. "Pis'mo v redakciju." *Rul'.* No. 2679 (September 18, 1929), 5.

[470] Slonim, Mark. *Portrety sovetskix pisatelej.* Pariž, 1933, 48–61. First published as "Portreti savremenix ruskix pisaca; 1. Evgenije Zamjatin." *Ruski arxiv.* No. 3 (1929); 99–112; and reprinted in *M. Slonim, *Portreti savremenix ruskix pisaca.* Beograd, 1933.

[471] Slonim, Marc. "Preface." In E. Zamiatin, *We.* New York, 1959, xxi–xxv.

[472] Slonim, Marc. *Soviet Russian Literature; Writers and Problems.* New York, 1964, 80–89.

[473] Slonim, Marc. "Zamyatin." *Encyclopedia Americana.* International ed. Vol. XXIX (1964), 745.

[474] Souvarine, B. "Eugène Zamiatine." *Preuves.* No. 136 (June 1962), 78–82.

[475] Ssachno, H. "Nachwort." In J. Samjatin, *Die Geissel Gottes: Attila*. Hamburg und München, 1965, 113–119.

[476] Štejnman, Z. "Zamjatiny, ix algebra i naši vyvody." *Al'manax Udar*. Moskva, 1927, 194–198.

[477] Stender-Petersen, A. "Zamjatin." *Den Lille Salmonsen*. Vol. XII. København, 1940, 581.

[478] Strelsky, N. "Zamyatin." *Columbia Dictionary of Modern European Literature*. Ed. by Horatio Smith. New York, 1947, 887–888.

[479] Struve, Gleb. "Evgeny Zamyatin; Obituary." *Slavonic and East European Review*. Vol. 16, No. 48 (April 1938), 700–702.

[480] Struve, Gleb. "Evgeny Zamyatin (1884–1937)." *Russian Stories*. Ed. by Gleb Struve. New York, 1961, 290–291.

[481] Struve, Gleb. *Geschichte der Sowjetliteratur*. München, 1957, 56–64.

[482] Struve, Gleb. *Histoire de la littérature soviétique*. Paris, 1946, 40–45, 148–155.

[483] Struve, Gleb. "*My* Zamjatina v Čexoslovakii." *Russkaja mysl'*. April 29, 1967.

[483A] Struve, Gleb. "Notes Russian 'Anti-Utopia' Anticipated Huxley, Orwell." *New Leader*. March 9, 1953, 23.

[484] Struve, Gleb. "Novye varianty šigalevščiny; o romanax Zamjatina, Xaksli i Orvella." *Novyj žurnal*. No. 30 (1952), 152–163.

[485] Struve, Gleb. *Soviet Russian Literature*. London, 1935, 17–22, 130–138. Reprinted in enlarged edition *Twenty-five Years of Soviet Russian Literature*. London, 1946, 17–22, 130–138.

[486] Struve, Gleb. *Soviet Russian Literature, 1917–50*. Norman, Oklahoma, 1951, 37–45.

[487] Tamanin, T. "E. I. Zamjatin." *Russkie zapiski*. No. 16 (April 1939), 98–108.

[488]* Taranovski, K. "Evgenije Zamjatin." *Misao*. Vol. 16, No. 44 (1937), 341–344.

[489] Tarsis, Valerij. *Sovremennye russkie pisateli*. Leningrad, 1930, 83–84.

[490] Terapiano, Ju. "E. I. Zamjatin." *Russkaja mysl'*. No. 1810 (March 10, 1962), 6–7.

[491] Thorgevsky, Ivan. *De Gorki a nos jours; la nouvelle littérature russe*. Paris, 1945, 68–73.

[492] *Twentieth Century Authors: A Bibliographical Dictionary of Modern Literature*. Ed. by Stanley J. Kunitz and Howard Haycroft. New York, 1942. Article, "Zamayatin[sic]," 1567–1568. *See also* first supplement, 1955, 1119–1120.

[493] Txorževskij, Ivan. *Russkaja literatura.* Pariž, 1946, 563–566. Reprinted in 2nd ed., 1950, 567–570.

[494] Utkin, I. "O kom i dlja kogo?" *Komsomol'skaja pravda.* No. 196 (August 29, 1929), 4.

[495] V. "Večer pamjati E. I. Zamjatina." *Poslednie novosti.* No. 5879 (April 29, 1937), 3.

[496] Voronskij, A. "Literaturnye siluèty: III. Evg. Zamjatin." *Krasnaja nov'.* No. 6 (November–December 1922), 304–322. Reprinted in Aleksandr Voronskij, *Na styke; sbornik statej.* Moskva-Petrograd, 1923, 47–75; *Literaturnye tipy.* Moskva, 1927, 15–38; *Literaturnye portrety v dvux tomax.* Vol. I. Moskva, 1928, 76–110; *Literaturno-kritičeskie stat'i.* Moskva, 1963, 85–111.

[497] Voronskij, A. "Ob otšel'nikax, bezumcax i buntarjax." *Krasnaja nov'.* No. 1 (June 1921), 292–295. Reprinted in A. Voronskij. *Na styke; sbornik statej.* Moskva-Petrograd, 1923, 227–235.

[498] *Die Weltliteratur.* Ed. by E. Frauwallner, H. Giebisch, and E. Heinzel. Vol. III. Wien, 1954. Article, "Zamjatin," 1953–1954.

[499] Werth, A. "The Film Abroad; A Soviet Writer Takes to Cinema." *Cinema Quarterly.* Vol. 2, No. 2 (Winter 1933–1934), 101–103, in Z*A* 6:3–5. See also [434].

[500] White, J. "Mathematical Imagery in Musil's *Young Törless* and Zamyatin's *We.*" *Comparative Literature.* Vol. 18, No. 1 (Winter 1966), 71–78.

[501] Wilczkowski, Cyrille. *Ecrivains soviétiques.* Paris, 1949, 213–217.

[502] Woodcock, G. "Utopias in Negative." *Sewanee Review.* Vol. 64 (1956), 81–97.

[503] Zajcev, B. "Pamjati Zamjatina." *Russkaja mysl'.* No. 1810 (March 10, 1962), 7.

[504]* Zamjatina, L. "Pis'mo v redakciju." *Russkie novosti.* August 5, 1955.

[505] Zavalishin, Vyacheslav. *Early Soviet Writers.* New York, 1958, 179–187.

[506] Zavališin, Vjačeslav. "Evgenij Zamjatin." *Novoe russkoe slovo.* No. 17926 (April 8, 1962), 2, 8.

[507] Zavališin, Vjačeslav. "[Vstuplenie k vtoromu izdaniju]." In E. Zamjatin, *Rus'* (2nd ed.). [Petrograd, 1923], 3.

[508] Žiglevič, E. "*My* i my." In E. Zamjatin, *My.* N'ju-Jork, 1967, vii–ix.

[509] Zilboorg, G. "Foreword." In E. Zamiatin, *We.* New York, 1924, v–xii. Reprinted in the 1959 ed., xiii–xviii.

[510] Zilboorg, G. "Thirty-five Years Later." In E. Zamiatin, *We.* New York, 1959, xix–xx.

Books and articles of a more general character in which Zamjatin is mentioned.

[511] Adamovič, G. " 'Na dne'." *Poslednie novosti*. No. 5733 (December 4, 1936), 4.

[512] Aleksandrova, Vera. "K 40-letiju sovetskoj literature." *Novyj žurnal*. No. 51 (1957), 87–104.

[513] Anikst, A. "Slander in the Guise of Scholarship." *Soviet Literature*. No. 10 (October 1947), 62–65.

[514] Anon. "Berlin, ot našego korrespondenta: vypuskajut pisatelej." *Poslednie novosti*. No. 3904 (November 30, 1931), 2.

[515] Anon. "Le groupe des Ecrivains Prolétariens recoit Barbusse, Zamiatine et Ehrenbourg." *Bulletin des Ecrivains Prolétariens*. No. 1 (March 1932) in *ZA* 6:21.

[516] Anon. "Itogi i perspektivy; iz rezoljucii dramaturgičeskoj konferencii." *Rabočij i teatr*. June 5, 1930, in *ZA* 6:81–82.

[517] Anon. "Leningradskie pisateli odobrjajut rešenie ispolbjuro FOSP o Vseross. sojuze pisatelej; postanovlenie ispolbjuro Leningradskogo otdela FOSP ot 16 sentjabrja." *Literaturnaja gazeta*. No. 23 (September 23, 1929), 1.

[518] Anon. "Leningradskie pisateli solidarizirovalis' s moskovskimi; soprotivlenie reakcionnyx èlementov (èkstrennoe obščee sobranie Leningradskogo otdela VSP)." *Literaturnaja gazeta*. No. 24 (September 30, 1929), 1.

[519] Anon. "Na literaturnom fronte. Protiv kapituljanstva, protiv političeskoj besxrebetnosti, protiv komčvanstva i prisposoblenčestva. Otkrytoe pis'mo RAPP." *Komsomol'skaja pravda*. No. 176 (August 3, 1929), 3.

[520] Anon. "Ne tol'ko ošibka, no i prestuplenie! Postanovlenie pravlenie Vseross. sojuza pisatelej." *Literaturnaja gazeta*. No. 21 (September 9, 1929), 1.

[521] Anon. "Ot redakciej *Komsomol'skoj pravdy*." *Komsomol'skaja pravda*. No. 176 (August 3, 1929), 3.

[522] Anon. "[Peredovaja]." *Literaturnaja gazeta*. No. 21 (September 9, 1929), 1.

[523] Anon. "Postanovlenie ispolbjuro FOSP ot 12 oktjabrja." *Literaturnaja gazeta*. No. 26 (October 14, 1929), 1.

[524] Anon. "Postanovlenie Moskovskogo otdela Vserossijskogo sojuza sovetskix pisatelej ot 11 oktjabrja." *Literaturnaja gazeta*. No. 26 (October 14, 1929), 1.

[525] Anon. "Postanovlenie pravlenija Leningradskogo otdela VSP ot 22 sentjabrja." *Literaturnaja gazeta*. No. 26 (October 14, 1929), 1.

[526] Anon. "Protiv političeskogo dvurušničestva i literaturnogo vreditel'stva. Postanovlenie ispolbjuro FOSP." *Literaturnaja gazeta*. No. 21 (September 9, 1929), 1.

[527] Anon. "Severnaja ljubov'." *Rabočij i teatr.* No. 32 (1927), cover, 13, in *ZA* 6:175–176.

[527A] Anon., "Smena geroev." *Literaturnaja gazeta.* No. 52 (September 25, 1931), 1.

[528] Anon. "Sovetskij pisatel' ne možet stojat' v storone ot socialističeskogo stroitel'stva . . ." *Literaturnaja gazeta.* No. 22 (September 16, 1929), 1.

[529] Anon. "Sovremennaja kritika o vol'nyx i nevol'nyx poputčikax; opyt xrestomatii." *Kniga o knigax.* No. 3 (May 1924), 21–22.

[530] Anon. "Uroki i zadači" *Literaturnaja gazeta.* No. 26 (October 14, 1929), 1.

[531] Antonini, G. "Russische Romans 1934." *Den Gulden Winckel.* December 1934, 183–187, in *ZA* 6:189–194.

[531A] *Arxiv A. M. Gor'kogo* (Vol. XI, *Perepiska A. M. Gor'kogo s I. A. Gruzdevym*). Moskva, 1966.

[532] Asad. "Na doroge v 'zavtra'." *Krasnaja gazeta* (večernij vypusk). No. 13 (January 15, 1931) in *ZA* 6:51.

[533] Aseev, N. "Xudožestvennaja literatura." *Pečat' i revoljucija.* No. 7 (September–October 1922), 68–80.

[534] Ašukin, N. "Sovremennost' v literature." *Novaja russkaja kniga.* No. 6 (June 1922), 4–6.

[535] Averbax, L. "O besprincipnom skločničestve i slovesnoj treskotne." *Oktjabr'.* No. 11/12 (November–December 1926), 194–215.

[536] B., H. "Hostující básníci." *Zvon.* March 9, 1932, in *ZA* 6:183–185.

[537] Baluxatyj, S. "Komentarii." *M. Gor'kij; materialy i issledovanija* (Vol. I). Ed. by V. Desnickij. Leningrad, 1934, 111–112.

[538] Berberova, N. "Iz peterburgskix vospominanij; tri družby." *Opyty.* No. 1 (1953), 163–180.

[539] Bezdomnyj, N. "Predteči sovetskoj 'naučno-texničeskoj' fantastiki." *Russkaja mysl'.* No. 2452 (April 16, 1966), 2–3.

[540] Bjuro frakcii LAPP i Bjuro frakcii FOSP. "Na literaturnom fronte. Za dejstvitel'nuju perestrojku." *Leningradskaja pravda.* July 30, 1931, in *ZA* 6:42.

[540A] Bljum, È. "Buržuazno-liberal'naja kritika za rabotoj; kritičeskaja produkcija 'Perevala'." *Pečat' i revoljucija.* No. 5/6 (1930), 18–29.

[541] Blok, Aleksandr. *Sobranie sočinenij v vos'mi tomax.* Moskva-Leningrad, 1960–1963. Vol. III, 424; Vol. VI, 481; Vol. VII, 381.

[542] Blok, Aleksandr. *Zapisnye knižki, 1901–1920.* Moskva, 1965.

[542A] Bojadžiev, G. "Sojuznik ili vrag? (Vmesto recenzii.)." *Na pod"eme.* No. 6 (1931), 154–167.

[543] Bonnard, André. *Vers un humanisme nouveau; réflexions sur la littérature soviétique (1917–1947).* Lausanne, 1948.

[544] Borev, J., "Modernizm, čelovek, razum." *Voprosy literatury.* No. 3 (March 1963), 64–77.

[545] Borisova, V. "Rannee tvorčestvo V. Kaverina." In Veniamin Kaverin, *Sobranie sočinenij v šesti tomax* (Vol. I) Moskva, 1963, 461–477.

[546] Borland, Harriet. *Soviet Literary Theory and Practice During the First Five-Year Plan, 1928–1932.* New York, 1950.

[547] Boženko, K. "Na pomošč' starym pisateljam." *Vestnik literatury.* No. 9 (1921), 19.

[548] Braun, Jak. "Bez pafosa — bez formy." *Novaja Rossija.* No. 1 (January 1926), 85–94.

[549] Braun, Jak. "Desjat' strannikov v 'osjazaemoe ničto'." *Sibirskie ogni.* No. 1 (January–March 1924), 201–240.

[550] Brodskij-Krasnov, M. and V. Druzin. *Kratkij očerk istorii russkoj literatury XIX i XX vekov.* Saratov, 1931, 82, 83, 93.

[551] Brown, Edward J. *The Proletarian Episode in Russian Literature, 1928–1932.* New York, 1953.

[552] Buznik, V. "V poiskax novogo (zametki o pervyx sovetskix romanax)." *Russkaja literatura.* No. 3 (1964), 171–200.

[553] C-l, S. "Tri principial'nyx doklada; na V plenume Oblrabisa." *Žizn' iskusstva.* No. 4 (1928) in *ZA* 6:80.

[554] Cetlin, M. "Plemja molodoe; o 'Serapionovyx brat'jax'." *Sovremennye zapiski.* No. 12 (September 30, 1922), 329–338.

[555] Cingovatov, A. "Bibliografija: *Sibirskie Ogni* . . . Kniga V–VI . . . 1923." *Žizn'.* No. 1 (June 1924), 418–419.

[556] Čukovskij, Kornej. *Sobranie sočinenij v šesti tomax* (Vol. II). Moskva, 1965–1968, 754.

[557] Čumandrin, M. "Itak, čto že takoe Sojuz pisatelej." *Krasnaja gazeta.* August 31, 1929. Article continued in next issue.*

[558] Čumandrin, M. "Zametki o diskusii." *Krasnaja gazeta* (večernij vypusk). September 1931 in *ZA* 6:41.

[559] Cybenko, E. "Problemy literaturovedenija na V Meždunarodnom s"ezde slavistov." *Vestnik Moskovskogo universiteta.* Serija 7, No. 2 (1964), 30–39.

[560] Dement'ev, A. "A. M. Gor'kij i sovetskaja žurnalistika (po neopublikovannym materialam)." *Novyj mir.* No. 11 (November 1964), 213–231.

[561] Dox, Georg. *Die russische Sowjetliteratur; Namen, Daten, Werke.* Berlin, 1961.

[562] Edgerton, W. "The Serapion Brothers: An Early Soviet Controversy." *American Slavic and East European Review*. Vol. 8, No. 1 (February 1949), 47–64.

[563] Eng-Liedmeier, A. *Soviet Literary Characters: An Investigation into the Portrayal of Soviet Men in Russian Prose, 1917–1953*. 'S-Gravenhage, 1959.

[564] Èrenburg, I. "Novaja proza." *Novaja russkaja kniga*. No. 9 (September 1922), 1–3.

[565] Ermilov, V., A. Selivanovskij, V. Sutyrin and A. Fadeev. "Otkrytoe pis'mo RAPP *Komsomol'skoj pravde*." *Komsomol'skaja pravda*. No. 176 (August 3, 1929), 3.

[566] Evgen'ev-Maksimov, Vladislav. *Očerk istorii novejšej russkoj literatury; ètjudy i xarakteristiki*. Leningrad-Moskva, 1925, 150, 237, 255.

[567] Fadeev, Aleksandr. *Sobranie sočinenij v pjati tomax* (Vol. V). Moskva, 1959–1961, 237.

[568] Farber, Leonid. *Sovetskaja literatura pervyx let revoljucii, 1917–1920 gg*. Moskva, 1966, 90.

[569] Fedin, Konstantin. *Sobranie sočinenij v devjati tomax* (Vol. IX). Moskva, 1959–1962, 158–160, 227–228.

[570] Furmanov, Dmitrij. *Sobranie sočinenij v četyrex tomax* (Vol. IV). Moskva, 1960–1961, 404–405. First published in *Voprosy literatury*. No. 5 (1957), 202–203.

[571] Gej, Nikolaj and Vladimir Piskunov. *Èstetičeskij ideal sovetskoj literatury*. Moskva, 1962, 205.

[572] Gifford, Henry. *The Novel in Russia: From Pushkin to Pasternak*. London, 1964.

[573] G[izetti], A. "Diskussija o sovremennoj literature." *Russkij sovremennik*. No. 2 (1924), 273–278.

[574] Gizetti, A. "Stixija i tvorčestvo; russkaja literatura pred licom revoljucii." *Mysl'*. No. 1. Petrograd, 1918, 226–248.

[575] Gizetti, A. "Vozroždenie ili vyroždenie? (O žurnale *Letopis'*)." *Ežemesjačnyj žurnal*. No. 4 (April 1916), 299–318.

[576] Gladkovskaja, L. "Primečanija: *Železnyj potok*." In Aleksandr Serafimovič. *Sobranie sočinenij v semi tomax* (Vol. VI). Moskva, 1959–1960, 668.

[577] Golikov, V. "Bessleznye glaza." *Vestnik znanija*. No. 7 (July 1913), 683–691.

[578] Gorbačev, Georgij. *Dva goda literaturnoj revoljucii; kritičeskie i polemičeskie stat'i 1924–26 gg*. Leningrad, 1926, 195–199.

[579] Gorbačev, Georgij. "K jubileju odnoj rezoljucii." *Al'manax udar*. Moskva, 1927, 173–192.

[580] Gorbačev, Georgij. *Očerki sovremennoj russkoj literatury* (2nd ed.). Leningrad, 1925, 24, 26, 36, 70, 90, 96, 174, 183.

[581] Gorbačev, Georgij. *Sovremennaja russkaja literatura* (2nd ed.). Leningrad, 1929, 7, 10, 16, 25–27, 80, 81, 133, 145.

[582] Gor'kij, M. "Gor'kij o molodyx." *Žizn' iskusstva*. June 5, 1923, 19–20, in *ZA* 6:114–115. A condensed retranslation from the French in *Disque vert*, No. 4/6 (1923). For the complete original Russian text, see *Literaturnoe nasledstvo*, Vol. 70, (Moskva, 1963), 561–563.

[583] Gor'kij, M. "Istorija kul'tury v inscenirovkax dlja teatr i kartinax dlja kinematografa." *M. Gor'kij; materialy i issledovanija* (Vol. I). Ed. by V. Desnickij. Leningrad, 1934, 108–110.

[584] Gor'kij, M. "[O Zamjatine]." *Letopis' žizni i tvorčestva A. M. Gor'kogo*. Vypusk 3 (1917–1929). Moskva, 1959, 350, 362, 378, 705.

[585] Hare, Richard. *Russian Literature from Pushkin to the Present Day*. London, 1947.

[586] Hayward, Max and Crowley, Edward (eds.). *Soviet Literature in the Sixties: An International Symposium*. New York-London, 1964.

[587] Hayward, Max and Labedz, Leopold (eds.). *Literature and Revolution in Soviet Russia, 1917–1962: A Symposium*. London, 1963.

[588] Hollis, Christopher. *A Study of George Orwell: The Man and his Works*. London, 1956, 199–200.

[588A] Howe, I. "The Fiction of Anti-Utopia." *New Republic*. Vol. 146, No. 17 (April 23, 1962), 13–16.

[589] Ingolin, S. "*Dom iskusstv*, No. 2." *Novyj mir*. No. 1 (1922), 272–273.

[590] *Istorija russkogo sovetskogo romana* (2 vols.). Moskva-Leningrad, 1965.

[591] *Istorija russkoj sovetskoj literatury* (Vol. I). Moskva: Izdanie Moskovskogo universiteta, 1958, 146, 154, 182, 295.

[592] *Istorija russkoj sovetskoj literatury* (Vol. I). Moskva: Izdatel'stvo Akademii nauk SSSR, 1958, 14–16, 67, 86, 96, 506, 507, 518, 581, 676, 714, 716.

[593] Ivanov, Vasilij. *Formirovanie idejnogo edinstva sovetskoj literatury 1917–1932*. Moskva, 1960, 79–82, 138–141.

[594] Ivanov, Vasilij. *Iz istorii bor'by za vysokuju idejnost' sovetskoj literatury 1917–1932*. Moskva, 1953, 28, 99, 109.

[595] Ivanov-Razumnik, R. "Literatura i obščestvennost'; russkaja literatura v 1913 godu." *Zavety*. No. 1 (January 1914), 87–99. Reprinted in Ivanov-Razumnik, *Zavetnoe o kul'turnoj tradicii; stat'i 1912–1913 gg*. Peterburg, 1922, 35–56.

[596] Ivanov-Razumnik, R. *Pisatel'skie sud'by*. N'ju-Jork, 1951, 7, 10, 27, 28.

[597] Ivanov-Razumnik, R. *Tjur'my i ssylki.* N'ju-Jork, 1953, 39–42.

[598] Ivanov-Razumnik, R. "Zemlja i železo; literaturnye otkliki." *Russkie vedomosti.* No. 79 (April 6, 1916), 2.

[599] Jaščenko, A. "Literatura za pjat' istekšix let." *Novaja russkaja kniga.* No. 11/12 (November–December 1922), 1–7.

[600] Jirásek, Josef. *Přehledné dějini ruské literatury.* Brno-Praha, 1946. Vol. III, 140–143, 159, 163; Vol. IV, 163–164.

[601] Jurgin, N. "O novatorstve v xudožestvennoj literature." *Krasnaja nov'.* No. 8 (October 1925), 224–233.

[602] Karlinsky, S. "Pis'ma M. Cvetaevoj k V. Xodaseviču." *Novyj žurnal.* No. 89 (1967), 102–114.

[603] Kašin, A. "Protiv bessmertnogo gvozdja." *Mosty.* No. 2 (1959), 312–326.

[604] Kiparsky, Valentin. *English and American Characters in Russian Fiction.* Berlin, 1964.

[605] Kogan, Petr. *Literatura ètix let, 1917–1923 gg* (4th ed.). Ivanovo-Voznesensk, 1925, 44–46, 49.

[606] Kogan, Petr. *Literatura velikogo desjatiletija.* Moskva-Leningrad, 1927, 30, 41, 48–49, 67.

[607] Kogan, Petr. "O russkoj literature 22 goda." *Petrogradskaja pravda.* No. 20 (January 28, 1923).

[608] KR. "Vybrosim zaval' iz bibliotek." *Literaturnaja gazeta.* No. 21 (May 26, 1930), 1.

[609] Kułakowski, Sergiusz, *Pięćdziesiąt lat literatury rosyjskej 1884–1934.* Warszawa, 1939.

[610] Kuzmin, Mixail. *Uslovnosti. Stat'i ob iskusstve.* Petrograd, 1923, 156, 158–159, 163, 166.

[611] Kuznecov, M. "Socialističeskij realizm i modernizm." *Novyj mir.* No. 8 (August 1936), 220–245. Reprinted in: M. Kuznecov. *Sovetskij roman; očerki.* Moskva, 1963, 99–148.

[612] L., T. "Dans 'Les Bas-Fonds,' avec Jean Renoir." *Pour vous.* September 1936 in *ZA* 6:25.

[613] Lavrin, Janko. *An Introduction to the Russian Novel.* London, 1942.

[614] Lelevič, G. "Nesovremennyj 'Sovremennik'." *Bol'ševik.* No. 5/6 (1924), 146–151.

[615] Lelevič, G. "Po žurnal'nym okopam." *Molodaja gvardija.* No. 7/8 (July–August 1924), 261–273.

[616] Lettenbauer, Wilhelm. *Kleine russische Literaturgeschichte.* München, 1952.

[617] Lettenbauer, Wilhelm. *Russische Literaturgeschichte.* Frankfurt/Main-Wien, 1955. 2nd ed., Wiesbaden, 1958.

[618] Ležnev, A. "Na pravom flange; o žurnalax *Rossija* i *Russkij sovremennik.*" *Pečat' i revoljucija.* No. 6 (November–December 1924), 123–130.

[619] Ležnev, A. "Xudožestvennaja literatura." *Pecat' i revoljucija.* No. 7 (October–November 1927), 81–118.

[620] Ležnev, I. "Gde že novaja literatura?" *Rossija.* No. 1 (February 1924), 179–203.

[621] Libedinskij, Jurij. "Pis'mo v redakciju." *Literaturnaja gazeta.* No. 61 (December 24, 1930), 4.

[622] Libedinskij, Jurij. "Segodnja poputničeskoj literatury i zadači LAPP; pervaja čast' doklada tov. Libedinskogo na plenume RAPP." *Zvezda.* No. 1 (1930), 177–190.

[623] Libedinskij, Jurij. *Sovremenniki; vospominanija.* Moskva, 1961, 147.

[624] Liberman, G. "[Bakinskij rabočij teatr]." *Zarja vostoka.* October 5, 1928, in *ZA* 6:168.

[625] *Literaturnoe nasledstvo.* Vol. 70 (*Gor'kij i sovetskie pisateli; neizdannaja perepiska*). Moskva, 1963.

[626] *Literaturnyj arxiv; materialy po istorii literatury i obščestvennogo dviženija* (Vol. V). Ed. by K. Muratova. Moskva-Leningrad, 1960, 215, 236, 242.

[627] Lo Gatto, Ettore. *Storia del teatro russo* (Vol. II). Firenze, 1952.

[628] Lo Gatto, Ettore. *Storia della letteratura russa* (4th ed.). Firenze, 1950. Condensed ed., Torino, 1956.

[629] Lo Gatto, Ettore. *Storia della letteratura russa contemporanea.* Milano, 1958.

[630] Lo Gatto, Ettore. *Il teatro russo.* Milano, 1937.

[631] Lunačarskij, A. "Tezisy o politike RKP v oblasti literatury." *Literaturnoe nasledstvo.* Vol. 74. Moskva, 1965, 29–37.

[632] Lundberg, Evgenij. *Zapiski pisatelja.* Berlin, 1922, 117–118.

[633] Luther, Arthur. *Geschichte der russischen Literatur.* Leipzig, 1924.

[634] L'vov, L. [Title unknown]. *Rossija i slavjanstvo.* September 3, 1932, in *ZA* 6:145.

[635] L'vov-Rogačevskij, Vasilij. "Gorod i derevnja v novejšej russkoj literature." *Gorod i derevnja.* No. 1 (1923), 9–11.

[636] L'vov-Rogačevskij, Vasilij. *1917–1927, xudožestvennaja literatura revoljucionnogo desjatiletija.* Leningrad, 1927, 13, 33, 45, 56.

[637] L'vov-Rogačevskij, Vasilij. "Velikoe ožidanie; obzor sovremennoj literatury." *Ežemesjačnyj žurnal.* No. 1 (January 1916), 155–180.

[638] Mackin, Aleksandr. *Obrazy vremeni; stat'i o literature i teatre.* Moskva, 1959, 357, 361, 365.

[639] Majzel', Mixail. *Kratkij očerk sovremennoj russkoj literatury.* Moskva-Leningrad, 1931, 22, 29–31, 33, 120, 155, 201.

[640] Maksimov, Aleksej. *Sovetskaja žurnalistika 20-x godov; křatkij očerk žurnal'noj periodiki.* Leningrad, 1964, 46–49, 81, 118.

[641] Mar'jamov, A. "'Net' i 'da'." *Novyj mir.* No. 1 (January 1957), 238–246.

[642] Markov, P. "Moskovskaja teatral'naja žizn'." *Pečat i revoljucija.* No. 3 (May 1925), 145–157.

[643] Menglet, G. P. and Z. V. Vladimirova. "Dikij." *Teatral'naja ènciklopedija.* Vol. II. Moskva, 1963, 439–441.

[644] Messer, R. "Poputčiki vtorogo prizyva." *Zvezda.* No. 4 (1930), 203–211.

[645] Messina, Giuseppe. *La letteratura sovietica.* Firenze, 1950.

[646] Miller-Budnickaja, R. "Potomki ludditov." *Zvezda.* No. 4 (1934), 177–193.

[647] Mjasnikov, A. "A. M. Gor'kij — organizator izdatel'stva 'Vsemirnaja literatura' (1918–1921 gg.)." *Istoričeskij arxiv.* No. 2 (March–April 1958), 67–95.

[648] Motyleva, T. "Dvadcat' šest' dnej v SŠA." *Novyj mir.* No. 5 (May 1964), 154–186.

[649] Nefelov, K. S. (ed.). *Russkaja literatura v biografijax i obrazcax; s portretami pisatelej.* Praga, 1946, 366.

[650] Nikitina, Evdoksija. *Russkaja literatura ot simvolizma do našix dnej; literaturno-sociologičeskij seminarij.* Moskva, 1926, 197–198, 318–319.

[651] Nikonov, A. "Zapretnaja sovetskaja literatura." *Vozroždenie.* No. 39 (March 1955), 142–147.

[652] Nilsson, Nils. *Sovjetrysk litteratur 1917–1947.* Stockholm, 1948.

[653] Novickij, P. "O buržuaznom vlijanii na sovetskuju xudožestvennuju kul'turu." *Izvestija.* No. 219 (September 22, 1929), 2–3.

[654] *Očerk istorii russkogo sovetskogo dramatičeskogo teatra* (Vol. I). Moskva, 1954, 371, 418, 596.

[655] Ol'din, P. "Slovo o dnjax našix." *Vestnik literatury.* No. 2/3 (1922), 18–19.

[656] Ol'xovyj, B. "Klassovaja bor'ba v literature; o položenii vo Vserossijskom sojuze pisatelej i o zadačax sovetskoj literatury v rekonstruktivnyj period." *Izvestija.* No. 212 (September 14, 1929), 2.

[657] Ol'xovyj, B. "O poputničestve i o poputčikax." *Pečat' i revoljucija.* No. 5 (May 1929), 3–18.

[658] Orlov, V. "Istorija odnoj 'družby-vraždy'." *Letopisi Gosudarstvennogo literaturnogo muzeja.* No. 7 (Aleksandr Blok i Andrej Belyj; perepiska). Moskva, 1940, lvi.

[659] Oulanoff, Hongor. *The Serapion Brothers; Theory and Prac-*

tice. The Hague-Paris, 1966, 10, 16, 90, 117–121, 146, 147.

[659A] Piotrovskij, A. "Sovetskaja dramaturgija 1928 goda." *Žizn' iskusstva*. No. 2 (1928) in *ZA* 6:79.

[660] Plotkin, L. "Propovednik bezidejnosti — M. Zoščenko." *Protiv bezidejnosti v literature; sbornik statej žurnala* Zvezda. Leningrad, 1947, 89–104 (see also 44).

[661] Poggioli, Renato. *The Poets of Russia, 1890–1930*. Cambridge, Mass., 1960.

[662] Poljanskij, Valer'jan. *Na literaturnom fronte; sbornik statej*. Moskva, 1924, 134–136 (see also article on Zamjatin, 164–172).

[663] Polonskij, Vjačeslav. *Očerki literaturnogo dviženija revoljucionnoj èpoxi* (2nd ed.). Moskva-Leningrad, 1929, 21–22, 49, 139–141, 150, 248.

[664] Pozner, Vladimir. *Panorama de la littérature russe contemporaine*. Paris, 1929.

[665] Pravduxin, V. "Èstetstvujuščie politiki i literatura." *Sibirskie ogni*. No. 5/6 (September–December 1923), 215–224.

[666] Pravduxin, V. "Literaturnye tečenija sovremennosti." *Sibirskie ogni*. No. 1 (January–February 1925), 205–215.

[667] Pravduxin, V. "O kul'ture iskusstv; literaturnye perspektivy." *Krasnaja nov'*. No. 1 (January–February 1924), 290–310.

[668] Pravduxin, V. "Pafos sovremennosti i molodye pisateli." *Sibirskie ogni*. No. 4 (September–October 1922), 147–160. Reprinted in Valer'jan Pravduxin, *Tvorec — obščestvo — iskusstvo*. Novonikolaevsk, 1923, 59–85.

[669] Pravduxin, V. "Pis'ma o sovremennoj literature." *Sibirskie ogni*. No. 2 (May–June 1922), 139–151. Reprinted in Valer'jan Pravduxin, *Tvorec — obščestvo — iskusstvo*. Novonikolaevsk, 1923, 35–56.

[670] Pravduxin, V. "Xudožestvennaja literatura za sem' let; proza 1918–1924 gg." *Sibirskie ogni*. No. 5 (November–December 1924), 213–227.

[671] Rajx, B. "K itogam teatral'nogo sezona." *Na literaturnom postu*. No. 11/12 (June 1927), 66–74.

[672]* Raškovskaja, A. "Novejšie iskaženija v sovremennoj literature." *Vestnik znanija*. No. 21/22 (1925), 1279–1282.

[673] Remizov, A. "Krjuk; pamjat' peterburgskaja." *Novaja russkaja kniga*. No. 1 (January 1922), 6–10.

[674] Rest, B. "Diskussija v Leningrade: 'formula perexoda'— doklad Zel. Štejnmana." *Literaturnaja gazeta*. No. 38 (July 15, 1931), 2.

[675] R[est], B. " 'Formula perexoda' ešče ne raskryta: kakova

rol' pisatelja v èpoxu rekonstrukcii?" *Krasnaja gazeta*. July 7, 1931, in *ZA* 6:46.

[676] Rest, B. "Literaturnyj Leningrad — 9." *Literaturnaja gazeta*. No. 18 (April 9, 1931), 1. [The April 4, 1931, issue is also listed as No. 18.]

[677] R[est], B. "Na fronte literatury i iskusstva. O 'prologe' v tvorčeskoj diskussii; Sojuz sovetskix pisatelej aktivno obsuždaet tvorčeskij metod." *Krasnaja gazeta* (večernij vypusk). July 11, 1931, in *ZA* 6:43.

[678] Rodov, S. "Literaturnoe segodnja; stat'ja pervaja; literaturnoe okruženie." *Molodaja gvardija*. No. 6/7 (October–December 1922), 307–312.

[679] Rozanov, I. "Obzor xudožestvennoj literatury za dva goda." *Literaturnye otkliki*. Moskva, 1923, 71–76.

[680] Rubaškin, A. "K voprosu ob idejnoj èvoljucii Èrenburga načala 30-x godov." *Učenye zapiski Leningradskogo gosudarstvennogo pedagogičeskogo instituta*. Vol. 184, vypusk 6 (1958), 184.

[681] Rühle, Jürgen. *Das gefesselte Theater; vom Revolutionstheater zum sozialistischen Realismus*. Köln-Berlin, 1957.

[682] *Russkaja sovetskaja literatura*; *očerk istorii*. Ed. by A. Boguslavskij and L. Timofeev. Moskva, 1963, 20, 21, 52, 71, 87–88, 303.

[683] Š., K. "Mečtuny." *Gorn*. No. 2 (1922), 141–142.

[684] S., O. [Title unknown] *Izvestija Tambovskogo soveta rabočix, krest'janskix i soldatskix deputatov*. No. 169 (October 4, 1918) in *ZA* 6:125.

[685] Šaginjan, M. "Pis'mo iz Peterburga." *Rossija*. No. 1 (August 1922), 29–30.

[686] Sajanov, Vissarion. *Sovremennye literaturnye gruppirovki*. 1st ed., Leningrad, 1928, 13–15, 17, 81. 3rd ed., Leningrad-Moskva, 1931, 15–16, 22, 24, 27–29, 39.

[687] Samarin, R. "Iskaženie istorii sovetskoj literatury v literaturovedenii SŠA." *Sovremennaja literatura SŠA*. Moskva, 1962, 208–227.

[688] Samsonov, A. "Nova ruska proza." *Nova Evropa*. Vol. 9, No. 13 (May 1, 1924), 411–416.

[689] Schmerl, R. "The Two Future Worlds of Aldous Huxley." *Publications of the Modern Languages Association*. Vol. 76, No. 3 (June 1962), 328–334.

[690] Schwartz, H. "For Class War on Mars." *New York Times Magazine*. October 19, 1958, 81–82.

[691] Sekretariat RAPP. "Ko vsem členam Vserossijskogo sojuza pisatelej." *Na literaturnom postu*. No. 17 (1929), 2–3.

[692] Selivanovskij, A. "Tribuna tvorčeskoj diskussii VSSP; 7-go sentjabrja, v Moskve otkrylas' tvorčeskaja diskussija ot

poputničestva k sojuzničestvu: doklad tov. Selivanovskogo." *Literaturnaja gazeta*. No. 49 (September 10, 1931), 3.

[693] Setschkareff, Vsevolod. *Geschichte der russischen Literatur in Überblick*. Bonn, 1949.

[694] Širmakov, P. "K istorii literaturno-xudožestvennyx ob"edinenij pervyx let sovetskoj vlasti; Sojuz dejatelej xudožestvennoj literatury (1918–1919 gody)." *Voprosy sovetskoj literatury* (Vol. VII). Moskva-Leningrad, 1958, 454–475.

[695] Sizif. "Otkliki." *Poslednie novosti*. No. 5,844 (March 25, 1937), 3.

[696] Šklovskij, Viktor. "Pis'mo o Rossii i v Rossiju." *Novosti literatury*. No. 2 (October 1922), 97–99.

[697] Šklovskij, Viktor. *Sentimental'noe putešestvie; vospominanija 1917–1922*. Moskva, 1923, 262, 377. Leningrad, 1924, 67, 177.

[698] Šklovskij, Viktor. "Serapionovy brat'ja." *Knižnyj ugol*. No. 7 (1921), 18–21.

[699] Skobelkin, Vladimir. *Rol' partii v razvitii sovetskoj xudožestvennoj literatury v poslevoennyj period, 1945–1952 gg*. Erevan, 1955, 37.

[700] Slepnev, N. "Ot kružka — k širokoj obščestvennoj organizacii; o pisatel'skix nastroenijax." *Al'manax* [priloženie k *Krasnoj panorame*]. No. 2 (1930), 109–114, in *ZA* 6:54–60.

[701] Slonim, Mark. "Desjat' let russkoj literatury; stat'ja vtoraja." *Volja Rossii*. No. 11/12 (1927), 92–119.

[702] Slonim, Mark. "Literatura našix dnej." *Novosti literatury*. No. 1 (August 1922), 6–7.

[703] Slonim, Marc. *An Outline of Russian Literature*. New York-London, 1958.

[704] Slonim, Mark. "Struje savremene ruske literature (svršetak)." *Ruski arxiv*. No. 2 (1928), 140–159.

[705] Slonim, Mark. "Xudožestvennaja literatura." *Trudy Komiteta russkoj knigi*. Vypusk 1, čast' 1 (1924), 99–109.

[706] Smirnov, I. "Pis'mo A. K. Voronskogo V. I. Leninu." *Novyj mir*. No. 12 (December 1964), 213–219.

[707] Smirnov, N. "Po žurnal'nym stranicam; obzor." *Krasnaja nov'*. No. 6 (November–December 1922), 323–342.

[708] Sobolev, Ju. "Literaturnaja sovremennost'; o pticax mertvyx i živyx." *Žurnalist*. No. 1 (September 1922), 36–40.

[709] Struve, Gleb. "Čelovečestvo v 1984 godu; novyj roman o totalitarizme." *Russkaja mysl'*. No. 148 (June 24, 1949). Reprinted as "Čerez 35 let; novaja satira na totalitarizm." *Novoe russkoe slovo*. July 10, 1949.

[710] Struve, Gleb. "Dead Souls and Living Reputations: Re-

Assessing the Past of Soviet Literature." *Soviet Survey*. No. 23 (January–March 1958), 10–17.

[711] Struve, Gleb. "The Double Life of Russian Literature." *Books Abroad*. Vol. 28, No. 4 (Autumn 1954), 389–406.

[712] Struve, Gleb. "From Chekhov to Zhdanov." *New Leader*. September 28, 1953, 24.

[713] Struve, Gleb. "V. Pozner. Panorama de la littérature russe contemporaine." *Rossija i slavjanstvo*. April 6, 1929.

[714] Struve, Gleb. *Russkaja literatura v izgnanii*; *opyt istoričeskogo obzora zarubežnoj literatury*. N'ju-Jork, 1956, 18–19, 29n, 64–65n.

[715] Svjatopolk-Mirskij, D. "O nynešnem sostojanii russkoj literatury." *Blagonamerennyj*. No. 1 (January–February 1926), 90–97.

[716] Tan, V. "Obilie talantov." *Novaja Rossija*. No. 2 (February 1926), 81–90.

[717] Timofeev, Leonid. *Sovetskaja literatura*; *metod*, *stil'*, *poètika*. Moskva, 1964, 104, 106, 196, 220.

[718] Trockij, Lev. *Literatura i revoljucija*. Moskva, 1923, 24, 34, 58.

[719] Turincev, A. "O novoj russkoj literature." *Gody* (Praga). No. 2 (1926), 27–29.

[720] Turincev, A. "Opyt obzora." *Versty*. No. 1 (1926), 213–228.

[721] Tynjanov, Ju. "Literaturnoe segodnja." *Russkij sovremennik*. No. 1 (1924), 291–306.

[722] Udušev, I. [pseud. of Ivanov-Razumnik] "Vzgljad i nečto; otryvok." *Sovremennaja literatura*; *sbornik*. Leningrad, 1925, 154–182.

[723] V., B. "Uroki pil'njakovščiny." *Žizn' iskusstva*. No. 39 (1929), 2–3.

[724] Vinogradov, Ivan. *Bor'ba za stil'*; *sbornik statej*. Leningrad, 1937, 286.

[725] Volin, B. "Nedopustimye javlenija." *Literaturnaja gazeta*. No. 19 (August 26, 1929), 1.

[726] Voronskij, A. "Literaturnye otkliki." *Krasnaja nov'*. No. 2 (March–April 1922), 258–275.

[727] Xodasevič, V. "Meloči." *Vozroždenie*. September 7, 1933.

[728] Yarmolinsky, A. "Russia's New Literature Still in the Future." *New York Times*. No. 24,494 (February 15, 1925), Section 3, p. 5.

[728A] Zamoškin, N. "Ličnoe i bezličnoe; iz nabljudenij nad sovremennoj literature." *Novyj mir*. No. 6 (June 1929), 201–212. Reprinted in N. Zamoškin, *Literaturnye meži; stat'i*. Moskva, 1930, 129–160.

[729] Zavališin, V. " 'Strannik i vremja'." *Novoe russkoe slovo.* No. 18094 (September 23, 1962), 5.

[730] Zavališin, V. "Zametki o sovetskoj literature: 2. Novyj oblik sovetskoj satiry." *Vozroždenie.* No. 17 (September–October 1951), 164–174.

[731] Zonin, A. "Ešče o Federacii." *Žizn' iskusstva.* No. 48 (November 30, 1926) in *ZA* 6:96.

[732] Žukov, P. "Čem kritika živa." *Žizn' iskusstva. No. 23* (1924), 8–9.

[733] Žukov, P. "Literaturnaja diskussija; protiv kliček." *Zvezda.* No. 6 (1924), 255–263.

Reviews, listed alphabetically by author under the title of the work reviewed (reviews of translations are listed after reviews of the Russian originals).

[734] "Alatyr' "

a. Jakovlev, Ja. *Žurnal žurnalov.* No. 27 (October 1915), 19–20.

[735] "Belaja ljubov' "

a. Glagolev, A. *Oktjabr.* No. 8 (August 1925), 153.

b. Medvedev, P. *Zvezda.* No. 2 (1925), 287–288.

[736] *Bič Božij*

a. B. In *ZA* 6:136–138.

b. Os[orgin], M. *Poslednie novosti.* No. 6,625 (May 18, 1939), 3.

c. S., B. *Russkie zapiski.* No. 19 (July 1939), 200–202.

[737] *Bol'šim detjam skazki* and individual fables

a. Anon. *Izvestija po literature, naukam i bibliografii.* No. 6 (June 1916), 89.

b.* Anon. *Literaturnyj eženedel'nik* pri *Krasnoj gazete.* No. 20/21 (1923), 12.

c. Vengerova, Z. *Novaja russkaja kniga.* No. 2 (February 1922), 6–8.

[738] "Č
revo" and *Čevo. Zemlemer*

a. Anon. *Žurnal žurnalov.* No. 3 (1915), 21–22.

b.* Anon. *Bjulleten' knigi.* No. 3/4 (1922), 90.

[739] "Detskaja"

a. S[lonim], M. *Volja Rossii.* No. 5 (November 15, 1922), 83–85.

b. Tynjanov, Ju. *Kniga i revoljucija.* No. 4 (1923), 70–71.

[740] "Drakon" (*The Dragon*)

a.* Anon. *Booklist.* Vol. 63 (July 15, 1967), 1183.

b.* Anon. *Kirkus Service.* Vol. 35 (January 1, 1967), 31.

c. Bannon, B. *Publishers' Weekly.* Vol. 190, No. 25 (December 26, 1966), 95.

d. Blake, P. "Literature As a Lash." *New York Times Book Review*. Vol. 72 (February 26, 1967), 1, 32–34.
e. Davenport, G. "Dry Rot and Tovarisch Stalin." *National Review*. Vol. 19, No. 17 (May 2, 1967), 479–480.
f. Ehre, M. "A Free Imagination." *New Leader*. Vol. 50, No. 6 (March 13, 1967), 22–23.
g. Gaines, E. *Library Journal*. Vol. 92, No. 4 (February 15, 1967), 799.
h.* Hattman, J. *Best Sellers*. Vol. 27 (April 1, 1967), 11.
i. Heiney, D. "Russian Novelist's Slightly Out-of-Focus World." *Christian Science Monitor*. June 15, 1967, 11.
j. Kern, G. *Novyj žurnal*. No. 87 (June 1967), 328–330.
k. Lask, T. "The Times Changed, but Not the Man." *New York Times*. Vol. 116, No. 39848 (March 1, 1967), 41C.
l. Marshall, R. *Catholic World*. Vol. 205, No. 1228 (July 1967), 248–249.
m. Muchnic, H. "The Literature of Nightmare." *New York Review of Books*. Vol. 8, No. 11 (June 15, 1967), 4–6.
n. Oberbeck, S. "Bread, Salt, and Acid." *Newsweek*. Vol. 69 (March 6, 1967), 92–94.
o. Pryce-Jones, A. "A New Collection of Stories by Russia's Exiled Zamyatin." *World Journal Tribune*. Vol. 1, No. 183 (March 16, 1967), 30.
p. Shane, A. M. *Slavic and East European Journal*. Vol. 12, No. 2 (Summer 1968), 240–241.
q. Spector, I. "Heir to the 'Overcoat.'" *Saturday Review*. Vol. 50, (April 1, 1967), 36.

[741] *Gerbert Uèlls*
a. Alapin, E. *Kniga i revoljucija*. No. 6 (1922), 52.
b.* Anon. *Bjulleten' knigi*. No. 3/4 (1922).
c. Šapošnikov, B. *Žizn'*. No. 1 (1922), 220.

[742] "Glaza"
a. D[amanskaja], A. *Novaja russkaja kniga*. No. 3 (March 1922), 10–11.

[743] "Ja bojus'"
a. Anon. *Načalo*. 1921, 86, in *ZA* 6:166.
b. Evgen'ev, A. *Vestnik literatury*. No. 3 (1921), 5–6.
c. Fedin, K. *Kniga i revoljucija*. No. 8/9 (February–March 1921), 85–86.
d. Lunačarskij, A. *Pečat' i revoljucija*. No. 2 (August–October 1921), 224–227.
e. Voronskij, A. [497].

[744] "[Kak my pišem]" — later, "Zakulisy"
a. Anon. *Kniga — stroitelem sozializma.* No. 10 (April 1931), 77–78.
b. Anon. "Novoe v samorazoblačenii Pilnjaka i Zamjatina." *Na literaturnom postu.* No. 5 (1931), 33, in *ZA* 6:44.
c. P-in, L. "Zamaskirovannyj rejd buržuaznogo pisatelja." *Kommuna* (Voronež). May 12, 1931, in *ZA* 6:48.
d. Rest, B. *Krasnaja gazeta* (večernij vypusk). No. 103 (May 3, 1931) in *ZA* 6:45.
e. Štejnman, Z. "Texnologija besprincipnosti." *Smena.* December 7, 1930, in *ZA* 6:52.
f. Vladimirov, I. "'Mersi'." *Krasnaja gazeta* (večernij vypusk). January 29, 1931, in *ZA* 6:50.

[745] "Končina Bloka"
a. Al'medingen, G. *Kniga i Revoljucija.* No. 8 (1922), 22–24.
b. Lutoxin, D. "Krizis èstetizma." *Vestnik literatury.* No. 10 (1921), 4–5.

[746] "L. Andreev"
a. P., I. *Volja Rossii.* No. 3 (October 15, 1922), 81–82.
b. Šamurin, E. *Žizn'.* No. 1 (1922), 217–220.

[747] *Lica*
a. A., G. *Opyty.* No. 6 (1956), 94–96.
b. D — skaja, A. "Posmertnaja kniga." *Russkie novosti.* No. 529 (July 22, 1955), 4.
c. Epp, J. *Slavic and East European Journal.* Vol. 14, No. 3 (September 15, 1956), 78–79.
d. Struve, G. *Novyj žurnal.* No. 42 (1955), 297–302. Included in *Russkaja mysl'*, No. 788 (August 12, 1955), 2–3; and in *Books Abroad*, Vol. 27, No. 3 (summer 1955), 263.

[748] "Lovec čelovekov"
a. Anon. *Kniga i revoljucija.* No. 4 (1922), 43–45.
b. Ingolin, S. *Novyj mir.* No. 1 (1922), 272–273.
c. Šamurin, E. *Žizn'.* No. 1 (1922), 206–207.

[749] *My*
a. Ajxenval'd, Ju. "Literaturnye zametki." *Rul'.* No. 1,931 (April 6, 1927), 2–3.
b. Andreev, N. "Perpetuum mobile." *Grani.* No. 16 (1952), 171–173.
c. Slizskoj, A. "Iz novejšej xudožestvennoj literatury." *Vozroždenie.* No. 29 (September–October 1953), 176–177.
d. Anon. *Booklist.* Vol. 21 (May 1925), 305.
e. Anon. *Boston Transcript.* April 22, 1925, 4.

f. Anon. *Independent* (Boston). Vol. 114, No. 3897 (February 7, 1925), 162.
g. Anon. *New York Times Book Review*. January 18, 1925, 16–17.
h. Anon. *Open Shelf* (Cleveland Public Library). No. 7/8 (July–August 1925), 82.
i. Anon. *Springfield* (Mass.) *Republican*. March 8, 1925, 7a.
j.* Borg, D. *New York World*. February 1, 1925, 4m.
k. Brewster, D. "Fiction of the Revolution." *The Nation*. Vol. 121, No. 3,138 (August 26, 1925), 237.
l. Brickell, H. *New York Evening Post Literary Review*. January 17, 1925, 4.
m. Deutsche, B. "Tonic Laughter." *New Republic*. Vol. 42, No. 537 (March 18, 1925), 104–105.
n. Latimer, M. *New York Tribune Books*. February 15, 1925, 9.
o. Orwell, G. "Freedom and Happiness." *Tribune* (London). No. 471 (January 4, 1946), 15–16. In German translation: "Wenn D-503 die Liebe erfaβt." *Heute* (Wien). May 24, 1958.
p. Parton, E. *Outlook*. Vol. 139 (February 11, 1925), 229.
q. Porterfield, A. "Retrospect." *Bookman*. Vol. 61, No. 1 (March 1925), 110–111.
r. Sorokin, P. "A Challenge to Utopias." *Saturday Review of Literature*. Vol. 1 (February 7, 1925), 507.
s. Anon. [A comparison of *Nous autres* and *Le meilleur des mondes*]. *ZA* 6:37.
t. Anon. *Illustration*. September 28, 1929, in *ZA* 6:35.
u. Bolander, C. *Dagens Nyheter*. August 10, 1932, in *ZA* 6:33.
v. Marion, D. *La nouvelle revue francaise*. Vol. 34 (January–June 1930), 428–430.
w. Membré, H. *Avenir d'arras*. February 6, 1930, in *ZA* 6:36.
x. Truc, G. "Rêves et réalités russes." *ZA* 6:34.
y. Anon. "Utopie; vor 1984." *Der Spiegel*. Vol. 12, No. 51 (December 17, 1958), 51–54.
z. Hahnl, H. "Utopie und Wirklichkeit." *Die Zukunft*. No. 9/10 (September–October 1958), 282–284.
aa. Lo Gatto, E. "Noi." *Dizionario letterario Bompiani delle opere*. Vol. IV. Milano, 1948, 71. In French translation: "Nous autres." *Dictionnaire des oeuvres*. Vol. 3. Paris, 1955, 547.
bb. Terras, V. *Slavic and East European Journal*. Vol. 4, No. 3 (Fall 1960), 264.

[750] *Na kuličkax*

a. Anon. *Bjulleten' knigi*. No. 3 (March 1923), 41–43.
b. Baxrax, A. *Novaja russkaja kniga*. No. 3/4 (March–April 1923), 13–14.
c. Oksenov, I. *Kniga i revoljucija*. No. 2 (1923), 63.
d. Pereverzev, V. "Na frontax tekuščej belletristike." *Pecat' i revoljucija* No. 4 (June–July 1923), 127–133.
e. V[enu]s, G. *Nakanune*; *Literaturnaja nedelja*. No. 28 (February 3, 1924), 6.
f. Voronskij, A. *Krasnaja nov'*. No. 2 (March–April 1923), 333, 344.
g. B[rlić], I. *Novosti* (Zagreb). Vol. 25, No. 39 (1931), 9.
h. D., A. *Jutarni list*. Vol. 20, No. 6,824 (1931), 22.
i. Draganić, J. *Riječ*. Vol. 27, No. 18 (1931), 14–15.
j.* Esih, I. *Obzor*. Vol. 72, No. 9 (1931), 3.
k.* Janež, S. *Jugoslovan*. Vol. 2, No. 78 (1931), 11.
l. Livadić, B. *Hrvatska revija*. Vol. 4, No. 6 (1931), 354–357.
m. Vračarević, B. *Socijalna misao*. Vol. 3, No. 12 (1930), 174–175.

[751] "Navodnenie"

a. Adonc, G. *Leningradskaja pravda*. February 24, 1931, in *ZA* 6:47.
b. Anon. *Komsomol'skaja pravda*. July 27, 1930, in *ZA* 6:53.
c. Anon. *Proletarskij avangard*. No. 3 (March 1929), in 6:67.
d. [illegible]. *Večernjaja Moskva*. September 13, 1929, in *ZA* 6:71.
e. Krasil'nikov, V. *Krasnaja nov'*. No. 4 (April 1929), 232–235.
f. Messer, R. *Rezec*. 1929. *ZA* 6:66.
g. Palej, A. *Literaturnaja gazeta*. No. 2 (April 29, 1929), 4.
h. Raškovskaja, A. *Žizn' iskusstva*. No. 17 (1929) in *ZA* 6:74.
i. Šafir, A. *Izvestija*. No. 139 (June 20, 1929), in *ZA* 6:68. *See also* [336], [540A], [542A], [728A].

[752] *Nečestivye rasskazy*

a. B-fel'd, V. [*Žizn' iskusstva*] No. 25 (1927) in *ZA* 6:95.
b. Friče, V. Pravda. No. 125 (June 5, 1927), 6. Reprinted in Vladimir Friče, *Zametki o sovremennoj literature*. Moskva-Leningrad, 1928, 22–29.
c. P., N. *Volja Rossii*. No. 11/12 (November–December 1927), 294–296.
d. Sosinski, B. *Ruski arxiv*. No. 1 (1928), 177–179.

[753] "Neputevyj"
a. Anon. "Slabyj i sil'nyj." *Bjulleteni literatury i žizni.* No. 12 (February 1914), 714–721.
b.* Š[iškov], V. *Sibirskaja žizn'.* No. 64 (March 25, 1914).

[754] "Novaja russkaja proza"
a. Sventickij, A. "Šemjakin sud." *Literaturnyj eženedel'nik.* No. 39 (1923), 10–11.

[755] "O. Genri"
a. Bobrov, S. *Pečat' i revoljucija.* No. 4 (June–July 1923), 273–276.
b. P[etrovskaja], N. *Nakanune.* No. 480 (November 7, 1923), 7.

[756] "O literature, revoljucii, èntropii i o pročem"
a. Gruzdev, I. *Russkij sovremennik.* No. 3 (1924), 274–275.
b. Ležnev, A. *Krasnaja nov'.* No. 3 (April–May 1924), 321–324.
c. Osorgin, M. *Sovremennye zapiski.* No. 21 (1924), 365–375.
d. Poljanskij, V. *Pod znamenem marksizma.* No. 3 (March 1924), 230–239. Reprinted in Valer'jan Poljanskij, *Voprosy sovetskoj kritiki.* Moskva-Leningrad, 1927, 143–155.
e. R[emizov], A. *Blagonamerennyj.* No. 2 (March–April 1926), 166–167.
f. Tukalevskij, V. "Žar-ptica; o sovremennoj russkoj literature." *Volja Rossii.* No. 14/15 (September 1924), 235–243.

[757] "O segodnjašnem i o sovremennom"
a.* Averbax, L. "Polemičeskie zametki." *Prožektor.* No. 22 (1924), 24–26.
b. Gorbačev, G. "Edinyj front buržuaznoj reakcii." *Zvezda.* No. 6 (1924), 247–251.
c. Knigočec. *ZA* 6:109.

[758] "O sintetizme"
a. Lukaš, I. *Russkaja mysl'.* No. 3/4 (1923), 419–421.

[759] "O tom, kak iscelen byl inok Erazm"
a. Anon. *ZA* 6:107.
b. T., V. *ZA* 6:108.

[760] *Obščestvo početnyx zvonarej*
a. Anon. "Po literaturnym kružkam; novaja p'esa." *Izvestija.* No. 34 (February 11, 1925), 6.
b. Poggioli, R. *Leonardo.* December 1931, 561–562, in *ZA* 6:187–188.

[761] *Ogni svjatogo Dominika*
a. Piotrovskij, A. "Novye p'esy." *Kniga i revoljucija.* No. 3 (1923), 45–46.
b. Zuev, O. "Tetrad' primečanij i myslej." *Russkij sovremennik.* No. 1 (1924), 349.

[762] "Ostrovitjane" and *Ostrovitjane*
a. Anon. *Polesskaja pravda.* No. 32 (April 10, 1929) in *ZA* 6:69.
b. Filippov, A. *Novosti literatury.* No. 1 (Aug. 1922), 51–53.
c. Gatov, A. "Evgenij Zamjatin." *Teatr* (Xar'kov). No. 8/9 (September 1922), 13–14, in *ZA* 6:123–124.
d. Kaverin, V. *Kniga i revoljucija.* No. 1 (1923), 54.
e. Levidov, M. *Novaja žizn'.* No. 27 (February 17, 1918), 3.
f. Lutoxin, D. *Utrenniki.* No. 2 (1922), 143.
g. Potapenko, N. *Novaja russkaja kniga.* No. 9 (September 1922), 16–17.
h. S[lonim], M. *Volja Rossii.* No. 1 (September 15, 1922), 86–87.
i. Vygodskij, D. *Rossija.* No. 2 (September 1922), 24–25.
j. Resnevich, O. "Isolani." *Dizionario letterario Bompiani delle opere.* Vol. IV. Milano, 1947, 140. In French translation: "Les insulaires." *Dictionnaire des oeuvres.* Vol. III. Paris, 1955, 47.

[763] "Peščera"
a. Aseev, N. "Po morju bumažnomu." *Krasnaja nov'.* No. 4 (July–August 1922), 244–245.
b. Degterevskij, I. *Žizn'.* No. 2 (1922), 170–171.
c. Osinskij, N. "Pobegi travy." *Pravda.* No. 95 (April 30, 1922), 4–5.
d. Raškovskaja, A. *Letopis' Doma literatorov.* No. 8/9 (February 25, 1922), 11.
e. S[lonim], M. *Volja Rossii.* No. 5 (November 15, 1922), 85.
f. Svjatopolk-Mirskij, D. *Sovremennye zapiski.* No. 23 (1925), 473–475.

[764] *Povesti i rasskazy*
a. Terapiano, Ju. *Russkaja mysl'.* No. 1,966 (March 9, 1963), 6–7.
b. Zavališin, V. *Novyj žurnal.* No. 73 (1963), 300–302.

[765] "Rasskaz o samom glavnom"
a. A., S. *Oktjabr'.* No. 2 (July–August 1924), 215–216.
b. Itin, V. *Sibirskie ogni.* No. 2 (April–May 1924), 184–186.
c. Ležnev, A. *Krasnaja nov'.* No. 4 (June–July 1924), 303–308.

d. Os[orgin], M. *Sovremennye zapiski.* No. 20 (1924), 426–429.
e. Postnikov, S. *Volja Rossii.* No. 1 (January 1925), 230–240.
f. Semjakin, A. "Solenoj stolb." *Kommuna* (Samara). June 29, 1924, in *ZA* 6:102–105.
g. Smirnov, N. "Literatura i žizn'." *Izvestija.* No. 186 (August 17, 1924), 4–5.
h. Strelec [pseud. of M. Stoljarov]. "Pis'ma o sovremennoj literature." *Rossija.* No. 4 (1925), 392.
i. Urièl [pseud. of O. Litovskij]. "Literaurnye zametki." *ZA* 6:110.

[766] *Robert Majer*
a. A., G. *Novaja russkaja kniga.* No. 11/12 (1922), 26.
b. Zavadovskij, M. *Krasnaja nov'.* No. 1 (January–February 1923), 345–348.

[767] *Sensacija*
a. BIB. *Zvezda Altaja* (Bijsk). December 11, 1930, in *ZA* 6:134.
b. Rozencvejg, B. *Sovetskoe iskusstvo.* May 18, 1931, in *ZA* 6:132.
c. Šabanov, G. *Novaja žizn'* (Ostrogorsk). No. 9 (May 28, 1931) in *ZA* 6:135.

[768] "Serapionovy brat'ja"
a. Tatarinov, V. *Rul'.* No. 487 (June 25, 1922), 7.
b. V[ol'skij], A. *Nakanune.* No. 72 (June 23, 1922), 6.

[769] "Sever" and *Sever*
a. Loks, K. *Pečat' i revoljucija.* No. 2 (April–June 1922), 359–360.
b. Voronskij, A. *Krasnaja nov'.* No. 3 (March 1922), 267–268.
c. Salazar y Chapela, E. *El sol* (Madrid). No. 3,034 (April 26, 1927), 2.

[770] *Severnaja ljubov'*
a. Anon. *Rabočij i teatr.* No. 26 (1927), 16, in *ZA* 6:171.
b. F., A. *Iževskaja pravda.* February 9, 1928, in *ZA* 6:173.
c. Šatov, L. *Novyj zritel'.* No. 49 (1927), in *ZA* 6:172.

[771] "Slovo predostavljaetsja tovarišču Čuryginu"
a. Friče, V. *Pravda.* No. 178 (August 7, 1927), 6.
b. Nikolaev, Ja. *Na literaturnom postu.* No. 13 (July 1927), 55–56.
c. Sl[onim], M. *Volja Rossii.* No. 8/9 (August–September 1927), 207–208.
d. Smirnov, N. *Novyj mir.* No. 9 (September 1927), 217–218.

[772] "Sovetskie deti"
a. Anon. "O tom, o sem . . ." *Vozroždenie*. No. 2775 (January 6, 1933) in *ZA* 6:150.

[773] "Sovremennyj russkij teatr" (lecture and translations)
a. Anon. "Jevženij Zamjatin o ruském divadle." *České slovo*. December 31, 1931, in *ZA* 6:9.
b. Anon. "Zamjatin o novém ruském divadle." *Lidové noviny*. January 1, 1932, in *ZA* 6:6.
c. Anon. "Evgenij Zamjatin o savremenim ruskim piscima." *Narodne novine*. Vol. 98, No. 19 (1932).
d. Anon. 'O soudobém ruském divadle." *Narodní listy*. December 31, 1931, in *ZA* 6:12.
e. Anon. "Prednáška nesovětského spisovatele ze SSSR v 'Umělecké besedě'." *Rudé právo*. No. 1 (January 1, 1932) in *ZA* 6:206.
f. Čeliščev, V. "V Prage; Evgenij Zamjatin o sovremennom sovetskom teatre." *Rossija i slavjanstvo*. January 9, 1932, in *ZA* 6:154.
g. Kd. "O ruském divadle." *Narodní osvobození*. No. 357 (December 31, 1931) in *ZA* 6:7.
h. Kbk. "Zamjatin über das russische Theater." *Prager Presse*. December 31, 1931, in *ZA* 6:13.
i. M[ejsne]r, D. "Evg. Zamjatin o teatre v sov. Rossii; pis'mo iz Prage." *Poslednie novosti*. No. 3,942 (January 7, 1932), 6.
j. P. "Ruský dramatik o dnešním ruském divadle." *Právo lidu*. December 31, 1931, in *ZA* 6:10–11.
k. Šmeralova, S. "Slovo má spisovatel Zamjatin." *Tvorba*. No. 2 (January 14, 1932), 23, in *ZA* 6:205.
l. W., J. "O současném ruském divadle." *Venkov*. December 31, 1931, in *ZA* 6:8.
m. Anon. *Flandre libérale* (Gand). November 20, 1932, in *ZA* 6:15–16.
n. Anon. *Journal du departement de l'Indre* (Chateauroux). December 11, 1932, in *ZA* 6:19.
o. Anon. *La Province* (Mons). November 25, 1932, in *ZA* 6:17–18.
p. Anon. *La Volonte*. November 16, 1932, in *ZA* 6:14.

[774] "Spodručnica grešnyx"
a. L[oks], K. *Pečat' i revoljucija*. No. 6 (July–August 1922), 297.
b. Neverov, A. *Krasnaja nov'*. No. 3 (May–June 1922), 269–271.

[775] *Tri dnja*
a. Anon. *Bulleten' knigi*. No. 4 (April 1923), 39.
b. V[ygodskij], D. *Rossija*. No. 3 (October 1922), 29.

[776] "Tulumbas"
a. Kogan, P. *Pečat i revoljucija*. No. 2 (April–June 1922), 157–163.

[777] "Uezdnoe" and *Uezdnoe*
a. Ajxenval'd, Ju. *Reč'*. No. 54 (February 25, 1916), 2.
b. Anon. *Bulleten' Glavlitprosveta*. No. 4 (1929), in *ZA* 6:70.
c. Anon. "Komu na Rusi žit' xorošo." *Bjulleteni literatury i žizni*. No. 1 (September 1913), 10–16.
d. Anon. *Bjulleteni literatury i žizni*. No. 21/22 (July 1916), 415–416.
e.* Anon. *Černozem*. No. 106 (1916).
f. Anon. *Krasnaja niva*. No. 46 (1923) in *ZA* 6:122.
g.* Anon. *Odesskie listy*. No. 159 (1916).
h. Anon. *Russkie zapiski*. No. 4 (April 1916), 303–305.
i. Anon. *Vestnik znanija*. No. 7 (July 1916), 453.
j. Batjuškov, F. "Bytovoe; po povodu nekotoryx proizvedenij molodyx pisatelej." *Vestnik Evropy*. No. 6 (June 1916), 325–330.
k.* Bersenev, È. *Utro Rossii*. No. 100 (1916).
l. Derman, A. *Russkie vedomosti*. No. 155 (July 6, 1916), 5.
m. Ganžulevič, T. *Ežemesjačnye literaturnye i populjarnonaučnye priloženija k žurnalu Niva*. No. 6 (June 1916), 306–308.
n. Gizetti, A. *Ežemesjačnyj žurnal*. No. 6 (June 1916), 245–246.
o.* Grigor'ev, R. "Baryba." *Den'*. No. 243 (September 8, 1913).
p. Gvozdev, A. *Severnye zapiski*. No. 6 (June 1916), 137–139.
q.* Izmajlov, A. "V literaturnom mire." *Birževye vedomosti* (večernij vypusk). No. 13621 (June 28, 1913).
r.* Izmajlov, A. *Birževye vedomosti*. No. 15428 (1916).
s. Pil'skij, P. "Vnuki. (Literaturnye nabljudenija)." *Argus*. No. 9 (1916), 84–87.
t. Vasilevskij (Ne-Bukva), I. "Grjaduščaja sila." *Žurnal žurnalov*. No. 7. (February 1916), 6–7.
u.* Vojtolovskij, L. "Žurnal'noe obozrenie." *Kievskaja mysl'*. No. 176 (June 28, 1913).
v. Xrapovickij, L. [pseud., Larisa Rejsner]. *Rudin*. No. 8 (April–May 1916), 9–11.
w. Zvenigorodcev, N. *Svobodnyi žurnal*. No. 2 (1916), 31.

[778] "Vstreči s B. M. Kustodievym"
a. Z., V. *Russkaja mysl'*. December 12, 1951, in *ZA* 6:32.

"Zakulisy," see "[Kak my pišem]," [745].

Other works cited in the discussion of the campaign against the VSP.

[779] Anon. "Ispolbjuro FOSP o *Literaturnoj gazete*." *Literaturnaja gazeta*. No. 17 (August 12, 1929), 1.

[780] Anon. "Mesto sovetskogo pisatelja." *Literaturnaja gazeta*. No. 25 (October 7, 1929), 1.

[781] Anon. "Na novyx putjax; sobranie aktiva Vserossijskogo sojuza sovetskix pisatelej." *Literaturnaja gazeta*. No. 28, (October 28, 1929), 1.

[782] Anon. "Na novyx putjax; v Leningradskom otdele VSSP." *Literaturnaja gazeta*. No. 28 (October 28, 1929), 1.

[783] Anon. "Načalo pereloma." *Literaturnaja gazeta*. No. 22 (September 16, 1929), 1.

[784] Anon. "Ob antisovetskom postupke B. Pil'njaka; rezoljucija Leningradsk. otd. Sojuza pisatelej ot 10 sentjabrja." *Literaturnaja gazeta*. No. 23 (September 23, 1929), 1.

[785] Anon. "Obsudim plan raboty FOSP." *Literaturnaja gazeta*. No. 27 (October 21, 1929), 1.

[786] Anon. "Ot redakcii." *Literaturnaja gazeta*. No. 20 (September 2, 1929), 1.

[787] Anon. "Pisatel' i politika." *Literaturnaja gazeta*. No. 20 (September 2, 1929), 1.

[788] Anon. "Postanovlenie ispolbjuro Leningradskogo otdela FOSP." *Literaturnaja gazeta*. No. 10 (June 25, 1929), 4.

[789] Anon. "Povest' B. Pil'njaka — kleveta na Sovetskij Sojuz i ego stroitel'stvo; postanovlenie pravlenija Sojuza pisatelej o *Krasnom dereve* B. Pil'njaka ot 6 sentjabrja 1929 g." *Literaturnaja gazeta*. No. 21 (September 9, 1929), 1.

[790] Anon. "V Leningradskom otdele VSSP." *Literaturnaja gazeta*. No. 34 (December 9, 1929), 3.

[791] Anon. "Vserossijskij sojuz pisatelej o stat'e B. Volina." *Literaturnaja gazeta*. No. 19 (August 26, 1929), 1.

[792] Anon. "VSP pereimenovan vo Vserossijskij sojuz sovetskix pisatelej; načalas' pereregistracija členov VSP," *Literaturnaja gazeta*, No. 24 (September 30, 1929), 1.

[793] Ermilov, V. and V. Sutyrin. "V redakciju *Literaturnoj gazety*." *Literaturnaja gazeta*. No. 12 (July 8, 1929), 2.

[794] Ermolaev, Herman. *Soviet Literary Theories, 1917–1934; the Genesis of Socialist Realism* (Volume 69 of the University of California Publications in Modern Philology). Berkeley and Los Angeles, 1963.

[795] Leont'ev, B. "Novyj dom na starom bolote." *Literaturnaja gazeta*. No. 24 (September 30, 1929), 2.

[796] Lomov, I. "Klassovyj mir v 'literaturnoj promyšlennosti'; *Literaturnaja gazeta* — primiritel'naja kamera po politiko-

xudožestvennym delam." *Komsomol'skaja pravda.* No. 165 (July 21, 1929), 2.

[797] Pravlenie L. O. VSSP. "Pis'mo v redakciju." *Al'manax* [priloženie k *Krasnoj panorame*]. No. 2 (1930), 114–115, in *ZA* 6:59–60.

[798] Revjakin, A. "Na novyx putjax (K itogam Vserossijskogo s"ezda krest'janskix pisatelej)." *Izvestija.* No. 148 (July 2, 1929), 3.

[799] Volin, B. "O *Literaturnoj gazete*; v porjadke samokritiki." *Literaturnaja gazeta.* No. 17 (August 12, 1929), 1.

[800] Zozulja, E. "O Vserossijskom sojuze pisatelej; pis'mo v redakciju." *Literaturnaja gazeta.* No. 18 (August 19, 1929), 1.

Index

This index contains the names of persons and journals mentioned in the text. Titles of Zamjatin's works, organizations important in his biography, and some subject headings have been included, but fictional characters have not been indexed.